# Developments in British Politics 4

*Also available from St. Martin's Press*

Peter Hall, Jack Hayward and Howard Machin (eds)
DEVELOPMENTS IN FRENCH POLITICS

Gillian Peele, Christopher Bailey and Bruce Cain (eds)
DEVELOPMENTS IN AMERICAN POLITICS

# Developments in British Politics 4

*Edited by*

**Patrick Dunleavy**
**Andrew Gamble**
**Ian Holliday**
**Gillian Peele**

St. Martin's Press      New York

Evans

Scholarly and Reference Division,
St. Martin's Press, Inc., 175 Fifth Avenue,
New York, N.Y. 10010

First published in the United States of America in 1993

Printed in Great Britain

ISBN 0–312–10087–6 (cl.)
ISBN 0–312–10088–4 (pbk.)

Library of Congress Cataloging-in-Publication Data
Developments in British Politics 4 / edited by Patrick Dunleavy . . .
[et al.].
p.   cm.
Includes bibliographical references and index.
ISBN 0–312–10087–6. — ISBN 0–312–10088–4 (pbk.)
1. Great Britain—Politics and government—1979–   2. European
Economic Community—Great Britain.   I. Dunleavy, Patrick.
II. Title: Developments in British Politics four.
JN231.D493   1993
941.085'9—dc20                                    93–10892
                                                  CIP

JN
231
D493
1993

# Contents

# List of Contributors

**Les Back** is Lecturer in the Department of Cultural Studies, University of Birmingham. He has published a number of articles on race, youth and identity, and on the politics of race and social change.

**David Beetham** is Professor of Politics at the University of Leeds and consultant to the Rowntree-funded Democratic Audit of the UK. Among his works on social and political theory are *Bureaucracy* and *The Legitimation of Power*.

**Ivor Crewe** is Professor of Government at the University of Essex. Recent publications include *The British Electorate 1963–1987* (co-authored) and *Political Communications: The General Election Campaign of 1992* (co-edited).

**Keith Dowding** is Lecturer in Politics at Brunel, the University of West London. Recent publications include *Rational Choice and Political Power* and *The Civil Service*.

**Gavin Drewry** is Professor of Public Administration and Head of the Department of Social Policy and Social Science at Royal Holloway University of London. Recent publications include *The New Select Committees* (second edition) (editor and principal author) and *The Civil Service Today* (second edition) (co-author).

**Patrick Dunleavy** is Professor of Government at the London School of Economics and Political Science. Recent publications include *Democracy, Bureaucracy and Public Choice* and *Replaying the 1992 General Election* (co-authored).

**Andrew Gamble** is Professor of Politics at the University of Sheffield. Recent bookss include *The Free Economy and the Strong State* and *Britain in Decline* (third edition).

**Ian Holliday** is Lecturer in the Department of Government, University of Manchester. Recent publications include *The NHS Transformed: A Guide to the Health Reforms*, and a series of articles on British politics and policy.

**Desmond King** is Fellow and Tutor in Politics at St John's College, Oxford. Recent publications include *The State and the City* (co-authored).

**John McCormick** is Assistant Professor of Political Science at Indiana University–Purdue University at Indianapolis (IUPUI). Recent publications include *The Global Environmental Movement* and *British Politics and the Environment*.

**David Marsh** is Professor in the Department of Government, University of Strathclyde. Recent publications include *The New Politics of British Trade Unionism* and *Implementing Thatcherism: Audit of an Era* (co-edited).

**Neill Nugent** is Reader in Politics at the Manchester Metropolitan University. Recent publications include *The Government and Politics of the European Community* (second edition) and articles on the changing nature of the European Community.

**Gillian Peele** is Fellow and Tutor in Politics at Lady Margaret Hall, Oxford. She is co-editor of *Developments in American Politics* and author of numerous books and articles on British and American politics.

**Chris Pierson** is Senior Lecturer in the Department of Political Studies, University of Stirling. Recent books include *Beyond the Welfare State?* and *Market Socialism*.

**David Sanders** is Reader and Head of the Department of Government, University of Essex. Recent publications include *Lawmaking and Co-operation in International Politics* and *Losing an Empire, Finding a Role*.

**John Solomos** is Reader in Public Policy in the Department of Politics and Sociology, Birkbeck College. Recent publications include *Race and Racism in Britain* (second edition) and *Racism and Migration in Western Europe* (co-edited).

**Stephen Wilks** is Professor of Politics at the University of Exeter. Recent publications include 'Science, Technology and the Large Corporation', in *Government and Opposition* and *The Promotion and Regulation of Industry in Japan*.

# Preface

This is the fourth *Developments in British Politics* volume. All the chapters are once again new, with a new set of contributors. The editorial team has remained the same as *Developments 3* except that Ian Holliday has joined us and has quickly proved himself indispensable.

As in previous volumes individual authors were asked both to analyse recent developments in policy and events, and to review some of the crucial theories and models available for interpreting them. All authors were asked to concentrate in their chapters on the period since the downfall of Margaret Thatcher and the ending of the Cold War. We have continued the practice begun in *Developments 3* of including an Introduction which surveys major perspectives for understanding the present condition of British politics. This is followed by individual chapters on the political system, public policy, and current issues, and a final chapter, this time written by David Beetham, which provides reflections on some major themes in the study of political theory and British politics – the nature of sovereignty, the meaning of democracy, and the character of political representation. Two innovations this year are separate chapters on the Constitution and Territorial Politics. We have also chosen three new topics for the current issues section – organised interests after Thatcher, migration and the politics of race, and the media and politics.

We would like to thank our authors for cooperating with what is always a tight publishing schedule. Our publisher, Steven Kennedy, has once again provided first-class support and encouragement. We are very grateful to him. Suggestions for improving *Developments* in the future, as well as comments on – and criticisms of – the present volume are very welcome.

*Patrick Dunleavy*
*Andrew Gamble*
*Ian Holliday*
*Gillian Peele*

# 1

# Introduction: Stability, Crisis or Decline?

Is British politics in the 1990s different from the 1980s? As one event piles upon another, and a long train of issues successively dominate the news headlines, it is easy to emphasise the extent of change. Add in some circulation of political personalities, with Thatcher and Kinnock displaced by Major and Smith respectively, and a certain stylistic alteration in the political scene is inevitable. On the other side, it is also easy to point to evidence of continuity, notably the Conservatives' fourth election victory in April 1992 on a programme of consolidation, and the consequent continuation of many policies. But behind both these sets of symptoms, the underlying shape of British politics and the basic health of its political system are more disputed than ever before. The scope for conflicting interpretations was highlighted in autumn 1992, when the Major government's honeymoon period was dramatically curtailed as its economic strategy collapsed and its political stability was rocked by a succession of policy disasters. We review three longer-term interpretations of the fundamental situation of the British political system, the implications of which can be traced out in many of the chapters in this volume. The first argues that the UK is a stable democracy, indeed 'super-stable'; the second view detects many signs of 'latent crisis'; and the last view concludes that the country is locked into a long-run, more gradual cycle of 'managed' decline, politically stable but slipping backwards in economic and social terms.

## Super-stability

It has long been part of the conventional wisdom that British politics displays all the hallmarks of a mature democracy. It

1

resembles a slow-moving meandering river, which has long since left its precipitate mountain descent, and now winds inertly across the plain. The institutional arrangements which provide the constitutional skeleton for the political system are long-established, well-entrenched and not seriously contested by significant social groups or political forces. Political life more generally is marked by a strong continuity of style and substance, with familiar patterns of 'moderate' controversy and political change predominating. Thatcher's fall from power and Labour's new 'moderation' both dramatise the strength of underlying forces of gradual rather than radical change.

At the level of political alignments and citizen attitudes an influential argument for super-stability denies that any significant process of 'class dealignment' has occurred in British politics since the 1960s (Heath *et al.*, 1985, Chapter 3). Although the growth of third-party voting since 1970 has eroded non-manual Conservative and working-class Labour support, these two different occupational classes remain as different from each other as they ever were in terms of the relative proportions of Conservative and Labour voters. This view of public attitudes as changing only in 'glacially slow' ways has been extended to other areas. On this account, party identifications remain strong amongst British voters, and no significant 'dealignment' has occurred; the privatisation of nationalised industries and council house sales have not benefited the Conservatives electorally; and British voters in general never embraced 'Thatcherite' values, even at the peaks of the Conservatives' political hegemony in 1987–88 (see Chapter 5). Thatcherism hence appears almost as an electoral 'blip'; the 1983 electoral landslide was an artificial result produced by Labour's weakness, not a 'critical election' bespeaking a fundamental transformation of the political scene. Equally the tactical implications for Labour were quietist – if the party simply stopped alienating voters, a class-based appeal could still resonate with the British public.

At the level of the party system, the super-stability interpretation also pointed out strong continuities. The left-wing sound and fury over democratising Labour's internal constitution in the early 1980s culminated in changes which actually entrenched a completely traditional Labour style of leadership, with trade union leaders providing undefeatable support for a succession of deradicalised leaders (first Kinnock and now Smith) virtually immune from challenge because of the cumbersome electoral college process. Similarly, the Social Democratic Party set up with such fanfares in 1981 dwindled away into final amalgamation with the Liberals. The Liberal Democrats now look identical to the former Liberal party, and they poll much the same level of support as they have since 1972. Finally, in ejecting Thatcher and choosing Major as leader, Conservative MPs made a switch back to a traditional Tory pragmatism, clearly assigning priority to electoral success over ideology.

Looking more broadly, the super-stability view points to the stark divorce in the 1992 election between 'chattering class' criticism of the British political system, and voters' actual endorsement of the Conservatives. The governing party adopted an absolutely clear-cut policy of rejecting constitutional change – ruling out electoral reform or change in the government of Scotland, substituting a weak 'Citizen's Charter' for demands for a bill of rights, and making no significant change to freedom of information. Even with John Major's initial attempt to put Britain 'at the heart of Europe', British policy resisted any significant democratisation of EC machinery, ruled out the UK's participation in the 'social chapter' providing various social rights, and impeded the progress of all forms of 'federalist' schemas which would take power away from Westminster (see Chapter 3). On all these fronts, the stability view argues that the public at large either actively supports the continuation of the status quo, or has only diffuse grumbles about the machinery of government, which culminate in no fixed or established preference for changes and have very little salience compared with the basic bread-and-butter issues of normal politics. The consensus for maintaining institutional arrangements draws strength from contrasts with political crises elsewhere in Europe. In the UK there are no prolonged crises over coalition government formation (unlike Belgium), and no crises of public finance or governability (unlike Italy where public deficits are large and the mafia has become a serious threat to state legitimacy). British voters even shifted away from accepting the mild uncertainty of a hung Parliament that a minority government in 1992 would have generated.

The super-stability view also argues that Britain's economy remains as well-founded and stable as other countries'. Economic doom-mongering is fashionable in cycles but ignores strong forces for underlying stability and general trends. For example, the alleged 'crisis' in British manufacturing industry has been part of a general trend towards service industries, and while UK-owned plants have certainly closed down in some periods (like the early 1980s), inward investment by foreign (especially Japanese) companies has often reproduced a 'British' presence in sectors previously declining (such as the manufacture of TVs or cars). Similarly, British society remains very stable, despite patches of urban decline and related social problems. For example, in the 1990s overtly racist parties command sizeable votes in many other West European countries, and an upsurge of racial harassment and chauvinistic nationalism seems widespread. But ethnic relations in Britain are generally good, and ethnicity plays little or no part in mainstream party politics (see Chapter 15). If European politics in the 1990s seems set to rerun some unsavoury aspects of the 1930s, Britain's role looks familiar too – as an offshore island remote from the wider tensions and travails of 'the Continent'.

## Latent Crisis

The capacity to change so as to meet new conditions is an important indicator of the health of a liberal democracy. A political system in which surface phenomena show recurring patterns and apparent institutional lack of movement may lack legitimacy and be vulnerable to sudden eruptions of protest, as the collapse of the previously frozen regimes of East European communism demonstrated at the end of the 1980s. The latent crisis view argues that the political foundations and consequences of unbroken Conservative rule from 1979 to the mid-1990s provide no grounds for proclaiming the stability of British democracy. Successive governments based on 43 per cent support have forced through non-consensual changes, dramatically increased social inequality, and eroded many traditional institutional arrangements, while putting nothing equivalent in their place. The gulf between people in employment and relatively well-off and the rest of society has widened, and social bonds between the majority and a variety of 'underclass' groups have weakened. Writing mainly about the USA, but equally relevant to Britain, Galbraith (1992) discerns the emergence of a 'culture of contentment' in which the electoral majority vote in narrowly self-interested ways, and insulate themselves by distance and various forms of social closure from poverty and urban stress. A two-thirds/one-third split of society on these lines now provides a fragile basis for political stability, while the erosion of welfare state provision recreates endemic social problems which had previously been thought to have disappeared – such as large-scale street begging and people sleeping rough in major cities.

One-party government adds an extra element of immobilism, since the constitutional structure in Britain allows – even fosters – the possibility of narrowly sectarian government based on satisfying interests close to the dominant party at the expense of other social groups. Britain has 'the fastest law in the West', with the fewest formal or codified restrictions on government action of any liberal democracy. Governments with secure Commons majorities can short-circuit or ignore public consultation, guillotine parliamentary debate, over-rule unfavourable judicial rulings by retrospective legislation, and even bulldoze through patently unimplementable policies for a time, as happened with the poll tax.

Unresponsive central government creates unnecessary social tension, evidenced by the emergence of an 'electoral/riot cycle' in Britain's inner cities. The mechanisms involved are similar to the much-discussed political/business cycle, whereby governments are supposed to rig the economy so that good times economically arrive in election years, and unpopular economic measures are taken immediately after the government has been re-elected and is furthest away from facing the voters. Under Conservative governments in the 1980s this pattern implied post-election squeezes on public expenditure and increases in unemployment, impacting particularly on inner city areas. In mid-term years between elections this distribution of economic 'pain' triggered large anti-government votes in local council elections. It also helped to create supporting conditions for violent urban riots in 1981 (when disturbances occurred in over thirty towns and cities), in 1985 (with fewer but more intense riots linked to tensions between the police and ethnic minorities), and in 1990 over the poll tax. This recurring pattern of events may indicate that Britain has become what Crozier (1970) calls 'a stalled society' – with communication channels between government and significant minorities of citizens so disrupted that normal flows of representation and policy response cannot occur, stimulating isolated violent protests in particular locales amidst a more general climate of repression of discontent by government.

One-party dominance also rests increasingly on a sequence of 'artificial' election results. The 1992 Tory victory was the sixth successive occasion on which third parties polled 20 per cent or more of votes in Great Britain, yet secured no remotely proportionate Commons representation. The UK's system of plurality rule ('first-past-the-post') elections in local constituencies protects the Conservative and Labour parties from other challengers. It is true that the national figure for 'deviation from proportionality' dropped to just over 17 per cent in 1992 (from a peak of 23 per cent in 1983). But this result was largely an artefact of Labour over-representation in Scotland being offset by Tory over-representation across southern England, the two effects artificially cancelling each other out in the overall national statistic. At a regional level, the disproportionality of the electoral system, its capacity to deliver Commons seats to parties whose share of the vote had not earned them, remained as marked as ever. Elections in Britain handle the major parties in a much more distorted way than in any other West European liberal democracy (see Chapter 5).

The major parties routinely discount such worries, assuming that third-party voters are catered for adequately by Tory–Labour debates, or that their support reveals only diffuse 'protest' votes. But the long-term implications of permanently excluding over a fifth of voters from effective representation are bound to be adverse for the legitimacy of government, even if the effects are diffuse. Within months of its unprecedented 1992 victory, Conservative government popularity collapsed to lag Labour by 20 percentage points, and John Major's victor's laurels were replaced by the lowest Prime Ministerial score on record. Such volatile shifts highlight the very restrictive way in which the voting system now counts citizen preferences in choosing governments.

Critical observers have also detected more general signs of unusual public disaffection from Britain's political institutions. Compared with the early 1970s (another period of dissatisfaction) more voters – and notably the young – now respond that the system of government needs a great deal of change or requires modernisation on more European lines (Dunleavy and Weir, 1991). During Britain's long decline the monarchy was one institution in the British state which had seemed almost immune from criticism, a beacon of stability and legitimacy. This began to change during the 1980s, mainly because of the behaviour of some of the younger royals which was seized on gleefully by the tabloid press. How far attitudes were changing towards the monarchy was shown by the publicity given in 1992 to the Queen's finances, the size of the civil list, and the question of whether the Queen should pay tax.

In the component countries of the UK, discontents also take forms which Major's election rhetoric correctly identified as threatening the Union. In Northern Ireland the IRA campaign for independence and sectarian killings by Protestant and Catholic paramilitaries show no signs of abating, while IRA terrorism in mainland Britain remains a threat. In Scotland, the Scottish National Party (SNP) got nowhere in the general election, and the Conservative vote rose very slightly. But Scottish nationalism still represents the most powerful pressure for the 'break-up' of Britain forecast by Nairn (1981). Developments such as the SNP's conversion to independence within the EC, the Labour–Liberal Democrat convergence in the Scottish Constitutional Convention, and the emergence of the 'Scotland First' campaign uniting Labour radicals and outside forces, will all have long-run significance. The government's masterly inactivity can probably hold the line against divided opposition in a four-party Scottish system for a little while, but not indefinitely (see Chapter 4).

Development of the EC is another source of potential political upheaval and conflict. Deep divisions have emerged within the Conservative party over the EC. These were a major factor in Thatcher's downfall in 1992 and continue to pose difficult problems of party management (see Chapter 6). A gulf has also emerged as in other EC countries between the attitudes of the political elite and popular opinion towards the development of the Community, and in particular towards the Maastricht Treaty. This gulf has already caused severe strains within several other EC countries. A third related problem concerns the economic strains which plans for economic and monetary union are imposing on the weaker regions within the Community. Attempts to keep Britain at the heart of Europe and on equal terms with the leading members of the Community might impose economic costs that could not be borne politically. However, the alternative would be to accept that Britain belonged to the second rank of a two-tier Community.

By the end of 1992 many observers thought that the EC was over-reaching itself and that even if the Maastricht Treaty were successfully ratified implementation would prove very difficult. Convergence criteria written into the Treaty were beginning to look unattainable by all but one or two states, and instances of discord among the governments of the Twelve were increasing. By the time of the Edinburgh Summit of December 1992 the major task which faced Community leaders was to keep the EC together as a cohesive political entity. Strains on the EC were becoming intense as recession across Europe (and particularly in Germany) threatened to stoke both ethnic conflict and racist political movements. At the same time the increasing gulf between political elites and the mass of the people in all EC states was capable of provoking a populist backlash against further progress towards economic and political union (see Chapter 3).

Finally, Britain's economic position remains very poor. In mid-1992, academic commentators were still arguing cautiously and almost defensively against Conservative claims to have wrought an economic miracle in Britain's economic prospects in the 1980s (Jackson, 1992; Healey, 1993). The forced ejection of sterling from the European Exchange Rate Mechanism (ERM) in the autumn 1992 currency crisis dramatically demonstrated the underlying fragility of Britain's economic prospects. Not only was the central plank of government policy overturned by 'Black Wednesday', but days of observable panic ensued in Whitehall as ministers faced up to their inability to control financial markets. The strong public reaction against proposals for massive pit closures necessary for coal privatisation to proceed also demonstrated the bankruptcy of 'new right' solutions. This experience has prompted a wide-ranging reassessment of the 1980s, experience by critics who argue that Thatcher's crusade to transform the economy once-and-for-all into a new enterprise phase culminated only in the inflationary boom of 1986–88 followed by the prolonged recession of 1989–93. Economic recovery is now problematic because the erosion of British manufacturing has created a situation in which any upturn triggers a crippling jump in imports, worsens the trade balance, and precipitates currency depreciation. In addition, a decade of financial deregulation in the 1980s geared up consumer markets to depend on rising property markets for debt-financing (people raising loans for consumption secured on their houses) and equity-release (people selling high-priced houses and trading down to smaller ones, or selling inherited properties, to finance other consumption). The collapse of property markets in the period 1989–92 created a huge debt crisis, devastated consumer confidence and locked the economy into a recession which could become semi-permanent. In these circumstances, even the confidence that economic downturns are followed by upturns may be misplaced.

The latent crisis view thus identifies a number of dimensions on which Britain's apparent political stability may fracture: social polarisation, unresponsive one-party governance, a progressive loss of institutional legitimacy, the re-emergence of substantial separatism, and economic malaise. The terminology of 'crisis' does not necessarily mean that collapse or decline is inevitable. A crisis is a point of decision. If a patient is ill, doctors refer to a 'crisis' when the illness enters a phase from which the patient either recovers for good *or* declines irrecoverably. The UK crisis (point of decision) remains latent. The branching of pathways confronting British voters could have become manifest in 1992 had Labour formed a minority government in a hung Parliament. The Conservative victory postpones crucial choices, but probably not for long.

## Managed Decline

Labour lost the 1992 general election with a manifesto which promised economic regeneration for Britain, a promise which was apparently not believed. By contrast, Conservative pledges were simply of an end to recession. Margaret Thatcher's victories all owed a good deal to her messianic rhetoric of stemming Britain's economic decline for good. In 1979, after the 'winter of discontent' in 1978–79, this appeal for fundamental change meshed with the public desire to throw Labour out. It was believed again in 1983, partly on the basis of 'feelgood' factors such as the Falklands war victory a year previously, and in 1987 the good times which the Conservatives had heralded seemed to have arrived, at least for middleclass voters. But in 1992, the Conservative election campaign concentrated only on attacking Labour, not on promising any remarkable improvements ahead. Voters' economic optimism did turn up in the run-up to the election, but primarily because people were relying on political/business cycle influences from the election itself to pull the economy (especially the housing market) out of recession, an effect which in practice proved almost negligible.

The managed decline view argues that this change of tone is a key difference from the 1980s, marking the realisation that the decade of North Sea oil and Thatcherism have both done little or nothing to change the basic downward trajectory of the British economy. Political stability may not be a virtue if is bought at the price of continuing decline in the UK's per capita gross domestic product (GDP) and living standards relative to other liberal democracies. In the early 1980s many Conservatives were surprisingly unconcerned about the decimation of manufacturing industry by high values for sterling on currency markets, reinforced by government-led high interest rates. They argued that currency appreciation was a natural corrollary of the pound becoming a petro-currency with North Sea oil; that manufacturing industry was anyway bound to decline vis-à-vis the expanding service sector; and that a range of 'sunrise' industries would grow up to replace the declining steel mills, shipyards and so on. Ten years on the three main 'sunrise' industries seemed to have failed of their promise. Financial services indeed expanded fast following the deregulatory 'big bang' in the City of London, but have contracted spectacularly in the current recession as well. Tourism has similarly ceased to grow. And the UK's information technology industry has largely ceased to have any significance in world market terms, after a short programme of government support inaugurated in 1982 was discontinued in the middle of the decade. The new 'sunrise' industries of the 1990s have yet to be identified, although ministers still hope that the Single European Market can be relied on to create 'dynamic' effects which will strengthen British industry – rather than see it further eroded by foreign competition.

The managed decline view also points to evidence of continuity in many of the worst aspects of British policy-making between the last fifteen years and earlier periods. This general argument can best be illustrated by an example. Many policy areas could be chosen – for example, training, industrial policy, regional policy and so on – but the management of exchange rates during the 1980s provides in retrospect a perfect case of the characteristic style of British decision-making. In 1979 the incoming Thatcher governmment seriously considered joining the ERM, a regime of fixed exchanges with the currencies of other EC nations: they decided not to do so because it was inconsistent with the Tories' then fashionable monetarist doctrine. Over the next three years sterling appreciated sharply against other currencies (reaching a value of $2.40), making British exports very expensive in world markets, and triggering otherwise avoidable factory closures and job losses. Then still floating against all other currencies, sterling began to decline, and in 1985 it fell disastrously low for a time, touching $1.03. This shift triggered a massive currency crisis which belatedly convinced the Treasury and Bank of England to back Britain joining the ERM, a policy choice vetoed by Thatcher. Nonetheless the Treasury began a policy of 'shadowing' the German mark on currency markets, which it pursued until 1988, contributing to greater British inflation. A hidden five-year argument about joining the ERM between the Prime Minister and her Chancellor of the Exchequer and Foreign Secretary paralysed British policy on Europe for much of this time. Then in autumn 1990 Britain eventually did join the ERM, but at a rate which valued sterling against the German mark at least 15 per cent too high. As her condition for withdrawing her block on ERM entry, Thatcher insisted on fixing sterling high as a means of artificially creating 'zero inflation' in the UK. Instead, the exchange rate chosen proved unsustainable in world financial markets, and the pound was eventually sent crashing out of the ERM on 'Black Wednesday' after barely two years inside, in the process destroying much of the Major government's remaining economic strategy. Within weeks this defeat was itself being rationalised, however. The government resolved that Britain should not re-enter the ERM until 1994 at the earliest, but some anti-European Tory MPs suggested instead that the pound should continue to float on currency markets indefinitely.

This brief story of prolonged dithering and inconsistency producing missed opportunities and incomplete commitments is sadly typical of the contemporary British State. Political control of decision-making by government is very complete in the UK, but far from having any consistent macro-economic objectives the Thatcher government continued a tradition of ad hoc and short-term policy-making. There are no strong independent institutions in Westminster policy-making (unlike the German Bundesbank), and no strong or consensually-agreed policy objectives (such as the Japanese attachment to growth). Instead British policy debates are orientated to an ever-changing set of short-term conundrums, the perfect political counterpart of the UK's 'casino capitalist' economic system, dominated by an over-large and highly volatile Stock Exchange.

The main kind of stability in British political life is thus the unhealthy recurrence of policy dilemmas, a repeated gnawing over unresolved problems, and a preoccupation with short-term issues. British government has continued to cope with basic survival problems, with few serious threats to the political system, and no real cumulation of difficulties which would justify characterisation as a crisis. In many respects the British political elite admirably fulfils the basic criteria for democratic government. Political leaders and senior civil servants are remarkably incorrupt, and can still be held responsible for their behaviour in basic ways. Yet this otherwise admirable political system seems incapable of producing decisive government appropriate to Britain's social decay, relative economic stagnation, and environmental degradation. Through all these adverse changes, not least in the Thatcher years, the political class has been content to avoid or hide the worst manifestations of slippage, to operate a policy of 'managed decline'.

## Conclusion: Future Prospects

The debate between these three views cannot easily be resolved by evidence alone. Underlying it there are profound differences of values, which determine what criteria of acceptable or unacceptable performance are in a liberal democracy. There are also important variations in patterns of explanation, in the 'theories of the State' being deployed (Dunleavy and O'Leary, 1987), as well as in applied accounts of the workings of the British political system. Pluralist writers, who once rather unquestioningly subscribed to the super-stability view, have now become more critical, veering off to embrace both the other viewpoints, and leaving the new right increasingly to defend the status quo on its own. The new right has revised downwards its expectations of feasible change in the light of the 1980s experience, as its messianic edge has been knocked off through seeing its ideas applied in practice to little effect. And Marxists too have changed course, drifting away from the latent crisis viewpoint towards the picture of managed decline, reacting to the general drop in morale amongst left theorists about the possibility of constructing any non-capitalist future after the collapse of Soviet and East European communism. Thus the perspectives covered here lie at the heart of many applied and intellectual debates in British politics.

The problem at the heart of the different perspectives on British politics has been the need to explain why the long record of policy failure and national decline has been accompanied by such a high level of institutional continuity and political stability. Much attention from a variety of political stand-points (Johnson, 1980; Nairn, 1981; Marquand, 1988) has focused on why Britain has failed to produce a political class with the will or ability to provide more effective government. During the 1970s the discontinuity created by frequent alternation of the two main parties in government became a popular target for constitutional critics of British political arrangements (Finer, 1975), but many of these voices were stilled after 1979, when the Conservatives proceeded to win four elections in a row.

Political scientists continue to be divided as to whether the Conservative success in the 1980s reflected fundamental changes in the structure of the British electorate, or whether it was due to a number of accidental and transitory features (see Chapter 5). Key issues are whether a dominant party system has emerged in Britain, despite the continuing rituals of two-party politics, and whether the policy changes of the 1980s constitute a genuine modernising revolution, which has successfully laid the foundations for reversing decline (see Chapter 10).

Political leaders in the 1990s will be tested by their handling of the economy and by their response to three major challenges – the constitution, the EC, and the environment. Constitutional issues are gaining increasing prominence. Various proposals for constitutional change had already been aired by the end of 1992 (see Chapter 2), although popular demand for change has been slow to emerge. But there remain a number of pressure points, identified in this Introduction and in the chapters that follow, any one of which could trigger change in the years ahead: the crisis in the monarchy; the electoral system; Britain's membership of the EC; and the fragility of the Union in Scotland and Northern Ireland.

Continuing uncertainty over the direction of the EC threatens not only domestic political and constitutional upheaval, but also goes right to the heart of what kind of role Britain seeks for itself in the post-Cold War world, and what kind of society Britain wants to be (see Chapter 3). Instability in the EC is in part a reflection of instability in the wider world order, in which issues of trade, migration, famine, poverty, and debt are interlinked.

A third challenge is environmental decay. Although the Green movement failed to establish a successful Green party in the UK, as had briefly seemed possible at the end of the 1980s, it did succeed in the perhaps more important task of 'greening' the political agenda of all modern states. As a result, traditional political parties found themselves faced with an agenda for environmental change to which they were frequently uncertain how to respond. The growth of environmental awareness and environmental lobbies looks set to continue.

Meeting these challenges will not be easy in a political culture in which the decline of public-mindedness and civic culture substantially narrows the range of possibilities open to policy-makers. In societies in which George Bush's famous 'Read my lips' pledge not to increase taxes is the central theme of electoral politics, policy initiative is severely curtailed. On both sides of the Atlantic many have greeted the Clinton victory in the American presidential election as marking a possible reversal of the political mood and the policy programmes of the 1980s, although others are sceptical. Clinton successfully projected the image of a new form of politics built on civic values which had been denied political space in the 1980s, but he may find it hard to retain public support if his brand of the civic culture generates substantial demands on American incomes.

At a time when policy-makers find themselves faced by some of the most important challenges of the post-war era, their ability to act is diminished both by a shift in the public mood towards individualistic concerns, and by a diminution of the range of policy instruments with which they might seek to direct change. The challenge of contemporary policy-making – not just in Britain but also elsewhere – is to construct new political coalitions which are able to break out of political deadlock.

In Britain the Conservative Government under John Major, having abandoned the radical ambitions of the Thatcher decade to reverse British economic decline and having lost both direction and coherence in the autumn of 1992, appears to have settled into the reactive mode typical of British governments in the post-war period. The underlying electoral position of the Conservatives remains extremely strong, but their prospects for continuing success will depend on whether the constitutional problems facing the government stay manageable, on how the EC crisis is resolved, and on how the economy performs. In the millenarian climate which will inevitably grow stronger as the end of the century approaches British politics is not likely to be dull.

# PART ONE
# The Political System

# 2

# The Constitution

**GILLIAN PEELE**

In the UK political debate is rarely focused directly on the constitution. Yet the early 1990s have witnessed wide-ranging debates both about institutions whose position had long been taken for granted (such as the monarchy and the Church of England) and about many of the country's basic constitutional arrangements. In the 1992 general election both Labour and the Liberal Democrats (who had long put constitutional issues at the top of their agenda) campaigned extensively on constitutional reform issues, putting on the agenda such topics as electoral reform, reform of the second chamber, a bill of rights, regional reform and the position of Scotland within the UK. In addition, the election campaigns in Northern Ireland and Scotland were inevitably suffused with constitutional questions. The distinctiveness of the 1992 election is well illustrated by estimates that electoral reform was the second most-discussed issue of the last week of the campaign.

Had Labour formed a minority government in a hung Parliament, as most commentators expected until the very end of the campaign, some significant changes in UK government would have been in prospect. Labour was committed to creating a Scottish Parliament with extensive devolved powers, to establishing a Greater London Authority, and to promulgating a Charter of Rights, while its position on electoral reform was in the process of transition, making some form of post-election deal with the Liberal Democrats feasible for the first time in more than sixty years. John Major's campaign explicitly rejected any form of electoral reform and argued that devolution could lead to the break-up of the union with Scotland.

19

The surprise Conservative victory removed the likelihood of a radical institutional transformation of the British polity. But it did not altogether remove these issues from the public agenda, as some Conservative commentators initially supposed it would. The Tories' narrow overall majority of 21 seats on the same minority vote (42 per cent), and Labour's failure for the third time in succession to oust an apparently unpopular government, both seemed likely to fuel further dissatisfaction with a political system which concentrated such power in its central government. Moreover John Major is said to be committed to doing something more for Scotland in terms of modestly strengthening its existing distinctive administrative and legal arrangements (see Chapter 4). And relations with the EC returned to centre stage at the end of 1992, after being suppressed by both major parties'.leaders during the campaign. The Conservative government also quickly became enmeshed in furious political controversy as it attempted to secure ratification of the Maastricht Treaty which heralded a new level of European integration fiercely opposed by Conservative and Labour Euro-sceptics.

Some of the government's own post-election initiatives seemed likely to set in motion a series of further changes of constitutional significance. The Citizen's Charter was inaugurated by the White Paper *Competing for Quality* published in November 1991, which promoted the idea that consumers of public services have a right to know what standards of service to expect, and outlined procedures to make complaints and secure compensation of some kind if standards are breached. With a special unit set up under William Waldegrave after the election promoting it throughout the public sector, the 'consumerist' Charter model was designed to head off much of the pressure for a bill of rights (see Chapter 8). The Major government also tried to deflate demands for Freedom of Information legislation by publishing details of the Cabinet committee system after the election, and rules governing Cabinet ministers' behaviour in the document 'Questions of Procedures for Ministers'. The new heads of the Security Service (MI5) and the Secret Intelligence Service (SIS or MI6) were also publicly named, and moves to bring the security services under some form of general policy scrutiny by a committee of Privy Councillors or possibly Parliament were mooted. A general push towards more open government was suggested by these moves, although how much further they will progress remains uncertain. However, even the modest changes made so far towards openness and the Citizen's Charter will improve the way in which some key parliamentary institutions such as the select committees and the Ombudsman operate (*Second Report of the Select Committee on the PCA, 1991–92*, C.158).

There were three main sources for the new constitutional debate: one-party dominance; the erosion of traditional constitutional theories; and the activities of groups pressing for constitutional reform.

## One-party Dominance

The constitutional implications of the Conservatives' long period of government, from 1979 through perhaps to 1996 or 1997, were exacerbated in the 1980s by the radical character of the policies pursued by Margaret Thatcher's governments and by the style of her premiership. These were not governments which sought consensus or practised consultation extensively (see Chapter 14). Far from adopting the mantle of 'one nation' Conservatism, Tory governments from 1979 to 1990 celebrated a tough-mindedness in implementing policies which departed from the consensual policies of their predecessors. Battle lines between the parties were more tightly drawn; demarcation lines between those included in and those excluded from government were more apparent.

Crucial to the dissatisfaction was that these sweeping policy changes were introduced by governments which never enjoyed more than minority support (42–43 per cent of the vote). A majority of people consistently voted for one of the opposition parties, but the Conservatives still won under plurality rule elections (misleadingly called 'first-past-the-post'), because of fragmentation of the non-Tory vote. Regular exclusion of the Liberals/Alliance/Liberal Democrats from effective Commons representation (despite the 1983 Alliance vote of 26 per cent, for example) also added to the legitimacy problems associated with the electoral system. The statistic for 'deviation from proportionality' measures how many MPs in the Commons would not have been there if seats had been allocated in proportion to votes. In 1983 this index reached 23 per cent, a post-war high (Dunleavy, 1992). Deviation from proportionality remained at 20 per cent in 1987 and fell in 1992 to 18 per cent (because of a lower Liberal Democrat vote), still a high level historically (see Chapter 5). British elections are much more disproportional than elections in any other European democracy (Mair, 1992).

Thus although the government was making increasingly dramatic uses of central government power, the legitimacy of its right to govern in this way was obviously open to question. By the late 1980s there was also concern that the alternation in government which had marked the post-war years had been transformed into a Conservative-dominated party system (Gamble, 1988).

The radical policies pursued by the Conservative governments after 1979 themselves seemed calculated to strengthen the power of central government and to weaken the role of any institutions which might act as a countervailing power to the government. The powers of local government were drastically reduced by successive legislation (see Chapter 9) and the government mounted what seemed like a frontal assault on the civil service (see Chapter 8). The dramatic strengthening of the central executive (and its appointed quasi-governmental agencies) at the expense of democratically-elected local bodies undermined any residual belief there might have been in a balanced constitution. Parliament was not entirely quiescent and the House of Lords in particular challenged the government with relative frequency. However in the 1987–92 Parliament, the government seemed determined to squash any claim by the upper chamber to balance the Commons. The one defeat which the peers inflicted on the government (the War Crimes Bill) was reversed, reminding the Lords of its vulnerability (Shell, 1992) (see Chapter 7).

The judiciary's ability to check executive power during this period also fluctuated. The bench appeared more conservative as a result of a series of political appointments by Conservative Lord Chancellors. And a previous movement by judges to expand administrative remedies seemed to have slowed or stopped as result of number of cases in the mid-1980s (Graham and Prosser, 1988). In 1992 the new Lord Chief Justice, Lord Taylor of Gosforth, delivered a Dimbleby Lecture which was critical of the status quo but directed the judiciary's attention to a series of problems more concerned with the administration of justice than the substance of the law. In addition, traditional approaches to civil liberties offered increasingly poor protection for individuals and minorities when the government was giving the highest priority to strengthening the powers available to fight crime, terrorism and subversion. The potential for abuse of government powers in the civil liberties area was underlined in a 1992 case about a deportation order which saw the Home Secretary (then Kenneth Baker) cited for contempt of court.

The power of mediating institutions – finance, business, the universities, the professions – was also weakened indirectly as policies designed to create more extensive competition in the various spheres of British life were imposed, often against the wishes of the relevant professional groups. In some ways Conservative ministers prided themselves on their willingness to challenge producer interests in the name of the public good. Moreover, some of the Tories' initiatives had the potential to affect the balance of strength between the parties. The trade unions, the key source of Labour funds, were the targets of a series of laws aimed at limiting their financial and political muscle (see Chapter 14). The sale of council houses and the increase in home ownership seemed calculated to diminish an important source of Labour strength. And the reduction of local authority power weakened the capacity of the public sector to build up clientele groups. In addition the electoral system itself seemed likely to produce further difficulties for Labour as a result of population shifts. Indeed the general assumption that the next redistribution of constituency boundaries would favour the Conservatives prompted the government in 1992 to inject additional money into the otherwise slow process of boundary review.

These developments did not just reduce faith in the existing mechanisms of party competition to provide future alternations in government. They also highlighted the fragility of constraints on the power of the executive in the UK, and extent to which the system relies on the executive itself exercising self-restraint.

## The Erosion of Traditional Constitutional Theories

Although some observers have seen the emphasis on a strong state as a logical consequence of the Thatcherite goal of extending the market economy, others have noted the extent to which weak protection of civil liberties in Britain predates 1979 by a long way (Brazier, 1991). The exhaustion of the common law as a source of substantive values; the unwillingness of the judiciary to challenge the executive especially in cases involving national security (as for example in the banning of unions from GCHQ Cheltenham and the censoring of Sinn Fein speakers); the dominance of Parliament by the executive through the party system and the absence of a bill of rights enforceable in domestic courts – none of these traits was the product of Thatcherism.

What the Thatcher period did was to draw attention graphically to these features of the British constitution and to underline the extent to which many of the most vaunted concepts of British constitutional theory were empty. The 'hole at the centre' of British constitutional theory was most evident in relation to Parliament. Clearly, the ability of Parliament to act as an independent check on government had long been a fiction. But 'parliamentary sovereignty' was frequently invoked in the 1980s as the reason for not introducing new protections for the citizens, such as a judicially-enforceable bill of rights (see Chapter 7). It was British integration into the EC which produced the strongest challenges to this doctrine – both in formal terms and pragmatically.

In term of practical politics, the problem facing the British Parliament in the early 1990s was how to prevent itself from being marginalised as the competence of the EC expanded and key decisions were increasingly taken not in Westminster but in Brussels. During the 1987–92 Parliament the issue was addressed by the House of Commons, and it was decided to establish new standing committees to deal with EC issues (see Chapter 7). But these new procedures are unlikely to resolve the problem, especially given the difficulty of making the committees work. How best to link the British political system with the wider European one is bound to remain a crucial issue for the 1990s.

There has been an increasing awareness of the British Parliament's legal subordination to Brussels. Section 2 of the European Communities Act, passed in 1972 when Britain first joined the EEC, pronounced that Acts of Parliament 'both past and future' would take effect subject to Community law. Until the early 1990s the force of this provision was masked by the fact that major conflicts between Community law and parliamentary legislation were very rare. In 1990 this situation was changed by a major legal case, *R*. v. *Secretary of State for Transport ex parte Factortame Ltd*. (no. 2) 1991 CMLR 3, which emphasised the change in the British legal system that had occurred as a result of EC membership. At issue was the power of the British Parliament to change its rules governing the registration of fishing vessels for EC fishing quota purposes. As a result of a ruling from the European Court of Justice (ECJ), the House of Lords effectively had to suspend the operation of the nationality provisions of a British Act of Parliament (the 1988 Merchant Shipping Act). There were two further implications of *Factortame* for the subordination of British to European laws. First, suspension of the nationality provisions provided only an initial remedy for the company which sued the UK government. But because of the need for certainty in such matters, it is not enough that sections of the law struck down by the European Court of Justice are made non-enforceable. Ultimately these provisions will have to removed from the British statute book. Secondly, following a 1991 case brought against the Italian government in the European Court of Justice, the way is open for plaintiffs to claim substantial damages where national governments do not give effect to rights under EC laws.

The *Factortame* case itself occasioned much debate in Parliament, despite the fact that its verdict had been inherent in the logic of British membership of the EC. Many legal authorities saw in it the final demise of Dicey's notion of parliamentary sovereignty (Wade, 1991). The doctrine whereby one Parliament could not bind its successors seemed dead, for in this case an act dating from 1972 had rendered illegal provisions passed through Parliament in later years. This change has important implications for those campaigning for a British bill of rights, because it seemed that past arguments that such a bill could not be entrenched under the British system were now invalid (Wade, 1991).

The *Factortame* case was only one indication of how membership of the EC had changed the British constitution. Less visible to the lay public was a series of European Court of Justice rulings which suggested that, although the UK had not formally incorporated the European Convention on Human Rights into its domestic legal system, the effect of so doing might be achieved indirectly, at least in those areas where the EC's competence was accepted, that is, in the broad area of economic policy. The European Convention on Human Rights came into force in 1953 when the UK signed it along with all other members of the Council of Europe (see Bogdanor, 1987, pp.213–15). British citizens can take cases against the government to the European Court of Human Rights (a very costly and lengthy process), and if they are successful the government will usually amend its policies and even legislation to conform to the Convention's requirements. But in all this time the Convention itself has not been incorporated directly into British law, a move resisted by Conservative and Labour governments alike.

Although the Convention long pre-dates the EC, it was recognised as part of the constitutional foundation of the European Communities and its importance as a source of law was also emphasised in the Single European Act. Increasingly it seemed likely the European Court of Justice might apply the Convention as a constraint on member states in policy areas where the EC had competence, thus giving Britain a bill of rights in a sense by the back door. British courts have recognised the implications for the UK of the status of the European Convention on Human Rights in the law of the EC, and have thus far attempted to set limits to this indirect incorporation or infiltration of the Convention into domestic law (Grief, 1991; Browne-Wilkinson, 1992). For example, UK judges would not accept the argument that Article 10 of the Convention which protects free speech could be used to prevent the Home Secretary banning Sinn Fein from the airwaves (*Brind* v. *Secretary of State for the Home Department*, 1991 AC 696). But the extent to which acknowledged areas of European Court of Justice jurisdiction may affect civil liberties was seen in 1992 when the Court ruled against Britain's use of the 'primary purpose' rule in determining the right of individuals to bring spouses to reside in the UK.

## Pressure Groups for Constitutional Reform

The various small concessions made by the Major government in promoting constitutional change were chiefly a by-product of the Conservative commitment to extending the ideas of consumerism to the public sector and improving the quality of services there through a blend of market forces and political initiatives. Nonetheless, the Tories themselves acknowledged a need to make some response to demands for changes in the structure of government, reflecting the strengthening of media and pressure group criticism, and changes made in other parties' programmes.

Traditionally the theme of constitutional reform has excited only a few academics, lawyers and the Liberal Democratic Party. In the current debate, however, in addition to some important single issue groups, the think-tanks and policy institutes which became a feature of British politics in the 1970s and 1980s became significant protagonists in the debate. Those involved include:

- The Constitutional Reform Centre, a non-partisan body which is, however, closely associated with senior Liberal Democratic figures such as Lord Holme. The Centre has sponsored a large number of seminars and discussion documents on applied constitutional topics.
- The Institute for Public Policy Research (IPPR), a left of centre think-tank set up in 1988 to provide the Labour party with a think-tank capability. In 1991 the Institute produced an influential 'draft constitution' for Britain, complete with a bill of rights, provision for PR elections to the Commons using the German-style additional

member system, and a House of Lords elected using the single transferable vote (IPPR, 1991).

- The Institute of Economic Affairs (IEA), a right-wing think-tank previously influential in promoting the market liberal agenda. Frank Vibert, the Deputy Director, has argued that traditional objections to a written constitution have become somewhat jaded. Some codification would help buttress Britain's institutions from erosion at EC level and domestically. He also emphasises the need for greater accountability and transparency in Britain's political processes, and argues that change in these directions would be consistent with new right ideas, such as securing the independence of a central bank (Vibert, 1990).

- Charter 88, the largest movement active on constitutional reform issues. It was created in 1988, a year which marked the tercentary of the British bill of rights and occasioned a good deal of academic and polemical writing about the woeful state of existing guarantees of constitutional liberty. The group's approach was to publish a minimum list of constitutional demands (the Charter) and ask people to write in supporting it, and sending cash donations to keep the campaign going. Explicitly designed to be cross-party, the campaign combined its populist strategy with efforts to engage the 'great and the good' (such as Lord Scarman) and cultural elites (novelists, actors, etc.). By the time that Charter 88 held its Constitutional Convention in Manchester 1991, some 25 000 people had signed the Charter. Around 10 000 people also participated in the group's Democracy Day event during the 1992 general election campaign.

Liberal Democrat activists have traditionally dominated discussion of constitutional issues in British politics, and their influence remained considerable in the late 1980s and early 1990s. Two bodies controlled by influential Liberal Democrat figures, the Rowntree Charitable Trust, and the Rowntree Reform Trust, provided much of the funding that sustained the constitutional debate in all three major parties, demonstrating the importance of philanthropic patrons in sustaining new interest groups already uncovered by American research (Walker, 1983).

What is new about current debates, however, is the increased involvement of Labour Party figures and groups. Traditionally Labour leaders have expected that in time they will gain office and be able to use the strong executive powers and light constitutional constraints in the British system to further the speedy implementation of their programmes. As a result they have been suspicious of efforts to restrict the authority of central government. Moreover, the history of hostility between the labour movement as a whole and the British judiciary made many Labour politicians and academic sympathisers hostile to measures which might enhance the role of the courts in British public life (Griffith, 1991).

These predispositions began changing after 1987, as Labour's long period out of power underlined the absence of safeguards in the British system. Labour leaders also gradually realised the extent to which legal regulation had become a permanent part of the British political process, especially in relation to local government. And as the party's commitment to Europe also strengthened it saw too that the role of law would be bound to increase in EC affairs. However, a series of spectacular miscarriages of justice revealed in the late 1980s and early 1990s – most notably the cases of the Birmingham Six, the Guildford Four and Judith Ward – strengthened the resistance of Labour opponents of vesting more power in the judiciary, especially the then Deputy Leader Roy Hattersley, together with many union leaders. Largely as a result of Hattersley's veto, Labour's 1992 election manifesto showed a new emphasis on personal freedom and individual rights, but still opposed the idea of a bill of rights justiciable in British courts. Instead Labour proposed a kind of advisory bill backing up a whole series of laws in different areas of the public service, a kind of stronger version of Major's Citizen's Charter. Not surprisingly, such a complex stance brought the party few extra votes and made little impact on public debates. One of the first changes in Labour's approach made by John Smith as leader was to accept that Britain should incorporate the European Convention on Human Rights into its domestic law, abandoning Labour's traditional hostility to this step.

In other areas Labour's policy evolution was also considerable, but uncertain and complex on critical issues. The party advocated a full Freedom of Information Act in its 1992 manifesto, again a commitment which it had historically opposed when in government. Labour was also *de facto* committed to extensive constitutional reform as a result of its commitments on local and regional government, on Scotland and on the House of Lords. The party also began to give serious consideration to the question of electoral reform, setting up the Plant Commission to undertake a lengthy investigation which remained uncompleted at the general election (see Chapter 17). However, Labour's general approach to enhancing the powers of individuals and reforming aspects of the British state was clearly different by the 1990s from a decade earlier, reflecting a major change of mood amongst the party's activists and voters towards constitutional radicalism as a corrective to the perceived excesses of Thatcherism.

Conservative interventions in the constitutional reform debates were rarer. With the exception of the IEA, only isolated individuals warned the party that it could not stand pat on the status quo. The former head of Thatcher's Policy Unit in 10 Downing Street, Ferdinand Mount, was one such lone voice (Mount, 1992). Having set its face against any form of electoral reform, the Major government still confronted new difficulties, such as the decision about Britain's six extra seats in the European Parliament secured at the Edinburgh EC summit in 1992 (see Chapter 3). Pressure to make them 'top-up' seats distributed proportionately was intense, as was Conservative opposition to any introduction of a PR element into mainland British elections.

The individual components of Britain's constitutional reform debate inevitably receive differing amounts of attention. Given the UK's capacity to divorce essentially inter-related issues, it is best to look at some of the main topics of current debate separately, while recognising that such treatment is abbreviated.

## Electoral Reform

Few issues were as central to the new constitutional debate as electoral reform. Replacing Britain's plurality rule elections in single-member constituencies (the first-past-the post system) was seen as fundamental to transformation of Britain's party system and political culture. The issue had been around since the nineteenth century, when the precursor of the still influential Electoral Reform Society was first established. In 1917 there were long Parliamentary debates on changing the system, with a Labour–Liberal coalition voting a change through the Commons, but Conservative peers successfully obstructing any action, a pattern repeated under the 1929–31 Labour minority government, which depended on Liberal support (Hart, 1992; Butler, 1953). In both cases, the reform proposed was to introduce the alternative vote, a system which retains single-member constituencies but asks voters to indicate multiple preferences (numbering candidates on their ballot papers 1,2,3, etc.). If no candidate has a majority of first preferences then the second preferences of low-ranked candidates are distributed until one person secures majority support (that is, over 50 per cent of the votes). This system remains the only reform which Labour traditionalists will consider, but is rejected by everyone else in the reform movement. A 1992 study found that in current conditions it would make virtually no difference to election outcomes, transferring 10 seats net from the Tories to the Liberal Democrats (Dunleavy *et al.*, 1992). It is not a proportional system.

The system advocated by both the Liberal Democrats and the Electoral Reform Society (the best known group campaigning for change) is the single-transferable vote (STV), as used in Ireland. STV entails completely redrawing the electoral map of the country, probably into around five-member constituencies, inevitably much larger than those currently in use. Again voters number preferences. First preferences are counted, and a quota of votes is calculated. All candidates who meet the quota are elected, and any 'excess' votes they have are redistributed to other candidates in line with second preferences. When no further candidates can pass the quota level this way, the system switches to eliminating the low-placed candidates and redistributing their second preferences until all seats in the constituency have been filled. The effects of STV have been simulated authoritatively using the 1992 votes, and produced a basically proportional outcome (Dunleavy *et al.*, 1992). Surprisingly the Labour party would have benefited most had the system been in operation, an ironic result since virtually the only decision made by the party's Plant Commission on electoral reform was to reject STV, because Labour is basically committed to retaining much more local constituencies.

The final electoral system under active discussion is the German-style additional member system (AMS). Essentially this involves reducing the number of locally-elected MPs by half (thereby doubling the size of constituencies). The remaining half of 'top-up' MPs are allocated at a regional level so that each party's share of seats in that region would equal their share of votes. In the 1992 election AMS would have produced a near-perfect proportional result, giving all the major parties seats which mirrored their share of the vote (Dunleavy *et al.*, 1992). First recommended by the Hansard Commission in the mid-1970s, and later included in the IPPR's draft constitution, AMS voting is now the preferred system of most Labour reformers. Because it keeps reasonably small local constituencies, it was the only system of PR which the Plant Commission has kept in play as Labour's possible choice. It is the majority choice of the Labour Campaign for Electoral Reform, now one of the largest organised groups in the party and counting 53 MPs amongst its sponsors. The main barrier to Labour accepting AMS is suspicion in the parliamentary Labour Party about the role to be played by the 'top-up' MPs, and the possibility of creating two 'classes' of MP.

So far the electoral reform movement has been divided on party lines, with the Liberal Democrats and Electoral Reform Society single-mindedly advocating STV, the Labour party torn between AMS and the minimal change Alternative Vote, and a variety of other groups (such as the Greens and the SNP) backing any proportional system. Whether the issue develops depends largely on how Labour reacts to the Plant Commission's final report, and on whether Labour and the Liberal Democrats can achieve any form of cooperation. One possible avenue for change is a Labour commitment to a referendum on the electoral system, such as that held in New Zealand in autumn 1992, where 85 per cent of voters opted for change away from plurality rule elections, and 70 per cent opted for a German-style AMS system.

Also keeping the issue alive will be the growing debate about the 'democratic deficit' in the European context. Whatever else this means it must surely involve increased awareness of the role of the European Parliament which is elected by member states all of which, with the exception of mainland Britain, use proportional representation. (Northern Ireland's Euro-MPs are elected by STV.) Thus despite the Conservative victory in 1992 questions of electoral fairness and the legitimacy of the first-past-the-post system are unlikely to disappear from the constitutional debate. However, it remains the case that the debate will be mediated through the political parties and even if there is a conversion to changing the system, as seems possible in the case of Labour, the kinds of change advocated will depend on calculations of party interest.

## A Scottish Parliament

In 1979 the comprehensive devolution measures introduced by the Labour government were rejected by voters in Wales, and narrowly accepted in Scotland – but with too little support to meet the criterion laid down by Parliament that at least 40 per cent of Scottish voters must approve the plan. During the 1980s, however, support for Scottish devolution increased enormously. By 1991 the movement for devolution commanded support from a much wider range of Scottish opinion than in the 1970s, including the Scottish TUC, the majority of Scottish local authorities, and the Churches as well as the Labour and Liberal Democratic parties (IPPR, 1991). All of these groups were represented in a cross-party Scottish Constitutional Convention which undertook detailed work on the future government of Scotland. The key point of the eventual agreements was the creation of a Scottish Parliament, elected on a form of AMS ensuring proportionality, and with competence over most domestic policy areas and substantial tax-raising powers. The Scottish National Party (SNP) stayed out of the Convention, and its support surged in the election run-up after it adopted a platform of Scottish independence within the EC, considerably blunting the devolution momentum.

The Scottish Conservative Party opposed devolution, despite some misgivings within its ranks. The Conservatives did rather better than had been anticipated in the 1992 general election but still remained very much a minority party in Scotland (see Chapter 4). Since demands for a more radical form of devolution than that enacted in the Scotland Act 1978 are still strong, the Major government is likely to have to make some new arrangements for Scottish government, although they will not be anything like the Scottish Constitutional Convention proposals. The restoration of a Scottish committee of parliament to debate the nation's affairs is one possibility. The government resisted pressure for a multi-option referendum on Scotland's future government, fearing an overwhelming majority for change and additional legitimacy being accorded to the referendum device. The fragmentation of pressure for change across Scottish parties has been addressed by a number of proposals including the Scotland First campaign, and calls for an unofficial referendum on devolution – none of which has yet progressed far. But it is unlikely that debate about the government of Scotland will simply disappear or be abated by minor concessions.

**Regional Reform**

As in the 1970s, proposals for handling the Scottish issue inevitably raise wider constitutional questions with repercussions for the UK as a whole. If a separate Scottish Parliament were ever established, would Scottish MPs be able to vote on domestic policy issues before the Westminster Parliament? If they could, then the Scots would in effect have double representation. If not, then Labour in particular might never again command a majority on domestic policy issues affecting England. In the run-up to the 1992 election, Labour coped with this difficulty rather inadequately, promising immediate action on a Welsh Assembly and creation of a new Greater London Authority, with regional assemblies for the rest of England in the fullness of time. If at least some English regions had dual representation then the Scottish anomaly could be got round, Labour leaders hoped. Liberal Democrat plans similarly involved regional assemblies throughout the UK. In the event these ideas never got close to implementation, but the basic problem for the reforming parties remains if Scottish devolution moves back onto the agenda.

The general context of debate is more favourable to elected regional assemblies for several reasons, even though the idea as yet remains unpopular and relatively poorly understood by most voters. The dominance of central executive power over local government, the growth of public service budgets being administered by unelected quasi-governmental authorities, and the abolition of metropolitan county councils and the Greater London Council in 1986, all reinforced arguments that regional democratic institutions could fill a gap and play a useful role. In the early 1990s, local government structures outside the conurbations in England, and in Scotland and Wales, will be reformed piecemeal as a result of the work of a Local Government Commission appointed to create a single tier of local government – most probably by phasing out most of the county councils and transferring their responsibilities to district councils. A change on these lines might open up more space for strategic regional authorities to undertake work such as macro-planning schemes and economic development that fragmented district authorities could not carry through.

EC developments are also boosting the case for regional reform. Across a wide range of EC developments the UK is theoretically becoming committed to the principle of subsidiarity, which argues that government tasks should always be carried out at the lowest feasible level. Although the Conservative government presents this idea as applying only to EC–nation-state relations, and hence stopping at Westminster, many aspects of EC policy encourage regional democratic institutions. For example, the EC Commission is very anxious to channel assistance from its Social Fund directly to regional bodies, rather than have national governments use EC money as simply replacement funding for their own programmes. Without a regional tier of government, the UK may be losing out on such EC funds, a controversy which keeps bubbling to the surface despite Conservative government denials.

The main argument against new elected tiers of government is that further structural reform would be disruptive and costly. The functions which a regional tier would perform are adequately discharged by local and/or central government without creating another level of government which would probably arouse no more electoral enthusiasm than local government. In addition, there would be complex issues about powers and financing to overcome. If local government structures do not become unitary in a simple way, but are composed of some counties and some districts, then any attempt to impose a regional blueprint on top of the local government system would also be awkward.

Any structure of regional government implemented in England would almost certainly fall prey to the problems of central–local relations, although some schemes such as the IPPR's draft constitution do basically adopt a federal system and solve the financial problem by giving all personal income tax revenues to the regions. All proposals for regional bodies tend to become enmeshed with considerations of party advantage, and if opposed by the Conservatives would almost certainly prove unstable. Yet regional reform is a commitment which the Labour and Liberal Democratic parties are unlikely to abandon in the 1990s, although it is not clear how high up the agenda of a future Labour government such structural changes would be.

## The House of Lords

Not surprisingly the new constitutional debate has also addressed the question of the House of Lords, whose mixture of hereditary and life peers, and permanent dominance by the Conservatives, have made it a target for reformers for most of this century. Many critics of Britain's constitutional arrangements now recognise that a legitimately constructed second chamber could be a useful countervailing force against the concentration of powers in the executive-dominated House of Commons, but few if any want to strengthen the position of the existing second chamber.

Liberal Democrat suggestions for reform comprise a Senate elected by proportional representation, with only a part of its membership coming up for re-election in any given year. By the early 1990s Labour too had abandoned its earlier policy position of outright abolition, and proposed an elective assembly with limited powers and linked to the regional assemblies. However, Neil Kinnock admitted in the run-up to the general election of 1992 that reform of the House of Lords would not be a priority for Labour's first Parliament, presumably because such reform could completely sidetrack a Labour government.

Labour's position on the second chamber in a sense underlined the fragility of its commitment to constitutional reform and the party's continuing preference not merely for domination of the policy process by the House of Commons but also to avoid any change calculated to give the second chamber more teeth. Even the proposal that the chamber should be elected is itself threatening to many Labour MPs, since it is almost inevitable that some form of proportional representation would be used. But then the second chamber might acquire greater legitimacy than the Commons, especially given the current tendency of multiparty politics to allow governments to gain overall majorities with relatively low shares of the popular vote.

The Conservative victory in 1992 precluded direct reform of the House of Lords and ensured that for the next four years at least the Lords would continue as before – revising the government's legislation and inflicting the occasional defeat on the government. The advent of the former prime minister to become Baroness Thatcher of Kesteven, along with the advent of Lords Tebbit, Ridley, Parkinson and others, underlined the opportunity provided by the Lords as a platform for expressing points of view that are not in line with existing government policy. Debate about the second chamber will undoubtedly continue from a number of perspectives but the likelihood is that, apart from some tinkering with the nomination process, little change will occur, short of a future circumstance like a hung Parliament where a major constitutional overhaul could be in prospect.

**The Monarchy**

The explosion of public criticism of the monarchy in 1992 reflected the damage wreaked on the previously powerful symbolic concept of a 'Royal Family', which has been the mainstay of the monarchy's popular appeal since Queen Victoria's time. The marriages of Prince Charles and Prince Andrew both collapsed, with immediate separations, and probable divorces in the future. The strong press interest in projecting both Prince Charles' and Princess Diana's account of their break-up, along with numerous invasions of privacy (such as transcripts of telephone calls) kept the monarchy at the centre of a complex, almost self-sustaining controversy. Subsidiary issues pulled into the argument included whether a divorced Prince Charles could legitimately become 'supreme head' of the Church of England, whether a separated Princess Diana could ever become Queen in future (as John Major initially insisted she could), the question of the Queen paying income tax for the first time, and the possibility of republican feeling growing in the future (as foreseen by at least one Labour front bencher). How long press obsession with royal stories will persist remains uncertain, but some serious constitutional issues have undoubtedly been raised and may not go away.

The most important in political science terms concerns the continuing existence of a number of royal prerogative powers which are still personally and directly exercised. In particular, the choice of a potential Prime Minister in a hung Parliament is inherently not a prerogative power which could be transferred to ministers, and yet one which could have political salience. Some left-wing commentators (such as Tony Benn) also believe that the monarch could conceivably play a role if a government was failing but refusing to resign, as happened in Australia in 1975 when the Governor General (acting a role analogous to the Crown in the UK itself) intervened to dismiss a Labour government unable to get its budget through the upper house, an incident which generated enormous controversy. Both Benn, and the right-wing commentator Frank Vibert, have suggested a decisive modernisation of the constitution by vesting the slim remaining prerogative powers of the monarch concerning the selection of the Prime Minister (or the possible dismissal of a government reluctant to go) in the Speaker of the House of Commons.

The second fundamental issue underlying the current controversy, and especially notable in the demand that the Queen pay tax, concerns the whole idea of an 'extended' monarchy, deeply and permanently enmeshed with other elite institutions – such as the House of Lords, large landowners, the top levels of the armed forces, and the worlds of horse racing, polo games and the very wealthy. Critics of the existing system cite the 'limited monarchies' of Scandinavia and Holland as an alternative, less elitist, more 'democratic' and radically less expensive form in which a constitutional monarchy could operate. If the media and public opinion backlash against the collapse of the 'Royal Family' mystique continues for any sustained period, then it could be that the 'extended' monarchy pattern of the past, in which the monarch is simultaneously both head of state and a linchpin of what remains of the British aristocratic system, may be unsustainable.

## Conclusion

It would be surprising if constitutional debates generated during the 1980s and 1990s were to fade from public consciousness. Apart from the imbalance caused by such a concentration of power in executive hands, external pressures – notably from the EC – seem likely to change both the climate in which constitutional discussions occur and their substance.

# 3

# The European Dimension

**NEILL NUGENT**

EC politics go to the heart of British politics. Debates about Britain's future in Europe were not only central to the tensions which engulfed British politics at the end of 1992, but are also integral to the future of Britain in all key spheres. Despite the events of 'Black Wednesday', when under intense speculative pressure sterling was withdrawn from the Exchange Rate Mechanism (ERM) of the European Monetary System (EMS), Britain's economic fortunes continue to rely heavily on those of the EC as a whole. In the political sphere, many important decisions are now made not in London but in Brussels. In consequence, domestic political debate – in Parliament, in the media, and elsewhere – is increasingly dominated by the EC, and many senior British decision-makers – both politicians and civil servants – have to spend a considerable amount of time deliberating and negotiating with their counterparts from the other eleven EC states (Belgium, Denmark, France, Germany, Greece, Ireland, Italy, Luxembourg, the Netherlands, Portugal and Spain).

Central to many of the issues which arise in regard to British membership of the EC is the Maastricht Treaty, which was negotiated at the end of 1991, and became in 1992 the focus of political debate not only in Britain but throughout the EC. In Britain, as in other EC countries, Maastricht was quickly seen as the most important development of the Community in years, and provoked a wide-ranging debate about the nation's place in Europe. British debate was given added impetus by the events of 'Black Wednesday', and reached a point of climax in November 1992 when a procedural vote on the Maastricht

Treaty in the House of Commons came close to provoking a government defeat. The drama of this parliamentary occasion was generated by very important conflicts of opinion concerning the way forward for Britain. Whilst no more than a few MPs were prepared to advocate British withdrawal from the EC, among those who wished Britain to retain its EC membership significant differences emerged concerning the terms and conditions of membership. John Major's contention that Britain should place itself 'at the heart of Europe' was strongly challenged by Euro-sceptics in his own party and indeed was brought into question too by the actions of his own government when it indicated that sterling would spend an extended period outside the ERM, and when it promised to slow down the process of ratifying the Maastricht Treaty as part of the concessions which were necessary to get the November 1992 vote through the Commons.

The result is that Britain's place in the European Union which will be created by ratification of the Maastricht Treaty remains highly uncertain. In part, this uncertainty reflects larger questions which hang over the entire process of European Union. In part, it is the product of domestic misgivings. This chapter begins by investigating the Maastricht Treaty in detail, and then moves to consider the impact that EC membership has already had on British politics and policy, and ways in which that impact might alter in the future.


## The Maastricht Treaty

*Background*

Since the EC was founded in the 1950s cooperation and integration between its member states have progressively developed. The pace of this development was steady in the 1960s, slow in the 1970s and early 1980s, and has been extremely rapid since the mid-1980s.

The increased pace since the mid-1980s stems in many ways from the Commission's 1985 White Paper *Completing the Internal Market*. This set out a legislative programme aimed at enabling goods, services, capital and labour to move freely throughout the EC on the basis of free and fair competition. Once the European Council (as EC summits are known) had accepted the programme, and set December 1992 as the deadline for its completion, the way was opened for a major legislative advance on market-related measures. But the way was also opened for other reforms of an integrationist kind because completion of the Single European Market (SEM) was seen to require both institutional changes (if the '1992 laws' were to be approved in time) and also policy developments (in the form of extensions of the EC's policy competence so that market measures would be accompanied by appropriate economic and social measures).

It was thus within the context of an 'integrationist surge' that three key developments occurred in the second half of the 1980s. First, in 1986 the Single European Act (SEA) was signed. Amongst other things the SEA increased the EC's ability to take decisions by qualified majority vote and extended the EC's legal policy competence. Second, in 1989 the *Community Charter of the Fundamental Social Rights of Workers* – commonly known as the Social Charter – was accepted by the governments of all EC member states except Britain. The Charter provided a political base from which the EC could develop social legislation in matters relating to employment. Third, in 1988–89 the foundations of Economic and Monetary Union (EMU) began to be laid. As part of this Britain entered the ERM in October 1990, with the consequence that the exchange rate of the pound was permitted to move only within specified limits in relation to other ERM currencies (except if there was a formal devaluation) and the macro-economic policy options available to the government were narrowed because of the need to defend sterling within the ERM.

Accompanying this 'integrationist surge', and in response too to an increasing number of countries applying to join the EC, an intense debate has been conducted since the late 1980s as to how the EC should develop. Much of this debate has focused on the balance to be struck between deepening (the further development of integration between the member states) and widening (the enlargement of the EC through the accession of new member states). The British government's position has been to favour widening but to be very cautious in respect of any deepening which is intended to take the EC beyond being an integrated internal market with a limited amount of intergovernmental cooperation in specified policy spheres tacked on. Most other EC governments, by contrast, have wished to see both deepening and widening proceed but, aware that there are potential conflicts between the two processes, they have tended to the view that deepening must be guaranteed before widening can be permitted.

Against the background of this debate it was decided at European Council meetings in 1989–90, against the wishes of the UK government, to establish Intergovernmental Conferences (IGCs) on EMU and on Political Union. The IGCs began their work in December 1990 and presented their reports to the European Council meeting at Maastricht in December 1991. At Maastricht a new Treaty on European Union was agreed. The Treaty was formally signed in February 1992 and was then referred to the member states for ratification.

*Contents of the Treaty*

The Treaty on European Union – now commonly referred to simply as the Maastricht Treaty – consolidates and develops political and economic integration between the EC member states. It does so both symbolically and substantively: symbolically by the very use of the word 'Union' – under the Treaty the EC becomes part of a broader European Union; substantively by making provisions for policy and institutional developments at the Union level.

It is not possible to examine in detail the many different aspects of the Treaty here, so attention will be restricted to an outline of its more important features. There are four such features:

(1) The Treaty is based on three pillars. The most important of these pillars is the EC itself. Provisions of the Treaty falling under this pillar take the form of amendments to the EC's three founding treaties (the 1951 Treaty of Paris and the two 1957 Treaties of Rome). The second pillar is a

'Common Foreign and Security Policy' (CFSP). The third is 'Cooperation in the Fields of Justice and Home Affairs'. The significance of having three pillars is that policy spheres which are not placed within the framework of EC treaties cannot be the subject of EC law, are not so subject to the control or influence of the Commission and the Court of Justice, and are generally conducted on the basis of intergovernmental cooperation – which means that national sovereignty can be said to be preserved. In the negotiations leading up to Maastricht the UK government took a leading role in resisting the pressure from some governments to place foreign policy and justice and home affairs policy under the umbrella of the EC.

(2) The Treaty, like the SEA before it, broadens the EC's, or more accurately in this case the Union's, policy competence. The EC pillar extends the policy competence to bring in, for example, aspects of education, public health, consumer protection, and industrial policy. The CFSP pillar greatly stiffens the general aim that was set out in the SEA whereby the member states would 'endeavour jointly to formulate and implement a European foreign policy' by specifying that the member states 'shall define and implement a common foreign and security policy ... covering all areas of foreign and security policy', and by further specifying that the common policy 'shall include all questions related to the security of the Union, *including the eventual framing of a common defence policy, which might in time lead to a common defence*' (italics mine – *Treaty on European Union*, 1992, pp.172, 175). The CFSP pillar also allows for some matters to be the subject of joint action and declares that the Western European Union (WEU) (which is made up of all EC countries apart from Denmark and Ireland) will be developed as the defence component of the Union. The Justice and Home Affairs pillar provides a legal base for coordination, and for the adoption of joint positions and joint actions, in certain areas of activity which, in the past, have been dealt with purely on a national basis or have been the subject of only rather loose and informal cooperation between member states. Areas of activity so identified in the Treaty include asylum policy, immigra-

tion policy, the combating of drug addiction, the combating of international fraud, and judicial cooperation in civil and criminal matters. To further the effectiveness of this pillar, police cooperation is to be enhanced through a Union-wide police intelligence office (Europol).

(3) Regarding the particularly important policy area of EMU, and in what many view as the most important aspect of the Treaty, the main features of EMU are defined and a timetable for establishing it is specified (see Chapter 10). EMU is to include, in its final stage, the introduction of a single currency and the establishment of a European Central Bank operating within the framework of a European System of Central Banks. It is to be established in three stages, with the final stage beginning – for those countries which are willing and which meet specified convergence conditions – by as early as 1997 and, for all countries which meet the convergence conditions, by no later than 1999. (See below for special conditions applying to Britain.)

(4) The Treaty incorporates institutional reforms which seek both to make the EC's decision-making processes more efficient and to address the problem of the 'democratic deficit' which has been identified by critics (and even supporters) of the EC. It does so, most notably, in the following ways: there are further increases in the range of policy areas where decisions can be taken by qualified majority vote in the Council of Ministers; the powers of the European Parliament are strengthened, in particular by the establishment of a new co-decision legislative procedure for certain categories of legislation which gives to the European Parliament, for the first time, the ability to veto legislative proposals; and the Court of Justice is given the power to impose fines on member states for not complying with its judgements or for failing to implement EC law.

## The Significance for Britain of the Treaty

In the period leading up to the Maastricht Summit the British government was concerned not only that the new Treaty should not move the EC too much further down the road of political and economic integration, but also that it should not be seen to do so. For this reason British negotiators devoted a great deal of time and effort to ensuring that a phrase which appeared in Treaty drafts was removed: namely, 'This Treaty marks a new stage in a process leading gradually to a Union with a federal goal'. In the event the phrase was indeed removed, to be replaced by 'This Treaty marks a new stage in the process of creating an ever closer union among the peoples of Europe, in which decisions are taken as closely as possible to the citizen' (*Treaty on European Union*, 1992, Article A). With the removal of the offending phrase the government became better equipped to defend itself against those critics who claim that the Maastricht Treaty is but the latest piece of evidence that Britain is involved in an evolutionary process that will eventually lead to some sort of federal system.

Whatever the government might claim, however, the essence of the EC is not to be found in the words it uses to describe itself. The word 'federal' is, after all, open to different interpretations. In Britain it is generally taken to imply a considerable degree of centralism, but this is not so on the Continent where the definition given by the. influential President of the Commission, Jacques Delors, to the European Parliament in July 1992 would be widely accepted: 'The concept of "federalism" is one in which power is shared between a number of political and administrative tiers [in our case, the Community, the Member States, and the regions], on the principle that any decision should be taken at the tier closest to the grass roots' (*Official Journal*, 1992, p.8). The reality of the EC must be sought, therefore, not in emotive or controversial words and phrases but rather in the substance of how it is organised and what it does. In regard to this substance, there can be no doubt that there are centralising aspects of the Treaty, both in respect of the functioning of the EC itself and in respect of transfers of policy responsibilities from member states to the EC level. These centralising aspects of the Treaty go to the very heart of the British 'problem' with the EC, namely concern over loss of sovereignty.

There are two main ways in which membership of the EC involves a weakening of national sovereignty. First, many of the decisions made by the EC are not just rules which are internal to the organisation, but are laws which constitute part of the legal framework of member states. The range of these laws has grown considerably over the years as the EC's policy interests and responsibilities have increased, with the consequence that member states have found their control and manoeuvrability restricted in many policy spheres. The Maastricht Treaty, by extending the EC's policy competence, provides a potential for further EC legislative expansion. Second, EC decision-making procedures are such that governments cannot always prevent unwanted decisions being taken and imposed upon them. It is not possible here to examine EC decision-making procedures in detail but, as Figure 3.1 shows, the basic process in regard to most important legislation is that the Commission makes a proposal and the Council of Ministers – in various forms of association with the European Parliament – takes the final decision. Whatever the Treaties specify about the way in which the Council is to take that final decision – and it varies between policy sectors – efforts are always made to reach a consensus. However, since the early 1980s the practice has developed of taking decisions by qualified majority vote when no consensus can be found and where the Treaties so permit. The circumstances in which the Treaties do so permit were considerably expanded by the SEA (in particular, by extending qualified majority voting to internal market measures) and are expanded further by the Treaty on European Union.

But if there are aspects of the Maastricht Treaty which the British government would rather were not included, there are other aspects which it has welcomed; which indeed it has presented as 'victories won'. Three such aspects are especially important:

(1) Deepening has not progressed as far as many member states and many key EC actors would have liked. For example, qualified majority voting is not extended to all policy areas, and is excluded most notably from fiscal policy. The European Parliament, of which the British government has long been wary, is not given the full co-decision-making powers with the Council it wanted. And

FIGURE 3.1   Principal features of the Community's law making procedures

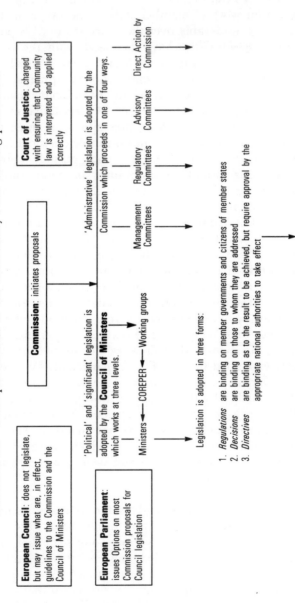

## The Institutions

**The Commission** is headed by 17 Commissioners – two each from France, Germany, Italy, Spain and the UK, and one from each of the other seven member states. The supporting bureaucracy, which is sectionalised along functional lines into 23 Directorates General (DGs), is tiny compared with national bureaucracies, numbering only around 13 000 staff. In addition to proposing policies the Commission's responsibilities also cover aspects of policy management and policy execution.

**The European Council** is made up of the twelve Heads of Government, the twelve Foreign Ministers, and the President and one Vice-President of the Commission. Major decisions of a constitutional and strategic nature are referred to it for approval. It meets at least twice a year.

**The Council of Ministers** is composed of national representatives who vary according to the subject matter being discussed. The Council's main function is to take decisions on important legislative proposals. When EC laws are being made the relevant Treaty articles determine whether Council decisions are taken by qualified majority vote or by unanimity. Where the former applies, the UK has 10 votes out of the total of 76; 54 votes constitute a majority.

**The European Parliament** has 518 MEPs, with 81 from the UK. Although it does not enjoy the legislative powers of the UK Parliament, the European Parliament in practice exercises much more influence over legislation than does Westminster. Under the Treaty on European Union the European Parliament is given, for the first time, veto powers over certain categories of legislation.

**The Court of Justice** consists of 13 judges, one from each member state plus another to avoid tied votes. The Court has various responsibilities connected with the interpretation and application of the Treaties and EC law. Under the Treaty on European Union the Court is given the power to impose financial penalties on member states which do not apply EC law in the proper manner.

policy and defence, and justice and home affairs, though part of the European Union's agenda, are to be based on an essentially intergovernmental, as opposed to a supranational, basis.

(2) An Article which the British government claims marks a significant turning away from the principle of EC centralisation is included in the Treaty. The key passage of the relevant Article reads: 'In areas which do not fall within its exclusive competence, the Community shall take action, in accordance with the principle of subsidiarity, only if and insofar as the objectives of the proposed action cannot be sufficiently achieved by the Member States and can therefore, by reason of the scale or effects of the proposed action, be better achieved by the Community' (*Treaty on European Union*, Article 3b). This passage does not, it should be said, provide a clear guide to action in all circumstances: partly because it can be disputed as to when results can be 'better achieved' by the Community, and partly because the much-debated term 'subsidiarity' is open to different interpretations – with the British generally taking it to mean that decisions should be taken at the Community level as little as possible and at the national level as much as possible, but many other countries taking it to mean that decisions should be taken at the most appropriate level, be that Community, national, regional or local level. Nonetheless, despite these difficulties, the passage does provide a legal basis for challenging Community initiatives, and especially Commission initiatives, if they seem to be unwarranted.

(3) Special provisions designed to allow Britain to stand aside from very important projected developments in respect of EMU and social policy are also included in the Treaty. In respect of EMU, whereas all other countries, except Denmark, committed themselves to entering the single currency by 1999 at the latest provided they meet the specified convergence criteria, the UK reserved the right to enter the currency only if Parliament, near the time of possible entry, gives its explicit authorisation to do so. In respect of social policy, the UK was, in effect, permitted to opt out of any further expansion in the EC's commitments.

(This was achieved by the other member states signing a separate Treaty protocol on social policy. Because the protocol is based on EC procedures and mechanisms, but is not incorporated into the EC Treaties, it may run into legal difficulties.)

## Post-Maastricht Uncertainties

The Maastricht Treaty was scheduled, subject to national ratifications, to come into effect in January 1993. However, the schedule was upset in June 1992 when Danish voters – who, unlike the voters of most other member states, were given the opportunity to participate in their national ratification process via a referendum – decided, by 50.7 per cent to 49.3 per cent, not to approve the Treaty. This was the first occasion in the EC's history that a major agreement between the governments of the member states had failed to be ratified at national level.

As well as jeopardising the Treaty, the Danish vote had the immediate effect of obliging EC elites to temper their integrationist rhetoric and to recognise that in some respects they were getting too far in advance of public opinion. The referendum thus introduced a new element of caution, and indeed of uncertainty, into the integration process. This caution and uncertainty were fuelled further by two very important events in the late summer/early autumn of 1992. The first event was a referendum in France on the Treaty which witnessed a sharply contested campaign and a very close result: 51 per cent voted for ratification and 49 per cent voted against. The closeness of this result, in one of the supposedly more pro-European member states, naturally provided valuable ammunition to the growing numbers of those who were arguing that there should be a slow-down, and perhaps a change of direction, in EC integration as it was conceived at Maastricht. The second event was extreme turbulence in the exchange rate markets which resulted, amongst other things, in sterling and the lira being forced to suspend their membership from the ERM. The system which was supposed to provide a key platform for the projected movement towards EMU was thus seen to be not as effective as had been supposed, and this had the effect of bringing the credibility of the whole EMU enterprise into question.

The Danish and French referenda and the partial collapse of the ERM had beneficial consequences for the British government insofar as they promoted second thoughts throughout the EC about aspects of the Maastricht Treaty. They also, however, had three quite undesired and unwanted consequences:

(1) They threatened to unravel the whole Treaty and that the British government most certainly did not wish to see, for if negotiations were to be reopened it was by no means guaranteed that the outcome would be as satisfactory as the deal which had been concluded at Maastricht. Certainly, as has been shown above, the Maastricht Treaty contained provisions that the British government would have preferred not to have had to accept, but on the whole it was regarded as constituting what Major described as 'a very good result for Britain'. Foremost amongst the dangers of a second round of negotiations would be a split in the EC between a fast integrationist inner core and a slow integrationist outer core. In the event of such a split Britain would almost certainly find itself in the outer core.

(2) They seemed likely to delay the anticipated widening of the EC. As a long-standing proponent of widening, the British government had hoped to see accession negotiations with countries such as Austria, Sweden, Switzerland and Finland open during the six-month period of the British Presidency of the Community in the second half of 1992, but the leaders of the other member states made it clear at the June 1992 Lisbon Summit that accession negotiations would have to await ratification of the Maastricht Treaty.

(3) They provided a significant boost to British opponents of the Treaty. It had been decided at an early stage that British ratification would be via parliamentary approval and in May 1992, shortly before the Danish referendum, opposition in the House of Commons to the Bill giving

effect to ratification was contained at second reading – with most Labour MPs following their Party's official position which was to abstain (the abstention being justified in terms of hostility to the social chapter opt-out clause) and only a handful of Conservatives defying Party whips and voting against. The Danish and French referenda however, plus what was seen by many to be the fortuitous release from the ERM, led many MPs to reconsider their position. Euro-scepticism became more open in both of the major parties, and was seen even to reach sections of both the Cabinet and Shadow Cabinet.

It was thus against the background of considerable difficulties, both at Community and domestic levels, that the British Presidency of the Community was exercised between July and December of 1992. (The Presidency – which, strictly speaking, is the Presidency of the Council of Ministers – rotates between the member states on a six-monthly basis. It offers considerable opportunities to the incumbent state to shape the direction and pace of Community affairs.) Notwithstanding the difficulties however, and notwithstanding also widespread accusations throughout the Presidency of inept management, Britain's tenure of office was generally judged to be ultimately successful in that it concluded with a highly productive European Council meeting in Edinburgh. The Edinburgh Summit was productive in the sense that the twelve member states, under Major's chairmanship, were able to reach agreement on a range of pressing and important issues. In so doing, they seemingly cleared the way both for ratification of the Maastricht Treaty (the key element of the agreement in this respect being the granting of certain opt-out clauses to Denmark) and for the widening process to begin. (The opening of accession negotiations was authorised to start with Austria, Finland and Sweden in early 1993, and with Norway later in 1993. Switzerland was not included because in a referendum held only days before the Summit the Swiss people had voted not to ratify a new wide-ranging agreement with the EC, thus bringing into question whether Switzerland's application was still realistic.)

## The Impact of the EC on British Political Processes

As the EC has grown in importance so has it become necessary for the many different parts of the British political system to adjust in terms of both organisational arrangements and behaviour. With decisions on key matters increasingly being made at EC level, the various institutions and agencies of government, and the political actors which are part of or which seek to influence government, have increasingly had to develop a European dimension.

### Central Government

In Brussels the British government's input into the Community is channelled via the UK Permanent Representation to the EC (UKREP). Around forty or so diplomats are based at UKREP and their job is essentially to see that British interests are promoted and safeguarded in EC fora. At a general level they do this by acting as a sort of information intermediary between the EC and Whitehall. More particularly they do it by taking a leading role in controlling Britain's input into the Council of Ministers: officials from UKREP, supported when appropriate by expert officials from national ministries flown out for the purpose, represent Britain in the many Council working parties which undertake the detailed analyses of Commission proposals for EC legislation; the UK Permanent Representative and/or his Deputy represent Britain in the Committee of Permanent Representatives (COREPER) which has as its main purpose the preparation of ministerial meetings; and before and during ministerial meetings UKREP officials have an important part to play in briefing ministers.

At home, arrangements vary between ministries for dealing with the EC dimension of their affairs. In general, ministries which have a great deal to do with the EC – such as the Foreign Office, the Treasury, and the Department of Trade and Industry (DTI) – have European departments or sections of some kind, while ministries which are less affected – such as Education, Health, and the Home Office – tend to deal with issues through normal processes as they arise. Coordination of the many different interactions which take place between national ministries and the EC is channelled primarily via the European Secretariat of the Cabinet Office, working closely with UKREP and the Foreign Office. The European Secretariat convenes around 200 interdepartmental meetings of civil servants each year, including a regular weekly meeting which is attended by the UK Permanent Representative.

Beyond the specific organisational arrangements which have been put in place to manage the government's relations with the EC, the governmental machine is also being affected in a more general way by EC membership. With only a few ministries not now having an EC dimension of some kind to their affairs, with many officials going back and forth to Brussels to attend meetings, with an increasing number of officials having working experience in the EC (on secondment usually to UKREP or to the Commission), and with the Civil Service College now running countless numbers of courses on aspects of the EC, the Civil Service as a whole is being increasingly penetrated by an EC awareness and sensitivity. As this is happening the traditional distinctions between domestic and external policies, and between the Home and the Diplomatic branches of the Civil Service, are breaking down.

*Parliament*

As the influence of the EC has increasingly penetrated across the policy spectrum so have EC-related matters increasingly come to play a part in the work of Parliament. It has become commonplace for the EC to be the subject of, or to arise in, debates, for it to be an issue in prime ministerial or ministerial question time, and for it to touch on the work of standing and select committees. EC business is thus becoming part of normal parliamentary business.

But EC business also receives special treatment insofar as there are EC committees in both the House of Commons and the House of Lords. Their job, essentially, is to scrutinise EC documents, and in particular proposed EC legislation. They undertake their responsibilities in rather different ways.

The House of Lords European Communities Committee, working through sub-committees, tends to concentrate on producing substantive reports on matters which it considers raise important questions of principle or policy. In compiling its reports it examines relevant EC documents, calls for information from government departments, and receives written and oral evidence from outside interests and experts. The Committee has developed a reputation for producing authoritative reports which are influential both within government and EC circles.

The House of Commons Select Committee on European Legislation does not produce such weighty reports but concentrates rather on scrutinising EC documents and proposals for legislation with a view to identifying those which raise matters of importance and need to be considered by the House. Until the 1990–91 session, consideration by the House took the form of late night debates, attended usually only by hardened pro- and anti-Europeans. Following, however, a report by the Select Committee on Procedure in 1989 consideration may now also take the form of reference to one of two standing committees (each composed of 13 MPs). Whether the consideration is via a debate on the floor of the House, via an examination in a standing committee, or via both procedures, the purpose is usually to try and influence the position adopted by the government when the matter in question is considered by the Council of Ministers.

*Regional and Local Government*

*Regional government* in the UK is restricted to Scotland and Wales, and even there it is of only a very limited and centrally controlled kind. As such, the links which have been established between the EC and the regions of some member states – the German *Länder* for example and the Spanish *autonomias* – have not been developed in the UK context. Indeed, until recently, the national government took steps to ensure they did not do so by insisting that dealings between Scottish and Welsh public sector bodies and the EC be conducted through UKREP.

This situation is, however, beginning to change. One reason for this is an increasing interest on the part of the EC in national regions – seen most clearly in a new advisory Committee of the Regions which is to be established under the Treaty on European Union. Another reason is that the government has had to accept that many Scottish and Welsh local authorities and public bodies are not inclined to be mediated by national government on all EC matters and have begun to deal directly with the Commission.

As part of this 'regionalisation' process, Wales and Scotland, with discreet government approval, established their own representative offices in Brussels in 1992: the Wales European Centre and Scotland Europa. Their purpose is not to replace UKREP for Welsh and Scottish EC affairs, but is rather to exercise information gathering, coordination, and lobbying functions on behalf of their 'clients' – which in the case, for example, of the Wales European Centre are the Welsh Development Agency, the University of Wales, and Welsh local authorities.

*Local government* is affected by the EC in three main ways. First, local authorities, especially those in less developed areas, are eligible to apply to the EC for financial assistance for various types of projects. Second, EC law requires local authorities to change some of their policies and practices – such as, for example, in relation to public procurement where most large contracts must now be open to tender from throughout the EC. Third, in respect of services such as consumer protection and waste disposal, local authorities have responsibilities to act as the agents of EC policy implementation.

There are considerable variations in the way in which local authorities have reacted to the opportunities and obligations which stem from Britain's membership of the EC. Many have appointed EC liaison officers of one sort or another, often as part of Economic Development Units. Some have appointed lobbyists to work on their behalf in Brussels, with a handful even maintaining their own office in Brussels. For the most part, however, as a 1991 Audit Commission report on local authorities and the EC revealed, the picture is patchy: the Commission found that fewer than a third of councils had undertaken reviews of their needs and organisation in relation to Europe, and of those which had there was little consistency in subsequent approaches (HMSO, 1991).

*The Political Parties*

In organisational terms the most obvious way in which political parties have been affected by the EC is in regard to the existence of the European Parliament.

Elections to the European Parliament are held on a fixed five-yearly basis. In the 518-member European Parliament which was elected in 1989 Britain had 81 seats, each of which was contested on the basis of the traditional first-past-the-post system (apart from in Northern Ireland where a form of proportional representation was used for the three available seats). At the Edinburgh Summit, it was agreed, as part of the deal which increased German representation following reunification, that the size of the European Parliament would be increased to 567 in the 1994 elections, and that this would include an increase in the number of British seats to 87. With Euro-constituencies usually consisting of between 5 and 8 Westminster constituencies, parties have been obliged to develop a new organisational level, at least for electoral purposes. MEPs themselves have usually been anxious to consolidate the strength of this organisational level and in many Euro-constituencies this has had the effect of producing general benefits for the candidate's party, not least in terms of enhanced political and administrative support for Westminster constituency organisations.

In the European Parliament itself, Labour MEPs – of which there have been 45 since the 1989 European elections – sit as members of the Socialist group. This is the largest single group in the European Parliament and the European Labour Party (as Labour MEPs call themselves) are, in their turn, the largest national group within the Socialist group. Conservative MEPs – of which there are 32 – have sat since spring 1992 as members of the European People's Party, which is the second largest group in the European Parliament and is better known as the Christian Democratic group. The acceptance, after a long campaign, of the Conservatives by the Christian Democrats symbolises the rather better relations that Britain has enjoyed with the EC since Thatcher's removal from office. (The majority of Conservative MEPs have long been strongly pro-European but they had been denied entry to the Christian

Democratic group because of the perceived negative European stance of their party and government at home.)

Links between British MEPs and their national party organisations have traditionally been weak, with the consequence that many MEPs have felt somewhat frustrated with, on the one hand, being on the fringes of the national mainstream whilst, on the other hand, not having the value of their work in the European Parliament fully recognised. In recent years, however, this problem has begun to be addressed by both main parties, with channels of communication and, to a lesser extent, institutional integration, being developed. The Labour Party has gone furthest in forging ties with, for example, the leader of the European Labour Party being an *ex officio* member of the Party's National Executive Committee, with MEPs being permitted to attend Westminster backbench meetings and being members of the parliamentary section of the electoral college for leadership elections, and with meetings between MEPs and national spokesmen being held on an increasingly regular basis. The legacy of Thatcher – who never had much time for what she thought was an overly 'wet' and pro-EC group – has meant that ties in the Conservative Party have not been so developed. Nonetheless, Conservative MEPs can attend meetings of the backbench 1922 Committee and since Major assumed the Party leadership a more conscious effort has been made to improve channels of communication.

## Pressure Groups

'Pressure groups go where power goes.' This much used description of pressure group activity is clearly demonstrated in the way in which transfers of power to the EC have produced organisational and behavioural changes in British pressure groups.

The extent to which pressure groups have developed a European dimension naturally depends in large measure on the extent to which policy matters which concern them are now determined at EC level. An obvious example of a pressure group which has had to adjust is the National Farmers' Union (NFU). With most important agricultural decisions now taken by the EC rather than by the British government, the NFU is obliged to lobby EC institutions as effectively as it can – which, in practice, means lobbying the Commission and the European Parliament, both of which are relatively open and receptive to representations from pressure groups, and lobbying the Council of Ministers through the British government. To enable it to undertake such lobbying, and to generally keep itself informed of EC developments, the NFU acts both directly through a small office it maintains in Brussels, and less directly through active involvement in appropriate Euro-groups – of which the Committee of Professional Agricultural Organisations (COPA) is the most important.

A rather different example of pressure group attention turning to Brussels is seen with the environmental lobby. Environmentalists have been attracted to the EC partly because the EC has shown itself to be willing and able to pass legislation on a range of environmental matters – from the emission of toxic substances into the atmosphere to the protection of flora and fauna – but partly also because the British government has not been seen to be very sympathetic to the environmentalists' cause. Organisations as various as Friends of the Earth (FoE), the League Against Cruel Sports, and Greenpeace have thus increasingly lobbied at EC level – both for more and stiffer EC legislation, and for the Commission to be more active in ensuring the effective implementation in the UK of existing EC legislation. An example of such lobbying bringing success was seen in November 1992 when a judgement was made against Britain in the European Court of Justice for failure to meet minimum health standards for nitrates in drinking water: the case had been brought to the Court by the Commission following complaints and representations by FoE.

## The Policy Impact of the EC

In just one week, in early January 1992, the following were included amongst the many announcements and decisions of the EC:

- The Commission decided that the agreement between Walt Disney, the *Guardian* and *Manchester Evening News*, Scottish

Television, London Weekend Television and Carlton Communications in respect of their holding of shares and control of the joint venture company Sunrise Television was not a concentration within the meaning of the EC Merger Regulation and was therefore authorised. (Sunrise Television had recently been awarded the licence to provide national British breakfast-time television on ITV Channel 3 from January 1993.)

● Following comments by British ministers concerning the possible creation of an Enterprise Zone in Lanarkshire to help offset the effects of the announcement of the closure of the Ravenscraig steelworks, it was made clear in Brussels that an application for approval of the creation of an Enterprise Zone would need to be made to the Commission to ensure there was no infringement of EC rules on regional policy.

● Under the Seventh Directive on Aid to Shipbuilding the Commission approved a number of UK aid schemes applicable to the shipbuilding sector.

● The Council of Ministers issued a statement reaffirming the EC's strong desire that there be an early successful conclusion to the Uruguay Round of GATT negotiations on international trade. They repeated earlier statements to the effect that the EC was prepared to be flexible, but non-EC countries would have to make concessions too – notably in respect of the EC's agricultural price support system. (The EC's Common Commercial Policy means the EC countries must negotiate as one in respect of the terms and conditions of trade with non EC countries.)

● The EC recognised the independence of Croatia and Slovenia. (The UK Foreign Secretary, Douglas Hurd, subsequently made it clear in interviews that Britain would have preferred to delay recognition of Croatia, but went along with the majority in the interests of presenting a common EC position.)

The range of matters covered in this list, in what was a quite typical week, gives a flavour both of how widely the EC's policy writ now runs, and how extensively British authorities are no longer sole decision-makers in many policy areas. The fact is that although EC policies continue to be primarily economic in character, there are now very few policy areas in which there is not an EC involvement of some kind. Moreover, that involvement extends increasingly to even the most sensitive, and hitherto guarded, of policy spheres – as was no more clearly demonstrated than in July 1992 when, after years of insistence by British governments that tax rates are solely a matter for national governments, EC Finance Ministers unanimously agreed to set a minimum 15 per cent rate for Value Added Tax for four years from 1 January 1993. (The British government claimed that the decision would have little practical effect in Britain where the minimum rate was 17.5 per cent. Nonetheless, the door of EC policy competence was unquestionably opened just a little further by the decision.)

Of course, the extent of EC involvement in particular policy areas, and the consequent balance of policy responsibilities between the EC and member states, varies considerably. Figure 3.2 demonstrates this in the form of a spectrum of Community policy involvement. It is a spectrum, it should be stressed, that is in constant transition as the EC's policy competence grows. So, for example, a decade or so ago competition policy was located towards the centre of the spectrum, but in recent years – under the impetus of the SEM programme – it has moved towards the 'extensive EC involvement' end as the EC has gained new powers and has become much more active in areas such as the authorisation of proposed large company mergers, the granting of state aid to business undertakings, the outlawing of restrictive practices, and the specification of product standards. A graphic example of competition policy in action was seen in July 1990 when the Commission instructed the UK government to recover £44.4 million worth of concessions ('sweeteners' as they were described in the media) which had been granted to British Aerospace at the time of its acquisition of the Rover car group in 1988. (On appeal, the Court of Justice in February 1992 overturned the Commission's decision on procedural grounds but the Commission quickly announced that it would continue to pursue its demand for the repayment to be made.)

In addition to varying in its extent, EC policy involvement also varies in its nature. It does so most particularly with regard

FIGURE 3.2 The extent of EC policy involvement

| Extensive EC policy involvement | Policy responsibility shared between the EC and the member states | | Limited EC policy involvement |
|---|---|---|---|
| Trade | Agriculture | Regional | Energy | Health |
| Fishing | Competition | Transport | Education |
| | Industrial | Macroeconomic | Defence |
| | Foreign | Combating terrorism and drugs | Law and order |
| | Monetary | | Social welfare |
| | Environmental | | |
| | Equal opportunities | | |
| | Working conditions | | |
| | Consumer protection | | |

*Note*: The policy areas which involve heavy public expenditure are grouped mainly at the 'limited EC policy involvement' end of the spectrum. In consequence the EC budget is tiny relative to national budgets – 66 billion ECU (£46 billion) for 1992, which amounts to only just over 1 per cent of total EC GNP.

to the balance that exists between legal and non-legal policy instruments. EC law is most commonly found in those policy areas which are well developed and where uniform rules and practices are required for the policy in question to be properly effective. Clearly, for example, the SEM could not function in its intended manner on the basis of free and fair competition if member states retained the legal power to impose tariffs on imports from other EC countries when they judged it to be economically desirable, or if governments were empowered to give national businesses a trading advantage in the form of subsidies from public funds. Figure 3.3 indicates the nature of the legal/non-legal balance across the policy spectrum.

The making of EC law does not, of course, always ensure its effective implementation. The UK's implementation record, both in incorporating EC law into national law and in applying that law in practice is, it should be said, better than that of most member states: a fact that has often been cited by government spokesmen as evidence that the UK is a good European despite the reluctance to join in with the integrationist rhetoric that frequently is heard from elsewhere. It is a record, however, that is far from perfect. In respect of EC environmental legislation, for example, the UK has been subject to a number of highly publicised actions by the Commission – including referrals to the Court of Justice – for non-implementation. One reason for such non-implementation is that compliance with some EC environmental legislation necessitates heavy capital expenditure, as with bringing British standards up to EC standards in regard to the purity of drinking water and the safety of sea bathing water. Another reason for non-implementation is that in some cases EC legislation may be regarded as being, for one reason or another, awkward or unwanted (though the public reason for non-implementation is likely to be presented in other terms – such as a belief that the legislation does not apply to the case in question). Recent examples of the UK getting into difficulties with the Commission for this second sort of reason include permitting the mass planting of conifers in parts of Scotland (which the Commission has alleged breaches EC legislation designed to protect areas of special scientific and ecological interest), and the row which first erupted in the

FIGURE 3.3   The nature of EC policy involvement

| Heavy reliance on legal regulation | A mixture of legal regulation and inter-state cooperation | | Largely based on inter-state cooperation |
|---|---|---|---|
| Trade | Regional | Industrial | Macroeconomic |
| Agriculture | Competition | Environmental | Health |
| Fishing | Consumer protection | Transport | Education |
| | Working conditions | | Foreign |
| | | | Defence |
| | | | Energy |
| | | | Law and order |
| | | | Combating terrorism and drugs |
| | | | Social welfare |

summer of 1991 when the Commission claimed that seven major construction projects – including the highly controversial scheme to extend the M3 motorway through the ancient chalk hills of Twyford Down – breached EC environmental law because the plans for the schemes did not incorporate environmental impact assessments (see Chapter 12).

As for EC policies that rest primarily on non-legal instruments, they are found in policy areas where no consensus has emerged that it is necessary or desirable to move beyond domestic policy-making coupled with intergovernmental co-operation. In such policy areas, recommendations, communications and opinions are frequently issued by the Commission and the Council to the member states with the purpose of encouraging the different national systems to develop in line with one another: policy matters so covered range from urging higher motoring taxes in the interests of the environment to identifying common objectives in the field of social welfare. Non-legal policy instruments do not, of course, have the same force as Community law, but over time pressures tend to build for them to be placed on a legal footing. Furthermore, even when they remain non-legal, and therefore non-binding, political pressures to bow to the majority view can be powerful – as for example, in the foreign policy field where the EC attempts to reach common positions on virtually all major international issues.

## Future Prospects

EC integration has advanced considerably in recent years, with institutions being strengthened and policy competence being broadened. The Treaty on European Union lays the basis for these processes to continue in the 1990s.

In what direction and at what speed they will continue is not, however, altogether clear. For the fact is that there is no consensus amongst either the leaders or the peoples of EC states about how far and how fast they wish the integration process to go. The Maastricht Treaty was a compromise which left most national governments at least partially dissatisfied – either because the outcome was regarded as being generally too cautious (the Benelux and Italian view), or because it was regarded as being too cautious in particular respects (the German view on the increased powers of the European Parliament and the French view on defence policy), or because it was regarded as furthering the integration process rather too much (the UK view, notwithstanding its belief that the Treaty does offer the opportunity – mainly via the subsidiarity principle – of slowing down, and possibly even reversing in some respects, the integration process). The debates, the manoeuvrings, and the negotiations on the nature and pace of EC integration, which have so long been a feature of the Community, thus seem certain to continue. This makes the future highly uncertain, particularly when there is always the possibility of unforeseen events blowing the best laid plans off course – as, for example, happened in 1992 when the Danish and French referenda forced EC and national leaders to become both more circumspect in their approach to the process of integration and more sensitive to popular concerns about perceived threats from the EC to national sovereignty and identity.

European integration processes in the next few years will be concerned, however, not only with the deepening of the EC but also with its widening. Pressures for enlargement are coming from three directions: from European Free Trade Association (EFTA) states (Austria, Sweden, Finland, Switzerland and Norway had all applied by the end of 1992, though the result of the Swiss referendum at the end of 1992 put this application in question); from the EC's southern flank (Turkey, Cyprus and Malta have made applications); and from states which were members of the former Soviet bloc or were part of the former Soviet Union (all these states realise that their political and economic 'backwardness' precludes immediate accession but Hungary, the Czech and Slovak republics which came into existence on 1 January 1993, and Poland have expressed their hopes for membership by 1996–97, and others have indicated their wish to be members by around the turn of the century). The EC's plan is to grant accessions in waves, with EFTA countries – which have political and economic structures which are broadly comparable to those of EC countries – becoming members some time in the middle of the decade. Clearly, as such accessions occur, and the EC grows to an organisation of 16, 18, 20, and perhaps even more members, its very nature will be subject to radical change. A more complicated structure of European integration is likely to emerge, probably involving some form of overlapping, fast and slow, integrationist streams. In such circumstances, Britain will be faced with very difficulty choices as to which stream it wishes to be in. John Major's stated desire to locate Britain 'at the heart of Europe' will be put firmly to the test.

# 4

# Territorial Politics

**ANDREW GAMBLE**

The UK is a unitary state, but it is also multinational. The territorial dimension of UK politics is a fundamental element in understanding both political change and how power is exercised in the UK. During the 1992 general election the primary focus as far as most of the London media was concerned was which of the two main parties, Conservative or Labour, would form the next government at Westminster. But in other parts of the UK, particularly in Scotland and Northern Ireland, a very different election was taking place, with a different agenda, different issues, and in some cases different parties.

## The 1992 General Election

The outcome of the 1992 General Election confirmed the territorial diversity of political behaviour in the UK. Northern Ireland, Scotland and Wales all voted differently from England, and within England itself there were significant regional variations (see Table 4.1). The differences were most stark in Northern Ireland and Scotland. Northern Ireland returned 17 MPs to the Westminster Parliament, none of whom was prepared to take the whip of any of the mainland British parties. The gulf between the politics of the province and the politics of the rest of the UK remained as wide as ever. Northern Ireland was defined once again by the election as a separate territory, with its own parties, and its own distinct concerns.

**TABLE 4.1** Regional distribution of seats and votes in the UK at the 1992 general election

| | Conservative | | | Labour | | | Liberal Democrat | | | Scottish National Party | | | Plaid Cymru | | | Other | |
|---|---|---|---|---|---|---|---|---|---|---|---|---|---|---|---|---|---|
| | % Votes | % Seats | Seats | % Votes | % Seats | Seats | % Votes | % Seats | Seats | % Votes | % Seats | Seats | % Votes | % Seats | Seats | % Votes | Seats |
| South East | 55 | 97 | 106 | 21 | 3 | 3 | 23 | 0 | 0 | | | | | | | 1 | 0 |
| South West | 48 | 79 | 38 | 20 | 8 | 4 | 31 | 13 | 6 | | | | | | | 2 | 0 |
| Greater London | 45 | 57 | 48 | 37 | 42 | 35 | 15 | 1 | 1 | | | | | | | 3 | 0 |
| East Anglia | 51 | 85 | 17 | 28 | 15 | 3 | 20 | 0 | 0 | | | | | | | 2 | 0 |
| West Midlands | 45 | 50 | 29 | 39 | 50 | 29 | 15 | 0 | 0 | | | | | | | 1 | 0 |
| East Midlands | 47 | 67 | 28 | 38 | 33 | 14 | 15 | 0 | 0 | | | | | | | 1 | 0 |
| Yorks and Humb. | 38 | 37 | 20 | 44 | 63 | 34 | 17 | 0 | 0 | | | | | | | 2 | 0 |
| North West | 38 | 37 | 27 | 45 | 60 | 44 | 16 | 3 | 2 | | | | | | | 1 | 0 |
| North | 33 | 17 | 6 | 51 | 81 | 29 | 16 | 3 | 1 | | | | | | | 1 | 0 |
| England | 46 | 61 | 319 | 34 | 37 | 195 | 19 | 2 | 10 | | | | | | | 1 | 0 |
| Scotland | 26 | 15 | 11 | 39 | 68 | 49 | 13 | 13 | 9 | 22 | 4 | 3 | | | | 1 | 0 |
| Wales | 29 | 16 | 6 | 50 | 71 | 27 | 12 | 3 | 1 | | | | 9 | 11 | 4 | 1 | 0 |

| Northern Ireland | Ulster Unionist Party | | | Democratic Unionist Party | | | Popular Unionist Party | | | Alliance Party | | | SDLP | | | Sinn Fein | | | Conservative | | | Other | |
|---|---|---|---|---|---|---|---|---|---|---|---|---|---|---|---|---|---|---|---|---|---|---|---|
| | % Votes | % Seats | Seats | % Votes | % Seats | Seats | % Votes | % Seats | Seats | % Votes | % Seats | Seats | % Votes | % Seats | Seats | % Votes | % Seats | Seats | % Votes | % Seats | Seats | % Votes | Seats |
| | 35 | 53 | 9 | 13 | 18 | 3 | 3 | 6 | 1 | 9 | 0 | 0 | 24 | 24 | 4 | 10 | 0 | 0 | 6 | 0 | 0 | 2 | 0 |

In Scotland the disaster that many had predicted for the Conservative Party did not materialise, but the party that was comfortably re-elected to a record fourth term could only secure the election of 11 Conservative MPs in Scotland (out of 72). Scotland voted again for a different government from the one England elected. Wales was closer to the English pattern, but as in Scotland, a nationalist party advocating the separation of Wales from the UK continued to attract significant support. As Table 4.1 shows the Conservatives have a much higher percentage share of seats than votes in many of the English regions and conversely a much lower share in the northern English regions and in Scotland and Wales. The Conservatives are not as weak as they appear in Scotland nor as strong in the South East. Nevertheless there remains a significant unevenness in the way support for both the Conservatives and Labour is regionally distributed, a bias which works to the Conservatives' advantage. The Liberal Democrats are the losers – the only region in which they are over-represented in Parliament is Scotland.

**Territorial Management**

Territorial politics has always been an important dimension of UK politics, although at one time it was ignored by political scientists, who argued that Britain had one of the most homogenous electorates in the world, and that British electoral behaviour was shaped predominantly by social class. Other factors which were still very important in other political systems such as regional and religious identities were regarded as weak and declining in Britain (Blondel, 1963).

The weakening of social class as an explanatory model of voting behaviour in the 1970s and 1980s was partly due to the re-emergence of old territorial problems. A new territorial model of British politics was proposed, which accepted that the UK contained several national and regional identities, and marked regional variations in party allegiances, voting behaviour, economic structure and performance. This model recognised that constitutional questions were not marginal but central for understanding the dynamics of British politics. The different institutions of government that have been evolved for Scotland, Wales, and Northern Ireland are not just historical curiosities but essential aspects of territorial management (Madgwick and Rose, 1982; Bulpitt, 1983). Through them the British State acknowledges that Northern Ireland, Scotland and Wales can all legitimately lay claim to an identity that is separate from that of England. All these territories have different traditions, and different institutions. They tend to vote differently, and they have come to be governed differently.

A key aspect of British territorial management is that although the Westminster Parliament still claims unlimited sovereignty over all parts of the UK, and has consequently always resisted federalism, it has not chosen to enforce its claims through a uniform pattern of central administration. Significant regional differences do exist. This has encouraged some political scientists to describe territories such as Scotland as distinct political systems (Kellas, 1989) but it is perhaps more accurate to see Scotland, Wales and Northern Ireland as integral parts of the *British* political system, which present particular problems that must be constantly managed by the central government (Midwinter *et al.*, 1991).

In England many powers taken by the Westminster Parliament are devolved to local authorities and other public bodies (see Chapter 9). Implementation of central government policy depends on the competence and support of subordinate bodies which have varying degrees of autonomy from the centre, and may regard themselves as accountable to local and regional communities rather than to Westminster. Such a pattern of territorial politics has always reduced the degree of control that the centre can exercise, and has ensured that in practice governments have always required a strategy for territorial management (Bulpitt, 1982).

The detail of the territorial problems facing governments at Westminster often changes, but the fundamental objectives they pursue remain the same – to secure continuing consent to the Union between the four territories and to ensure compliance with the policies of the centre. During the last twenty-five years these objectives have become harder to achieve. The revival of nationalism in Scotland and Wales, and the renewed outbreak of sectarian conflict in Northern Ireland, have severely tested the strength of the Union, while conflicts between central and local government have threatened the implementation of central policies.

The overwhelming dominance of England within the Union in modern times in terms of population and wealth has tended to obscure the deep-seated problems of managing the periphery that must still be solved if the old British constitutional state is to continue to exist. Westminster governments might like to forget territorial problems altogether, but they have a habit of breaking in, and still have the capacity to make and unmake governments. The 1974–79 Labour government was not brought down in 1979 by the Winter of Discontent but by the outcomes of referenda on devolution in Wales and Scotland. The Scots voted narrowly in favour of devolution but not in sufficient numbers to meet the condition that 40 per cent of the electorate had to be in favour. The SNP withdrew its support from James Callaghan's minority Labour government which then lost by one vote the motion of confidence tabled by the Conservative opposition.

## National Identity

Problems of territorial management in multinational states have been highlighted recently because of the disintegration of states like Yugoslavia and the USSR which were based on a union of several territories with distinct national identities. In the modern era the main source of legitimacy for states has been nationhood (Gellner, 1983). Multinational states which were established before the modern era on different principles have in most cases succumbed to the principle of national self-determination. Britain, however, has so far been an exception. Although two-thirds of Ireland was lost in the 1920s the British State has been successful in keeping the rest of the British Isles within its jurisdiction.

The future success of this policy is not guaranteed. Nation-states in the modern era have always encouraged where they could the joining together of national identity and citizenship. In Britain nationality and citizenship have been growing apart. The English, the Welsh and the Scots are all British citizens, yet all have a distinct national identity (Crick, 1991b) They belong to the same state but different countries. States which contain separate national identities often have to confront the problem of rival allegiances. The UK has experienced this once before over Ireland. The Irish problem could only be handled ultimately by separation.

In the past the various national identities within the UK were complemented by a more inclusive and over-arching British identity, which linked the British State to the British Empire and Britain's world dominance. Maintaining a British identity was always thought indispensable for preserving the Union. The disappearance of the Empire has raised afresh the problem of what such an identity now is. What is the British project which unites all the inhabitants of the UK? For the English the problem is less since English and British are often treated as synonymous. But a very different position exists, for example, in Scotland. One of the reasons why the future of the Union is once again in doubt is that many Scots have begun to reject some of the key symbols such as the flag and the national anthem which express Britishness. Once a gulf opens between citizenship and national identity, support for the continuation of political Union can be swiftly eroded. There may be arguments of self-interest or convenience for continuing the Union, but as far as legitimacy is concerned the logic of the case for self-determination tends to sweep all before it.

A further difficulty in preserving the Union in its traditional form has been development of the EC. The way in which the EC works has put a spotlight upon regional government, by offering regions within the Community the possibility of a relationship with Community institutions that bypasses their own nation-states. (The Commission itself acknowledges the special character of the British state by maintaining separate offices in Cardiff, Edinburgh and Belfast.) Many regions including Scotland and some of the English regions which felt that the Westminster government was discriminating against them have become keen to develop their links with Brussels. The existence of the supranational institutions of the Community also undermined the argument that small regions needed to be part of strong powerful nation-states in order to survive. Membership of the EC could provide both external support and self-determination at the regional level. The idea of an independent Scotland in Europe is one expression of this.

As the British economy became more integrated into the EC so the prospect emerged that the South East of England might merge into the richest and most rapidly growing area of the Community, while other parts of the UK would become part of the periphery of the Community and experience slower growth, higher unemployment, and lower standards of living (Martin, 1989). Such possibilities also tended to create new political perceptions and political alliances, as well as conflicts of interest within nation-states. They tended to encourage regions to look beyond their own nation-states to find policies that would benefit them.

## Scotland

Territorial management in the UK has always been extremely diverse because it has been very responsive to local issues and circumstances. Yet this ability to create consent has been declining, most notably in Scotland, where the union has come under increasing strain. Scotland occupies a special place within the UK, because while both Wales and Ireland were incorporated through conquest, Scotland negotiated the terms of its entry into the parliamentary Union in 1707. As a result it was able to retain its own distinctive institutions – a separate legal system, church, schools and universities – which have helped to nurture the strong sense of national identity in Scotland. Scots are well aware that they were once an independent nation and could be so again. The Union with England that was considered so advantageous at one time could be broken if it ceased to work to Scotland's benefit.

This pragmatic view of the Union treats it as the Union of two sovereign nations, united under a common Crown and a common Parliament, but which did not result in the creation of a new nation which replaced the older nations. Because the national identities have remained separate the possibility of the states splitting apart has continued to exist. For much of the period of the Union the chance of it happening has not been strong. Scotland benefited as much as any part of the UK from the prosperity and power that accrued to Britain in the nineteenth century. The problem for the Union has come with the decline in British competitiveness and the collapse of so many of its former great industries. The relative enfeeblement of the British economy has reduced the attractiveness of the Union in pragmatic terms, while at the same time the rise of the EC and the discovery of oil in the North Sea have given Scotland other options. A future separate from England has gradually come to be embraced by more and more Scots during the twentieth century (Marr, 1992).

In the 1970s the favoured solution for Scotland was devolution, which meant devolving specific powers from Westminster to Edinburgh. After the failure of the 1979 referendum to deliver devolution the idea has fallen into discredit, condemned as a strategy of the Westminster government to concede as little power as possible to a Scottish Parliament. The current debate in Scotland on the future of the Union centres on three main options: the status quo; Home Rule; and independence. The supporters of reform are not united, but all wish to repudiate the unlimited sovereignty over Scotland which is claimed by the Westminster Parliament.

*The Decline of Conservative Support*

The Conservative Party after briefly favouring devolution has reverted to being a staunch defender of the status quo. But the Union is no longer the rallying cry it once was. Conservative support in Scotland has suffered a long-term erosion, which accelerated during the Thatcher decade. Scotland was traditionally a stronghold of Liberalism, but the Conservatives had built up their strength during the twentieth century in the rural areas and among the Protestant and Unionist working class. From the 1920s until the 1960s Conservative support in Scotland was normally equal to Labour's and often greater. In 1955 for example the Conservatives had 50 per cent of the Scottish vote and more than 50 per cent of the seats (36 to Labour's 34). By 1992 they had only 25 per cent of the Scottish vote and only 15 per cent of the seats (11 to Labour's 49).

1992 could however have been much worse for the Conservatives. They managed to cling onto their seats, and even made a net gain of one, as well as slightly increasing their share of the vote. The Scottish Nationalists, while substantially raising their share of the vote, failed to increase their parliamentary representation. Labour saw its vote fall. But although disaster was averted the Conservative performance in 1992 was hardly a triumph. It could only be judged a success when measured against the collapse that many of their opponents had been predicting, which would have margin- alised the Conservatives as a political force in Scotland. If the Conservatives had been reduced to only three or four seats and had seen their percentage of the Scottish vote drop below 20 per cent, then the implications for the authority of the Westminster government in Scotland would have been ser- ious. There would no longer even have been enough Scottish MPs to fill the ministerial portfolios in the Scottish Office.

The Conservative Secretary of State for Scotland, Ian Lang, immediately claimed that the government had won the argument on the Union, and that there was no longer any need for constitutional change in Scotland's position in the UK. Formally he was correct. He pointed out that the lack of Labour support in Sussex did not mean that a Labour government elected on a national vote had no mandate for its policies in Sussex. The problem for Unionists however is that Scotland feels itself to be quite different from Sussex. If Sussex votes differently from the rest of England it is a matter of little consequence to the ability of the government to carry through its policies, because Sussex voters do not have a national identity and therefore the possibility of an allegiance that is different from the rest of English voters.

Scottish voters do have a separate national identity and therefore it is a more serious matter for the stability of the constitutional order if they vote repeatedly in a way that is significantly different from the English electorate. It might not matter if they supported one party more than another, provided the parties to which they gave their support upheld the Union and alternated in power. But many Scots have begun supporting the SNP, which is an anti-Unionist party and advocates independence for Scotland. The Unionist party which has lost most popularity in Scotland, the Conservative Party, has now won four elections in a row at Westminster.

The possibility that the party which enjoys the highest level of support among Scots, the Labour Party, may never win enough English votes to form another Westminster government has swollen the ranks of those demanding constitutional change in Scotland.

### The Impact of the Thatcher Government

The reasons for the erosion of Conservative support in Scotland are complex. Scotland is by no means the poorest region in the UK, or the region with the highest unemployment. It has been hit hard by the decline in manufacturing, particularly in shipbuilding and engineering, but it has developed many new hi-tech industries as well as receiving a substantial boost from North Sea oil. Conservative policies emphasising enterprise and disengagement of the state from the economy were expected to appeal to Scots as much as to voters anywhere else in the UK. Indeed Margaret Thatcher always expressed surprise that the Scots were not active converts to Thatcherism, since Scottish presbyterianism and Scottish political economy were the origins of so many of the free-market and individualist ideas she espoused.

Despite having one of the most vigorous think-tanks of the Thatcher era named after Adam Smith, and the establishment of Thatcherite cells in a few places like the University of St Andrews, the Scots never embraced Thatcherite ideas (Holliday, 1992a). One of the main reasons was that the Thatcherite programme appeared to be predominantly English. Although Thatcher proclaimed the Conservative Party the Unionist party, the Thatcherite programme and the style of the Thatcher government, particularly the personalities and attitudes of Thatcher herself and most of her ministers were seen as profoundly English, dominated by English concerns. John Major, despite making symbolic gestures like holding the December 1992 European Summit in Edinburgh, has done little to dispel this image. The Conservative party has very few politicians in Scotland who are still in touch with the working-class Scottish electorate in the way that traditional Unionists used to be. In addition substantial sections of the professional and business classes who used to be natural Tory voters have abandoned the Conservatives and begun voting either for the Liberal Democrats or the SNP. Identification of the Conservatives as an English Party which cares little and does less for Scotland explains this shift.

This perception was reinforced by a series of policy decisions by Conservative governments which appeared to take no account of legitimate interests in Scotland. The most resented was the decision to introduce the poll tax in Scotland twelve months before it was introduced in England and Wales. The impression that Scotland was being used as a test-bed for new policies was deeply damaging (Midwinter *et al.*, 1991). The accusation was only partly true – the real reason for the early shift to the poll tax was the urgent need to introduce something to replace the rates after rates revaluation in Scotland had so badly misfired. But once a government has lost legitimacy and trust it is very difficult to regain them. Events and policies now tend to be interpreted on the assumption that Scotland is either being ignored or exploited in some way by unscrupulous English governments. In many political systems the loss of trust and legitimacy on such a scale is remedied through defeat of the government at a general election and the installation of a new one. In Scotland's case this possibility for the moment is closed off. However much the Scots disapprove of the way in which they are being governed, their votes are not sufficient to elect an alternative.

## The Constitutional Debate

Because the pendulum has failed to swing Scotland has become a fertile area for proposals for constitutional change. The Labour Party is the largest party in Scotland. Although it does not have an absolute majority of the vote, it has an overwhelming majority in seats. In the 1987 Parliament Labour had 50 of the 72 Scottish seats (70 per cent). But since the Conservatives had a Commons majority of 100 Labour's 50 MPs were powerless to influence policy relating to Scotland, and were promptly dubbed by the SNP 'the feeble fifty'. Labour is a Unionist party, and has strong centralist, anti-devolutionist and anti-Home Rule traditions. But those traditions have been losing ground, the more the Conservative position at Westminster has come to seem unassailable, and the more Labour has come under attack from the SNP. In the last few years Labour has supported the Scottish Constitutional Convention. The Convention brought together the main opposition groups in Scotland (apart from the SNP who participated at first and then withdrew) to discuss constitutional change. Labour has gradually moved to become a firm part of the coalition pressing for radical constitutional change in Scotland. The old pattern of two Unionist parties competing against one another for the votes of the Scottish electorate has been shattered (Marr, 1992).

The constitutional argument in Scotland is very far advanced. The government which led to the establishment of the Constitutional Convention grew out of disappointment with the failed attempt to get devolution in the 1970s. The main emphasis of the new approach is Home Rule – a Parliament in Edinburgh with substantial powers, including fiscal powers, and elected under a PR system (the additional member system, AMS). This programme of constitutional change has the full support of the Liberal Democrats, but has come under attack from the SNP for whom it does not go far enough. While Ian Lang fears that a Home Rule Parliament if it was ever set up would be the start of a slippery slope to complete independence, the SNP fears that it could be used to shore up the Union and deny Scotland any real autonomy.

One of the ironies of the recent run of Conservative success at Westminster is that it has complicated the problems of territorial management in Scotland, by encouraging a great deal of anti-English and anti-Unionist sentiment, and by obliging Labour to abandon its support for the status quo. The Conservatives are now a minority in Scotland, and a clear majority of the electorate and the political elite want substantial constitutional change, although it is an advantage for the Conservatives that there is not as yet a consensus on what that change should be.

The immediate prospects for change are not high. After the election political agitation quickly subsided. Attempts by the pressure group Scotland United to organise campaigns of civil disobedience did not materialise. But underlying support for change remains strong and is unlikely to decline. The national question in Scotland will not go away, and may erupt again at any time.

If constitutional change does come eventually, its consequences will go far beyond Scotland. Would a Home Rule Scotland still be entitled to its present 72 MPs? Scotland's population entitles it to 59 MPs, while Wales should have 32 instead of 38 (see Chapter 5). Would Scottish members still be allowed to vote on legislation affecting England (Tam Dalyell's West Lothian question)? If there was a change on either it would have a serious effect on the Labour Party, since it depends for so much of its support on Scotland. Almost one-fifth of the PLP is Scottish, and so now are several key members of the Shadow Cabinet, including John Smith.

Labour faces a cruel dilemma over Scotland. It needs Scotland's present level of representation to be preserved in order to keep alive its hopes of winning power again at Westminster. At the same time the party in Scotland has been won over to the case for constitutional change. If Scotland's position is altered there will be strong pressure to reduce Scotland's representation at Westminster. If the Scots opted for full independence the consequences could be still more serious for Labour. The UK political system was decisively biased towards the Conservative Party when Eire left the Union, because it removed 80 Irish MPs who might well have continued to support anti-Conservative coalitions at Westminster as they did before 1914. It would have made the dominance the Conservatives have exercised for so much of this century much harder to achieve. If either Scotland or Wales were to be removed from the UK political system the difficulties for anti-Conservative forces would be compounded. If calculations of electoral self-interest were the only factor involved, Conservatives should be arguing for the early independence of Scotland.

## Wales

In Wales territorial politics assumes forms very different from either Scotland or Northern Ireland. Wales, the oldest member of the Union, was conquered by the English and substantial parts were resettled. A determined attempt was made to suppress the Welsh language and other expressions of Welsh nationhood. It was unsuccessful, because the language survived in the remoter parts of Wales, but in other respects Wales was much more fully integrated into England than Scotland ever was. The native Scottish language, Gaelic, practically died out as a spoken tongue, but the Lowland Scots while disdainful of the language and the religion of the highlands were careful to preserve their distinctive institutions. The Scottish sense of nationhood came to be expressed through its civil society, but in Wales nationhood came to be understood in terms of Welsh culture, the most important symbol of which was the Welsh language.

Many of the modern battles of Welsh nationalism have therefore been around the status of the Welsh language. Wales has an estimated 500 000 Welsh speakers out of a total population of 2.7 million. Much of the effort of Welsh nationalists has been to ensure that the Welsh language is protected and that its official status is recognised. Legislation has been passed to ensure the parity of Welsh and English in official documents and public notices and signs. Channel 4 in Wales is reserved for Welsh language programmes. Campaigns to bring temperance reform to Wales have also been organised, and Wales was allowed its own legislation so that referenda could be held to determine the wishes of local communities.

Apart from these expressions of cultural nationalism, Wales has been affected only to a small extent by nationalist movements. The referendum on devolution for Wales in 1979 was rejected by a very large margin. Only 11.9 per cent voted in favour, 46.9 per cent voted against, and 41.2 per cent did not vote. The fear of the consequences for a small territory like Wales being separated from England persuaded most voters to vote against or abstain.

*The Welsh Office*

As a result of its different history Wales has experienced very little administrative devolution. Wales has been treated for the most part as a region of England. But the demand for Wales to be treated the same as Scotland and accorded a similar constitutional status has led to innovations in the way Wales is governed without there being any particular surge of support for them. These innovations include the setting up of a Welsh Office to parallel the Scottish Office by the Labour government in 1964. (The Scottish Office was set up much earlier in 1885.) At the same time a Secretary of State for Wales was appointed with an automatic seat in the Cabinet. Similarly the Welsh were given a Grand Committee like the Scots to consider parliamentary legislation that affected Wales. But there was little to parallel the substantial administrative devolution that Scotland enjoyed in areas like agriculture, and fishing, local government, health and education (Madgwick and Rose, 1982; Midwinter *et al.*, 1991).

Plaid Cymru, the Welsh Nationalist party, has built up a solid core of support, and won four parliamentary seats in 1992, but its main areas of support have been in the Welsh-speaking areas of the country. It does not have the broad appeal of the SNP. Since only a minority of the Welsh speak Welsh, and many resent having to learn it, there are limits to the party's electoral base. Many parts of Wales, particularly along the northern coast, have large numbers of inhabitants of English origin.

Establishment of the Welsh Office in 1964 was widely seen as a sop to Labour's Welsh supporters. But the institution has developed in interesting ways. Having a Cabinet Minister heading the Office has allowed the development of coherent interventionist policies for the whole region. The most striking example of such strategic thinking came paradoxically in the Thatcher years, under first Peter Walker, and more recently David Hunt (the only Cabinet Minister openly to support Michael Heseltine on the second ballot for the leadership in 1990). Under Walker and Hunt the Welsh Office has practised not the disengagement favoured by Thatcherite ideology but an interventionist industrial policy, the Valleys Initiative, aimed at reconstructing the economy of South Wales after the run-down of the coal and steel industries by attracting inward investment from British, European, and most strikingly Japanese companies. During Walker's three years as Secretary of State, Wales with 5 per cent of the UK population received

22 per cent of the inward investment, and unemployment was reduced by 50 per cent, to below the national average. The kind of regional strategy denied to the regions of England, particularly after abolition of the metropolitan counties in 1986, has been allowed to flourish in Wales.

*Public Expenditure*

Another feature of this special position which applies to Scotland also is the formula that has evolved for determining how much Scotland and Wales should receive in public expenditure. Some spending programmes, such as defence, are determined centrally, often without much consideration being given to their territorial impact (even though this can be substantial). But other expenditure is allocated in a block to be distributed at the regional level. In the nineteenth century a Treasury formula, the Goschen formula, was devised which allocated Scotland a budget of 11 per cent of the UK total, roughly the size of Scotland's population. A formula-based system was revived in the 1970s. Wales and Scotland each receive a block grant, which is adjusted in line with changes in expenditure in England. Wales receives 5/85ths and Scotland 10/85ths of any increase or decrease in English programmes (Midwinter *et al.*, 1991, p.101). Although the spending of much of this block grant is heavily constrained by existing commitments, the Secretaries of State for both Wales and Scotland do have some freedom to determine priorities. Welsh Secretary Peter Walker, for example, set his own, fairly generous, levels for rate support grant.

Why Wales with a population of 2.7 million is entitled to its own regional administration headed by a Minister with Cabinet rank while Yorkshire with a population of 4.6 million enjoys neither, is one of the many anomalies of the British constitution, which can only be satisfactorily explained by the requirements of territorial management based on the recognition that the UK is made up of several national identities. After many centuries of refusing to recognise any special distinctiveness of Wales, in the twentieth century the Westminster State has recognised the separate national status of Wales within the UK and accords it certain institutional and legislative privileges. Nationalist forces in Wales would like to go further and dream like the Scots of a Europe of the regions. The Plaid Cymru council at Aberystwyth flies the flags of all the smaller nations of Europe at present imprisoned within larger state structures. But there are few signs at present that the Nationalists can expand beyond their heartlands in Gwynnedd and Dyfed to capture a majority of Welsh support.

## Northern Ireland

For the last twenty-five years Northern Ireland has been by some distance the most intractable territorial problem with which British governments have had to deal. It is easily forgotten that establishment of the Stormont Parliament after enforced partition of Ireland in 1921 came to be regarded as a reasonably successful experiment in administrative and political devolution. Westminster did not need to concern itself with the drains of Fermanagh. Every election in Northern Ireland returned a Unionist government and every general election sent a solid block of Unionists to Westminster to take the Conservative Whip and be a loyal component of the party that was in government for thirty-five of the fifty years that Stormont existed. After the traumas of the long and bitter conflict with Ireland, partition appeared to have strengthened the Union by creating a loyal and dependable satellite.

Westminster proved unable to distance itself from Irish affairs for ever. The fifty years of one-party government at Stormont successfully removed Ulster from the attention of British politicians, but one of the costs was widespread discrimination against Catholics. The abuses of the Stormont regime helped create civil rights protests in the 1960s which were followed by the eruption of civil disorder and sectarian conflict that have continued up to the present. By 1993 3000 had died, equivalent to 100 000 in the rest of the UK.

### Direct Rule

The Westminster government responded first with military intervention in 1969, and then with political and administrative intervention. Stormont was suspended in 1972 and direct rule imposed. Northern Ireland has since been ruled directly though a Northern Ireland Office, headed by a Secretary of State who like his Welsh and Scottish counterparts has a seat in the Cabinet. The old Northern Ireland civil service has been incorporated into the new office with the addition of a layer of civil servants from Westminster.

The role of the Northern Irish Secretary is very different from that of the Scottish Secretary or Welsh Secretary. It is more like that of a colonial governor or proconsul sent out from London to govern a troublesome province than of a representative of the territory itself. The Scottish Secretary has always been Scottish, and the Welsh Secretary usually Welsh (Peter Walker was an exception). The Northern Ireland Secretary has rarely had any Irish connection at all (although the present incumbent, Sir Patrick Mayhew, is a partial exception) and certainly has not been drawn from Northern Ireland itself.

The powers of the Northern Ireland Secretary are also different. In part this reflects the security situation, for which no parallel exists in Scotland or Wales. In part it reflects the divided nature of the community. A territory which was allowed a greater degree of devolution of power than any other part of the UK now has considerably less. Not just Stormont has been suspended; powers have also been stripped away from local government. The refusal of the two communities to share power has meant that the normal political process has been suspended, and all significant administrative and political decision-making has been centralised in the Northern Ireland Office which is a direct arm of Westminster. The Scots may describe the Conservative Scottish Secretary as the agent of an alien Westminster government, but the position is quite unlike that in Northern Ireland, because the Scottish Secretary is always an elected Scottish MP, and a leader of a substantial if minority part of Scottish public opinion. Even this limited form of self-government has been denied Northern Ireland since 1972.

Since the imposition of direct rule successive British governments have enforced a tough security policy while searching for a political solution that could isolate the terrorists and extreme sectarians on both sides and restore civil peace. The key British government objective has been to contain the violence, while experimenting with political initiatives in the hope that a settlement may eventually emerge which would allow Britain's financial and military commitment to be drastically reduced. Northern Ireland currently costs the British Treasury $£1.7$ billion per annum more than is raised in taxation (Cunningham, 1992).

## The Anglo–Irish Agreement

The recent period has been dominated by the signing of the Anglo–Irish Agreement (AIA) in 1985 by the Thatcher government. This agreement led to fierce protests from Unionists in Northern Ireland, because for the first time it gave the Republic of Ireland a formal status in the search for a political solution. To Unionists the AIA was a sign that the British were preparing to disengage from Northern Ireland. In the Republic the agreement was strongly attacked by Nationalists who saw it as a betrayal of Irish Nationalism since it conceded that there were two communities in Northern Ireland and that Unionists did have a right of self-determination (O'Leary, 1990).

The British government rode out the storm and has persisted with its attempt to involve the Republic, amidst signs that the Unionist side had begun to accept the necessity for compromise if some form of self-government was ever to be restored to the province. When Peter Brooke was Northern Ireland Secretary patient diplomacy established a new round of talks between the parties in Northern Ireland over how to restore self-government to the province. Brooke's proposal was that talks should have three stages: talks between constitutional parties in the province; talks between Northern Ireland parties and the government of the Republic; and talks about the London–Dublin relationship. Initial agreement on the terms and sequence of discussion was obtained, but the process stalled because of Unionist objections to the stage at which the government of Ireland would be admitted to the talks. Peter Brooke's unwise appearance and impromptu cabaret act on a Dublin chat show soon after an IRA atrocity reduced his credibility as an intermediary. He lost his post in the government after the 1992 election. His successor Sir Patrick Mayhew restarted discussions, but the process came to a definite halt a few months later, the Unionists insisting that there was no point in further discussions until the Irish government was prepared to remove the territorial claim to Northern Ireland which still appears in the Irish Constitution. Hopes of movement now rest on the new coalition government in Dublin formed by Fianna Fail and Labour.

*Nationalist and Unionist Perspectives*

Despite the weariness induced by twenty-five years of sectarian conflict and the widespread desire, at least on the part of politicians, to end direct rule, a lasting solution still looks very difficult to achieve. Traditional interpretations of the politics of Northern Ireland are polarised between Nationalist and Unionist perspectives. The Nationalist view sees the main problem as the British presence in Ireland. Unionism it is alleged is the creation of the British to perpetuate their control of the territory. Without British support Unionism would collapse. The corresponding Unionist view blames the problem on the Nationalists for refusing to recognise that Protestants have their own national identity and refusing to give them the same right of self-determination that they claim for themselves (Whyte, 1990). As John Whyte points out both views share a similar model of politics. Both assume that there is a single self-evident appropriate unit of self-determination for Northern Ireland. For the Nationalists it is Ireland – a geographical and historical entity, the natural unit of self-government for the whole island. For the Unionists it is Ulster, the territory of the Ulster Protestants, a distinct community which has nothing in common with the southern republic. Neither view is prepared to concede the legitimacy of the other. Both argue as though the other community did not exist.

The stubborn reality of the division of Northern Ireland into two communities is what strikes many observers. Most recent writing and research on Northern Ireland has accordingly strongly favoured an internal conflict model (O'Leary, 1985; Whyte, 1991). Although there is still much debate as to which particular factors are most important there is agreement that the problem is endogenous rather than exogenous. Its basic causes stem from internal factors, the existence of two communities whose identities and allegiances are irreconcilable, rather than from external factors, such as the roles of Britain or Ireland.

An internal conflict model does not ignore the important part played by external powers. One of the reasons why the conflict is so intractable is precisely because Northern Ireland is a border territory (Wright, 1987). The two communities in the province divide their allegiance between the two nation-states that adjoin them. The desire of the British government to involve the Republic of Ireland in a search for a solution to the problem of Northern Ireland is belated recognition of the actual nature of the conflict. The Government of Ireland Act 1920 which established the Stormont Parliament in the North partitioned Ireland so as to ensure that Northern Ireland would have a secure Protestant majority. That aim was achieved – Protestants still outnumber Catholics 2:1 in a population of 1.5 million. But the allegiance of the majority of Catholics to the British state was never secured.

Nationalist fervour in the Catholic community can be exaggerated. Many Catholics show no enthusiasm for uniting with Ireland, but neither can they accept the Unionist conception of nationhood, which as many observers have pointed out is a pre-modern, pre-nationalist form of allegiance of a particular community to the British Crown. The Unionists are not individual British nationalists. Their primary loyalty is to their own distinctive community, whose identity they link indissolubly with Britain rather than the Irish Republic.

Both communities are themselves internally divided, which complicates the search for political agreement. The Unionists have fractured into a variety of parties, the Official Unionists (OUP), the Democratic Unionists (DUP), and the Alliance; while the Nationalists have an even deeper split between the Social Democratic and Labour Party (SDLP) and Sinn Fein (which is directly linked to the IRA). In the 1992 election the OUP and DUP held their ground while the SDLP recaptured West Belfast from Sinn Fein with the help of some support from Unionist voters. One new development in 1992 was that Ulster

Conservatives, with little support or encouragement from Conservative Central Office, ran some candidates. In North Down they obtained 23 per cent of the vote. Despite such attempts however to integrate Northern Ireland into mainstream UK politics it remains a realm apart, with its own parties and voting habits. Little has changed in elections since the 1920s since the fundamental determinant of voting behaviour is the community to which the voter belongs. This gives great stability to Northern Irish politics but as in divided polities elsewhere makes the search for political consensus and institutions that are both legitimate and representative extremely difficult.

## Conclusion

The territorial dimension in British politics is important because the institutions and the ideology of the state have been founded on a particular kind of territorial management. The unlimited authority of the Westminster Parliament has been asserted at the same time that local arrangements have evolved to maintain the loyalty of national groups which remain outside the dominant English national identity. Northern Ireland, Scotland and Wales are all very different from one another, as well as from England. The problems of governing them highlight the provisional and fragile nature of the constitutional order. The form of the UK state is not immutable. In the last hundred years Ireland has left the Union. In the text of the Anglo–Irish Agreement the British government concedes that if a majority of the inhabitants of Northern Ireland ever vote for separation or unification with the Irish Republic that vote will be binding on the British government. The same right of self-determination could hardly be denied to Wales and Scotland if they chose to exercise it.

Relationships between the different parts of the UK have entered a new phase with the dismantling of the British Empire and development of the EC. The viability of smaller national units has increased as well as the possibility of forging a different and more equal relationship with England. The budgetary advantages that the separate parts of the UK receive are outweighed by the restrictions that the central government imposes.

The scope for genuine autonomy of even large nation-states is limited, and it is not certain how successfully territories would fare if the break-up of Britain became a reality. The Westminster government remains committed to holding the Union together, and it is not likely to allow referenda or any other means for opposition to show itself. Whether it can frustrate change forever is doubtful. Given the attitude of the British State and the birth-rate of the two communities Northern Ireland is the territory least likely to remain within the UK indefinitely. In Scotland and Wales the ties are much closer. In Scotland it is probable that some new constitutional arrangement with the rest of the UK will eventually have to come if the Union is to be preserved at all. When it does it may well be the catalyst for a more general constitutional upheaval.

# 5

# Voting and the Electorate

**IVOR CREWE**

Election results are easier to describe than interpret. The result of the 1992 British general election – which the Conservatives unexpectedly won for a fourth consecutive time, though with a drastically reduced majority (see Table 1) – is open to two radically different interpretations. The first regards it as a reversion to the two-party system of the 1960s and emphasises the scale of Labour's advance. It points to Labour's gain in seats (its largest since 1966), its second successive percentage increase in the vote since its 1983 debacle, its replacement of the centre parties as the main challenger in most Conservative seats and its above average recovery in the urban South. With 'one more heave', it is argued, Labour could easily overcome the Conservatives' modest 21-seat majority at the next election.

The second interpretation regards 1992 as confirmation of the new dominant-party system ushered in by the watershed election of 1979. It points to the continuity of 1992 with recent elections, emphasising the Conservative Party's unprecedented run of four successive wins, the rock-like stability in its vote since 1979, and the fact that its 7.5 per cent winning margin of the popular vote was the third largest since the war, exceeded only by 1983 and 1987. It notes that the Labour vote did not return even to its 1979 level, that its advance was wholly at the expense of the centre and that its vote fell below 40 per cent for the sixth election running. And it also notes that the Conservative government was forced to call the election when the severe recession, the abortive poll tax and Labour's new-found unity and moderation made political conditions unusually adverse. If Labour could not win in 1992, it is argued, it could never win.

TABLE 5.1   The result of the 1992 general election in the UK

|  | *MPs elected* | *Share of UK vote (%)* | *Share of GB vote (%)* |
|---|---|---|---|
| **Conservative** | 336 | 41.9 | 42.8 |
| Change from 1987 | −39 | −0.3 | −0.4 |
| **Labour** | 271 | 34.4 | 35.2 |
| Change from 1987 | +42 | +3.6 | +3.7 |
| **Liberal Democrat** | 20 | 17.8 | 18.3 |
| Change from 1987[a] | −2 | −4.8 | −4.8 |
| **Welsh/Scottish Nationalists** | 7 | 2.3 | 2.4 |
| Change from 1987 | +1 | +0.6 | +0.7 |
| **Others** | 0 | 1.4 | 1.5 |
| Change from 1987 | 0 | +0.9 | +1.0 |
| **Northern Ireland parties** | 17 | 2.3 | n.a. |
| Change from 1987 | 0 | +0.1 | n.a. |
| **Total** | 651 | **UK turnout** 77.7% | |
| Change from 1987 | +1 | +2.4% | |

*Note*: [a] The Liberal Democrats in 1992 are compared with the Liberal/SDP Alliance in 1987.

*Source*:   *The Times* (1992).

These interpretations differ because they adopt different baselines (1945, 1979, 1983), indicators (vote, seats) measures of success (change over time, margin over opponent) and prior expectations. Choosing between interpretations requires a coherent framework of analysis grounded in theories of voting.

## Interpreting Election Results

### The 'Normal' Vote

Every election result is the product of (1) trends in voters' long-term *partisanship*; (2) fluctuations in the parties' short-term *political fortunes*; and (3) the operation of the *electoral system*. Partisanship determines the size and composition of each party's 'normal' vote. It is rooted in the enduring features of voters' everyday lives – their class, community and deep-laid values – and also in the political institutions that structure the voters' choice. Political fortunes temporarily supplement or erode each party's normal vote. They depend on the parties themselves – their agendas, policies, leaders, record and image – and on an element of chance. The electoral system converts votes into seats. In most countries it does so proportionately: Britain's single-member, simple-plurality system, however, is non-proportional, unpredictable, biased and therefore crucial to understanding an election result.

An assessment of 1992 therefore rests on assumptions about the normal vote. The actual Con–Lab percentage vote gap was 42 to 34. The first interpretation of the election would be supported if the two parties' normal vote is similar or if the gap is considerably narrower. It would mean that strictly short-term factors – the tax issue, perhaps, or Neil Kinnock's leadership – heavily favoured the Conservatives in 1992 without eliminating Labour's prospects of victory next time. It would imply that Labour could win by modest changes – a new leader, different policy emphases and cleverer presentation. The second interpretation would be supported if the normal vote corresponds to the actual vote and the net impact of short-term factors in 1992 was neutral. It would not rule out an occasional Labour victory, because temporary political fortune might overcome Labour's in-built disadvantage. But it would suggest that the Conservatives would usually be in office, that Labour success would take the form of minority or coalition government and that collaboration with other opposition parties might be the right strategy. The second interpretation would also be supported if the normal vote gap is *larger* than the 42–34 vote gap, implying that, as many believed at the time, short-term factors in April 1992 benefited Labour. This would suggest that Labour's support was more likely to fall than rise in 1996–97, and that short of a radical self-transformation it is destined to serve as the permanent opposition under a Conservative hegemony.

*Measures of the Normal Vote*

One measure of a party's normal vote is the average of its vote across recent elections. Electoral trends since 1945 suggest that the current structure of party competition began in February 1974 when, for the first time, the centre parties and, in Scotland and Wales, the nationalists contested every seat (Table 5.2). The pattern of competition before then was of stable and balanced duopoly. The Conservative and Labour parties won over 90 per cent of the vote, but neither party was dominant: Labour averaged 46 per cent, the Conservatives 45 per cent and their vote fluctuated within a narrow band of plus or minus 3 per cent (excluding the exceptional 1945 election). The pattern thereafter has been one of uneven and volatile multi-party competition. The combined Conservative plus Labour share of the vote dropped from 90 to 75 per cent. Fluctuations around the average have risen to plus or minus 4 per cent for the Conservatives and plus or minus 6 per cent for the Labour and centre parties, which suggests that short-term factors have had more impact in recent elections. And the averages have shifted: the centre parties' vote has risen from 7

TABLE 5.2  The means and fluctuations of the parties' share of the UK vote, 1945–70 and 1974–92

|  | *1945–70* | *Feb. 1974–92* |
|---|---|---|
| **Conservative** | | |
| Mean vote (%) | 45.3 | 40.7 |
| Min to max | 39.8 to 49.7 | 35.8 to 43.9 |
| **Labour** | | |
| Mean vote (%) | 46.1 | 34.3 |
| Min to max | 43.1 to 48.8 | 27.6 to 39.2 |
| **Liberal**[a] | | |
| Mean vote (%) | 7.2 | 20.0 |
| Min to max | 2.6 to 11.4 | 14.1 to 26.0 |

*Note*: [a] Liberal/SDP Alliance in 1983 and 1987; Liberal Democrat in 1992.

to 20 per cent (of which 7 per cent was due to the increase in Liberal candidates), the Conservative vote has fallen from 45 to 41 per cent and the Labour vote from 46 to 34 per cent. Both major parties lost support, but Labour's decline was by far the steeper, leaving the Conservatives dominant.

The 1992 election closely fits the post-1974 pattern, as the following comparison in Table 5.3.

TABLE 5.3    Major party support, 1992 general election

|  | Five elections Feb. 1974–87 (mean) | 1992 election | Six elections Feb. 1974–92 (mean) |
|---|---|---|---|
| Conservative | 40.4 | 41.9 | 40.7 |
| Labour | 34.3 | 34.2 | 34.3 |
| Centre | 20.3 | 18.3 | 20.0 |
| Nationalists | 2.3 | 2.3 | 2.3 |

This suggests that the normal vote is Con 41, Lab 34, Lib Dem 20 and that 1992 produced a 'normal' result in which short-term factors largely cancelled out but marginally advantaged the Conservatives and damaged the Liberal Democrats. If the post-1974 size of short-term fluctuations – plus or minus 4 per cent for the Conservatives, plus or minus 6 per cent for Labour and the Centre – is added to the normal vote, the normal *range* for each party is Con 37–45, Lab 28–40, Lib Dem 14–26. These ranges corroborate the second interpretation of the 1992 election: a Conservative win is far more probable than a Labour win in the foreseeable future but is not guaranteed because the top of Labour's range overlaps with the bottom of the Conservative range.

A preferable indicator of the normal vote is the trend in party identification (i.e., the party that people generally 'think of themselves as') because it is largely independent of (and less volatile than) the actual vote and can reveal any change in the normal vote since February 1974. Figure 5.1 suggests that the Con–Lab gap in the normal vote has been gradually *widening*.

In 1992 the level of Conservative identification was at its highest since measures were first taken in 1964, the level of Labour identification at its lowest. The comparison between 1979 and 1992 is particularly telling because the Conservatives' popular vote margin over Labour was about the same (7–8 per cent) at both elections. In 1979, Conservative identifiers outnumbered Labour identifiers by 43 to 40 per cent; in 1992 by 45 to 33 per cent. Equally revealing is the fact that although the Labour vote has recovered by 6 percentage points since 1983, Labour identification has remained flat.

The party-identification measure of the normal vote, unlike the actual-vote measure, implies that short-term political factors in 1992 favoured the opposition parties: the Conserva-

FIGURE 5.1   The party identification of voters, 1964–92

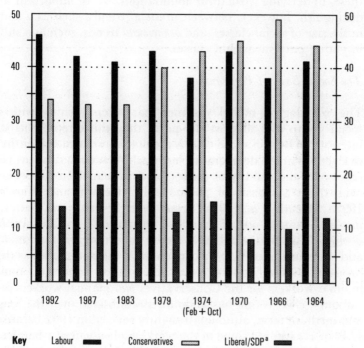

**Key**   Labour ▬▬▬   Conservatives ▭▭▭   Liberal/SDP[a] ▬▬▬

*Note*: [a] Liberal/SDP Alliance in 1983 and 1987; Liberal Democrat in 1992.

tives under-performed while the Liberal Democrats substantially over-performed and Labour did so marginally. But like the actual-vote measure it supports the second interpretation of the election, only more strongly. It infers that the Conservatives' 8 per cent lead was lower than 'normal', reflecting unfavourable political conditions that will not necessarily be repeated at the next election.

## Trends in Partisanship

A party's normal vote is formed by long-term partisanship, which is rooted in the enduring features of voters' everyday lives: their class or ethnicity, their neighbourhood, and their fundamental values. Trends in partisanship reflect changes in these underlying structural foundations. It is important to distinguish, however, between *structural* trends, such as a shift in the size of social classes, and *behavioural* trends, such as a shift in voting patterns within classes.

### The Social Basis of Partisanship

The 'sociological model' assumes that voters identify with a social group and support the party they think represents its interests; in Britain social class is the dominant form of identity, so elections are a 'democratic class war'. Academic controversy rages over the validity of the sociological model, in particular over the class basis of partisanship (Denver and Hands, 1992a). Heath *et al.* (1991) argue that the long-term pattern in class voting is one of 'trendless fluctuation', not inexorable decline. Much of the debate turns on definitions, measurement and statistical inference. By conventional measures, such as the proportion of all voters voting along class lines (i.e., non-manual workers for the Conservatives *plus* manual workers for Labour), class voting has undoubtedly subsided over the long and medium term, although it slightly revived in 1992 because Labour recaptured some of the working class voters it had lost to the Alliance in the 1980s (see Table 5.4). In the 1945–70 period, nearly two-thirds of all voters voted for their class party. From February 1974 the link slowly and fitfully weak-

TABLE 5.4  Social class and the vote, 1979–92

| | Average 1945–70 | | 1979 election | | 1983 election | | 1987 election | | 1992 election | |
|---|---|---|---|---|---|---|---|---|---|---|
| | Non-manual | Manual | Non-manual | Manual | Non-manual | Manual | Non-manual | Manual | Non-manual | Manual |
| Conservative | 65 | 30 | 55 | 36 | 51 | 35 | 49 | 37 | 49 | 35 |
| Liberal/Other | 10 | 8 | 19 | 17 | 31 | 28 | 31 | 23 | 25 | 20 |
| Labour | 24 | 62 | 26 | 46 | 18 | 37 | 20 | 40 | 26 | 45 |
| Non-manual Con plus manual Lab as per cent of total vote | 63 | | 51 | | 45 | | 44 | | 47 | |
| Odds ratio[a] | 5.6 | | 2.6 | | 3.0 | | 2.6 | | 2.4 | |

Notes: [a] The ratio of the odds of a non-manual voting Conservative rather than Labour to the odds of a manual worker voting Labour rather than Conservative; see Heath et al. (1985).

Source: Harris/ITN exit polls (3 May 1979; 9 June 1983; 11 June 1987; 9 April 1992).

ened and since 1983 the proportion has been under half (44–47 per cent) with a majority voting for either the 'class enemy' or for the non-class centre or nationalist parties. This trend should not be exaggerated, however: class remains the single most important social factor underlying the vote.

Class dealignment within the post-1974 era of party competition is illustrated by comparison of the 1979 and 1992 elections. At both elections the Conservative lead over Labour in the popular vote was 7–8 per cent, but the class basis of that lead changed. Among non-manual workers it narrowed from 29 to 23 per cent whereas among manual workers Labour's lead slipped by 1 per cent. Non-manual workers swung by 3 per cent from Conservative to Labour; manual workers by 0.5 per cent from Labour to Conservative. Notwithstanding the slight revival of class voting in 1992, both social classes have shifted away from their 'own' class party since 1979.

The changing social composition of the classes is the main explanation. The growth of the public service professions has eroded middle-class solidarity with the Conservative party. This new middle class tends to have working or lower-middle-class origins (and thus a Labour background) a higher education (and thus liberal values) and a work ethic that puts public service and professional standards before wealth creation and managerial authority. In the 1980s it came to regard the Thatcher governments as hostile both to the public sector and professional autonomy; many joined white-collar trade unions. Social and demographic changes within the working class have worked in the opposite direction. The rapid spread of home-ownership, the migration from North to South and from inner city to suburb, and the expansion of non-union private sector employment have undermined working class loyalty to the Labour party. Unionised council tenants in the North remain solidly Labour; but they are increasingly outnumbered by the 'new working class' of non-union home-owners in the South who are much more inclined to vote Conservative. Between 1979 and 1992 professional and managerial classes (the 'ABs') have swung furthest away from the Conservatives (−5.5 per cent); the skilled manual class (the 'C2s') furthest towards them (+2 per cent).

Class dealignment does *not* infer the decline of Labour: both parties have lost ground in their own classes. Structural changes in the size of the social classes is a different matter. The continuous embourgeoisement of British society relentlessly tilts the balance of partisanship in the Conservatives' favour. Almost all the predominantly Conservative groups in the British electorate are expanding; almost all the predominantly Labour groups are contracting. Between 1979 and 1992 the working class – defined as manual workers excluding the self-employed, supervisors and technicians – declined from 41 to 34 per cent of all voters while the professional and managerial salariat grew from 26 to 29 per cent. There are parallel trends in housing: between 1979 and 1992 the ratio of owner-occupiers to council tenants in the electorate almost doubled from 52:34 to 68:24. Trade union membership – another symbol and source of Labour partisanship – fell from 13.3 million (53 per cent of the labour force) in 1979 to 10.2 million (38 per cent of the labour force) in 1990 and will have gone on falling as the recession took its toll. Heath *et al.* (1991, Chapter 13) estimate that since 1964 the changing size of these class, housing and trade union groups has produced a 1 per cent swing from Labour to Conservative over a full parliament, *independently of any voting shifts within these groups*, but with the acceleration of these trends during the Thatcher governments Labour's base probably eroded more rapidly after 1979.

## New Social Factors

Class has diminished, without disappearing, as a basis for party choice. This would not weaken the sociological model if social class was replaced or supplemented by new social bases of partisanship. Economic self-interest, neighbourhood culture and party policies have combined to make housing – in particular the division between owner-occupiers and council tenants – a better predictor of the vote than occupational class. But housing is correlated with class and some of its impact disappears once class is taken into account (Marshall *et al.*, 1988, pp.249–50). Another new factor is race: the ethnic minorities vote along ethnic rather than class lines. In 1992 the overwhelming majority of Afro-Caribbeans (90 per cent) and Asians (71 per cent) voted Labour compared with below half their white neighbours (Harris/ITN exit poll). But only 4 per cent of the electorate is black, so the impact of race is confined to a few urban areas. The slow spread of higher education has created a new but still weak value cleavage within the middle classes: broadly speaking, materialist, nationalist and authoritarian non-graduates who vote Conservative *versus* libertarian, internationalist and anti-commercial graduates, who vote for the centre parties or Labour (Heath *et al.*, 1991).

These new social cleavages have cut across and weakened class voting, even if they have not replaced it. By 1992 four out of five voters belonged to 'mixed-class' categories – working-class home-owners, or middle-class trade unionists, or the white-collar wives of blue-collar husbands. Such voters tend to have weak group or class identities and to be ambivalent about their group interests. As a result, the electoral impact of the social structure taken as a whole has steadily declined. There has been a general social dealignment as well as a specific class dealignment (Rose and McAllister, 1986, p.91; Franklin *et al.*, 1992).

## The Geographical Basis of Partisanship

Partisanship is rooted not only in the jobs people do but in the places where they live. Geographical factors have become increasingly important since the 1970s (Johnston *et al.*, 1988). Once again, we need to distinguish between the structural impact of a geographical redistribution of the electorate and the behavioural impact of a change in the importance of geographical factors.

Steady post-war population movements from north to south and town to country have of course had a structural impact on the constituency map: between 1955 and 1992 the number of seats in the South grew from 334 to 350 while the number of MPs representing Birmingham, Glasgow, Liverpool and Manchester declined from 46 to 30 – and the forthcoming boundary revisions will extend these trends. But if the way people voted was unaffected by where they lived, migration would have no structural effects on the party division of the

national vote. In the 1950s and 1960s region and neighbourhood had a negligible impact on the vote once their socio–
economic composition was taken into account. Wales was more
Labour than the South East but because it was more working
class, not because it was Wales. But since 1970 geographical
milieu has exerted an increasingly independent influence on
the vote. Each election has been a 'two-nation' affair in which
the Conservatives have advanced most where there was
economic expansion and security and least where there was
deprivation and decline. There has been a long-term swing to
the Conservatives in the South and Midlands, the suburbs,
small towns and countryside; and a long-term swing to Labour
in the North and Scotland, the large towns, inner city areas
and outer fringe council estates.

In 1992 this twenty-year trend went into modest reverse.
The swing to Labour was above average in the Midlands and
some parts of the South and below average in Scotland and
some parts of the North – reflecting in part the uncharacteristic
geography of the 1989–92 recession. Given the recession's
severity, however, the reverse was remarkably limited. The
geographical axis has not tilted back to its pre-Thatcher
position: since 1979 the Conservatives have lost eleven seats
in Scotland, six in the North and five in Wales, but gained ten
in the Midlands (including East Anglia) and nine in the South.
During this period the South East and East Anglia have shifted
most to the Conservatives (with swings of 2.8 and 2.5 per cent
respectively) while the North West and North have shifted
most to Labour (with swings of 4.1 and 4.0 per cent).

The reason for these geographical effects is not entirely clear,
but they undoubtedly reflect more than the social and
economic structure of each region. The Glasgow bank
manager is much less likely to vote Conservative than the
Guildford bank manager, despite having the same income,
work and status. Geographical difference in economic optimism, reflecting short-term trends in the local economy, is
probably the most important factor (Curtice, 1988, 1992);
hence the de-polarisation in 1992. But other contributory
factors include the cumulative impact of *long-term* economic
change (hence the limits to the de-polarisation); the party
complexion of local government; tactical voting and partisan

patterns of migration. These have combined to produce a more enduring geographical polarisation, which can withstand short-term economic fluctuations, and which has an independent behavioural impact on the vote. Movers tend to embrace the partisanship of their adoptive region, irrespective of their original partisanship. North–South and urban–rural migration has slowly eroded Labour's normal vote and enlarged the Conservatives'.

*The Ideological Basis of Partisanship*

The relationship between partisanship and ideology is two-way. Political beliefs owe more to partisanship than vice versa but have some independent impact. Partisanship is sustained if a party's basic positions match those of its supporters; strained if they do not. The long-term effect has been to Labour's detriment, for two reasons.

The first is the greater ideological distance between politicians and voters in the Labour party than the Conservative party. Simplifying drastically, the political beliefs of British voters are structured by two dimensions: collectivist–individualist and liberal–authoritarian. Figure 5.2 maps the location of the three parties and their supporting voters on the two-dimensional ideological map. Two features stand out. Firstly, the middle classes are more ideologically polarised than the working class, especially along the liberal–authoritarian dimension. Secondly, all three parties are ideologically closer to their middle-class than to their working-class supporters, the result perhaps of the overwhelmingly middle-class composition of the parties at both parliamentary and activist levels. This ideological gap between parties and their working-class supporters poses a particular problem for the Labour party because the working class provides it with the great majority of its votes while the middle classes provide it with the great majority of its activists. Class differences on policy are particularly wide among Labour voters, most notably on immigration, nuclear disarmament, capital punishment and the rights of women, blacks and gays. This periodically presents the Labour leadership with electoral dilemmas and weakens Labour partisanship.

FIGURE 5.2 The ideological map of the British electorate

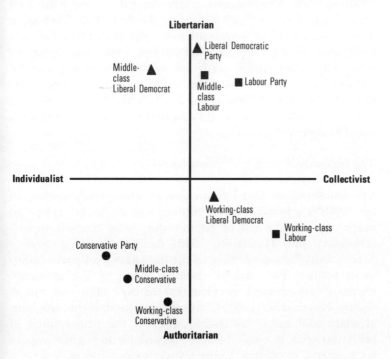

The second threat to Labour's partisanship has come from recent changes to the ideological map; the few available trend measures suggest that *voters'* positions have changed surprisingly little, despite Thatcher's ideological crusade in the 1980s. It drifted slowly leftwards, becoming *less* Thatcherite, especially on issues of social expenditure and welfare provision, job creation, trade union legitimacy and a range of 'civil liberties' issues such as abortion, racial equality and women's rights. Thatcherism's only ideological success was privatisation (Crewe, 1988; Studlar and McAllister, 1992).

But the parties changed position. Under Thatcher the Conservative party moved to the free-market 'west' and the populist–authoritarian 'south'. Overall it *reduced* the ideological distance between its policies and the beliefs of its supporters. Its vote increased among free-marketeers in the electorate but stayed the same among populist-authoritarians (Heath *et al.*, 1991, p.177). The Labour party moved to the Old Left collectivist 'east' until 1983 and to the New Left libertarian 'north' until 1987; it *increased* the ideological distance between itself and its working-class supporters while narrowing it, especially after 1983, with its middle class supporters. Labour's rapid move to the middle of the collectivist–individualist axis, following its 1989 Policy Review, appears to have recouped its previous losses to the centre parties (Heath and Paulson, 1992).

## The Institutional Basis of Partisanship

The Conservative and Labour parties' change of direction in the 1980s is a reminder that elites as well as demography can shape the distribution of partisanship. The 'radical model' (Dunleavy and Husbands, 1985) focuses on the governing party's exploitation of office to tilt the balance of partisanship in its favour. The various attempts made by the unusually partisan Conservative governments of the 1980s had mixed results. Heath *et al.* (1991, Chapter 8) argue that the extension of share and house ownership through the programmes of privatisation and council house sales had a negligible impact because it was existing Conservatives who disproportionately took up the opportunity; but in the case of housing, alternative estimates suggest that the Labour party was electorally damaged, at least in the short term (Crewe, 1991). The likely longer-term repercussion is that interest rates will become more sensitive electorally and their management a totem of governmental competence.

The Conservative government's exploitation of the popular media was probably more fruitful. A blind eye to monopolies and honours for owners and editors kept the press on the Conservatives' side. By 1992 75 per cent of voters read a Conservative newspaper, including the majority of working-class and Labour voters. Partisanship determines choice of newspaper more than vice versa; thus the press is an agency of reinforcement rather than conversion. But reinforcement is important: in the 'long campaign' prior to both the 1987 and 1992 elections the Conservative tabloids persuaded relatively non-political working class readers to swing behind the government. And there is some conversion: Harrop (1987) estimates that the press is worth a 1 per cent swing from Conservative to Labour at each election (see Chapter 16).

Whatever their base, long-term structural changes in the British electorate have helped the Conservatives and hurt Labour. They have also weakened partisanship, offering both parties greater rewards from the exploitation of short-term political opportunities. Structural change does not mean 'Labour cannot win', only that it must run faster up a downward-moving escalator.

## Short-term Influences on the Vote

The party system, shaping and shaped by partisanship, forms the framework within which elections are contested; the actual result depends on the impact of short-term factors on the uncommitted voter. In a typical election about 20 per cent of voters switch parties but that proportion almost doubles if movement to and from abstention is included: thus, in theory, about 13 million voters are 'up for grabs'. If all of them moved in the same direction, the favoured party would win by a landslide; in reality the vote switching largely cancels out and the net swing is small. Direct conversion from Conservative to Labour or vice versa is exceptional (typically 1 to 2 per cent of voters in either direction) and, while traffic to and from the centre parties is heavier, it rarely produces a *net* swing between the two major parties of more than 1 per cent either way. The national swing between two elections is therefore small – the post-war average is 2.8 per cent, the post-war record 5.2 per cent – and much of it arises from differential abstention and the physical replacement of the electorate. Of those eligible to vote in both 1987 and 1992, 16 per cent switched parties and another 20 per cent moved to or from abstention, but the national swing was only 2.0 per cent to Labour. Movement into and out of the centre accounted for most of the swing (1.7 per cent), supplemented by direct conversion (0.7 per cent) switches to and from other parties (0.3 per cent) and physical turnover of the electorate (0.3 per cent) but differential turnout benefited the Conservatives, reducing the swing by 1.0 per cent.

'Flux' rather than 'flow' characterises volatility for two reasons. Firstly, many switchers revert to their normal party loyalties after a one-off protest vote or unavoidable abstention at the previous election: the magnetic field of partisanship remains strong. Secondly, switchers tend to be the least interested and informed about politics and thus most exposed to random influences. Contrary to democratic myth, only a minority are model citizens who carefully assess the parties' qualities by paying close attention to the media. Nonetheless, these homing and random tendencies are largely self-cancelling. The net swing *does* reflect uncommitted voters' considered response to short-term political factors. What factors count most?

## Rules and Resources

The *radical model* focuses on institutional bias and unequal resources (Ridley, 1991). It claims that the impact of the State, capital and the media on long-term partisanship is parallelled by their impact on short-term voting choice. The rules and conventions of party competition are not neutral technicalities that ensure an even playing field but structured biases that systematically help some parties and hinder others.

Much of the radical model founders on the rock of fact. In principle, the Prime Minister's right to choose the election date when opinion polls and economic indicators suggest the time is propitious gives the governing party an unfair advantage. In practice, governments have lost six of the fourteen elections since the war. In theory, the extension of the franchise to UK citizens who left Britain up to twenty years previously to live abroad should help the Conservatives. In fact, only 30 000 expatriates registered in 1992 and they helped the Conservatives to retain, at most, one marginal seat (Butler and Kavanagh, 1992, p.232). In theory, the Conservative party should be advantaged by the much stricter regulation of trade union donations than of business donations, by its superior wealth, and by the absence of limits on national (as distinct from constituency) campaign expenditure. In practice lavish spending is a waste of money. In each of the four elections since 1979 it is the impoverished centre parties whose support has risen during the campaign while the relative standing of the two major parties (according to the campaign polls) has remained static. In theory the governing party can exploit its capacity to 'get two bites at the television cherry' (Miller *et al.*, 1990, p.231) – once as a competing party, once as the government. But this is a double-edged sword because government failures capture as many headlines as government successes, as the relentlessness of the recession in 1991–92 demonstrated. It is the centre that benefits most from the broadcasting rules in elections because by convention it receives disproportionately generous campaign coverage and usually a boost to its vote as a result.

There remain two institutional biases which may give the Conservatives a more serious advantage. Firstly, electoral under-registration is concentrated among Labour-inclined groups such as the unemployed, the mobile young, Afro-Caribbeans and inner city residents. Under-registration has risen since the mid-1980s and increased by 50 per cent in response to the poll tax, to about 1 million. In 1992 it was probably worth eight seats to the Conservatives; on a correct register their majority would have been down to five (Smith and McLean, 1992, p.32). Given that under-registration is unlikely to be rectified quickly and that the 1991 electorates shape the new constituency boundaries, the bias will survive into the next century.

Secondly, the increasingly right-wing slant of the press may well produce short-term swings to the Conservatives on top of its more enduring impact on partisanship. In his resignation speech Neil Kinnock blamed the Conservative press for his defeat ('Never has their attack on Labour been so comprehensive . . . this was how the election was won') and the *Sun*, for one, crowed in agreement: 'IT'S THE SUN WOT WON IT'.

But did it? The small late swing to the Conservatives in the campaign did coincide with a stepping up of the tabloids' offensive against the Labour Party, especially that of the *Sun* whose readership is concentrated among the working-class in the South – a large, key group of volatile voters. According to one estimate *Sun* readers swung by a massive 7.5 per cent to the

Conservatives in the last few days of the campaign. But one should avoid hasty conclusions. There were also above-average swings to the Conservatives among readers of the non-partisan *Independent* and of the stridently Labour *Daily Mirror*. The late swing was 'a national, not a newspaper, phenomenon' (Harrop and Scammell, 1992, pp.208–9). The most one can infer is that *some* Tory tabloids, like the *Sun* and *Today* gave an extra push to a Conservative bandwagon that was already rolling.

Local party membership is another unequally distributed resource, although not because of electoral laws or institutions. Current estimates suggest that Conservative Party membership (850 000) is more than double that of the Labour party (280 000) and Liberal Democrats (105 000) combined. Recent studies have revised the conventional wisdom that constituency organisation counts for nothing in the television age and suggest that local party activity does boost the Labour and centre vote at the constituency level (Denver and Hands, 1992b); one study claims that with double its membership Labour would have won in 1992 (Whiteley and Seyd, 1992). That is too bold. The Conservative party's superior numbers consist of inactive members in safe seats. What counts is the numbers who help at election time in marginal seats and in this respect all three parties are equally matched (Denver and Hands, 1992b, p.532). This is consistent with the above-average performances in 1992 of Labour and Liberal Democrat candidates in Conservative-held marginals and suggests that the Conservative party's much larger paper membership is a negligible advantage.

*Issues*

The *consumer model* of voting focuses on issues. It assumes that people vote for the party they prefer on the issues they care most about. Voters are as volatile as shoppers choosing between supermarkets, constantly in search of a better product. The party that advertises the more attractive range of goods increases its 'market share' and wins the election.

'Issue-voting' involves three different judgements about the parties. Consider the unemployment issue: voters might judge the parties by their *policies* for creating jobs ('policy-voting'), by their degree of *emphasis* on the problem ('priority-voting') or by their past *record* on unemployment ('performance-voting').

Policy-voting is the old-fashioned liberal democratic ideal – what politicians understand by 'voting on the issues'. But it is not what most voters, especially uncommitted voters, do: they have neither the information nor inclination to judge the parties' specific policy proposals. When they vote on issues they conduct post-mortems rather than confer mandates, because it makes more sense to judge parties on the hard evidence of their past performance than on flimsy speculations about their promises. At most, they can gauge which of the two major parties they are 'nearer' to on one or two general policy axes such as government control versus the free market, welfare versus self-sufficiency and 'progressive' versus 'traditional' morality.

The electorate has a clearer perception of the parties' priorities and past record. The prevalence of priority and performance voting is reflected in the historical constancy of the public's preference for one party over the other on each issue: the Conservative and Labour parties each 'own' certain issues but very rarely 'capture' one from the other (Budge and Farlie, 1983). In 1992, for example, voters preferred the Conservatives on taxation, defence and law and order and Labour on unemployment, the health service and pensions – as they have done throughout the past half century. The parties' history in government is part of the explanation: a Labour government established the NHS, Conservative governments have cut income tax. But sheer party rhetoric is another: the Conservatives talk more about crime, Labour about jobs, despite their poor track records in office. Priority-voting is the assumption behind the parties' electioneering, which is about setting the agenda, not winning the policy debate.

The issue-voting model failed in 1992, as it did in 1983 and 1987. If everybody had voted for the party they preferred on the two issues they cared most about, the result would have been a dead heat in 1983, a slender 2 per cent Labour win in 1987 and a runaway 11 per cent Labour victory in 1992 (Heath *et al.*, 1985, p.97; Crewe, 1987, p.7; Sanders, 1992, p.197). In fact Labour went down to its three worst defeats since 1931.

A more detailed analysis of the 1992 election is instructive. Labour easily won the agenda-setting competition: on the three issues that dominated voters' concerns – the health service, unemployment and education – it was preferred by a comfortable margin by those for whom the issue was important; Conservative defectors and Labour recruits were particularly likely to mention health and education as key issues (Table 5.5). But the bonus to Labour was limited for two reasons. Firstly, the continuous advantage of a recurrent issue to a party is incorporated in a party's normal vote; issues only contribute to the short-term swing if the importance or party preferences that voters attach to them have *changed since the previous election*. And in two of the three cases the changes worked *against* the Labour party. The proportion citing unemployment as important and, among them, the majority preferring Labour on the issue, actually declined while the proportion mentioning the health service as important increased but among them Labour's lead on the issue, although still substantial, was well down on 1987. These welfare issues are necessary for Labour's normal vote but insufficient for an additional, winning, boost.

Secondly, in answer to the general question 'taking everything into account, which party has the best policies?' voters chose the Conservatives (Sanders, 1992, p.195). The reason is that 'everything' includes the economy, which voters regard as too abstract and general to cite as an 'issue' but which in recent elections in Britain, even more than elsewhere (Lewis-Beck, 1988), is their first priority and the main basis on which they judge the government's record. They do engage in issue-voting, but of the special kind Americans call 'pocketbook-voting' – voting with one's wallet.

It might be thought that the 1992 election destroyed the idea of pocketbook-voting too: after all, voters re-elected a government that had presided over the longest recession since the 1930s. In fact, the election result confirmed its importance, while highlighting four of its facets. Firstly, pocketbook-voting is *prospective* as well as retrospective: voters gauge the future as well as assess the past. In the most successful economic model of British elections (the 'Essex model', which accurately forecast the 1992 result a year in advance) the single best predictor of

## TABLE 5.5 The issues that mattered in the 1992 election

Proportion (%) of respondents mentioning an issue as one of the two most important in influencing their vote[a]

| | All voters | Change since 1987 | Conservative recruits | Conservative defectors | Labour recruits | Labour defectors | Party advantage[b] 1992 | Party advantage[b] 1987 |
|---|---|---|---|---|---|---|---|---|
| NHS/Hospitals | 41 | +8 | 23 | 45 | 47 | 40 | Lab +34 | Lab +49 |
| Unemployment | 36 | −13 | 35 | 31 | 42 | 51 | Lab +26 | Lab +34 |
| Education | 23 | +4 | 15 | 30 | 27 | 23 | Lab +23 | Lab +15 |
| Prices | 11 | +5 | 15 | 9 | 7 | 10 | Con +59 | * |
| Taxation | 10 | +3 | 26 | 11 | 5 | 7 | Con +72 | Con +68 |
| Poll tax | 8 | +7 | 6 | 11 | 15 | 7 | * | * |
| Pensions | 6 | −4 | 7 | 10 | 6 | 6 | Lab +35 | * |
| Defence | 3 | −32 | 6 | 1 | 1 | 1 | Con +86 | Con +63 |

*Question*: 'Think of all the urgent problems facing the country at the present time. When you decided which way to vote, which two issues did you personally consider most important?'

'I am going to read out a list of problems facing the country. Could you tell me for each of them which party you personally think would handle the problem best?'

*Notes*: [a] This was an open-ended question; the first six issues listed were those most frequently chosed.
[b] The party advantage shows the lead of the party chosen as the best on that issue over the next party, among respondents for whom the issue was important.
* Figure is not available.

*Source*: Gallup post-election survey (10–11 April 1992).

the government's vote is people's optimism about their living standards over the next year, the so-called 'feel-good' factor (Sanders, 1991). In March and April 1992 Gallup's personal economic optimism index rose sharply from an average of –3 in January, February and March to +15 in April. Secondly, some elements of the real economy matter much more than others. The strongest influence on personal economic expectations is the recent trend in inflation and interest rates. Both were declining steadily in the nine months prior to the election. Moreover, by April 1992 the inflation rate (4.2 per cent) was only fractionally above that at the previous election (4.1 per cent) while interest rates were only 1 per cent higher (10.5 compared with 9.5). Unemployment, significantly, does not affect personal economic expectations, once inflation and interest rates are taken into account. It may be the symbol of recession, but it directly affects (and indirectly threatens) far fewer voters than rising prices or spiralling interest rates. Areas of rapidly rising unemployment did record above average falls in the Conservative vote (Johnston and Pattie, 1992), but these were largely confined to the urban South; nationally, unemployment was marginally *lower* in 1992 than 1987. Thus by polling day 1992 the health of the economy, judged by three indicators of inflation, interest rates and unemployment, was about as good as it was on polling day 1987. Thirdly, pocketbook-voting involves the assigning of credit and blame. Asked in the Harris exit poll who was responsible 'for the present state of the British economy' nearly half (47 per cent) blamed 'world economic conditions' and almost as many (46 per cent) 'Mrs Thatcher's government'. A mere 5 per cent blamed 'John Major's government' even though the majority of its cabinet served under Thatcher, including, of course, John Major himself as Chancellor. The Conservative party's replacement of Margaret Thatcher by John Major was a brilliant act of self-renewal: voters regarded it not simply as a change of Prime Minister but as a change of government, absolved of all responsibility for earlier mistakes. Fourthly, pocketbook-voting involves *comparison* and the Conservatives were still trusted more than Labour to run the economy. In the BBC/NOP exit poll the Conservatives led Labour by 53 to 35 per cent as the party most likely 'to take the right decisions on the economy' and by the even wider margin of 63 to 21 per cent among those saying the economy was an 'important influence on their vote'.These figures almost certainly represent more than a judgement about the parties' specifically economic competence. In the campaign's final days there was a surge of preference for the Conservatives over Labour in *every* policy area (Crewe, 1992, p.10; Sanders, 1992, p.210). People trusted Labour less than the Conservatives to run the economy because they trusted it less to run things in general.

*Competence, Trust and Leadership*

Consumer models of voting fail because they leave a party's perceived competence at governing out of the equation. Voters do not enter polling stations with a shopping list of policy preferences; they enter with an overall judgement about one preference – that the government should be competent, primarily (in peacetime) in the economic sphere, because the economy affects almost everything else. Voting is *not* like choosing a supermarket: dissatisfied voters cannot take back faulty policies or change governments the following week. It is more like choosing a solicitor or doctor: the voter is a non-expert, and must choose in ignorance of the problems that will require attention over the next few years; yet the wrong choice could be costly and irremediable (Harrop, 1990). Voters therefore assess the parties' general competence and trustworthiness. Credibility is everything.

In 1992 the Conservative campaign, aided by much of the popular press, successfully played on voters' latent fears about the Labour party: its poster theme was 'You can't trust Labour'. *Why* it succeeded is more difficult to explain. By 1992 Labour was as well endowed as the Conservatives with most of the ingredients that make up a party's governing credibility – unity, discipline, 'moderation', respectability and a distancing from special interests. The exception was the prime-ministerial plausibility of its leader. In 1992 the voters' judgement of the party leaders undoubtedly helped the Conservatives and hurt Labour, although by exactly how much is impossible to say. Asked who would make the 'best Prime Minister', 52 per cent of voters answered John Major and 23 per cent Neil Kinnock, who trailed in *third* place behind Paddy Ashdown (24 per cent) and who easily led the field as 'worst Prime Minister' (60 per cent). Judged by their combined 'best' and 'worst' scores, Kinnock ($-37$) was a serious electoral liability, while Major ($+30$) and to a lesser degree Ashdown ($+5$) were assets. Again, it is the *change* of voter opinions between two elections that particularly matters; and compared with 1987 Major was a bigger bonus to the Conservatives than Margaret Thatcher, and Kinnock a bigger drag on Labour. In 1987 Thatcher was 9 points ahead of Kinnock in the stakes for 'best Prime Minister'; in 1992, Major was 29 points ahead.

However, a leader-voting model works no better than the issue-voting model. The idea that televised politics has made British elections more 'presidential' is fashionable but wrong. Television does tend to portray a party's campaign in terms of its leader's electioneering, but no more so in the 1990s than 1960s (Crewe and King, 1993). The country voted Labour out of office in 1970 and again in 1979, despite preferring Wilson to Heath and Callaghan to Thatcher as prime ministers: popular prime ministers cannot save unpopular governments – although they might make them slightly less unpopular. A minority of voters do prefer the policies of one party but the leader of another, but no more so and with no greater electoral impact in recent elections: in the 1980s about a fifth of all voters were in this position and their vote split by five to one in favour of the first. That is why Major's 52–23 per cent lead over Kinnock as preferred Prime Minister did not enable the Conservatives to win by a landslide. Another, quite different, reason was the operation of the electoral system.

## The Operation of the Electoral System

*Single-member, Single-plurality*

Earlier we saw that most elements of the electoral system make a negligible difference to the result. The exception is the counting rules for determining how votes are translated into seats. Britain's single-member, simple-plurality (SMSP) system, known (misleadingly, because the post is not fixed!) as first-past-the-post, is a system of territorial rather than popular representation. What determines the number of seats a party wins is the distribution of its popular vote, not its overall level. It is designed to produce single-party government, not fair representation.

Three systematic properties of SMSP have enabled it to do so. The *high threshold* penalises minority parties, excluding or severely reducing their representation. The *winner's bonus* over-rewards the single most popular party more than any other, converting a plurality of votes into a majority of seats. And the related *multiplier* converts small net shifts of the popular vote into a much larger turnover of seats.

In 1992, however, all three biases failed to operate as expected. The high threshold penalised only some of the small parties. SMSP does not, as commonly thought, discriminate against all small parties, but only those that spread their vote evenly. The Liberal Democrats' 18 per cent vote secured only 3 per cent of the seats (20 as opposed to a proportional 116) and the Scottish Nationalists' 21 per cent of Scotland's vote won only 4 per cent of the area's seats (3 as opposed to 15). Both parties were penalised for attracting votes from across the social spectrum rather than from specific, and residentially concentrated, groups. But the four seats each won by the SDLP and Plaid Cymru were proportional to their vote because support for the former comes from Northern Ireland's Catholics, who live in increasingly segregated enclaves, and support for the latter comes from Welsh speakers, who are concentrated in north-western Wales. SMSP applies a high threshold to constituencies, not to the country as a whole, and in the geographical peripheries of Britain these do not stop the election of parties hostile to the Westminster system.

The winner's bias operated only in part. It allocated a decisive bonus to the Conservatives (9.7 per cent more seats than votes) but it gave barely less of a bonus to Labour (7.4 per cent more). This was reflected in the absence of the multiplier, at least for the two major parties. In the 1945–70 period the multiplier conformed to a 'cube law': the Con:Lab ratio of seats was the cube of the Con:Lab ratio of votes. In 1992 the cube law would have converted the Conservatives' 55 per cent of the two-party vote into 65 per cent of the two parties' seats, i.e. 395 seats and an overwhelming majority of 139. Instead the Conservatives won 336, 55 per cent, of the major party seats and a modest majority of 21. In this respect the SMSP system was, for the first time, proportional.

This gradual weakening of the multiplier was noted a decade ago by Curtice and Steed (1982), who attributed it to a decline in the number of marginal seats arising from the growing North–South, urban–rural polarisation of the vote. But in 1992 the number of marginal seats actually increased to 97, from 80 in 1983 and 87 in 1987, partly because the long-term geographical trend went into reverse.

The explanation for the electoral system rewarding the Conservatives' substantial 7.6 per cent lead with a mere 21-seat majority lies elsewhere. In 1983 and 1987 the Conservative Party's vote was the more effectively distributed; in 1992 Labour's vote was. One reason was probably peculiar to the 1992 election: the swing to Labour was above average in Conservative marginals partly as a result of tactical voting, partly because high-swing regions such as London and the East Midlands happened to include a disproportionate number of marginals. Normally more Labour than Conservative votes are 'wasted' because Labour wins more seats with large majorities and fewer seats with small ones; this time there was no difference. But the other reason reflects the permanent pro-Labour bias in the electoral system that arises from constituency boundaries. The statutory guidelines by which the Boundary Commissioners operate are meant to be impartial but in fact benefit Labour in two ways. Firstly, Scotland and Wales are deliberately allocated proportionately more seats than England. On a strict population basis Scotland is entitled to 59 seats and Wales to 32; in fact they are allocated 72 and 38 respectively. Given its dominance in both countries, Labour gains: in 1992 it 'won' 13 of the 19 bonus seats. Secondly, the boundaries lag behind population changes by anything from five to twenty years and the Boundary Commissioners are encouraged to give priority to 'natural community boundaries' over strict equality of size. As a result constituencies vary massively in size: as these disparities arise mainly from population drift from the Labour fastnesses of the inner city and industrial North to the Conservative heartlands of the suburban and small-town South, it is Labour that benefits. In 1992 the average size of a Labour seat was 62 000 electors, the average size of a Conservative seat 67 000 electors, the equivalent of the Conservatives forfeiting eight seats to Labour.

The implications of the electoral system's pro-Labour bias are shown in Figure 5.3, which shows the outcome from a range of nationally uniform swings (the Liberal Democrats' and other parties' vote is assumed to be unchanged). A uniform swing of only 0.6 per cent would be enough to

FIGURE 5.3   Uniform swing from the 1992 result

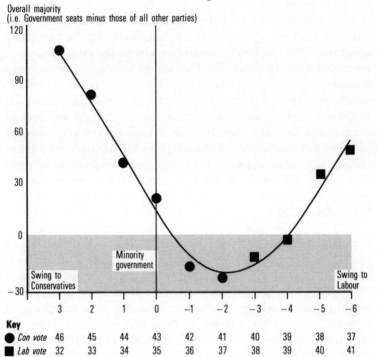

*Note*: These projections asssume that the vote share for the Liberal Democrats and smaller parties remains the same and that the swing between Conservative and Labour is uniform across all constituencies. The vote share figures are for Great Britain.

deprive the Conservatives of their overall majority, even though the Conservatives would have a 6.4 percentage point lead of the popular vote; Labour, however, could lag 3.0 per cent behind and become the largest party and would need only a 0.6 per cent lead in the popular vote to win an outright majority.

But these distortions are not as favourable to Labour's optimistic 'one more heave' school as they appear. For if Labour repeated its 1992 performance of a 2.1 per cent swing (but did *not* do better than average in Con–Lab marginals) it would still fail to be the single largest party (which requires a 2.6 per cent swing). And to obtain a bare overall majority it needs a 4.1 per cent swing – larger than anything it has achieved since 1945.

Moreover, by the next election the pro-Labour bias will be reduced (but not eliminated) by completion of the boundary revisions. The probable impact is currently estimated as a switch of 15 seats from the Labour to Conservative columns without a single vote changing. The Conservatives will be defending the equivalent of an overall majority of 51, not 21. Labour would require a uniform swing of about 2 per cent to deprive the Conservatives of their overall majority, of about 4 per cent to become the largest party and of about 6 per cent to obtain an overall majority for itself. By the standards of post-war Britain it would still have an electoral Everest to climb.

*Can Labour Win?*

A radical solution proposed by some Labour sympathisers is a joint commitment with the Liberal Democrats to a programme of constitutional reform, underpinned by an electoral pact: each party would withdraw its candidate from those Conservative seats where the other had the best prospects of winning. The idea carries a plausible electoral logic: in traditionally Conservative seats tactical voting has cumulatively concentrated the non-Conservative vote behind one or other of the opposition parties (Curtice and Steed, 1992, p.336): the Liberal Democrats are strongest where Labour is weakest (e.g., the South Coast and rural South West) and weakest where Labour is strongest (e.g., the urban Midlands and North West). The English and Welsh local elections of May 1993 dramatically confirmed this trend. Anti-Conservative tactical voting was so substantial that only one county council (Buckinghamshire) remained in Conservative hands. In a general election, however, a pact would probably deprive the Conservatives of, at most, only a handful of seats. In highly marginal Conservative seats the third-placed party cannot be squeezed much further. Moreover, parties do not own their voters: while most Labour supporters deprived of a Labour candidate would vote Liberal Democrat rather than Conservative, Liberal Democrats without a candidate would not reciprocate: in 1992 their second preferences split 38 per cent Conservative to 33 per cent Labour (although there were regional variations) (Dunleavy *et al.*, 1992, p.4). Nor do parties own their activists: local parties could not be stopped from fielding unofficial candidates. Indeed, a pact might well backfire to the Conservatives' benefit by driving anti-Labour Liberal Democrats into the arms of the Conservatives and by precipitating electorally damaging rows both within and across the opposition parties as the details of the pact were hammered out.

Nor is a policy of constitutional reform a plausible vote winner. For the vast majority of voters the issue is abstract, technical and remote from their everyday lives. Moreover, the comfortable majorities for electoral reform and devolution that are consistently recorded in the opinion polls are shallow and liable to ebb away when anti-reformers campaign vigorously on the alleged disadvantages (coalition government, the break-up of the Union) (Weir, 1992). This appears to be what happened in the final few days of the 1992 election campaign.

No simple or obvious solution for the Labour party presents itself. Social and cultural change is slowly eroding its normal vote. Demographic trends for the 1990s – embourgeoisement, de-unionisation, migration, ageing – are not on its side. The party has already moved to the ideological centre; a return to the left would lose votes to centre. It lacks the access to powerful media or local networks of influence outside the (declining) trade unions and (contracting) public sector bureaucracies that might enable it to expand its social base or launch a successful ideological crusade. Neither a change of leader nor a re-writing of policy nor an electoral pact is likely to bring more than marginal benefits. The best prospect for a Labour victory is the relapse of the economy into deep recession and, as a result, a decisive loss of public faith in the Conservatives' governing competence. But such circumstances are, of course, out of the Labour party's hands.

# 6

# The Political Parties

**PATRICK DUNLEAVY**

Party competition in the 1990s is much less overtly ideological than in the previous decade. John Major espousing a non-distinctive, apparently more 'moderate' Conservatism, faces John Smith, pursuing an equally pragmatic and overtly right-wing Labour stance, while a partly discredited and partly revitalised Liberal Democratic Party bobs uneasily on the sidelines. In fact, however, ideological differences remain vitally important in understanding internal processes in both main parties. There are quite complex patterns of enduring disagreement between different sets of MPs and major party interests, which define the basic contours of party faction fights.

Cutting across this background pattern there are a small number of key issues which do not fit neatly into the basic categories. In the modern period, EC policy has been the most conspicuously poorly integrated issue, one which divided Labour from the early 1970s to the mid-1980s, and then progressively sapped the cohesion of the Conservative government from 1985 to 1990, eventually helping to trigger Thatcher's demise. Conflicts over EC policy were suppressed in the run-up to the 1992 general election in both major parties following the Maastricht agreement, but they returned to haunt both Tory and Labour leaderships in the aftermath of Britain's exit from the European Exchange Rate Mechanism (ERM) in September 1992. Another perennial issue which cuts across each party's basic ideological map concerns its funda-mental methods of operating leadership and conducting its internal affairs – which Drucker (1978) termed a party's 'ethos', as opposed to its 'doctrine'. Meanwhile, the Liberal Democrats are permanently troubled and hamstrung by their relative *inability* to define a coherent ideological position widely visible to voters. Their internal conflicts about doctrine are consequently more muted, but their strategic difficulties and consequent disagreements about tactics have been accentuated.

## The Conservative Party

No understanding of the Tory party is possible without recognising explicitly that it is very close to being the dominant party in British politics. In the twelve general elections held since 1918 (when Labour first competed nation-wide as a party), the Conservatives have averaged 44 per cent of the vote, a full 6 per cent ahead of Labour's score. Over this time period, the Conservatives have formed secure majority governments in more than three years out of every five, and been in office even more frequently (Dunleavy, 1989). Conservative majority governments are four times more common than Labour majority governments (of which there have only really been two, 1945–50 and 1966–70). Even if we restrict attention to the post-1945 period, Conservative hegemony remains almost equally strong. If the Conservatives stay in government until 1996–7, the advantage will tilt even more in their favour, and Labour will have been out of government for almost two decades.

Conservative party politics are central to the government of Britain – they matter in a way in which ideological debates and conflicts in other parties do not. Conservative elites, MPs and activists clearly recognise this: a conviction of their own importance is one of the party's hallmarks. Their characteristic response in the past has been to exercise enormous discretion in publicly voicing disagreements from current leadership policies. Conservatives usually engage in ideological conflicts using sophisticated codewords and themes which resonate with the cognoscenti but cannot easily be picked up by outsiders. A normal Conservative party conference is rather like watching a convention of sixteenth-century alchemists at work – each contribution aims to persuade the initiated, while preventing dangerous knowledge from seeping out to the rest of humanity. And traditionally, explicit ideology itself has been disparaged by Conservative thinkers, who have preferred to stress either the need to operate within traditions of debate and institutional development (Oakeshott, 1962), or the need for flexible pragmatism in preserving Tory predominance in British political life (Gilmour, 1977). The Thatcher era, with the strong emergence of an explicit new right ideology, altered this situation for good, and for a time made 'economic rationalism' predominant in Conservative debates. But the older ways of working have crept back in as new right policies faltered or proved ineffective, and non-economic issues and questions of leadership style returned to prominence.

*Basic Ideological Conflicts*

Newspaper and television commentators commonly discuss Conservative thinking in terms of a surrogate left/right dichotomy famously formulated by Margaret Thatcher, who categorised her own party into 'wets' (her opponents, who lacked the courage of their convictions) and by implication 'dries' (her supporters, who were prepared to push through right-wing policies despite obstacles and opposition). Most academic accounts give only a more refined version of the same one-dimensional view, with more gradations of view distinguished and space for unthinking 'loyalists' to whatever leadership line prevails at any given time (Norton, 1990; Baker *et al.*, 1992).

The 'left' (or wet or 'damp') wing in Tory party terms consists of Conservatives who believe that some degree of state intervention to ameliorate the social inequalities of a market society is necessary and indeed inevitable. Government must regulate markets to preserve public interest concerns, and must redress the balance in favour of economically disadvantaged or socially deprived groups to some degree. Not to do this would create social conflicts and tensions, and is simply inappropriate in a modern industrial state.

By contrast, the 'right' (or 'dry', or 'Thatcherite') wing of the Tory party is overtly inegalitarian, regarding it as both

natural and desirable that there should be very wide differences in wealth, income and social status between people.
These variations set up incentives for people to work hard, and
help create a stable social hierarchy within which people can
function effectively. Government interference with market
allocations is always unjustifiable, undesirable and should be
minimised. Arguments for any form of egalitarian intervention
on grounds of social stability or 'fairness', or for any qualification of business predominance in the economy, should always
be resisted, and inequalities and privileges vigorously defended.

Cross-cutting this basic left/right split, however, and every
bit as important in its own way, is a second dimension of
Conservative ideology, shown as the vertical axis in Figure 6.1.
Traditional Conservatism, the Toryism of the aristocracy
which dominated the party right through to the 1950s, was
and is a philosophy in which the British nation-state featured
as the dominant unit of analysis. What matters to nation-state
Conservatives are a set of intangible and rather collective-
sounding entities, the British constitution, British culture,
British institutions, a British way of life. By contrast, since
Edward Heath became the first middle-class Conservative
leader in 1965, an alternative Conservative unit of account
has developed – the individual. In this approach, the way that
government is conducted and institutions are arranged should
be assessed primarily in terms of their impacts on individual
welfare, rather than in the semi-mystical terms of British
traditions, institutions or culture.

Combining the left/right split (those who accept a welfare
state versus those who favour greater inequality) with the split
between nation state Conservatives and individualist Conservatives, yields four basic groupings inside the Tory party,
shown in Figure 6.1.

The *traditional far right* is the pre-Thatcherite, aristocratic
right wing of the party. Its political philosophy is best
represented by the *Salisbury Review* and the works of Roger
Scruton (1980). Unversed in economics, the traditional far
right places the defence of hierarchy and tradition at the core
of its thinking, believing strongly in national autonomy,
defence of the realm, and strong, decisive government.

FIGURE 6.1 Ideological map of the Conservative Party

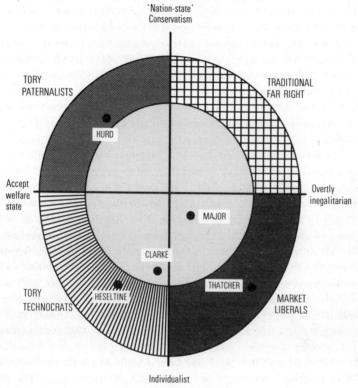

Tory loyalists and pragmatists, 'positional Toryism'

Contemptuous of local authorities or calls for devolution, the traditional far right instinctively opposes government intervention, except for farming subsidies vital to maintenance of part of the British way of life.

*Tory paternalists* represent the other long-lived current, believing strongly in 'one-nation' Conservatism in the Disraeli mould, accepting the need for a welfare state from a sense of *noblesse oblige*, almost completely pragmatic in their economic thinking, and committed to gradual reform of existing institutions. The apogee of this group's influence was under Harold

Macmillan in the late 1950s, and they have been a declining force in national politics since, although important still in Conservative local authorities. Perhaps the most important current exponent of this political style is Douglas Hurd.

*Tory technocrats* achieved their most complete influence under Edward Heath. For them, the welfare state is an inevitable (even if partly unwelcome and expensive) concomitant of modernity. Government's job is essentially to guide key aspects of national life in a way which promotes effective economic development, and to run the public sector effectively and cheaply. Heath's Toryism was interventionist, radically reorganising many institutions, attempting (but failing) to restructure industrial relations, and promoting economic efficiency as its watchword. Part and parcel of Tory technocracy is a strong commitment to Britain's involvement in Europe, and now the development of European Union. The crux of this group's differences from Thatcherism is the need for an active government industrial policy. Its greatest if now carefully-shrouded exponent remains Michael Heseltine. His willingness to promote sweeping pit closures in 1992–93 was widely seen as inconsistent with a belief in an interventionist industrial policy – in fact, he had simply concluded that a sizeable domestic mining industry could not play a role in the UK under modern conditions.

*Market liberals* are the final Conservative group, the heart of 'Thatcherism' and of new right thinking more generally. In many ways they stand outside older Tory traditions, not least in their commitment to unrelenting economic rationalism. Their chief commitment is to free markets and to cutting back the role of government to the absolute minimum. For them the extended welfare state is the chief symptom of fundamental defects in liberal democracies, and the major source of economic malaise and social decay. Initially committed to regenerating Britain's economy and transforming its society to embrace an 'enterprise culture', market liberals began the 1980s as monetarists, but lost their faith in the primacy of economics in setting a governing style by the middle of the decade. Market liberal (and new right thinking beyond the Tory party itself) increasingly ended up focusing on curtailing trade union powers and on a series of narrowly governmental reforms and changes – scrapping government regulation of markets, whittling away a few state-endorsed professional monopolies, privatising public corporations, and reorganising the civil service, NHS and education. When these changes failed to generate lasting economic growth, and the boom of 1986–88 was succeeded by recession, the market liberals' star waned. Like Margaret Thatcher herself, their economic policy focused increasingly on resisting further progress towards European unity, an issue where they could find common cause with the traditional far right. In the 1980s, figures such as Norman Tebbit, Nicholas Ridley, Sir Keith Joseph, and John Nott were important in this group, in addition to Thatcher herself. Thatcher and Tebbit remain active market liberal campaigners in the Lords, as Tebbit's speech to the 1992 Tory conference demonstrated. But after Thatcher's fall the solitary Cabinet exponent of their position was Michael Portillo, although Kenneth Clarke represented a centrist position close to theirs on domestic issues. Nonetheless, market liberal views have become the bedrock of modern Conservative right-wing thought. They are well expressed by think-tanks such as the Institute of Economic Affairs (IEA) and the Adam Smith Institute, and find powerful support in business circles, especially the financial sector, from which many Tory MPs and councillors now come.

*Leadership Change*

When Margaret Thatcher was deserted by just under half of all Tory MPs in the first round of the November 1990 leadership ballot, and subsequently urged to resign by many of her Cabinet, she was essentially a casualty of her inability to stay sufficiently close to the centre of the Tories' ideological map shown in Figure 6.1. Thatcher always lead the party from just inside the market liberal quadrant. She made least effort to draw support from the Tory paternalists, who she set out to marginalise from her earliest Cabinet changes in 1980 and 1981. They were weak and indecisive in organising to express their dissatisfaction with government policy, but calculations of electoral politics repeatedly prevented Thatcher from indulging her own desire to make large-scale cut-backs in key welfare state institutions such as the NHS. Her commitment to strong defence (especially in the Falklands war) together with her instinctive dislike of Europe and resolute style of government, all kept Thatcher onside with the traditional far right. And her economic rationalism provided a line to the Tory technocrats, especially as long as the attack on trade union powers and deregulation/privatisation seemed to be delivering growth dividends. But Thatcher's core support always came from the market liberals.

After the 1987 election Thatcher moved downwards and to right, away from the centre of Tory thinking and deeper into the market liberal camp, on two fronts. The first was the poll tax, a thoroughly misconceived and ill-thought-through 'reform' of local government finance (see Chapter 9). Its key feature was an overtly inegalitarian commitment to charging everyone the same head tax rate, irrespective of income, and thus moving local government away from being tax-financed towards a charging basis. This rationale collapsed long before the poll tax was implemented, while its enormous administrative expense made the new system economically irrational from the start. The second shift Thatcher made was towards an increasingly single-minded opposition to European unification, in a prolonged conflict with her Chancellor (Nigel Lawson) and Foreign Secretary (Sir Geoffrey Howe) from 1985 onwards focusing on British entry into the ERM. After removing Howe from the Foreign Office and forcing Lawson's resignation (mostly on this issue) in 1989, Thatcher's position became untenable in 1990. She conceded ERM entry to her new Chancellor John Major, albeit at a high value of the pound deliberately chosen so as to create 'zero inflation' in the UK economy. Howe's delayed resignation from the honorific role of 'Deputy Prime Minister' in autumn 1990 was provoked by Thatcher's attempt to obstruct progress at the Rome EC summit, and nicely timed to precipitate a challenge to her leadership from Michael Heseltine, representing the Tory technocrat wing of the party.

Thatcher's resignation forestalled a possible Heseltine victory, and was supposed to allow John Major to resume the pattern of leading the Conservatives from just inside the market liberal quadrant in Figure 6.1. In fact, Major turned out to be a less clear-cut figure than Thatcher herself supposed, much less market liberal-orientated and more pragmatic in his economic and social policy beliefs. Major's domestic policy initiatives came to little before the general election, except for removing the poll tax. The Citizen's Charter, with its muddled efforts to keep market liberals and Tory technocrats and paternalists happy, typified his approach (see Chapter 8). But it was his switch on European policy, and apparent acceptance of the substance of virtually all the Maastricht agreement, which really characterised his leadership, the commitment to 'put Britain at the heart of Europe', instead of being laggardly and marginalised.

*The Tory Feud over Europe*

Britain's forced ejection from the ERM under pressure from financial markets therefore represented an enormous defeat for Major, and for the initial members of his campaign team who had helped secure his election as leader, especially the Chancellor Norman Lamont. Had Margaret Thatcher remained an MP, Major's position in the autumn of 1992 could conceivably have been threatened. But the ex-premier and Lord Tebbit were among anti-Europeans who nonetheless wreaked havoc in Conservative ranks during the summer and autumn of 1992. In June immediately after Danish voters narrowly rejected the Maastricht Treaty, a total of 69 Conservative MPs signed the 'Fresh Start' early day motion which became the rallying document for Tory anti-marketeers. Together with thinly veiled attacks on the government's unwillingness to pursue new waves of market liberal ideas, anti-European feeling transfixed the Conservative Conference in October (after 'Black Wednesday').

It also produced the unprecedented parliamentary crisis on 4 November when the government depended on the votes of 19 Liberal Democrat MPs to get the Maastricht 'paving bill' through the Commons. A total of 21 Tory backbenchers resisted all the Whips efforts, and joined Labour in voting against the bill, with 6 more Tories abstaining (Baker *et al.*, 1993). This level of dissent is remarkable given that the vote was clearly a 'confidence' issue for the government: had it been lost John Major's survival as Premier would have been problematic indeed. Nor has the European issue gone away. At the time of writing, it seems likely that getting the Maastricht Treaty accepted by the Commons will involve a long parliamentary struggle. The Labour party will seek to commit Britain to the 'social chapter' of the Treaty, a move which Tory rebels might tactically support in a bid to make more Conservative MPs vote against the third reading of the bill. It is clear that the chasm over European policy which opened up under Thatcher will not be easily healed, especially if the EC itself confronts future difficulties (such as further delays in countries ratifying the revised Maastricht provisions agreed by EC leaders at Edinburgh in December 1992, or another crisis in the ERM). The unusually explicit and fiercely-fought character of this internal conflict naturally prompts comparison with historic Conservative battles, over the repeal of the Corn Laws in the 1840s, and over free trade versus imperial protection in the early twentieth century, the reverberations of which also stretched over many years.

Yet despite the passions aroused, pro- and anti-European feeling does not match up neatly with the basic ideological map of Toryism shown in Figure 6.1. Technocratic modernisers are uniformly pro-EC, but opposition to further European union draws scattered support in an arc which to some degree spans across the other three quadrants. The fiercest Conservative opponents are the traditional right, for whom the blow to British nationhood is unacceptable. But some Tory paternalists also dislike the regulatory and bureaucratic features of EC government, and the threat to British institutions. Many market liberals darkly suspect that European Union will usher in renewed bureaucracy, corporatism and social democratic notions via the back-door, after they have been successfully squashed in Britain by Thatcherism. However, other market liberals (especially those still in government, and hence bound to vote for Maastricht), accept that economic pressures for greater European convergence are too strong for Britain to stand aside. What seemed to distinguish the Maastricht rebels most as a group was their membership of the 'awkward squad', a set of stubborn individuals resisting government blandishments and threats alike, more than any coherent ideological view. This hetero-geneity limits the Conservative anti-Europeans' effectiveness. They know what they dislike, and hope that faltering EC momentum will let them obstruct the Major government's policy. But they find it hard to produce alternative policy scenarios of their own, beyond enlarging the EC (so as to dilute its central capacity to act), and narrowly restricting its scope of concerns to economic matters.

## *The Dominant Party?*

Outside the rarefied atmosphere of Westminster the Conser-vative party remains one of the strongest and most successful integrated parties of the right anywhere in the Western world. Its electoral machine in 1992 proved rusty and ill-experienced at the national level, but reliable enough in delivering increased votes outside the marginal constituencies almost everywhere. In local government the party made up some ground in 1992, and with the abandonment of the poll tax and commitment to piecemeal restructuring of county government may be poised to perform more competitively than during its long slow decline through the 1980s. And at the grass roots, Conservative membership continues to fall very gradually, but still dwarfs the individual membership of the Labour Party and the small numbers of Liberal Democrat activists. Party finances were hit by the return of recession, but election year funding showed a continued commitment from business to supporting a Tory government.

Whether their fourth election victory will precipitate new signs of the Conservatives assuming 'dominant party' status in British politics remains difficult to assess. In Japan the hegemony of the right-wing Liberal Democratic Party, and in Italy the presence of the Christian Democratic party continuously in government since the transition to democracy of the late 1940s have both been accompanied by the emergence of very strongly defined factions inside each party, and by an extensive growth of political corruption. The British Conservatives have so far been little touched by either phenomenon. In 1987–88 the party's MPs did exude over-confidence, with individual ministers or key figures showing signs of developing factions of 'clients' of their own – attracting sub-groups of followers, focusing on very applied issues in public debates, trying to steer issues away from 10 Downing Street and the Prime Minister by fixing up compromises between themselves. The growth of parliamentary lobbying by business, almost entirely using Tory MPs as conduits to ministers, added an unhealthy tinge.

Major's more consensual and collegial regime, combined with the prolonged recession, the loss of 42 Conservative MPs at the general election, and the tighter discipline needed with an overall majority of just 21, all focused Conservative energies again on the contest with Labour – apart from the European/ERM issues. With this huge exception, factionalisation remains low, chiefly because the main Tory leadership figures stand in rather muddy relationship towards the basic ideology map shown in Figure 6.1. Major himself is famously elusive ideologically, talking consensually if prosaically during the election, but adopting 'drier' attitudes immediately afterwards, and not qualifying many Thatcherite social policies in any radical way (see Chapter 11). The market liberal wing and the traditional far right inside the Tory Parliamentary party both resemble headless chickens, losing the clear Cabinet representation they had enjoyed in the 1980s (Baker *et al.*, 1992). Finally, Michael Heseltine's disastrous handling of the pit closure crisis, which also triggered a Tory backbench backlash for a time, seems to have largely dashed any future hopes he might have entertained of leading a Tory technocrat bid for the leadership. Major promoted his main rivals, Heseltine and Kenneth Clarke, after the 1992 election. But he carefully stripped the regulation of financial services out of the DTI before Heseltine took over (passing it to the Treasury), leaving him with a poisoned chalice of difficult industrial policy decisions. Clarke is a possible leadership contender if Major should crumble further in office as he seemed to do in autumn 1992, and could enjoy right-wing support in default of any better candidate. More 'dry' aspirants include Michael Portillo (who famously proclaimed his joy at having to implement the poll tax to the Conservative party conference when a junior minister), and Michael Howard.

More surprising perhaps is the Conservatives' apparent inability to recruit new leadership personnel of high calibre. Major initially made a push in his 1990 appointments to bring the average age of the Cabinet down, and reportedly asked the then Northern Ireland Secretary Peter Brooke to resign on these grounds, which he refused to do. After the 1992 election Brooke went to the backbenches, following an abortive Cabinet bid to get him elected as Speaker, only to be subsequently recalled by Major to take over the National Heritage department, from which David Mellor had to resign over sex and property scandals. Similarly, Sir Norman Fowler, who left Cabinet under Thatcher, returned to prominence as Party Chairman under Major. The Thatcher era is often portrayed as one of rapid turnover in Cabinet personnel, with opponents being chopped at will. In fact, Thatcher appointed only 55 people to an average of 22 Cabinet posts over her whole eleven and a half years in office. She certainly eliminated opponents, but she rarely let go other ministers. Most people who left the Cabinet moved into business, or were suffering from exhaustion with political life. Major's very gradual renewal of the Cabinet continues this record, suggesting that the circulation of elites inside the Conservative party continues to be relatively slow – itself a factor which may eventually promote backbench unrest.

## The Labour Party

Far more is written on internal Labour politics than about the Conservatives, perhaps because more academics are members, but also reflecting the more overt nature of conflicts inside the party, and the often more interesting character of its debates. Labour now is a fairly straightforward piece of machinery, dominated by the party leadership and Parliamentary party, but housed in the shell of an older and larger labour movement which grows less relevant as the years go by. This shell is responsible for the continuing federal structure of the party, the separation between individual members who join via the constituency parties, and members who belong via their affiliated unions. While constituency members cast their votes by appointing Conference delegates and voting directly on the choice of leader, union members' votes have traditionally been cast en bloc by each union's leadership, frequently controlled by one or a few powerful officials or executive members. Gaps between different branches of the party have widened, despite overlapping mechanisms, such as the integration of most middle-class trade unionists via the constituency parties, because their unions are not formally affiliated to the party. The mechanisms of the block vote remain a powerful source of delegitimation in the party, discrediting it as a democratic structure in the eyes of many voters. The leadership has made very slow progress in reforming the party's constitution. Like Kinnock before him, John Smith is caught by his dependence on trade union leaders for 'responsible' support, and the fear that (unless party membership could be dramatically boosted) constituency activists will remain more 'extreme' in their views than Labour voters. If reducing union barons' influence on policy gives 'unrepresentative' activists more power, then it could push Labour away from policies that make it electable.

*Basic Ideological Conflicts*

The fundamental left/right cleavage in the Labour party was historically about attitudes to nationalisation, a commitment to which is apparently incorporated in Clause IV of the party's Constitution. The left enthusiastically supported direct state ownership of the means of production, and the need for public ownership to often make non-commercial decisions, for example to safeguard employment. The Labour right by contrast believed in a mixed economy, where only industries with a particularly strong public interest involvement, or those of great strategic importance economically, would be taken under direct state control, and even then run on a basically commercial basis. This controversy played itself out in terms of nationalisation by the early 1980s, as most Labour leaders became disillusioned with nationalisation or public corporations as effective tools of state economic intervention. Arguments about whether to take back into public ownership some key public utilities privatised by the Conservatives (such as the national electricity grid or the water industry) are the main contemporary echo of these historical disputes. The left now favours creation of diverse forms of 'social ownership', much more decentralist in character than the old public corporations, and imposition of strict public interest regulation regimes on privatised utilities and major companies. The Labour right opts for much weaker forms of the same solutions, approving only those measures it sees as consistent with the maintenance of private sector capital investment.

Cross-cutting the left/right distinction is a second fundamental Labour cleavage, between the industrial and the welfare state wings of the party, shown in Figure 6.2. Historically Labour was founded by manual worker unions, most of whose membership worked in private sector industries.

FIGURE 6.2    Ideological map of the Labour Party

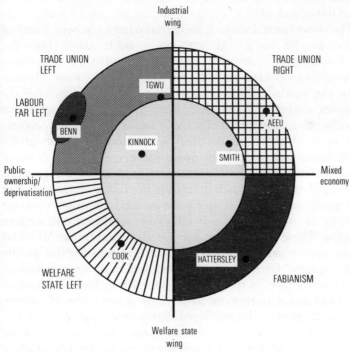

For a time, when public ownership was at its peak, many of these unions' members had moved into the public corporation sector, in large employment industries like mining, the railways, and the Post Office. Today public corporations have virtually disappeared because of privatisation, and employment in the few that remain has shrunk drastically. The other great source of Labour membership, especially in the post-war period, has been the growth of the welfare state, notably local government and the NHS. Public sector manual worker unions affiliated to Labour have expanded enormously, partly filling the gap left by the decline of traditional heavy industries and public corporations. More important still, the basis of Labour's constituency membership has been transformed, with white-collar public sector employees belonging to non-affiliated unions emerging as the bedrock of Labour's activists, and the source of most of the party's councillors, Parliamentary candidates and MPs.

The concerns of Labour's industrial wing have been first and foremost with industrial relations – trade union law, the mechanisms of collective bargaining, whether a Labour government operates an incomes policy, and so on. Historically the trade unions helped form Labour to defend the complex system of immunities from prosecution which alone permits them to operate effectively under British law. Reversing some of the Conservatives' anti-union legislation of the 1980s remains a priority for union leaders, especially those on the left. By contrast, the welfare state wing of the party is concerned essentially with defending the fabric of state benefits and public services built up by the Attlee Labour government of 1945–51 – the NHS, state education, pensions and welfare benefits. These two agendas are of course connected. Affiliated public sector manual worker unions and white-collar public sector unions formally unaffiliated but well represented in constituency parties have strong interests in both areas. And the trade union movement as a whole is protective of welfare state entitlements. Nonetheless differences of emphasis between the two wings are often decisive, for example, triggering coalitions of left and right union leaders in defence of their particular organisational concerns.

The intersection of the left/right and industrial/welfare state dimensions creates four key ideological groupings. The *trade union right* now focuses principally on the engineers and electricians union (the AEEU), whose policies express the most profound dissent from the traditional way of running Labour's and the unions' affairs. The AEEU has been aggressive in seeking to enlarge its membership by breaching the conventions that bind other unions, accepting no-strike deals, negotiating private health care benefits for its members, being reluctant to trigger industrial actions, and being willing to accept most 1980s' industrial relations laws. In party terms, the trade union right opposes public ownership, defends free collective bargaining (because these unions often represent higher-paid workers), is sceptical about government intervention and more sympathetic to private capital, and believes in strong British nuclear defence. Above all the union right is loyalist, believing in giving strong backing to the party leader and parliamentary party, and leaving them to get on with the job, so long as they do not affect the Labour right's icons.

The *trade union left* has diminished hugely in influence during the 1980s. At the start of the decade this wing of the party was enormously influential, pushing through constitutional changes which stripped Labour MPs of the sole right to elect the party leader, affirming the legitimacy of union and constituency party control via the annual conference, committing Labour to reverse privatisations, helping to force through a commitment against a British nuclear deterrent, and a pledge to withdraw from Europe. All these policy positions then disintegrated. The constitutional changes produced the election of Kinnock and Hattersley and the reimposition of a very traditional, leadership-dominated pattern of control over Labour policy. The EC and unilateral disarmament stances helped make Labour's 1983 manifesto 'the longest suicide note in history', and both stances were reversed within two years by Kinnock, with remarkably little effective union dissent. The trade union left in the 1990s has no strong policy ideas of its own, beyond repealing some aspects of previous Tory industrial relations laws, and preserving the unions' dominant position inside the Labour Party apparatus itself.

The *welfare state left* is in better shape. In the 1980s a key current was the 'new urban left', based in local government, which sought to develop a different kind of welfarism from Labour's traditional policies, based on community involvement, decentralisation, and the development of efficient services. As many new urban left figures have moved into Parliament, so these ideas have developed into a much broader 'soft left' strategy of breaking away from Labour's old industrial ties and repositioning the party as spokesperson for users of public services, state-dependent groups, the inner cities, the unemployed, women and ethnic minorities. In addition, the welfare state left was close to the peace movement in the 1980s and is the key source of environmentalist pressures inside Labour ranks. Its approach is a 'coalition of minorities' one, taking a 'rainbow' of different groups and bringing them together behind common purposes, chiefly by using the welfare state to bind together diverse interests. The 'soft left' has been the prime mover behind Labour's commitment to achieving a quota of 40 per cent women in all Party offices by 1996, and the changes giving women a quota of reserved seats in the shadow Cabinet, and it is the leading source of support for 'black sections' inside Labour's ranks. The welfare state left believes in drastic reduction of trade union representation at Party Conference to eliminate domination of party decision-making by the block vote. And it is the key source of grass-roots' pressure inside the party to drop support for first-past-the-post elections, to embrace PR, and to seek some form of understanding with the Liberal Democrats to overcome the record of four successive election defeats and get the Tories voted out of office – although these are all demands which Labour MPs have difficulty in accepting. By any standard, this is a coherent and dynamic programme, essentially seeking to disentangle Labour from its historic record and reposition it as a non-industrial party of the left.

The fourth Labour grouping is *Fabianism*, the core position of the party's non-industrial right wing. Historically, Fabianism was an intellectual viewpoint developed by the Fabian Society, a grouping of Labour parliamentarians, academics and activists, small in absolute numbers, but enormously influential in terms of defining Labour ideology. In the post-war period, Anthony Crosland's book *The Future of Socialism* (1956) defined the Fabian right's position as a defence of the mixed economy, opposition to further drastic nationalisation, and progressive achievement of socialist objectives via gradual extensions of the welfare state. This position thereafter became a conventional wisdom of 'moderate' Labourism, and remains the dominant view in the parliamentary Labour Party (PLP). The classic modern exponent is Roy Hattersley, who as deputy leader from 1983 to 1992 successfully pulled the 'soft left' closer to Fabian views during the 1980s, and blocked the welfare state left's pressure for constitutional change. In economic policy terms, Fabianism is pragmatic and conservative, while on defence policy its exponents advocated only multilateral nuclear disarmament throughout the Cold War era.

A final Labour grouping worth distinguishing is the *Labour far left*. At parliamentary level this group encompasses a fairly small number of MPs united chiefly by their intense almost paranoid suspicion of the Labour leadership, which they see as almost permanently 'selling out' core Labour beliefs and values, and as operating internal party politics in an authoritarian mode. Tony Benn has long been the unofficial leader of this group. Although the PLP 'hard left' is normally remarkably ineffective and elitist in its activities, its views resonate with a shifting variety of left-wing 'groupuscles' and sects, some of which are organised within Labour's ranks, while others are Trotskyist organisations debarred from membership, often organised around left newspapers or broadsheets. The Militant Tendency was the largest such group in the 1980s, and practised 'entryist' tactics of taking over particular constituency parties and organisations with some success in Liverpool, before being expelled from membership.

*Leadership Change*

The traditional pattern of Labour leadership is for a new leader to get elected in a centre-left position, but then to move progressively right the longer his tenure of office, a pattern which Neil Kinnock's career followed exactly. Left policies on unilateral disarmament, withdrawal from the EC, reversing privatisation and Tory trade union laws, were progressively dropped. But in addition, his whole leadership style became effectively right-wing for several reasons.

The first and in many ways most difficult task for any Labour leader is to stay sane and calm given the characteristically vituperative onslaught of the Conservative tabloid press, especially at election time. Kinnock coped with this problem by creating a small team in his office, which filtered out all information and policy ideas that reached him, but also seemed to have screened out the flow of new or more critical ideas which might have helped Labour positively to increase its vote. A second key leadership task is simply to run Labour's creaking and over-sized party machinery without mistakes and foul-ups, and despite disruptive activities from the PLP left and extra-parliamentary groups. The key task here is to bridge between the trade union leaders commanding the key block votes and the PLP. Kinnock devoted huge amounts of time to party management, partly because he was very skilled at it. Despite being elected and re-elected by the party machine as a whole using its complex electoral college arrangements, Kinnock effectively recreated the strongly centralised leadership patterns of Labour under Harold Wilson in the 1960s. The transition from left hegemony in the early 1980s to the reassertion of leadership domination seemed decisively to rehabilitate Robert McKenzie's controversial thesis from the 1950s, that Labour and Conservative patterns of effective leadership are strikingly convergent, despite the huge formal differences in the two parties' organisation (McKenzie, 1965).

The 'fake' leadership election of 1992 which brought in John Smith, with Margaret Beckett as deputy leader, continues this convergence. Smith and Beckett were effectively 'anointed' by the decision of virtually all other possible leadership candidates – such as Gordon Brown, Tony Blair, Robin Cook and Jack Cunningham – not to stand against them: Cook even ran Smith's election campaign. Bryan Gould did run, but lost badly, with union and PLP votes solidly decided in advance. Some trade unions resisted balloting their membership because of the expense, given that the outcome was a *fait accompli*. Although the biggest recalcitrants (the TGWU and AEEU) relented, some unions only 'consulted' their members, and the overall climate of the election tended to undermine the new leadership team's legitimacy, and the whole electoral college system. Smith's shadow cabinet duly promoted Brown, Blair, Cunningham and Cook while marginalising Gould, who subsequently resigned his front bench role at the 1992 Labour conference in a manner calculated to embarrass Smith. The leadership election 'stitch-up' may yet open up future problems for the party, because like James Callaghan before him Smith leads the party from the right. Having no left-of-centre credentials as protection, Smith may face more severe left dissent (as Callaghan did, especially after losing the 1979 election).

Smith's leadership position worsened as he proved highly reluctant to give any clear lead on big issues about Labour's future direction (see below), and rather colourless in opposition to the unimpressive John Major. To help change Labour's policy, he created new bodies, a Social Justice Commission (with some non-party figures on it) to look again at taxation and welfare policies, and a Democracy Commission to explore new constitutional arrangements. How effective they will prove (except in deferring hard decisions) remains a matter for conjecture. Smith's health also remains in question, and may have caused other leadership candidates to hold back in the expectation of perhaps having another bite at the cherry before the next general election. Finally in any future election campaign, Smith and Beckett may also be severely handicapped by the fact that they jointly masterminded Labour's 1992 'alternative budget', whose plans to increase taxes on the well-off were widely seen as contributing to a last-minute surge of opinion poll support for the Conservatives.

*Fundamental Re-think, or 'One More Heave'?*

The 1990s started badly for moderate left parties around the world. In Sweden a right-wing government was elected for only the second time in many decades; in Germany the SDP's efforts to slow down unification were swept aside by the conservative CDU/CSU victory; in New Zealand Labour lost power, blamed for the recession, a pattern almost certain to be repeated in France, and possibly in Australia. Labour's problems can be seen as part of a general problem of social democracy in coming to terms with a world where competitive tax rate cuts, increasing international integration, and the enormous institutionalised power of financial markets seem to have foreclosed the option of single-country 'socialism'.

Labour's situation is worse because it is still clawing back very painfully much of the ground lost in the disastrous 1983 election. But the party has at least rebuilt its Commons representation, even if its overall share of the popular vote improved only incrementally in 1987 and 1992. Within Labour's ranks, there are powerful forces pushing for simply a more intensive form of Labour's existing campaigning, the 'one more heave' syndrome. This 'traditionalist' position is fuelled by left-wing hostility to further deradicalising policy changes, by union leaders' opposition to internal party reforms cutting their power, by Labour's seat gains despite lagging nearly 8 per cent behind the Conservatives in votes, and Labour's revival in opinion polls following the government's policy crises at the end of 1992.

The apparatus of British parliamentary democracy systematically fosters the 'one more heave' illusion in the minds of Labour's leadership and MPs. There they sit in the Commons, almost touching their counterparts on the government benches. Assisted by at most a couple of researchers, shadow ministers find it possible to beat their ministerial counterparts at question time and in debates, despite the vast back-up provided by the civil service. The apparatus of two-party dominance remains intact in all spheres of the Commons' operations, so that Labour leaders and Whips can easily ignore the inconvenient presence of Liberal Democrat and Nationalist MPs in the certainty that they are *the* Opposition – even if voters in ballot booths have just allocated these third and fourth parties over 20 per cent support. And patterns of power in the Commons transmute into the mass media system, and the structure of the most mundane TV or radio debates. In this cosy, two-party world, the illusion of a Conservative/Labour 'straight fight' is religiously maintained, and Labour leaders repeatedly get deceived about the scale of the electoral mountain the party has yet to climb.

Many trade unionists also want to believe that Labour can win an overall Commons majority without facing up to fundamental questions about its role in British politics. For union elites, their established role in Labour's policy-making machinery is much more important, even sacred, than would seem sensible to outsiders. Why, one might ask, care so much about dominating the Conferences of a four-times defeated Labour party? This is a question most union leaders cannot ask: their commitment to the status quo is such as to render it almost unthinkable. And the party leadership's efforts to cut back their block vote, from its current level of 94 per cent of nominal party membership at Annual Conference to 70 per cent in the first instance and less in future, are likely to continue to meet with union resistance.

Pressure for the most fundamental rethinking of Labour's position comes from the constituency party membership, especially the centre-left disillusioned with Kinnock's failures. One central call is for Labour to remove all support for first-past-the-post elections, and to come out squarely for a system of PR, as the basis for positive cooperation between Labour and the Liberal Democrats to vote the Tories out of power. Electoral reform has been investigated by the Plant committee of the party since the leadership was defeated by party conference in 1990, and forced to extend an initially limited review to look also at Westminster elections. Before the 1992 election, and for the first year after it, the Plant Committee was a classic case of spurious inquiry, its chief job being to edge party opinion round to looking at the available choices for non-Westminster elections. Crunch year for Labour's debate will be the 1993 party conference, by which time the party must decide whether to accept PR elections and the likely necessity for coalition-building with the Liberal Democrats, or to try yet again to make voters feel confident enough to give Labour an overall majority. The strong pressure at the grass-roots and from Labour voters is for a thorough-going reappraisal of the party's historic stance. But the likely result under the Smith–Beckett leadership is for 'apparat' politics to triumph again, and for official Labour policy to fudge or evade the electoral reform issue. The Liberal Democrat decision to support Major over the Maastricht vote, despite its 'confidence' character, has powerfully strengthened Labour traditionalists' distrust of centre parties.

At the leadership level there are also right-wing Labour 'modernisers' who oppose or are indifferent to electoral reform, including Beckett, Brown, Blair and probably Smith himself. In their view the party's fundamental job is simply to reposition itself so as to win more votes from middle-class people and be less identified with either the trade unions or with people living on welfare state benefits. In early 1993, Labour interest in copying some of the techniques which helped elect Bill Clinton as the first Democratic Party president since 1976 in the USA provoked controversy. Left-wing MPs (notably John Prescott) alleged a plot by right-wing fixers (such as Peter Mandelson, Kinnock's former Campaign Director, now a Labour MP) to 'Clintonise' the party, abandoning historic Labour commitments and beliefs in favour of slavish deference to opinion polls and a quest for 'yuppie' votes.

The one area where Labour's internal debates have been relatively weak concerns EC policy where the party has basically backed the Maastricht deal, but demanded that the UK should not opt out of the 'social chapter'. Together with the mishandling of economic policy in autumn 1992, this allowed Labour to vote against the Maastricht 'paving' bill as a confidence issue, despite poll evidence that most Labour voters as well as Labour MPs are now solidly pro-EC in their general attitudes. More backbench dissent over the EC may yet emerge before the Treaty is finally ratified in 1993, or if the ERM mechanism should collapse completely. But so long as the EC itself continues to develop Labour looks set to remain less divided on this issue than the Conservatives.

## The Liberal Democrats

If electoral reform and future coalition-building raise problems for Labour, they are scarcely less troubling for the Liberal Democrats. The future of the electoral system is an absolutely critical issue for the prospering of any centrist politics in Britain. But although the Liberal Democrats can agree what they want as an end-goal – full PR using the single-transferrable vote (STV) system – the strategic dilemmas involved in getting there are manifold, as the 1992 election demonstrated.

## Ashdown's Mistake

Paddy Ashdown pitched the Liberal Democrat campaign from the start around the issue of 'fair votes' and constitutional reform, and the party had this corner of the policy field almost to itself until a week before polling day. Then Neil Kinnock began to drop very well-publicised hints about a possible Labour rethink on electoral reform, while insisting that he could envisage no post-election dealing with the Liberal Democrats. The danger for the Liberal Democrats was that their support could be nibbled away by defections to Labour, while at the same time they risked losing Tory waverers who saw them as just covert allies of Labour – a major theme of Conservative propaganda.

Ashdown responded in a series of TV and radio interviews, carried on virtually all channels the weekend before the election, and played up in Conservative newspapers. He warned that if Labour tried to form a minority administration and govern alone in a hung Parliament, as it had in 1974, then economic catastrophe could loom. Finance market confidence would be sapped, sterling's parity in the ERM would be jeopardised, and interest rates would have to rise with such an unstable government, stifling hopes of economic recovery. The *only* way to avoid this prospect, Ashdown argued, was for Kinnock to commit himself to negotiate a full, four-year term of government with the Liberal Democrats, in which case stability would be guaranteed.

It never seemed to have occurred to Ashdown (or his campaign manager Des Wilson) that doom-mongering about a hung Parliament played straight into the Conservatives' hands, and undermined the whole basis of the Liberal Democrats' campaign for a strong third-party vote. In 1974, the then Liberal leader Jeremy Thorpe had put quite the contrary case: he stressed that in a hung Parliament every Liberal vote was a vote for moderation, for an MP who would act always in the public interest, putting the country's welfare first. In Thorpe's campaign, a minority Labour government would be controlled by Liberal votes and so represented no threat to wavering Conservative voters. Ashdown's very different closing theme in 1992 saw a last-minute pick-up in Tory support, especially in their heartland areas.

The Liberal Democrats won seats only in the south-west (where they opened a sizeable bridgehead of six seats) and in Scotland (where they are the fourth-placed party but the electoral system for once treated their relatively low vote fairly). In every other region of the country the party secured at most one or two seats, whatever their level of support, and the electoral system continued to be as unfair to the Liberal Democrats as ever. Yet somehow the party must succeed in persuading voters to support it under the present system, even if the prospect of a 'wasted vote' looms. That is one part of the Liberal Democrats' policy dilemma.

The other part of their problem is that the underlying nature of Liberal Democrat support is not easily classified. When pushed for a second preference, 38 per cent of Liberal Democrat voters in 1992 chose the Tories, 33 per cent Labour, and 15 per cent the Greens (Dunleavy *et al.*, 1992, p.4). From this, Liberal Democrat voters can be identified as either preponderantly right-wing (with a net lead of 5 per cent for the Conservatives over Labour), or preponderantly left-wing (with Labour plus the Greens outstripping the Tories by 10 per cent). But in only three regions of the country did most Liberal Democrat second preferences go to Labour, suggesting that a 'left of centre' deal would help Labour little.

Objectively, if the Liberal Democrats are ever to achieve their goals, they must rely on a hung Parliament with a Labour minority government, or on a Labour conversion to electoral reform. There is simply no feasible scenario in which a Conservative Premier would ever agree the change, since the Tories are so clearly the chief beneficiaries of the status quo. Yet Ashdown could not say anything remotely like this during the election campaign itself, for fear of gifting Tory propagandists. And when he tried to say it immediately after the election, calling for a 'realignment of the Left' to get the Conservatives out, his lead raised predictable opposition within his own party's ranks, both in the Commons and at the 1992 party conference.

*Directional Voting and the 'Hotel Party' Syndrome*

A deeper-lying structural problem for the Liberal Democrats is their generally indistinctive ideological position. The party's central commitment to constitutional change – to STV elections, a Bill of Rights, devolution for Scotland and Wales, and action on regional decentralisation as well, used to be distinctive, but all these points except PR are now official Labour policy as well. In addition, the Liberal Democrats are overt Euro-enthusiasts, advocating further progress towards eventual European Union – even to the point of saving John Major's skin over the Maastricht paving bill. But on the economic and social issues which dominated the 1992 election campaign, the Liberal Democrats still have little public identity. The damaging but esoteric disputes between former Liberals and former members of the Social Democratic Party, about the control of inflation or the meaning of a 'social market' economy, flared and died in 1987–89, without ever being understood by ordinary voters. The public see the Liberal Democrats as being 'in the middle' between the Tories and Labour on virtually all economic and social issues. In one way this is a source of support, for then you can attract waverers from either of the other two parties. But in another way it is a key limitation, which is well explained by a recent rational choice argument – the 'directional model' of voting (Rabinowitz and Macdonald, 1989).

The model assumes that a voter visualises political space as a left/right spectrum, and can also identify a symbolically important neutral point. For example, suppose the issue is support for a well-funded National Health Service (shown on the left in Figure 6.3), set against a policy of privatising the NHS or letting it run down (shown on the right), with the neutral point at $N$. The voter also defines a zone of feasible policy solutions (the unshaded area in the diagram), and identifies where she stands on an issue, her personal optimum position: in the diagram I assume she moderately supports the NHS. Next she locates the parties on the same scale, Labour firmly over on the left, the Liberal Democrats somewhat over on the left (it does not matter that the party sees itself as very committed to the NHS), and the Conservatives somewhat over

FIGURE 6.3   Directional voting: the NHS

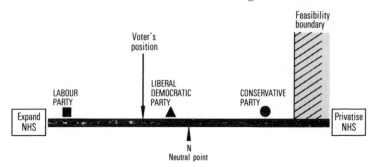

on the right. How should this voter choose to vote? The orthodox rational choice model says that she should choose the Liberal Democrats, because they are closest to her optimum position. But the directional model says that casting her vote this way would symbolically be going in the 'wrong' direction. Because our hypothetical voter sees herself as supporting the NHS, the Liberal Democrat's perceived position will not attract her, because it is a pull towards nothing distinctive, or towards privatisation if anything. So she is likely instead to choose Labour.

Consider another symbolically-charged issue, nuclear disarmament (Figure 6.4). Here the voter puts unilateral disarmament on the left of the scale but sees it as infeasible, while a more inside left position is given by active efforts at multilateral disarmament, through to further British nuclear weapons-building on the right. Labour is located well to the left, the Tories firmly on the right, and the Liberal Democrats are perceived (possibly wrongly given their commitment to building Trident nuclear submarines) as being just inside the left half of the spectrum. The voter takes a modestly right-wing position. How should she vote? Again, the Liberal Democrats should recruit her support if all that mattered was the perceived distance between the parties' different positions and the voter's best possible outcome. But for this voter to choose them, not only would she have to cast her vote in the 'wrong' direction, but in addition she would have to cross the symbolic neutral point to do so. The directional model predicts

FIGURE 6.4    Directional voting: nuclear disarmament

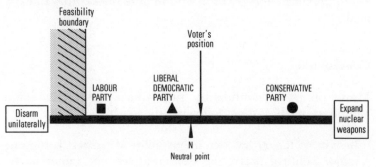

that instead she will end up supporting the Tories, even though their pledge is more 'extreme' than her modestly right-wing personal preferences.

Put simply, the directional model suggests that despite there being many centrist voters close to the Liberal Democrats' position, they will often end up not voting for them but for the Conservative or Labour parties, which can provide much stronger ideological leads on issues. The major parties can energise voters more, stirring up their personal commitments and articulating things that they feel – even if they often treat issues in more polarised ways than centrist voters' actual views. By contrast, the Liberal Democrats are seen by voters as indistinctive and cannot activate voters in the same way.

To try to avoid this structural trap Ashdown committed his party to one distinctive policy combination in the 1992 campaign, raising income taxes by 1p and spending the proceeds on education. Approved by most voters, these bolt-on ideas did little to fill the party's ideology/image gap. So long as this situation persists, the Liberal Democrats may be limited to the core support they can win over permanently by their stance on the EC and constitutional change, plus a shifting collection of voters disillusioned with the other major parties whom the Liberal Democrats can recruit temporarily at any given election. This situation is the 'hotel party' model – lots of people check in, but they check out again soon afterwards: the hotel can be regularly filled, but still have few long-term residents. If the directional model of voting is right, the Liberal

Democrats' handicap is not going to be easily overcome, even if electoral reform does occur in Britain later this century or early next.

## Conclusion

Many observers confidently proclaimed the arrival of a 'dominant party system' following the general election:

> Britain no longer has two major political parties. It has one major political party, the Conservatives, one minor party, Labour, and one peripheral party, the Liberal Democrats (King, 1992, p.224).

Yet within six months Conservative hegemony seemed very much less securely based, ministers' grip on power and John Major's premiership both seemed highly fragile, and Conservative party internal divisions far more serious. The *Financial Times* concluded just before the Maastricht vote:

> It is now clear that what was elected on April 9th was not a Conservative Government with a majority of 21, but a hung Parliament in which the parties that most loathe one another, the Thatcherites and Majorites, stand beneath the Tory flag (quoted in Baker *et al.*, 1993).

At the least the government's survival by three votes in the Commons (still more its dependence on Liberal Democrat support), the throwing back of initial pit closure proposals, and the reversal of its economic strategy, all point to a much more conditional Conservative dominance than was previously thought.

It is also clear that the opposition parties continue to create the basic conditions for Tory government, partly by their own efforts and omissions. Labour's halting and ill-conducted election post-mortem, plus Smith's indecisive and non-cerebral leadership, contributed to blowing the opportunities apparently open in autumn 1992. The Liberal Democrats' inability to admit publicly that they depend on cooperation with Labour to enact constitutional change and electoral reform, their unwillingness to stand clearly as a party of the centre-left, also undermines their position. And both parties' campaigning efforts are dulled by the certainty that only a measure of cooperation is likely to evict the Conservatives from office.

Meanwhile the Green Party gained less than 1 per cent of the vote nation-wide, but may yet stage a minor comeback at the 1994 Euro-elections (because of the base given by their 15 per cent vote in 1989, the past 'environmental' character of Euro-elections, and voters' disaffection from all other parties). Studies of voters' second and third preferences in 1992 suggest that the Greens do enjoy some support amongst younger age groups (Dunleavy *et al.*, 1992), which might revive if the party's activists could ever bring themselves to nominate a leader and build up a proper organisation.

Behind the appearance of 'moderate' leadership and loss of ideological impetus amongst all parties, it is hard to avoid the impression of a political stalemate. The Conservatives can win, but it is no longer clear *why* they want to. They can dominate party politics too, but whether the Major government still has any ideas left or can even govern competently remains open. So far it seems too that Labour cannot win, because Labour elites cannot bring themselves to want to win enough to bear the necessary costs involved (such as electoral reform and an accommodation with the Liberal Democrats). How long this deradicalised politics of deadlock will be maintained is the central political question of the rest of the decade.

# 7

# Parliament

**GAVIN DREWRY**

A distinction has been drawn by Nelson Polsby (1975) between 'arena' and 'transformative' legislatures. An arena legislature is one in which debate is conducted and issues are aired, but few decisions of any substance are taken. A transformative legislature plays a much more active role in policy-making. Given a straight choice between these two models, most commentators would almost certainly assign the UK Parliament to the former category. A 'parliament', as the word itself suggests, is for talking, rather than doing.

However, one contemporary defender of Parliament's residual capacity for influence, Philip Norton (1984, 1985, 1991), takes an intermediate position, arguing that Parliament falls into the category of a 'policy-influencing' legislature, able intermittently to reject or even amend executive-inspired measures, but with limited capacity to launch policy initiatives of its own. Even if one were to accept the Polsby dichotomy, it would surely be wrong to ignore entirely, in any analysis of recent political history, the parliamentary arena in which, for instance, many of the events that led up to Thatcher's resignation in November 1990, and the succession of dramatic episodes, two years later, surrounding the ERM crisis, the pit closures controversy, and the Maastricht debates, were publicly enacted.

It is certainly true that if one goes to the trouble of adding up all the small change of incremental procedural reform, along with shifting patterns of parliamentary behaviour, one ends up with what seems at first sight to be quite a tidy sum. Arguably, however, the process of 'adding up' a lot of disparate episodes and tendencies is a somewhat artificial exercise, and the end-product, rather than being a lump sum, may be separate piles of loose change, made up of a mixture of different currencies and earmarked for a lot of different purposes.

Norton's contentions about policy influence are plausible – though the extent of such influence is impossible to measure. Moreover, as this writer has argued elsewhere (Drewry, 1988, p.127), much of it has to do with the 'invisible' deterrent effects of Parliament upon ministers, who may shrink from the prospect of having to justify an unjustifiable policy in public (and nowadays, often in front of television cameras).

## Parliament, the Party System and the Prime Minister

The key to understanding the House of Commons is party politics. Its practices and procedures are essentially adversarial in character (though lubricated by covert collaboration through 'the usual channels' operating 'behind the Speaker's chair') and revolve around the continuing durability of the two-party system.

In the 1970s, Stuart Walkland (1976, 1977) scorned the notion that meaningful parliamentary reform could take place in the absence of political change. He argued that only if the rigidities of the two-party system were to break down, or were broken down by electoral reform, could Parliament acquire a meaningful role, sharing power with government and exercising effective scrutiny. In the 1980s, the temporary emergence of a new centre party grouping prompted speculation about hung parliaments – how they would work, and what effect they would have on the House of Commons. This speculation was linked in some quarters with the recent establishment, in 1979, of a new cluster of departmentally-related select committees (see below). For instance, Ian Marsh (1986), having conducted research into select committees in the early 1980s, foresaw a hung Parliament scenario in which committees might acquire 'independent powers of political initiative', serving as an antidote to what Samuel Beer termed 'pluralist stagnation', by facilitating the integration of pressure groups into the policy-making process.

The opinion poll predictions in 1992 that the Liberal Democrats might end up holding the balance of power never materialised, and the prospect of a hung parliament role looks, for the time being, remote. In any case, Marsh's prognosis seemed, even in the mid-1980s, to be highly speculative – though some of his empirical findings about the interplay between pressure groups and committees have been confirmed by subsequent research (Rush, 1990, Chapter 6). Indeed, a hung Parliament might diminish the influence of select committees, with parties bargaining among themselves behind closed doors, and governments being fearful of the risk of backbench committees driving wedges between coalition partners.

It may prove significant, in terms of the government's sense of vulnerability, and hence its willingness to listen to the House (and its committees), that the government returned in 1992 had an overall majority of just 21, compared with its predecessor's 101; but, on the other hand, experience suggests that the effect of this will be slight. Conservative backbenchers may pay more heed to government whips (and the latter may apply discipline more firmly) when the majority is small. And the overall majority is of less practical importance than the government's majority over the largest opposition party; in this Parliament the Conservatives have 65 more MPs than Labour. The latter is the largest of a cluster of opposition parties who on many issues will not be united among (or even within) themselves.

Nevertheless, even a Thatcher government which had secured a majority of 144 at the general election of 1983 was defeated in April 1986 on the second reading of the Shops Bill (which sought to liberalise Sunday trading laws) when substantial numbers of Conservative backbenchers defied government whips. More dramatically, Major's government survived the Commons Maastricht vote in November 1992 only because the Liberal Democrats voted with the government. The rebellion in Conservative ranks was sufficient to defeat the government had opposition parties been united. On occasion, the notion that Parliament is structured by party politics needs to be treated with some caution.

Small majorities may make more regular difficulties for government in select and standing committees than on the floor of the House; but committees can, in the last analysis, enforce their will against government only by carrying a majority, almost inevitably on a whipped vote, on the floor. As we shall see, the heavy hand of the whips was very much in evidence when the select committees were re-established in 1992.

## Scrutiny of Government: Recent Trends

There is a tendency for parliamentary reform to happen slowly and incrementally, and to lag behind changes in the context in which Parliament operates. Any radical parliamentary reforms tend to be initiated by governments in order to expedite the transaction of their business. The increasingly routine use since the beginning of the century of government-dominated Commons standing committees for the detailed scrutiny of primary legislation (and in recent years, of secondary and draft EC legislation) is a case in point. Predictably, the development of new devices to make Parliament a more effective scrutineer of government generates much less enthusiasm from ministers, and so tends to happen much more slowly.

One major contextual change in recent years, to which Parliament has had to adapt, is the EC, discussed below. Meanwhile, over a much longer period, the scale of government activity, and the size and complexities of ministerial workloads, have grown – and long ago relegated those aspects of parliamentary procedure (such as parliamentary questions) that are based on the fiction that ministers control, or even know about, more than a small fraction of what happens in their departments, to the 'dignified' rather than the 'efficient' part of the constitution. The public sector cuts in the Thatcher-Major years have not materially affected the validity of this statement; indeed, the hiving off and contracting out of public functions, and the Next Steps programme have, as will be discussed later, created new problems of accountability.

That said, most of the traditional procedural mechanisms remain firmly in place. Question time is a case in point. In the 1990–91 session, 5811 questions received oral replies, and 32 290 received written replies in *Hansard*. The procedure does not amount to much in terms of holding ministers effectively to account, and it is open to abuse, but its residual significance will remain so long as everyone involved continues to behave as if they take it seriously. And ministerial and civil service culture does still accord it some seriousness – if only because of its potential hazards. A careless answer can still cause ministerial embarrassment and offer dangerous or expensive hostages to fortune.

Parliamentary procedure has been slow to modernise itself in response to developments in Whitehall. This is particularly true of financial scrutiny. Development of new budgeting machinery (such as PESC in the 1960s; cash limits in the 1970s; and the FMI in the 1980s) was slow to impact upon Parliament's traditional machinery for holding the executive to account. Changes such as the introduction of Estimates Days (at the beginning of the 1982–83 session) have amounted only to token concessions to those who have lamented the irretrievable demise of Parliament's 'power of the purse'. The record of the departmentally-related select committees in undertaking financial scrutiny has been decidedly patchy.

The main procedural innovation in the Commons in the last two decades has been refurbishment of the select committee system in 1979. These committees – whose consensual, inquisitorial *modus operandi* is in sharp contrast to the Commons' usual adversarial, party-dominated way of doing business – have established themselves as important instruments of parliamentary scrutiny (though there is no question of their having significantly altered 'the balance of power' between Parliament and the executive, still less of their having shifted the Westminster system towards a US congressional legislative model). They have become a focus for specialisation by MPs, a piece of intermittently useful weaponry against taciturn government, and a useful point of contact for outside groups trying to make themselves heard. Their profile has been raised by the televising of House of Commons proceedings; but their weaknesses have thereby been rendered more widely visible.

Their role, ten years after the 1979 upheaval, was the subject of an inquiry by the Select Committee on Procedure, whose report, *The Working of the Select Committee System*, was published in October 1990 (HC 19, 1989–90) – more or less coinciding with the departure of Thatcher, whose long-standing dislike of the committee system (consistent both with her suspicion of consensus politics and with her minimal involvement with Parliament, Dunleavy *et al.*, 1990) was an open secret. Some of the Committee's seventy conclusions and recommendations – a solid, low-key defence of the status quo – are mentioned in the next section. Perhaps its most interesting proposal, now to be implemented, is to allow the departmentally-related select committees, as well as the Public Accounts Committee (PAC), to have limited access to unpublished National Audit Office papers.

There were various changes in select committee structure in the period before the general election. In May 1991 the remit of the Home Affairs Committee was extended to the Lord Chancellor's and Law Officers' Departments, whence it had hitherto been excluded by dint of dubious claims about possible threats to judicial independence. The potential capacity for the House of Commons to scrutinise aspects of the administration of justice (increasingly operating, like other public services, in the financial ethos of the 'three Es' (economy, efficiency and effectiveness)) was further enhanced by the appointment, after the election, of a new junior minister in the Commons to answer for the Lord Chancellor's Department.

Meanwhile, at the beginning of 1991, the Select Committee on Health and Social Security had been divided into two separate committees, following the splitting of the DHSS. There was some dispute about the division of existing members between the two committees, with Conservative members of the old committee apparently much keener to be drafted to Health than to Social Services. The motions to set up the new committees, on 21 January, were opposed by Scottish opposition MPs, protesting against the continuing absence of a Scottish Affairs Committee. The Health Committee elected as its Chairman the Conservative, Nicholas Winterton, who had fallen out with his party's whips because of his somewhat unruly voting record and his sometimes less than deferential demeanour towards ministers; he was elected by his own vote and the votes of Labour members of the

Committee, against those cast by his Conservative colleagues. However, as we shall see, his party's whips soon got their revenge.

Later, the same committee – shadowing a policy field characterised by substantial political controversy – hit the headlines when its draft report on hospital trusts was leaked to the Department of Health in advance of the final version (considerably watered down by Conservative amendments) was published. A Conservative member, Jerry Hayes, later resigned from the Committee, claiming that his research assistant had been responsible. The matter was being investigated by the Committee of Privileges at the time of the dissolution.

Numerous instances, in the 1987–92 Parliament, could be cited of the continuing struggle by select committees, with mixed success, to compel reluctant ministerial and official witnesses to appear as witnesses and/or divulge information. Perhaps the most publicised instance involved the Agriculture Committee's pyrrhic victory in persuading Edwina Currie to give evidence in connection with its inquiry, at the beginning of 1989, into salmonella in eggs, following Currie's imprudent media comments on the subject, which led to her resignation as junior Health minister. She eventually gave way to strong parliamentary pressure, following several previous refusals, and agreed (but only 'as a personal courtesy' to the Chairman) to appear before the Committee; but the result was a stonewalling performance, which the *Times* described as a 'display of defiance' and referred to her 'barely-concealed contempt'. Her evidence added nothing of substance to the Committee's knowledge and understanding of the salmonella controversy, and its Report (First Report, 1988–89, HC 108) said, with some justice, of Currie's attitude that 'the House would rapidly fall into disrepute if it expected everyone else to be accountable in this way, but not its own members'.

Another instance of witness resistance highlighted an important (and arguably necessary) limitation on the investigative role of select committees. In July 1991 the Social Services Committee, prompted in the first instance by the *Barber* decision (affirming the principle of gender equality in pension rights) in the European Court of Justice, embarked upon an inquiry into various matters to do with pensions. The inquiry's focus on the ownership and control of pension funds took on greater significance when the scandal surrounding Robert Maxwell's financial activities hit the headlines. In this context, the Committee decided to extend the remit of the inquiry to cover events surrounding the operation of the Mirror Group Newspapers and the Maxwell Communications Corporation pension funds, and to request evidence from Ian and Kevin Maxwell. The latter eventually appeared before the Committee but declined, though counsel, to answer questions, on the grounds that criminal charges were probably imminent and they did not wish to risk incriminating themselves.

A special report on the conduct of the Maxwell brothers in relation to the inquiry (1991–92, HC 353) makes clear that the Committee itself – like outside commentators – had mixed feelings about the matter. On the one hand, there is clearly the risk of prejudice in conducting televised interrogations of people who might soon be cast as defendants in a criminal trial. On the other, this case was not *sub judice* at the time the Committee made its request, and the House had resolved as long ago as 1947 'that the refusal of a witness before a Select Committee to answer any question which may be put to him is a contempt of the House and an infraction of the undoubted right of this House to conduct any inquiry which may be necessary in the public interest'. (Commons Journal, 1946–47, p.378). It is undeniable that parliamentarians have a legitimate interest in the Maxwell case. But there must be an obvious risk that a select committee may damage its credibility and the impact of its work if it sails as close to the boundaries of the trial process as happened on this occasion – even if, technically, it stays just the right side of the line.

## The Select Committees Re-established

This controversial matter may resurface in the post-1992 Parliament (the newly re-established Social Security Committee began its work with resumption of the inquiry into the Maxwell scandal). Meanwhile there was the usual hiatus in re-establishing the departmentally-related committees after the election, only a marginal improvement on the delays that had occurred in 1983 and 1987. As one MP observed: 'it is wrong that this Parliament, which was elected on 9 April, met for the first time on 27 April and had its state opening on 5 May should be considering this motion [see below] on 30 June' (Patrick Cormack, HC Debs., 30 June 1992, col. 815). The only committee re-established reasonably promptly was the PAC, which is a special case because the government regards it as an adjunct to the Treasury's machinery for enforcing financial discipline in departments.

The Procedure Committee had recommended a maximum interval of 30 days before the committees were re-constituted, but this objective is prey to the realities of party politics. The overall composition of select committees is largely a matter of party-political arithmetic. Thus the severe shortage of Conservative MPs from Scotland explained the non-appearance of the Scottish Affairs Committee for the duration of the 1987–92 Parliament. The quota of opposition party members is (particularly as regards the smaller parties) a matter of hard bargaining. In 1992, the Labour Party's elections of its new leader and shadow cabinet were not completed until July – and frontbenchers, by parliamentary convention, are ineligible for committee membership.

Departmentally-related committees must by definition mirror the current configuration of government departments. This principle was strongly reaffirmed in the 1990 report of the Procedure Committee, which quoted with approval evidence from the Clerk of the House to the effect that this arrangement was necessary 'to sharpen up the relationship between Parliament and the Executive and to keep the Government on their toes' (HC 19, 1989–90, para. 282). The Committee therefore rejected proposals for thematic committees on science and technology and on 'green' issues.

However, the list of committees does now include a departmentally-related committee on science and technology, following a Commons debate on 30 June 1992 on motions to amend the standing order relating to select committees in the light of recent changes in the machinery of government. The Department of Energy was abolished after the election, but a National Heritage Department was created, and William

Waldegrave, Chancellor of the Duchy of Lancaster, was put in charge of science policy and the Citizen's Charter, in a new Office of Public Service and Science. It was decided in consequence that the Energy Committee would be abolished, while new National Heritage and Science and Technology committees were created. The Scottish Affairs Committee was revived, with eleven members instead of thirteen, after Labour had withdrawn its former opposition to the Conservative membership of the committee being augmented by two English members. The net effect of these changes is that there are now sixteen departmentally-related committees (when the new system was launched in 1979, there were fourteen).

Several members who spoke in the debate, including Michael Clark, former Chairman of the Energy Committee, called for the retention of that committee (88 MPs had already signed an Early Day Motion in support of this), or at least the creation of an energy sub-committee of the Environment Committee. James Molyneaux renewed previous calls from the Ulster Unionists for the creation of a Select Committee on Northern Ireland. The standing orders require the departmentally-related committees to cover 'similar matters within the responsibilities of the Secretary of State for Northern Ireland', though in practice they have not given much attention to this aspect of their remits. This amounts to a glaring and regrettable gap in the coverage provided by the select committee system, though it must be conceded that there would be major problems in constituting a new committee. The Leader of the House said later in the debate that any such move could not be contemplated outside the context of the current talks about the future of Northern Ireland.

Much sharper controversy attended the debate that took place on 13 July, on the motion of the Chairman of the Committee of Selection, Sir Marcus Fox, to constitute the membership of the departmentally-related committees (96 Conservatives, 70 Labour and 10 others), in the wake of numerous press reports of behind-the-scenes jostling over chairmanships. Some Conservative backbenchers had complained, for instance, that allowing Labour to chair Trade and Industry (whose remit includes coal privatisation) as well as Employment and the PAC, puts three of the four main economic committees – the exception being Treasury and Civil Service -into the hands of the Opposition; conversely, Labour backbenchers objected to the chair of Trade and Industry being gained at the expense of Transport (which will shadow rail privatisation).

One area of grievance aired in the debate concerned the under-representation of the minor parties, excluded altogether from membership of eight of the sixteen committees. But the issue which generated the most heat concerned the invention by the Conservative members of the Committee of Selection of a 'three-Parliament rule' to exclude long-serving Conservative committee members (including some chairmen) from re-appointment to committees.

One of the casualties of this so-called 'rule' was Sir Nicholas Winterton, the outspoken former chairman of the Health Committee (see above), and several of those who spoke in the debate expressed the plausible belief that it had been devised by the Committee of Selection, at the behest of the Conservative whips, expressly for his disbenefit. According to press reports, Labour had been offered the chair of the committee, but had turned it down, saying that if the Conservatives did not want Winterton they should take steps to exclude him altogether from membership. This is precisely what they did.

Another notable victim was Sir John Wheeler who, as he himself said in the debate, had 'fully expected' to serve again on the Home Affairs Committee, of which he had been chairman; indeed his name had appeared on the Order Paper, in the original list of nominees to the Committee, but he had been rung up at 12 o'clock on the day of the debate by Sir Marcus Fox, who told him that his inclusion had been a mistake. Terence Higgins, who would presumably have been another casualty but for the fact that he had already decided not to seek reappointment to the Treasury and Civil Service Committee, of which he had hitherto been chairman, echoed the views of many when he said that he was 'deeply concerned about the way in which the matter has been handled'. He denied that there was any such thing as a three-Parliament rule.

Frank Field pointed out that the introduction of such a rule 'will de-skill our select committees', a view echoed by several other speakers. The Select Committee on Procedure had recognised the desirability of avoiding staleness in the membership of committees, but thought that this consideration needed to be balanced against the need for continuity in expertise and the development of a collective memory. It concluded that:

> The normal rate of turnover in Committee membership is, in any case, sufficient to ensure a fairly regular influx of fresh ideas and personalities and we do not favour any rigid ceiling on length of service (HC 19, 1989–90, para. 306).

The most serious implication of this episode is its stark exposure of the limitations of the Committee of Selection as a buffer against the party whips. Few people can ever seriously have imagined that, in an executive-dominated parliamentary system, select committees would be left alone by the whips, or indeed that the Committee of Selection would provide more than minimal protection. Indeed, the persistent evidence of such attentions that has emerged over the years can be interpreted positively, as evidence that they are doing a good job as gadflies of government.

But select committees need to retain at least a semblance of independence if they are to have any credibility as scrutineers of the executive. Many observers will share Sir Nicholas Winterton's view that in this case the Committee of Selection was 'seriously compromised' by its actions. Seasoned observers of the House of Commons will not be at all surprised about attempts by the whips to manipulate the process of selection, but here the crude cynicism and transparency of the collusion between the Conservative party managers on the one hand, and Sir Marcus and his colleagues on the other, suggests the need for long hard re-think about the whole committee selection process. Perhaps the time has even come to contemplate the possibility of backbench elections for committee membership?

A further danger of which select committees need to be wary is exploitation by ministers in times of political crisis. Heseltine's reference of the pit closure programme to the Trade and Industry Committee in November 1992 smacked not of a concern to involve Parliament in a genuine re-think of British energy policy, but of a desire to get ministers out of a particularly pressing political crisis (which was, moreover, almost entirely of their own making). Harold Wilson used to use Royal Commissions for much the same purpose in the 1960s and 1970s. As it turned out, this Committee was well prepared to debate the coal closure programme, having a series of carefully-researched reports from the now-defunct Energy Committee to draw on. Nevertheless, this is not the kind of role which champions of Parliament as a check on the executive would necessarily like to see extended.

## Parliament, the Citizen's Charter and the Next Steps Agencies

The development of new forms of public administration, based *inter alia* on devolved management, on 'empowerment' of the citizen and on contracting out public services, has raised important issues to do with parliamentary scrutiny and public accountability. In particular, the Next Steps programme, launched in 1988, following a report by the Cabinet Office Efficiency Unit, acknowledges as an otiose constitutional fiction – long recognised as such by modern constitutional scholars – the notion that ministers can (or indeed should) answer personally to Parliament for all that happens in their departments. Although the doctrine of individual ministerial responsibility remains nominally intact, the programme has progressively transferred many of the operational or service-delivery functions of central government to semi-autonomous agencies, headed by chief executives, leaving ministers directly responsible in practice only for the policy functions located in core departmental headquarters. At the time of writing, more than half the civil service is employed in Next Steps agencies, of which there are more than seventy.

There is a logical difficulty – and the obvious danger of an 'accountability gap' arising – in trying to fit such increased managerial autonomy within the traditional doctrine of ministerial responsibility. The new arrangements pose interesting challenges to a Parliament whose procedures have been predicated upon that doctrine. It is an important truism of traditional public administration that in practice, 'administration' cannot always be disentangled from 'policy'. The problem of trying to separate responsibility for policy from responsibility for day-to-day management is illustrated by the history of the nationalised industries.

The Select Committee on Procedure noted in its 1990 report that:

> Whilst the last decade has witnessed a significant reduction in the number of associated public bodies in general and of nationalised industries in particular, their place as legitimate targets for scrutiny by Select Committee will be taken increasingly over the next few years by the various agencies designated as part of the Government's 'Next Steps' initiative . . . It is clear that, as their numbers and scope grow, scrutiny of executive agencies, and of their relationships with their parent Departments, ought to play an increasingly important part in the work of Select Committees (HC 19, 1989–90, paras 42, 44).

MPs have from the outset been encouraged to establish direct contact with agency chief executives on operational matters and, following some persistent lobbying by MPs, steps have been taken to publish such correspondence as a supplement to *Hansard*. The published framework documents, which set out the goals and budgetary targets of the agencies, offer potentially useful starting points for select committee inquiry. The progress of the Next Steps programme has been monitored on an annual basis by the Treasury and Civil Service Committee. The PAC has also investigated agencies, and early in the life of the Next Steps initiative it was decided that agency chief executives could appear before the PAC as agency accounting officers.

Part of the Major government's mission is the promotion of improved and more consumer-sensitive public services. The Citizen's Charter, launched in July 1991 and featured prominently in the Conservative manifesto, was to be, according to the Queen's Speech in May 1992, 'at the centre of decision-making'. The Treasury and Civil Service Committee's remit will cover both the Next Steps and the Charter, which come under the responsibility of Waldegrave's new Office of Public Service and Management – apart from the Office of Science and Technology which, as already noted, falls within the purview of the new Science and Technology Committee.

One assumes that, if the Charter's promise of more open government, re-affirmed by both Major and Waldegrave, comes to fruition (and some scepticism is in order, given how often we have heard this sort of thing before), then Parliament and its committees should be major beneficiaries. But increased openness, though welcome for all kinds of reasons, is not by itself going to make any significant impact on the impotence of a subordinate, essentially reactive Parliament, in an executive-dominated system.

## The House of Lords

So far discussion has concentrated almost exclusively on the House of Commons. It should be remembered however that, in the 1980s, with the Thatcher government facing little effective resistance in the Commons where it had very large majorities, the House of Lords played a very significant role in checking the government; Shell records that, between 1979 and 1990 the government was defeated 155 times in the Lords, 148 of these defeats being on legislation (Shell, 1992, p.157). The House also has a well-developed and generally well-regarded committee system, complementing the coverage of Commons select committees, centring on the respected European Communities Committee which works through six specialised subject-related (rather than departmentally-related) sub-committees. Following a Lords debate on 3 June 1992, the House is moving towards some important reforms in its present committee arrangements – including the use of special standing committees to take evidence on Bills (a variant upon an interesting experiment tentatively tried, and now apparently abandoned by the government, in the Commons in the early 1980s).

There is of course a long-running debate about the legitimacy of a non-elected second chamber and the extent to which it should obstruct the will of the elected House (even one dominated by governments whose mandate is founded on only 40 per cent or so of electoral support). Exceptionally, the Parliament Acts were invoked in 1991 to secure the passage of the government's War Crimes Bill, denied a second reading outright (almost equally exceptionally) by the Lords, after it had passed through the Commons, in the preceding session. The constitutional reform sections of both the Labour and Liberal Democrat manifestos in 1992 featured proposals concerning the future of the House of Lords, though these proposals were of course rendered redundant by the outcome of the election. It remains to be seen if the House of Lords continues to be a major battleground in Major's 1990s; one factor that may make it so is the elevation of Thatcher to its membership, as a life peer, along with several of her closest former ministers (including Cecil Parkinson and Norman Tebbit) in the June 1992 dissolution honours list.

## Parliament and the EC

As already noted, most parliamentary procedure is founded on the mythology of ministerial responsibility. In most contexts it is assumed that (as is the case, for example, with government Bills) ministers bring to Parliament the proposals that they and their departments have formulated, and then defend them in debate. This assumption certainly applies to the Bills and statutory instruments giving effect to EC directives, though of course by the time a directive has been approved by the Council of Ministers, the UK minister and department involved are bound by the terms of the directive, and are therefore more in the position of interpreters than authors of the legislation.

This issue is compounded when Parliament is called upon to debate European draft directives, where the Commission and not the minister has paternity of the proposal. Much discussion has been going on since Britain first joined the Community about how Parliament can best handle EC business in circumstances where the familiar rules of ministerial responsibility do not apply. Moreover, even where ministers are left in no doubt about the balance of parliamentary opinion, the extent to which their submissions to the Council of Ministers reflect Parliament's views cannot be verified, because the deliberations of the Council take place *in camera*, and the proceedings are not published.

The Westminster Parliament's role as a scrutineer has further been diminished by the terms of the Single European Act (SEA), ratified in 1986, which greatly extended the range of issues decided by majority voting in the Council of Ministers. When the Council proceeds by way of unanimity, Parliament can (at least in theory) instruct a minister to use a veto, or threaten the use of such a veto to win concessions. In circumstances where ministers can be outvoted, this no longer applies.

The details of parliamentary procedure in relation to European legislation are described elsewhere (e.g., Bates, 1991), and need not be detailed here. The Westminster Parliament is accorded more prominence in the scrutiny of EC legislation than are the legislatures of most other EC countries (Denmark being one exception). Apart from the two new standing committees, whose origins are noted below, the House of Commons has, since 1974, had a Select Committee on European Legislation, whose task is to sift Community proposals, and identify ones which are of sufficient importance to call for debate in the House or the appropriate standing committee; until this debate has taken place, scrutiny procedures are not considered complete. There is a device called 'scrutiny reserve', whereby:

> the Government has undertaken not to give agreement in the Council of Ministers to the adoption of any document until the [parliamentary] scrutiny procedures are complete unless the Committee has indicated that agreement need not be withheld or the Minister decides that there are special reasons why agreement should not be withheld (Select Committee on Procedure, HC 622, 1988–89, vol. 2, p. 14, para. 19).

A good deal of the time and energy of officials concerned with Community policy is expended upon the requirements imposed by parliamentary scrutiny – e.g., the drafting of explanatory memoranda (EMs) to EC documents, explaining their policy significance for the UK, for the benefit of parliamentary committees, and briefing ministers for appearances before the Commons standing committees – and before the Lords Select Committee on the EC, a committee which, despite the perceived marginality of the Lords, seems to be widely respected both in Whitehall and in Brussels for the quality of its reports.

Apart from the important but limited function of the Joint Committee on Statutory Instruments in undertaking technical scrutiny (e.g., looking at *vires*, quality of drafting, whether an instrument imposes a charge or has retrospective effect), statutory instruments (the means by which most directives are given legal effect) are seldom effectively scrutinised by Parliament, and hardly ever rejected or obstructed. When primary legislation is required for implementation, government can normally mobilise its majority to ensure that such legislation is enacted quickly: this is in contrast to the more extended legislative processes of other EC countries, such as Italy and Belgium.

In November 1989 the Commons Select Committee on Procedure published a substantial report, *The Scrutiny of European Legislation* (HC 622, 1988–89, 2 vols). This identified 'a number of genuine problems facing the House in seeking to exercise scrutiny over European legislation', and proposed, *inter alia*, 'the creation of five subject-oriented Special Standing Committees, appointed for a session with the power to take evidence from Ministers prior to debating a [EC] document on a substantive Motion'. It rejected the proposition 'that the House should place a formal requirement on Select Committees to give a higher priority to the examination of European legislation'; but the Committee made plain its view that the House should 'send a clear signal to Select Committees that it wishes them to make a greater contribution to the scrutiny process'. It also called for the encouragement of closer links between MPs and MEPs in this context.

The Government's broadly sympathetic response, published in May 1990 (Cm 1081), recommended that initially just three Special Standing Committees should be established. The Procedure Committees's Report, along with a Special Report by the Committee on European Legislation (HC 512), was debated in the Commons on an adjournment motion on 28 June 1990. The three standing committees were later reduced to two, because of the difficulty in manning even three of them.

The tendency for pressure groups – certainly the better resourced and more influential ones – to by-pass Parliament is particularly marked in a European context. This is substantially for the reason already cited; that backbench MPs have little enough to offer by way of influence in a domestic context; they have even less in the context of EC proposals, for which UK ministers are not responsible. The unconstructive hostility of the House of Commons towards the Community and its institutions in the early years of UK membership no doubt contributed to a feeling that lobbying there was a waste of time. The considerable literature on the part played by interest groups in the EC (e.g., Butt Philip, 1985, 1992; Grant, 1989; Mazey and Richardson, 1992) makes clear the extent to which groups have targeted their efforts directly at Brussels (and to a growing extent, since the SEA, at the European Parliament); about the use of Westminster as a channel of influence there is for the most part an eloquent silence. However, Nicholas Baldwin, a contributor to a recent study of pressure groups and Parliament (Rush, 1990, p. 166) notes the recognition by some groups of the usefulness of the House of Lords Select Committee on the European Communities as a respected forum for influence in the Community.

A study by Stephen George concludes that Parliament has adapted to the EC more slowly than the civil service or the courts – a reflection of the difference between the roles of 'overviewer of the system' and of direct involvement in the day-to-day business of the EC. He suggests, however, that Parliament may now be 'catching up' in this respect, a trend that may, he thinks, be attributable to 'the weakening of the gatekeeper role of the Government' (George, 1992, pp.101–2).

## Parliament in the 1990s

In the absence of constitutional change, procedural reform of Parliament is unlikely to have any significant impact on the balance of functions between Parliament and the executive, or upon the capacity of the former to move from a reactive to a proactive role in decision-making. The 1980s saw the newly established, departmentally-related select committees carving out a useful role as scrutineers of government. The post-1992 committees, despite the cynical antics of the Conservative party managers in manipulating membership nominations, will probably consolidate this position: the cautiously supportive tone of the 1990 Procedure Committee Report does not suggest that, for the time being, significant change to the committee system is on the agenda.

One likely area of procedural change concerns the arrangements of House of Commons business, following the report of a Select Committee on Sittings of the House, chaired by Michael Jopling, published in February 1992 (HC 20, 1991–92). This proposes, *inter alia*, alterations to the working hours of the House, with longer notice of sitting times, earlier finishes and some morning sittings, and some Fridays designated as non-sitting days. Part of the thinking behind this is connected with long-standing recognition of the disruptive impact of the traditional parliamentary schedule on MPs' family lives, a consideration that may have deterred some people (particularly women) from seeking election. This change, if it comes about, may be accompanied by the fixed timetabling of government Bills – a change supported by party managers but opposed by some opposition party backbenchers. Time-tabling, if it happens (and it was considered and rejected by the House of Commons a few years ago), would probably help outside interest groups to organise themselves for parliamentary lobbying.

One prospective change in the financial timetable should also be noted. It was announced in the March 1992 Budget, and elaborated in a white paper (*Budgetary Reform*, Cm. 1867, 1992), that the Chancellor's autumn Financial Statement and the March Budget Statement are, from 1993, to be combined in a single Budget statement to be delivered each December, with the Finance Bill published soon after the Christmas recess. The government argued that this will result in an end to the unsatisfactory practice whereby spending plans are not presented alongside the tax proposals needed to pay for them; and that in future, taxpayers and employers will have longer notice of tax changes. Whether, as it also claims, this will result in improved opportunity for consultation and public debate is more debatable, given that there is little sign of any intention to relax the secrecy of budgetary preparation. The Finance Bill will, as now, be unveiled soon after the Budget, without its authors having engaged in much outside consultation – and then subjected to a tight parliamentary schedule.

But, given the essentially reactive character of Parliament, the only prospects of significant change lies in its having to adapt to external contingencies – perhaps to constitutional changes like electoral reform, or renewed pressure to reform the House of Lords, or the incorporation into domestic law of the European Convention on Human Rights; or to continuing developments in the institutional arrangements and the policy agendas of the EC; or to changes in the scope and processes of UK government (we have touched already on some of the implications for Parliament of the Next Steps programme and the Citizen's Charter). We should perhaps be looking also for behavioural changes as parliamentarians adjust to what looks, in the aftermath of the 1992, like the prospect of continuing one-party domination.

Meanwhile, those – and they include some parliamentarians – who talk loftily about the 'democratic deficit' as a defect of decision-making in the EC might appropriately turn their attention to some uncomfortably analogous shortcomings of parliamentary government in the UK.

# 8

# Government at the Centre

**KEITH DOWDING**

At the surface of political life the change from the dominant, decisive and strident Mrs Thatcher to the hesitant, indecisive and 'nice' Mr Major could hardly be more dramatic. But we should be careful with our comparisons. It is a standard error amongst sports writers to compare the first performance of newly-appointed captains with the final performance of those they have replaced. If we compare Major's first 18 months in office with the first 18 months of Thatcher's administration it is not Major who looks indecisive nor Thatcher who looks assured. But certainly there is a difference in their style, their relationship with their cabinet and senior civil servants, and the conduct of cabinet government.

During Thatcher's premiership the claim that the Prime Minister was becoming more presidential and less of a chair of the Cabinet – a debate started thirty years ago (Crossman, 1964) – grew in strength and stature. Thatcher dominated her later cabinets by her forceful presence and personality. She would open discussions by stating her views and then daring her colleagues to contradict her. She used cabinet committees and informal meetings to great effect, and when she turned her attention to any policy areas her influence was plain to see. But this was no more so than had been the case during Harold Wilson's premiership. He used the cabinet committee system to isolate colleagues, to manipulate debate as he desired, and if he had less influence overall on policy then that is due more to the fact that he had stronger colleagues and less interest in radically transforming the nation. Thatcher's apparent wish to by-pass her Cabinet when she could, and her privately stated desire to be President as it would make her job easier (Young, 1989, p.324) gave ammunition to proponents of the 'increasing presidentialism' argument. Thatcher behaved presidentially in the sense that she liked to do business on an individual basis when she could. She did this by the perfectly acceptable constitutional method of ministerial correspondence, and by the more unusual procedure of asking ministers to produce papers just for her (and her Cabinet Office, Policy Unit, the Downing Street Private Office and perhaps a Treasury official) purview. She halved the number of full Cabinet meetings to one a week, and developed a more informal additional structure of ad hoc groups. Another method of compartmentalising decision-making would have been to use the cabinet committee structure (best described in Hennessy, 1986), but Thatcher decided from the beginning to use fewer cabinet committees. She was forced by events to use them more than she desired. Even so cabinet committees were created at only half their previous rate, and cabinet papers were produced at only about one-sixth of their previous annual post-war rate (Hennessy, 1991).

It should be recognised that change in the nature of central governance occurred gradually as Thatcher gained in stature through length of tenure and was able to create a malleable Cabinet. It is also necessary to recognize that she did not always get her way in Cabinet, and certainly the system of British government slowed the programme of her radicalism even if it did not make it more conservative in the long-run. By doing so it probably made her radical programme more successful. Her instinct for immediate radical reform would have frightened more people, created greater dislocation and made her more vulnerable. By slowing the pace of reform and creating change more piecemeal, her colleagues stabilised her and her programmes.

Major has stated that he wishes to promote consensus in his Cabinet, to allow full and frank discussion of issues. He is much readier to listen to the advice of colleagues and advisers, which is an important advance. Chris Patten described the Conservatives' 1992 manifesto as 'packed full of ideas' – which it may have been – but the major policy problem under Thatcher was that, once generated, ideas were not sufficiently thought through. The 'Next Steps' reforms of the civil service are exceptional, having been thought about continually by the civil servants whom they were most going to affect (see Chapter 7). That is why they may well be among the most enduring of the reforms of British society undertaken during the Thatcher years.

Major had a striking rise through the ranks and was relatively inexperienced when he became Prime Minister. He was Foreign Secretary for only three months, appointed as a pliant plant whose most important task was to hold Thatcher's handbag at the Kuala Lumpur meeting of Commonwealth leaders. Four days later, on 27 October 1989, he became Chancellor following the resignation of Nigel Lawson. One of the reasons Major succeeded in the battle for the leadership of the Conservative Party is that he was perceived as Thatcherite by many on her wing of the party, though this was soon proven mistaken. He was her favoured successor from the candidates on offer, though his role as her 'yes man' could hardly be expected to continue once he got the top job himself. How far he moulds society and the structure of government to any predetermined plan will not emerge for many years yet, but so far he has bolstered cabinet government in the conventional constitutional mould.

## The Citizen's Charter

The Citizen's Charter was Major's big idea for the 1992 General Election. It was launched in the summer of 1991 when Major announced that he wanted it to become one of the central themes of public life in the 1990s:

> The Charter programme will be at the heart of government policy in the 1990s. Quality of service to the public, and the new pride that it will give to the public servants who provide it will be a central theme (Citizen's Charter, 1991).

The White Paper produced a programme of centrally-directed action. The charter is designed to institute expectations for citizens with regard to the services the state provides.

Individual charters include fairly detailed expectations about service delivery, though the main emphasis is on increasing the quality of public services. Charters now exist for NHS patients, parents of state school children, tenants of public housing authorities, and recipients of state financial benefits, as well as for customers' of public monopolies such as the London Underground and British Rail. All government departments (with the exception of the secret services) have been instructed to produce charters. William Waldegrave, Chancellor of the Duchy of Lancaster, has been given the task of 'harrying his cabinet colleagues' to ensure that each department takes the initiative seriously. The charters produced do not, generally speaking, increase individuals' legal rights though they do state what existing legal rights are, and include specifications of what consumers have a right to expect in terms of service delivery. Many of the proposals contained in the Citizen's Charter are merely a re-packaging of a range of existing initiatives, but they do include some new measures and try to generate a new consumer-oriented feel to publicly provided service delivery.

The Citizen's Charter is permeating government and beyond, allowing the centre to input policy pressures throughout government. Whilst the charter and, more generally, the new public management create opportunities for managers at all levels to demonstrate greater initiative, their central direction also allows for a hands-on approach by central government. To a much greater extent than before the offices of Prime Minister and Cabinet Office are demonstrating that they are the apex of the hierarchy, bullying other departments to provide services in a more flexible and consumer-oriented manner.

## The Core Executive

The core executive is defined functionally to include all of the elements which 'primarily serve to pull together and integrate central government policies, or act as final arbiters within the executive of conflicts between different elements of the government machine' (Dunleavy and Rhodes, 1990, p.4).

This executive has long tentacles which extend beyond what is often thought of as central government in Whitehall, though once we go outside Whitehall (and Edinburgh) we are leaving the core executive. We can see in Figure 8.1 that the prime minister is at the centre of an interlocking web of power.

As chair of the Cabinet the Prime Minister is a part of that Cabinet, and, additionally, is influential not only in largely deciding the agenda but also, with the Cabinet Secretary, in writing the minutes. Officially the Cabinet Secretary writes the minutes from his notebook and that of at least one other member of the Cabinet Office. Seldon (1990, p.113) reports of the period 1979–87 that 'His final record was never cleared with the PM or with the individual ministers concerned, contrary to the view of some'. However, given the nature of cabinet discussion under Thatcher she never needed to intervene. The Westland affair demonstrated that, with regard to minutes of a cabinet committee, Michael Heseltine felt that the record reflected the Prime Minister's intentions and not the actual discussion. Crossman, too, was in no doubt that Wilson's influence was at work in cabinet minutes, though this may have been due to his unique summing up rather than actually influencing the minute-writing itself. Steiner and Dorff (1980) have dubbed this form of decision-making 'decision by interpretation'.

Within the cabinet in Figure 8.1 is marked the 'Inner Cabinet'. At times this is a semi-official body which meets to conduct business with regard to a particular aspect of policy. More often, however, an unofficial 'Inner Cabinet' is identified by political observers when certain cabinet ministers are thought to be consulted and advise the Prime Minister in areas beyond their departmental briefs. The war cabinets set up during the Falklands and Gulf conflicts should not be confused with these despite sometimes being called inner cabinets – they were official cabinet committees.

Cabinet committees have been represented in Figure 8.1 by two different sorts of cabinet committee – those chaired by the Prime Minister and those not. Even in the latter, though, officials from the Cabinet Office will be present. Cabinet committees may be formed for any number of reasons. Some are standing committees which last for the length of a Prime

180

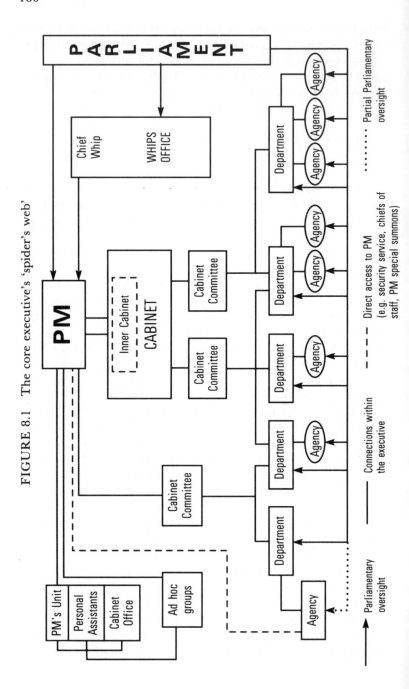

FIGURE 8.1  The core executive's 'spider's web'

Minister's tenure, whilst others may be formed to deal with specific problems or crises and meet only once or twice. Some are ministerial in that civil servants take minutes but do not participate; others include both ministers and civil servants. Figure 8.2 lists the cabinet committees identified by the Cabinet Office in May 1992, together with their respective chairs.

Shadowing cabinet committees are official committees consisting of civil servants alone. This complex web of meetings involving networks of ministers and civil servants is coordinated by the Cabinet Office. Only the Cabinet Office can really get a grasp on the whole edifice of government business. The Cabinet Office itself is divided into six secretariats: Economic, Overseas and Defence, European, Home Affairs, Science and Technology and Security and Intelligence. With the exception of the last, all are headed by civil servants at deputy- or under-secretary level on secondment from other departments.

Thatcher did not alter the structure of prime ministerial power to any great extent. Whilst she tinkered with various aspects by abolishing the Central Policy Review Staff (CPRS) in 1983 and strengthening the Policy Unit which served to enhance prime ministerial control (see below), too much can be made of these structural changes. Too many commentators have confused her radicalism with power – she changed much because that is what she wanted to do whereas previous prime ministers achieved less because they attempted less. The true source of her strength came from the length of her tenure and she left the office of Premier with much the same power resources as she found it. She may have created some conventions for future prime ministers to follow. Major has not yet reverted to twice-weekly Cabinet meetings, and it remains to be seen whether formal cabinet committees will return to their former rate of expansion or whether the informal meetings will continue unabated. If she has changed conventions in this 'ratchet' sense – that is, her successor largely follows what she did for that is all he knows – then she will have made it easier for prime ministers to manipulate their Cabinet colleagues. Most observers believe that the Cabinet is genuinely more collegial under Major, both because of his

FIGURE 8.2   Ministerial committees of the Cabinet, 1992

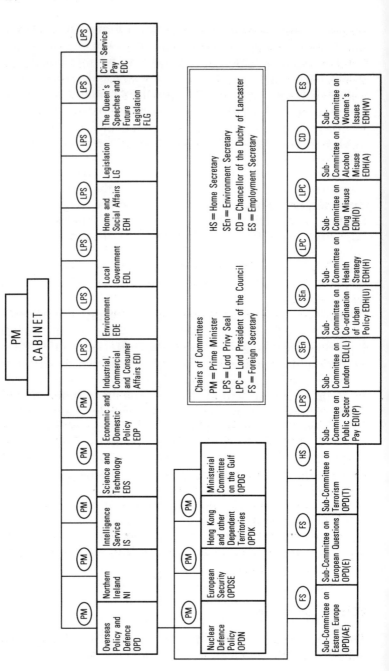

personality and because of the fact that his colleagues will not allow him to dominate in the Thatcher mode. Major's first Cabinet reshuffle after his election victory in April 1992 brought many new people into government – especially into the junior posts – and signalled that he felt that talented but forceful people who had been sidelined by Thatcher should be given a chance to demonstrate their talents. This signals a willingness to consider a broader set of attitudes and probably a new openness.

## Open Government

William Waldegrave has been given the job of encouraging greater openness in government. His first move was formally to identify the membership and chair of standing cabinet committees. Informed observers, of course, already had that information, so it is not a gigantic step towards open government. Also titbits of information such as the heads of the security services have been released and regulations governing the release of government papers under the thirty and hundred year rules are being re-examined. Even if Major and Waldegrave are serious in their desire for more open government, the higher civil service will fight tooth and nail in the knowledge that 'the bureaucracy's supreme power instrument is the transformation of official information into classified information by means of the notorious concept of the "official secret". In the last analysis, this is merely a means of protecting the administration against supervision' (Weber, 1978, p.1418). So whilst we may see many managerial aspects of civil service administration opened up by politicians in their desire for better management, only the naive can hope for the political aspects of administration to become more open. Only a Prime Minister planning retirement in a couple of years' time would desire that kind of openness.

## Private Advisers

The presidential side of Thatcher's tenure is arguably also indicated by the role of the Cabinet Office and that of her private advisers. There has been much talk of the Cabinet Office one day becoming a prime minister's department but there is little sign of that yet. Thatcher's private advisers were more controversial and in the public eye. This private advice, and its effect on cabinet government came to a head with the Lawson resignation, which was also the nadir of the relationship between the Treasury and the Cabinet Office.

Nigel Lawson's resignation raised questions both about the nature of cabinet government under Thatcher and about the role of private policy advisers. Lawson wanted an exchange rate policy which was part and parcel of the financial discipline of the government. To this end the pound shadowed the Deutschmark from early 1986 and Lawson favoured entry into the European Exchange Rate Mechanism (ERM). Thatcher, advised by her own economic guru Sir Alan Walters, preferred the market mechanism for the exchange rate as she favoured it for everything else. The problem for British government was not so much this dispute but the manner in which it was carried out. For the Chancellor and prime minister to give different public signals on this key issue of economic policy and for her views to be made plain by her own economic advisers against the virtual unknowns of the Treasury was quite extraordinary and made Lawson's position untenable. Moreover it seems obvious from various statements that this issue was never discussed in Cabinet – quite a remarkable situation given the supposed constitutional role of the Cabinet in the British system.

This debacle, which was just one of many in the latter years of Thatcher's premiership, seems unimaginable under John Major. Right from the start he stated that he believed in open discussion and collegial decision-making. Indeed his Cabinet Office has privately complained about his tendency to let Cabinet meetings over-run with consequent strains upon the rest of his day's programme. That is not to say that disagreements with colleagues do not leak into the open, nor that he does not get his own way. The Chancellor, Norman Lamont, reportedly favoured increasing personal allowances beyond the rate of inflation in the 1992 pre-election budget, but Major insisted upon the creation of a 20 per cent tax band as an election gimmick.

The Policy Unit contained within Number 10 has become very important at the heart of the core executive. Since Thatcher decided to abolish the CPRS in 1983 the Policy Unit has taken on a more structured and institutionalised role. The Policy Unit is there to help the Prime Minister exclusively whereas the CPRS was supposed to provide advice more widely throughout the government machine. The Policy Unit liaises closely with the Prime Minister's Private Office which passes on all domestic papers up to but not including the highest security classifications. The Unit sees itself having seven functions. First, it is a small, creative think-tank. Second, it advises the Prime Minister on all domestic policy emanating from departments. Third, it reports on the progress of central policies. Fourth, it raises issues which get ignored by the usual inter-departmental machinery. Fifth, it tries to focus the Prime Minister on crucial issues and liaise between departments and the Prime Minister to avoid conflict. Sixth it provides a non-Whitehall focus on issues. Finally, it operates as a source of new and grander ideas than those likely to come from traditional civil service sources (Willetts, 1987).

## Departmental Power

The higher civil service is often described as a 'village community' and the small number of permanent secretaries (around forty) ensures that all are well-known to each other. The Cabinet Office is the fulcrum around which other departments operate. There are a number of ways in which those departments could be ranked in terms of importance: their expenditure, their profile in the press, the numbers of new laws produced from the department annually or the numbers of jobs (both civil service and non-civil service such as armed forces or state teachers) under their expenditure headings. Some departments such as the Home Office affect everyone in the nation, others such as Health virtually everyone, whilst yet others such as Education affect only those in, or with children in, state education. The Treasury remains pre-eminent as the paymaster, and is involved in all policy-making to some extent, as is evidenced by its omnipresence on cabinet committees.

Looking purely at the number of civil servants in each department does not give a very good idea of their importance. Defence employs just over 25 per cent of the total number of civil servants, whilst the next largest department by this measure is the Department of Social Security at 14 per cent. Yet neither department has as much influence on policy as the Foreign Office (see the section on the EC below) which employs only 1.8 per cent of the total number of civil servants. The three great offices of State after the Prime Minister, the Foreign Secretary, Chancellor of the Exchequer and Home Secretary accurately reflect the influence accorded overall in the government machine. Large spending ministries such as Defence and Health do affect many people's lives but are not so important in overall policy terms.

**Policy Networks**

The organisation of the civil service into discrete departments headed by a minister gives them a certain amount of autonomy. The average length of tenure of ministers in the post-war period is about two years, even less if the four great offices of state are taken out of the calculation. Common wisdom amongst civil servants is that it takes a new minister eighteen months to find his or her feet in a new department – though that does not necessarily stop ministers from pursuing their own unique policies. However, this has usually been seen to give a bargaining advantage to civil servants and allow them to impose the departmental line upon their ministers (Kellner and Crowther-Hunt, 1980). Departments do develop reputations for pursuing certain policy lines as opposed to others. The Department of Transport is known for its single-minded pursuit of road as opposed to rail transport, the Foreign Office for its love of Europe, the Home Office for its 'liberal' culture. It is not surprising that civil servants soon take on the culture and stance of the department in which they work. It is much less costly for a civil servant to take on a policy stance already worked out than to spend time creating a new viewpoint for the ministry as a whole (Dowding, 1991, Chapter 7). Departments also create policy within a network of contacts, lobbyists, advisers and officials from other departments. Some departments have very close links with interest group organisations to whom they turn for advice and information, forming close-knit policy communities. Other policy areas are more open to the influence of a wider range of groups, though organisations which pursue policies too far away from the departmental line will have no influence and are apt to be no more than a minor irritant.

The static picture of departments pursuing policies in keeping with their traditions, consulting closely with allies within their policy network and ignoring other outside groups does not mean to say that departmental policy never changes. The close-knit community enjoyed by the Department of the Environment and local authorities was broken up, much to the chagrin of many civil servants, by fifteen years of Treasury and central pressure to reduce local authority spending and ever more frenzied legislation to reduce local authority powers. Similarly the DTI interventionist instincts were contained by twelve years of Thatcherite non-interventionist ideology, though it is notable how long it took her first Secretary of State, Sir Keith Joseph, to change the policies of the Department. Even the cosy relationship between the Ministry of Agriculture and the National Farmers' Union is beginning to be broken up. Here the policy community is breaking down into a wider issue network involving the powerful supermarket food lobby and the health lobby operating via the Department of Health. Edwina Currie was an early casualty of the attempts of these new lobbies to break into the agriculture policy community (Smith, 1991). Indeed the Agriculture minister John Gummer was grilled during the summer of 1992 under the auspices of the Citizen's Charter for his department's lack of concern for the consumer. Thus policy networks must not be seen as static and unchanging.

## The Next Steps Reforms

The 1988 Efficiency Unit report 'Improving Management in Government: The Next Steps' heralded a radical reform of the civil service. The revolutionary idea is to create agencies designed to deliver services entirely separated from policy-making core departments. The purpose is to produce a more flexible delivery structure in which local and individual initiative can create a better service for the recipients of state activity. By the end of 1992, over 50 per cent of civil servants worked in agencies, though the degree to which departments had created agencies differed substantially. The Department of Social Security had 97 per cent of its staff in agencies, whilst departments like the Home Office, Foreign Office and the three territorial offices (Scotland, Wales and Northern Ireland) had only small numbers of staff in agencies.

Individual agencies are run by Chief Executives who sign 'framework agreements', which specify the service and delivery targets the agencies must meet. This agreement gives conditions for reporting and accountability between the Chief Executive, the 'parent' department and the Treasury. Each agreement establishes a corporate plan covering current and future objectives as well as policy. Each also establishes the financial arrangements of the agency including how costs are to be controlled and delegated and accounting and auditing procedures managed. Even personnel requirements and basic conditions of employment are included in the framework agreements, as well as review procedures for the agency as a whole. Once the policy objectives and budgetary arrangements are established the Chief Executive (who generally is also the Agency Accounting Officer) has overall responsibility for the everyday executive functions of the agency. He or she is then accountable for meeting the conditions of the framework agreement and can be removed from post if the agency fails to do so.

The policy-making and policy-implementation functions of the civil service have thus been almost completely separated – almost but not entirely, since Chief Executives should have an input into policy-making in the restricted sense that they can point out that certain policies are not implementable under certain contractual conditions. Framework agreements are reviewed and re-formed every three years at present, but individual targets may be altered or added with the introduction of new government policies within the time period of the original framework agreement. Furthermore policy-makers should be aware of the nature of the agencies and so should never create policy which the agencies are unable to execute. However, it should be noted that the sentences above are all normative – what Chief Executives and policy-makers should do, not necessarily what they do do. There is a need for structures to allow Chief Executives to point out, without detriment to their own careers, that certain policies are not implementable. How far those structures are in place is not yet clear.

The ideology behind these changes is clear. The Next Steps approach, whilst not strictly market-oriented, is designed to mirror for Chief Executives the sorts of incentives which exist in private companies (Dowding, 1993). It is intended to create a service-based culture within agencies delivering goods to consumers as cheaply and efficiently as possible. However, whilst this ideology is undoubtedly Thatcherite, giving greater initiative to individual managers within the civil service was one of the proposals of the Fulton Committee (1968). Fulton recommended that managers should have a clear set of objectives and be given full responsibility for the most efficient use of resources entrusted to them. Fulton recognised that this would give greater autonomy to lower management; the agency concept takes this a stage further by separating policy-making and policy-implementation tasks. Indeed one reason why Next Steps has been well so received by many senior civil servants is that as juniors in the late 1960s and early 1970s they were horrified that the then senior civil service acted to destroy the aims of the Fulton Committee.

## Next Steps and Ministerial Responsibility

Creation of a two-tier civil service allows a clearer demarcation between those elements of the civil service which come within the core executive and those which are outside it. This is represented in Figure 8.1 by agencies lying outside the dotted line. Some have worried that the break-up of the civil service in this way has blurred the concept of ministerial responsibility (Chapman, 1988; Fry *et al.*, 1988; Drewry and Butcher, 1991). Chief Executives are directly responsible for service delivery.

They are accountable to Parliament in the sense that they can be called by select committees to answer questions within their arena of competence. MPs might find it preferable to deal directly with Chief Executives over constituents' problems rather than going through the minister with overall departmental responsibility. In this way ministerial responsibility is blurred, for ministers would seem to have the option of referring certain problems directly to Chief Executives rather than answering for them in Parliament. However, the only real disadvantage of such direct contact between a senior civil servant and an MP missing out the minister as middleman is that the answer will not appear in *Hansard*. As Chief Executives' answers are now to appear in official publications filed in the House of Commons library, an important loss of ministerial accountability has been avoided.

Generally worries over loss of ministerial responsibility are probably overplayed by academics (but see Chapter 7). The whole point of the agency process is to try to make clearer who is responsible for policy failure – the agency implementing the policy or the government/minister who created it. In fact the line of accountability between agencies and Parliament varies according to the framework agreements. There are some advantages for Parliament to be able to deal directly with Chief Executives. It is in the interests of Chief Executives to aid MPs where possible, within the constraints of the Osmotherly rules (drawn up by Edward Osmotherly in 1980 to combat the new select committees). These state that any civil servant appearing before a committee remains 'subject to Ministerial instructions as to how he should answer questions'. This problem for accountability is caused by the Osmotherly rules and not by the Next Steps changes.

Throughout the creation of the new agencies the first Project Manager Peter Kemp denied that there was a hidden agenda eventually to privatise large chunks of the civil service. However, Kemp was sacked by William Waldegrave on 8 July 1992 and since then privatisation has explicitly been on the agenda. Officially, Kemp retired early because, in his own words, he had worked himself out of a job by ensuring the smooth progress of the Next Steps reforms. Insiders suggest that Waldegrave wanted to move to the more radical privatisation agenda with which Kemp was uncomfortable. This more radical agenda seems to include the aim to put out to tender 25 per cent of all government activity both within central departments and new agencies within the lifetime of the current Parliament. Effectively civil servants will be competing for the jobs they currently undertake. Only the 'core functions' of offering advice on policy formation to ministers will be completely protected from competitive tendering, which would mean that eventually only 2 per cent of civil servants will retain their current status. This process comprises the most radical shake-up of central government this century.

## The EC

The EC provides both an opportunity and a threat to the civil service. On the one hand it provides an opportunity for individual civil servants and departments to utilise the authority and power of the EC to extend their sphere of influence. The opportunity for senior civil servants is that dealings with Brussels are complex and time-consuming, and broaden the policy network in which they operate. Ministers find it difficult to oversee this complexity, but civil servants do consult continually with their political masters as soon as any negotiations start to impinge upon the guidelines under which they are operating. When negotiations are taking place in Brussels there is constant consultation with Whitehall. The threat to individual civil servants is that the Commission presents another source of bureaucratic authority which may threaten their own authority, though this threat is not yet serious.

The EC can become an ally of a department if the aims of that department fit with the aims of the Commission. The first department to gain in this way was the Foreign Office. When Britain entered the EC the Foreign Office became the leading actor in dealings with the other member nations and the Commission. This was one of the major sources of conflict within government once Thatcher had taken a more sceptical stance towards Europe than her predecessor, especially since the EC moved swiftly into a developmental phase in the 1980s (see Chapter 3).

The Cabinet Office also set up a special division in 1972 – the European Secretariat – in order to deal with EC affairs and to coordinate the activities of all the other departments in their dealings with the EC. This is a source of strength for the Cabinet Office though it is now waning. British government has always had strong central coordination – largely due to the history of the Prime Minister overseeing the business of the Cabinet, helped by the convention of collective ministerial responsibility. The Cabinet Office is the key actor in this central coordination which has helped Britain in its negotiating stance within the EC. It is widely recognised in Brussels that Britain is a better negotiator than most of the other member states, and its strong central coordination is probably the key reason. It does lead to a degree of inflexibility within the negotiating stance of British officials, for they have stricter guidelines than most of their counterparts from other EC states. Furthermore, Britain does not have the overall goals of some other member states. Officials brought up in the university tradition of British empiricism as opposed to the grand theory of continental academia tend to look to current problems and their solution rather than developing a grand strategy under which to operate. This may lead to short-termism in government, with each problem being dealt with as it arises, rather than policies being created with regard to some over-arching goal beyond the life of the present administration.

As the role of the EC expands this provides opportunities for departments to gain strength vis-à-vis the centre. As the sphere of competence of the Commission expands into new policy arenas the work of individual departments both in carrying out directives and within policy-making is expanded. Most departments have now set up their own divisions for dealing with the Commission and so rely less upon both the Foreign Office and more importantly the Cabinet Office. This has made the role of the Cabinet Office as a central coordinating body more difficult and some control and power has been lost by the centre to the departments (though this has not reached the stage of decentralisation enjoyed by many bureaucrats in other member states). Thus the expanding area of competence of the Commission makes the central coordinating role of the core executive more difficult. This can explain some of the resistance of the core executive to the burgeoning strength of the EC. It is not merely the political instincts of Conservative politicians but also the self-interest of officials within the Cabinet Office. As the EC grows in power, the power at the core of the executive wanes. As each department within the civil service deals more directly with Brussels via its own section on EC affairs so the power of the Cabinet Office declines. This process is set to continue in the coming years.

## Conclusion

The central organs of government have not changed dramatically during or after the Thatcher years. The most radical reform of the civil service this century is altering the relationship between the central State and its policy-implementing periphery. But this is essentially a managerial change, though certainly one which enhances opportunities for the contraction of state activity which remains a major plank of Conservative policy. Its effects upon the central State itself and its relations with Parliament are slight if not non-existent. The Citizen's Charter, seen by John Major as the keynote of his administration in the 1990s, is unlikely to have much of an impact on administration of central government, nor for that matter on public service delivery.

Within the core executive itself there has been a constant evolution in which both the Prime Minister and the Cabinet Office have gained power at the expense of the cabinet and ministries, but neither the extent nor the novelty of this should be exaggerated. This concentration of power at the very heart of the core executive could be threatened by a bigger centralisation of power within the EC, which enables individual ministries to recoup some power. The EC allows ministries to develop new partners in expanding policy networks to use against the Treasury and Cabinet Office. So far the European Secretariat has managed to coordinate and control this expansion of EC competence, but just how autonomous individual departments may become within their own policy arena remains one of the key questions of British government for the 1990s.

# 9

# Government Beyond Whitehall: Local Government and Urban Politics

## DESMOND KING

A principal reason for Margaret Thatcher's replacement as Prime Minister was her calamitous reform of local government finances, the poll tax. It is apt that a recondite issue of local finances should displace a leader whose twelve-year premiership was marked by an unprecedented legislative programme of reform of local government. Despite rhetorical allusions to neoliberalism and limited government, the Conservatives have legislated enthusiastically and in detail to reform local government: since 1979 there have been almost 50 separate parliamentary Acts affecting local authorities (see Table 9.1). The aim of these reforms is to marginalise local government as a political institution by creating alternative local agencies to deliver policy and by denuding its representative role.

TABLE 9.1  Selected post-1979 legislation affecting powers of local government

| | | |
|---|---|---|
| 1980 | Housing Act | Privatisation of council houses to tenants of three years' standing |
| 1982 | Local Government Finances No. 2 Act | Abrogated the right of local authorities to levy a supplemental rate at mid-year |

| 1984 | Rates Act | Gave the Secretary of State for the Environment the power to 'cap' or limit the rates levied by local authorities |
|---|---|---|
| 1984 | Housing and Building Control Act | Broadened the policy of selling off council homes to tenants |
| 1985 | Local Government Act | Abolished the Greater London Council (GLC) and the six metropolitan county councils |
| 1985 | Transport Act | Limited the powers of local authorities to subsidise or regulate public transport |
| 1988 | Local Government | Abolished rates system and introduced the Finance Act community charge/poll tax system; non-domestic rates replaced by a Uniform Business Rate (UBR) set and collected centrally |
| 1988 | Local Government Act | Six services specified which local authorities were required to put out to competitive tendering |
| 1988 | Housing Act | New Housing Action Trusts (HATs) created by the government and imposed in areas of derelict council housing empowering tenants to replace council tenancy for a landlord of their own choice |
| 1988 | Education Reform Act | Abrogated the Inner London Education Authority (ILEA); empowers parents to vote to remove schools (opt-out) from local authority control; introduces mandatory national curriculum with compulsory testing of children at specified ages; ends local authority control of colleges of further education and polytechnics |
| 1992 | Local Government | Replaces the community charge/poll tax with a Finance Act council tax based on property ownership but retains UBR |
| 1992 | Education (Schools) Act | Every school to be inspected every four years |
| 1992 | Housing, Land and Urban Development Bill | Extends home ownership to more council tenants through rent to mortgage schemes; creates an Urban Regeneration Agency (URA) to coordinate government programmes for English inner cities by developing derelict and under-used land |

In this chapter I develop two theses about local government. First, the Conservatives' post-1979 legislation has created a new system of *informal local government* (ILG) composed of centrally-controlled agencies whose work parallels that of elected local authorities. Government policy since 1979 has centralised by weakening local government, and privatised either by transplanting functions to the private sector or by imposing market criteria within publicly funded activities. This trend is set to continue. With other reforms a new world of sub-central government has materialised. Second, local government's relationship with central government is becoming analogous to a Next Steps executive agency, as local authorities' activities are increasingly prescribed by Whitehall and local autonomy is correspondingly diminished.

Both claims have implications for the empirical and theoretical study of local government.

## The Crisis of Local Government Finances: From Poll Tax to Council Tax

Central–local finances have rarely lacked discord since 1979. The Conservative administration's introduction and subsequent abrogation of the poll tax altered cardinally the basis of local government finance in Britain. The extent of the local fiscal crisis was revealed by the Chancellor of the Exchequer Norman Lamont's need, in March 1991, to raise VAT by 2.5 per cent (from 15 per cent to 17.5 per cent) to offset the cost to local authorities of the poll tax they were compelled to levy from voters.

### Revenues

*Poll tax*: Conservative efforts to impose central priorities upon local authorities informed the legendary debacle of the Thatcher administration: the poll tax. Before the poll tax local government revenue-raising was restricted principally to the rate derived from property-owners and businesses with some additional income from user charges and fees (Table 9.2). Following a 1985 paper published by the Adam Smith

Institute (Mason, 1985) the government issued their proposals for a new local tax, termed 'community charge', in January 1986. The Green Paper, *Paying for Local Government*, emphasised the importance of local authorities' accountability to their voters:

> the main role of local government is to provide services in a way which properly reflects differences in local circumstances and local choice. A council's powers to raise taxes locally, and the grant it gets from the national Government, should be designed to ensure that the council can provide adequate services. They should also be designed to ensure that the local electors know what the costs of their services are, so that armed with this knowledge they can influence the spending decisions of their council through the ballot box. Effective local accountability must be the corner-stone of successful local government (Department of the Environment, 1986, p.vii).

In the Adam Smith Institute paper, Mason argued that many consumers of local services made no financial contribution to their provision: 'because of rate rebates, the operation of the housing benefit scheme, and the fact that only the head of household actually pays rates, a substantial majority of those who vote can do so in the confident knowledge that they will not have to pay a penny in rates towards their local authority's activities.' Consequently, 'high-spending programmes can be adopted, inflated services introduced, and generous benefits offered, in the safe and secure knowledge that someone other than the voters will have to pay for it' (Mason, 1985, pp.4–5).

The new community charge/poll tax system was supposed to foster a direct relationship of accountability between all citizens of voting age and their local authority by levying an equal tax from each voter (though residents with no voting rights were liable also) and allowing each local authority to set its own rate. In practice, the government quickly imposed limits upon local authority spending – community-charge-capping – and created a new business charge collected by the central government and distributed nationally. The poll tax changed the basis of local taxing in Britain by shifting from a

TABLE 9.2   Landmarks of local government revenue systems

| | | |
|---|---|---|
| 1601 | Poor Relief Act | Beginning of rates organised on a parish basis evolving from a 'poor rate' into a multipurpose rate |
| 1840s | General District Rate | Rate collected in urban areas; compound system: landlords made responsible for tenants' rate for a commission |
| 1925 | Rating and Valuation Act | Rating authorities to revalue property every two years, though rarely implemented |
| 1948 | Local Government Act | National standards established for valuation assessment |
| 1961 | Rating and Valuation Act | Assessment of rateable value based on current market values |
| 1966 | Local Government Act | Rate rebate schedule introduced giving poorer households partial or complete exemption from rate levies; introduced Rate Support Grant |
| 1988 | Local Government Finance Act | Replaced domestic and property rates with personal community charge/poll tax and uniform business rate (UBR) respectively |
| 1992 | Local Government Finance Act | Replaces the community charge/poll tax with a property-ownership-based council tax |

property-based tax to an individual one, ending the progressive element of local taxation and increasing considerably those eligible to pay the local levies irrespective of income.

The poll tax was a political rout, mobilising diverse constituencies in a common opposition. Not least amongst these opponents were Conservative backbenchers, often holding slim majorities, whose constituents suffered from the new, relatively indiscriminate, financial burden created by the new tax. The chairman of the Conservative Party, Chris Patten, discovered the power of this constituent resentment on election night in April 1992 when he lost his seat in Bath. The poll tax was introduced in Scotland on 1 April 1989, a year before its establishment in England and Wales, amidst wide opposition and resentment; about a fifth of the Scottish poll tax remains unpaid since its introduction. This opposition was mirrored in England and Wales, most dramatically in the London riot of 31 March 1991. In a period of eight hours, after a march organised under the auspices of the Anti-Poll Tax Federation, rioters looted 250 shops, overturned and burned vehicles and staged running battles with the police.

*Council tax*: The Local Government Finance Act 1992 introduces a new system for local taxes to replace the poll tax, the council tax. This new system does not begin until fiscal year 1993 and consequently a fresh round of poll tax bills were issued in March 1992. On average the 1992–93 poll tax rose by 13.8 per cent; in many districts non-collection surcharges pushed up the poll tax, that is, levies to cover the amount which poll tax payers have failed to provide. (For occupiers of 900 000 business premises the transitional relief for paying the uniform business rate introduced in 1990 has been extended to 1992.)

The council tax comprises both a personal element and a property element though each household will receive only one bill requiring payment. The average household bill will assume a two-person household and where this is inapplicable discounts can be procured. Single-adult households receive a personal discount (likely to be about 25 per cent of the bill) and about 4 million adults such as students and recipients of income support will be excluded entirely. The government has declined to establish a register of council tax payers. To evaluate property (a task supervised by the Valuation Office of the Inland Revenue) the government has established a banding system (composed of seven broad tax bands – see Table 9.3) which allocates all properties across a set of bands reflecting different values. Households falling within the same band should receive comparable council tax bills. In principle a two-adult household in the top band will pay two-thirds more than a similar household in the middle band who in turn pay two-thirds of the bill of a household in the lowest band. The government assumes that regional variations can be factored out of the designation of bands. What they are unable to factor out is the unanticipated and precipitous fall in house prices (and increase in number of repossessions) concentrated in the Conservative Party electoral heartland of

TABLE 9.3    Government projections of average council tax bills in England

| Band | Property value upper limit (£) | Bill[1] (£) | % of homes in band |
|------|-------------------------------|-------------|--------------------|
| A | 40 000 | 329 | 26 |
| B | 52 000 | 384 | 19 |
| C | 58 000 | 439 | 22 |
| D | 88 000 | 494 | 15 |
| E | 120 000 | 604 | 9 |
| F | 160 000 | 713 | 5 |
| G | 320 000 | 823 | 4 |
| H | 320 000 + | 988 | 1 |

[1] Houses containing only one adult are entitled to a 25% discount in each band.

the South East. Consequently, the robustness of the seven bands, based on property values two years ago, used for council tax evaluations will be severely tested.

*Spending*

The dominant trend during the 1980s was the diminution of local in favour of central control both in the size of grants to local government and in discretion about their deployment. These changes began with the Local Government, Planning and Land Act 1980 which modified the basis for the allocation of rate support grants. A new block grant system was introduced in England and Wales, removing the distinction between the needs and resources elements in central grants and replacing it with a single unitary grant. The new block grant was based upon a central estimation of each authority's 'true needs', and those authorities whose expenditures exceeded this level were penalised. The notion of 'over-spenders' was pivotal to this 1980 Act; it introduced spending targets and penalties for their transgression. The Local Government Finance Act 1982 consolidated the penalising process by empowering central government to hold back grants from over-spending authorities and ending the power of local authorities to raise a supplementary rate in mid-year to compensate for any rate shortfall. The 1984 Rates Act introduced rate-capping, the power of central government to reduce what it deemed 'excessive' rate levies by local authorities and to set rate levels for individual authorities. The central government acquired a determining power in local authority rate-setting and budgetary allocation. Eighteen rate-capping councils were identified and 80 councillors from Liverpool were fined a £5000 personal surcharge for failing to set a local rate and debarred from office for five years. The capping of local authorities' spending plans is still a feature of central–local relations with a number of councils' capped each year.

Local authorities used creative accounting devices to enhance local government financial independence, but these were mostly outlawed in the 1988 Local Government Finance Act. One notorious example of creative accounting was known as the 'swaps market', whereby local authorities exchanged fixed interest rate payments for floating rate payments. By exchanging debt service payments both borrowers improved their financial management. This swapping transaction was held to be *ultra vires* by the House of Lords in January 1991, a ruling with adverse fiscal implications for the 80 banks who had entered into such agreements with local authorities; to the chagrin of the bankers the government declined to legislate retrospectively to validate the millions of pounds' worth of swaps entered into by local authorities.

There are currently three types of grants to local governments. First, the revenue support grant is a general formula-based allocation to all local authorities. The criteria for allocation are allegedly objectives ones set in the Department of the Environment including factors such as population size, ethnic composition of the population, age of housing stock, health, and measures of the costs of service provision in different areas. In Scotland the Client Group system uses the number of clients for each service related to the expense of each service per client as an indicator of need. This objective-based component of the revenue support grant accounts for approximately 80 per cent of the allocation. Of the remaining 20 per cent, 15 per cent is given in grants to local authorities for specific activities including the police, education and short-term needs such as those costs associated with establishing the community charge/poll tax system. The remaining 5 per cent of central government revenue support grants goes for a miscellany of items, including recently technical education.

Second, transfer grants are allocations and assistance provided to citizens through local authorities the spending of which permits of no discretion. Third, capital allocation grants give permission to spend money but are not grants of money: instead, the central government confers upon local authorities the licence to borrow and to spend but does not provide the finances for these activities.

## Future Finances

It is implausible that local government finances will be settled by the new council tax scheme even under a new Conservative administration. Vexatious regional and personal inequities will persist and the retention of a personal element will assure similar difficulties to those associated with the poll tax. If the council tax is not to be as onerous as the poll tax local authorities will have to cut spending: the difficulties facing Sheffield City Council are a premonition of future fiscal problems for local authorities.

In 1992 Labour committed itself to a system of 'fair rates', a tax derived from the old rates system and under which Labour claims the average two-adult household would be better off compared with their council tax bill. A long-term issue is whether any government will introduce some sort of local income tax, either as supplement to or in place of the existing system. Such a tax is a necessary condition for local account-ability since it provides local government with autonomy and, if progressive, avoids the gross inequities of the poll and council tax systems (Jones and Stewart, 1985). Most European local governments have some form of local income tax. The Liberal Democrats are the only party consistently to express an interest in a local income tax.

## The Formal and Informal Local Government Systems

*Formal* local government consists of the district councils, regions, counties and London boroughs listed in Table 9.4: in Wales 8 county councils, 37 district councils and about 800 community and town councils; in England 29 counties, 296 districts and 900 local councils in non-metropolitan areas and in metropolitan areas 32 London boroughs, the City of London Corporation, and 36 districts within 6 metropolitan areas (Greater Manchester, Merseyside, South Yorkshire, Tyne and Wear, West Midlands and West Yorkshire); and in Scotland 9 regions, 53 districts, 1200 community councils and 3 island areas. Local authorities have a range of responsibilities including housing, transport, environmental health, leisure services, education, social services, local planning, fire services, police and garbage collection. There is also a Cabinet committee for London chaired by the Secretary of State for the Environment.

TABLE 9.4   Formal local government in Britain

|  | *England* | *Wales* | *Scotland* |
|---|---|---|---|
| *Top-tier authorities* | | | |
| County councils | 39 | 8 | – |
| Regions | – | – | 9 |
| *Second-tier authorities* | | | |
| District councils | 296 | 37 | 53 |
| *Unitary authorities* | | | |
| Metropolitan[a] district councils | 36 | – | – |
| London boroughs[b] | 32 | – | – |
| Island areas | – | – | 3 |
| *Third-tier authorities* | | | |
| Community and town councils | 900 | 800 | 1 200 |

*Notes*:
a These are in Greater Manchester, Merseyside, South Yorkshire, Tyne and Wear, West Midlands, West Yorkshire.
b Plus the City of London Corporation.

Within this formal system the Conservatives have changed the character of local government by privatising council housing and expanding the number of services provided by private sector organisations. The ubiquity of these initiatives has grown, commencing with council house sales and land privatisation, extending through contracting-out to include the removal of some service provision from the public to the private sector. The Local Government Act 1988 compelled local authorities to put the following services out to competitive tender: cleaning, rubbish collection, street cleaning, building cleaning, vehicle and ground maintenance, catering and the management of leisure services. One study in 1992 found that the private sector was winning an increasing proportion of these contracts (Chartered Institute of Public Finance and Accountancy, 1992). Combined with changes in contract compliance procedures competitive tendering measures are intended to force local authorities to rely upon private rather than public employers, to pursue economic cost efficiency in meeting the service requirements and, in the long term, to weaken the role of public sector trades unions. Cost efficiencies have been achieved principally by paying lower wages to the same workers no longer employed in the public sector.

Instead of envisaging local government as an institution representing a community and its local tradition, it is to be designed as an institution responsible for overseeing service provision. Local government is thought of as an enabling institution and not one of direct service delivery, not dissimilar to the Next Steps model implemented throughout Whitehall since 1988 (Efficiency Unit, 1988; see also Chapters 7 and 8). This new role maximises efficiency and profit criteria in local government. It treats citizens as customers of government services. Furthermore, local authorities are viewed as purchasers rather than providers of services. It is the job of local authorities to purchase and regulate the delivery of services but to be removed from the day-to-day provision of such services. In the run-up to the 1992 election the government promised arrangements for the publication of league tables ranking the performance of councils. For supporters of the user service role an 'entirely new type of local government officer [will develop]. Instead of managing or administering in house staff, he will need to be skilled in the arts of contract specification, purchasing and supply, and quality control' (Mather, 1988, p.17). This vision implies a professionalised and service-oriented tier of government increasingly remote from electoral accountability. Councillors will be required to act as part-time enablers instead of full-time providers of services.

Local authorities retain planning powers and discretion about the provision of some services, though these are all likely to be made subject to compulsory competitive tendering and many planning decisions are over-ruled. East Cambridge-shire district council is contracting out the collection of taxes and the payment of benefits, examples other authorities will emulate. This council's policy anticipates future government requirements that local authorities introduce compulsory competitive tendering in the collection of taxes, architecture and planning.

*Informal local government (ILG):* A series of authorities has been established independently of local government holding significant powers over the same jurisdictions and discharging policy-making functions which might logically have been assigned to local authorities. Thus institutions of further education and sixth form colleges were given corporate status in 1991 and removed from the control of their local education authority. Such changes and the creation of new agencies constitute the realm of *informal* local government and result in a sub-national governmental network. Figure 9.1 depicts the new arrangements.

The ILG includes non-elected authorities, self-governing hospital trusts and in metropolitan areas joint boards for police, fire and transport with members appointed by the government or nominated by public and private sectors. Part of the Conservative administration's strategy for local government is to centralise in the short term as the basis for decentralising, on its own terms, over the long term. Agencies constituting the *informal* local government system effect this strategy; they are complemented by government programmes to increase public–private partnerships in urban policy such as those associated with the City Challenge and enterprise agency schemes. The system is informal in that a range of agencies and

FIGURE 9.1   The new local governance system

| FORMAL LOCAL GOVERNMENT | | INFORMAL LOCAL GOVERNMENT | | |
| --- | --- | --- | --- | --- |
| *Locally controlled service delivery* | *Locally purchased services* | *Nationally controlled service delivery* | *Nationally regulated* | *Regulatory agencies* |
| Non-opted out schools | Private contractors delivering public services | Opted-out schools houses | Innercity initiatives | Privatised utilities |
| Planning | (e.g., rubbish collection and cleaning)[a] | Training | Local enterprise agencies | Private sector developers |
| Social services | | Enterprise Councils (TECs) | Urban Development Corporations (UDCs) | |
| | | Housing Action Trusts (HATs) | Public/private partnerships | |
| | | | Urban Regeneration Agency (URA) | |
| | | | Enterprise Zones | |

a To be extended to community care of the elderly and handicapped.

organisations enjoying significant policy-making powers and financial resources operate independently of formal local government institutions to which members are elected and held accountable by voters. Informal local government agencies are not directly accountable to local voters (and are indirectly accountable in only a few cases) yet they shape many of the policies – such as education, health, urban regeneration, and training – which affect citizens. Some examples of the ILG illustrate these changes.

(1) *Urban Development Corporations* (UDCs): These were initiated in the Local Government, Planning and Land Act 1980 which established two such corporations in the London and Merseyside dockland areas – named the London Docklands Development Corporation (LDCC) affecting the London boroughs of Tower Hamlets, Newham and Southwark, and the Merseyside Docklands Development Corporation (MDDC), affecting Liverpool and Wirral, with budgets (in 1981–82) of £40 million and £26 million respectively. These two UDCs were supplemented with eight more, five founded in 1987, whose budgets ranged from £100 million to £160 million: Trafford Park, the Black Country, Cardiff Bay, Tyne and Wear, Teeside, and in 1988 a UDC was established in Sheffield with a budget of £50 million. Mini-UDCs have been established in central Manchester, Leeds and Bristol with budgets of £15 million each over four or five years.

UDCs hold powers to acquire and own land within their jurisdiction, to construct factories and infrastructure, to invest in the environment and to provide housing and other necessary social facilities. Their objective is to 'regenerate' the area over which they exercise jurisdiction, though this term has never been defined precisely (National Audit Office, 1988). According to the 1980 Act, 'regeneration' can be achieved by four means: bringing land and buildings into effective use; facilitating new industrial and commercial development; creating an attractive environment; and ensuring the provision of housing and social facilities in which people can live. The UDCs are required to raise private funds and to develop the areas for which they are responsible, though they draw upon substantial public funding as well. They have had some success (Morison, 1987). The LDDC's 1988 *Annual Report* claims it had attracted

£4 400 million between 1981 and 1988 from the private sector against £400 million from the government (LDDC, 1988, p.5). However, the London UDC has enjoyed a greater opportunity for success than the other corporations and despite its favourable location its future is uncertain with the Canary Wharf project in turmoil. And ten years after the establishment of LDDC, the level of vacant property and the collapse of property prices paints a much less favourable picture of this approach to urban regeneration. Furthermore, government subsidies to developments within the LDDC area have been higher than a supposedly private sector strategy should have required.

UDCs have been the object of three main criticisms. First, their policies are ineffectively coordinated with those of the local authorities upon whose jurisdiction they impinge, a common problem of the ILG sector. Second it is unclear to whom UDCs are or should be accountable. Formally UDCs are accountable directly to the Department of the Environment with their boards nominated by the Secretary of State. There are no elected representatives. UDCs' accountability to central government constitutes a deliberate weakening of local authority power. This arrangement does not preclude effective working relations between UDCs and the relevant local authorities but it does preclude control of major local developments from the community most affected and limits community participation. Third, some critics claim that UDCs are failing financially as measured by losses on property transactions. On the basis of written replies to parliamentary questions Labour MP Stephen Byers concluded that UDCs had lost over £67 million (quoted in Wynn Davies, 1992). Property transactions have been the UDCs' core activity. Such a loss challenges the viability of the strategy underpinning UDCs as Bryan Gould, former Labour Shadow Cabinet member, has remarked: 'the problem has been that the policy is entirely based on property development rather than investment in the residents of the areas concerned in creating businesses' (quoted in Houlder, 1992).

(2) *Training and Enterprise Councils*: The system of sub-national government has been affected by the Conservatives's training policy (King, 1993). The government has shifted from

a centralised system controlled by the Manpower Services Commission with regional area manpower boards to a decentralised system administered through 82 local training and enterprise councils (TECs) and in Scotland 13 local enterprise councils (LECs) overseen by the Training Agency in the Department of Employment. This major policy change ends direct local authority involvement in training programmes and decisions, despite the importance of such measures for local labour markets. TECs are employer-dominated organisations to whom the government has devolved responsibility for the administration of training programmes throughout Britain. Each TEC has a contract with the government through the Department of Employment to spend its allocated budget on training programmes as it judges most appropriate for its local labour market; most TECs coordinate with local enterprise agencies from where many of their members have come. The average membership of a TEC is 50 of whom the majority are businesspersons. One analysis found that 722 members (from a total of 945) on 79 TECs were from the private sector. Trade union representation is limited and by invitation.

TECs and LECs have raised two key problems. First, the Department of Employment is ambivalent about how much autonomy it intends to devolve to TECs. TEC members are unprepared simply to act as a rubber stamp for Department of Employment policy; they have won independence to vary the weekly allowance they pay to participants in training programmes and to design programmes as they wish. Government pressure to push as many unemployed persons as possible into training programmes will continue to clash with the TEC members' preference for training employed persons. However, the G10 group (composed of a number of TEC chairpersons that represents the movement to the government) are a powerful pressure group who have exercised their muscle in relations with Whitehall, demanding to be included in the administration of Employment Action and in devising programmes most apposite for their local area. According to one report of G10's first meeting with the new Employment Secretary, Gillian Shephard, the TECs are demanding a role in policy-setting and resisting a purely implementing role

(Wood, 1992). Second, the relationship of TECs, administering large budgets and allegedly responsible for addressing unemployment a key concern of many local authorities, with local government is undefined. Local authorities enjoy only weak representation on TECs and little influence upon their budget allocations. In some areas cooperation has been achieved but in many others local authorities are excluded.

(3) *Education*: The informal local government system also operates in education initiated by changes in the Education Reform Act 1988 and advanced in the July 1992 White Paper. Under the 1988 Act responsibility for education has been steadily shifted from local education authorities to the suppliers of services, that is, schools themselves. Managerial and financial functions have been detached from the education authorities and given to headteachers and governors. It is planned that each school receiving public funds will have it own budget controlled by school governors, from which the full costs of operating the school must be satisfied, including purchasing equipment and books and paying teachers. This new local management of schools places principal responsibility upon headteachers and governors. Nominally governors are responsible for the school's financial management but in practice this burden falls upon headteachers. The Education Reform Act clause empowering schools to opt-out of the control of their local education authority – to acquire grant-maintained status – is an additional blow to the latter's power (schools taking this option will not be able to opt in subsequently). Opted-out schools retain a direct relationship with the Department for Education. The initial incentives to opt-out in the short term were substantial since grant-maintained schools receive a share of the local education authority's administration budget. However, only a small number of schools have yet availed themselves of the scheme (of over 21 000 schools in England and Wales only 277 had opted out by September 1992 and none in Scotland); and public spending pressures will erode the incentives to opting-out. (Council tenants received a comparable right to opt-out under the Housing Act 1988 which entitles them to substitute their council-tenancy with a landlord of their own choice, a very popular option.)

The White Paper entitled *Choice and Diversity – A New Framework for Schools*, published in July 1992, confirmed the government's determination to maximise hierarchical distinctions in the primary and especially secondary school systems and widely to diffuse self-management in schools. The latter implies a weakening role for local education authorities and stringent powers of intervention to protect standards for inspection services. The intellectual and administrative rationale behind these measures is thoroughly new right: the claim that enhancing choice and diversity in education, treating it as analogous to an economic market, fosters the conditions for individual satisfaction and attainment. The White Paper assumes that all schools will opt-out of local authority control and proposes establishing a new statutory Funding Agency for Schools (FAS) to allocate government grants to grant-maintained schools. Schools will be more susceptible to market forces and less controlled by government.

The implementation of a national curriculum by definition expands the role of the Department for Education and limits that of local authorities in school education. To whom will the schools opting out of local education authority control appeal? Under current legislation they must appeal direct to the Secretary of State. Regional education authorities analogous to regional health authorities are predictable. Furthermore, the Department for Education will become responsible for the allocation and monitoring of funds to opted-out schools, an unmanageable task if the numbers grow. From 1994–95 funds will be awarded to opted-out schools based on a government estimate of how much the local authority should be spending on its schools. Plainly if a local authority is spending less than this estimate each school's budget will be smaller.

Important changes not dissimilar in emphasis to these educational reforms have occurred in the health sector where power has been devolved to hospitals and general practitioners, internal markets created and hospitals accorded the power to become self-governing trusts (see Chapter 11). These reforms push health sector delivery agencies toward a rigorous managerial style dictated by market and profit criteria.

(4) *Urban Development and City Challenge*: The government has created a new agency to coordinate its urban regeneration

work (including the UDCs). This Urban Regeneration Agency (URA) (announced in the Queen's Speech in May 1992 and launched in July) is headed by Lord Walker, a former Conservative Minister, and holds similar compulsory purchase powers to the UDCs to develop derelict and under-used land. It will be given responsibility for city grants, housing corporation grants, city action teams, derelict land grants and English Estates, the government agency that builds offices and factories in deprived areas. The URA will have power to assemble parcels of land (if necessary through compulsory purchase) and make them available to developers. The URA will centralise the regeneration process for developers; however, whether development itself will remain a viable strategy as the British property market collapses is an unquestioned, but nonetheless tenuous, assumption. Such an approach undoubtedly neglects training, transport and social housing needs because developers and government prefer the tangibility and prestige of flagship property schemes.

The URA will assume responsibility for other government urban development programmes. These latter will be under increasing scrutiny from the Treasury determined to reduce government spending. The government has chosen to limit the powers vested in the new agency, leaving many important spending choices with ministers; the URA follows too closely the design of UDCs to be as innovative or effective as it ought to be.

The Department of the Environment has expended much energy on the City Challenge programmes (to remain independent of the new URA) through which it allocates regeneration funds to urban areas on the basis of bids from urban programmes' authorities. The twenty successful authorities, almost all Labour-controlled, in 1992 were: Barnsley, Birmingham, Blackburn, Bolton, Brent, Derby, Hackney, Hartlepool, Kensington and Chelsea, Kirklees, Lambeth, Leicester, Newham, North Tyneside, Sandwell, Sefton, Stockton, Sunderland, Walsall and Wigan. The allocation totals £750 million over a five-year period. These funds are used in partnership with private contractors, whom the government expects to contribute over £2 billion, and voluntary agencies. A recent Policy Studies Institute study of urban deprivation,

*Urban Trends*, reveals the challenge facing these authorities (Policy Studies Institute, 1992). The Institute's analysis demonstrated how profound the gap between deprived urban areas and the remainder of the country remains, measured by staff–pupil ratios, unemployment, and housing difficulties.

(5) *Public–Private Partnerships*: Since the urban riots of 1981 the government has sought to mobilise business interests and leaders in a partnership with government-funded urban programmes and agencies to revitalise derelict inner cities. This drive has resulted in a range of such partnerships among which enterprise agencies are prominent (Moore, 1990). The Business in the Community (BITC) group, founded in 1982, has been active. It acts as an umbrella organisation linking businesses, local government and local communities in collective attacks upon urban deprivation and economic decline (Jacobs, 1990, 1992).

Over 500 businesses have joined BITC and thousands have become involved in local partnerships. BITC-supported projects have focused upon improving the employment opportunities of the long-term and school-leaver unemployed. BITC has eleven regional offices. Its national organisation administers the Per Cent Club whose corporate members agree to contribute a half per cent of pre-tax profits or 1 per cent of dividends to the funding of community projects. BITC provides a framework through which business interest in addressing community needs can be harnessed. In the short term the relationship between BITC and TECs will be of crucial importance since their efforts should be complementary, but overlapping jurisdictions may encourage conflict, not cooperation. For local authorities, BITC initiatives impinge directly upon their jurisdiction and previous responsibilities.

(6) *Regulatory Authorities*: The massive post-1979 privatisation programme has resulted in the creation of US-style regulatory authorities to monitor formerly public sector utilities and to act as watchdogs in consumers' interest (see Chapter 10). Four prominent examples and their Director-Generals are: the Office of Electricity Regulation (Professor Stephen Littlechild); Office of Gas Supply (Sir James McKinnon); the Office of Telecommunications (Bill Wrigglesworth); and the Office of Water Services (Ian Byatt). The regulatory agencies'

powers were strengthened by the Competition and Service (Utilities) Act 1992, which established complaints procedures for customers. Savings have been won for gas and telephone consumers, and each agency has provided information about likely future costs in their sector.

The major omission in government restructuring has been any commitment to regional government. The Conservatives have stated repeatedly their opposition to such reform, including opposition to devolution for Scotland. Compared to European countries such as Spain, France, Germany and Italy which have 17, 22, 16 and 20 regional governments respectively Britain stands out particularly within the context of the EC which defines many of its policies and grants in regional terms. The Labour party is committed to some form of Scottish devolution and to regional assembles throughout England and Wales while the Liberal Democrats would go further toward a federal system. However, there is a good possibility that the civil service – as part of Next Steps – will be subject to increasing regionalisation.

Speculation prompted the suggestion that the government favoured eliminating county councils throughout England and Wales. Such a decision depends upon the Local Government Commission, chaired by Sir John Banham. The Banham Commission's review of local government boundaries is scheduled to take three years and its final proposals should provide an important framework to address the turbulent world of local government structures. These proposals will have to take account of the effects of the new council tax and education reforms.

In sum, since 1979 the Conservatives have striven to weaken local government, to impose private sector performance measures upon local authorities, and to establish organisations administering public programmes previously administered by local authorities. A novel separation of the 'client' and 'contractor' functions has been realised: that is, those officials responsible for specifying service delivery requirement and monitoring their implementation have been separated from those producing them. Service delivery standards are to be carefully defined and the new Citizen's Charter initiative will theoretically provide a basis for assessing performance as in other areas of government activity (see Chapter 8). The government has proposed establishing league tables of local authority performance based on over 150 indicators. These developments confirm the value of viewing local government as analogous to a Next Steps agency.

## The Study of Local Government

*New Community Regime*

The growth of *informal* local government and the weakening of formal local government will test approaches to the empirical study of local politics. As major parts of public policy and former local government functions are transferred to unelected agencies then these latter become increasingly important objects for study. The growth of unemployment and globalisation of labour market trends limit the capacity of local authorities efficaciously to formulate policy responses and encourage the formation of public–private development partnerships (King and Pierre, 1990; Stone and Sanders, 1987).

Figure 9.1 provided a preliminary view of the *informal* local government system. It emphasises the increasing importance of public agencies nationally controlled and of public–private partnerships to the structure of local politics. Collectively these institutions coalesce with the formal local government system to form a 'new community-regime' distinguished by (a) the increased presence of nationally-controlled agencies; (b) the integration of private sector representatives onto local agencies; and (c) new funding arrangements. This new regime poses two analytic challenges. First, more research needs to be undertaken about the informal local government system, an imperative which requires the introduction of new theoretical approaches developed to study public–private partnerships, unelected local agencies and local regimes (Dunleavy and King, 1990). Second, the traditional community power study approach pioneered by Robert Dahl (1961) in his pluralist analysis of New Haven Connecticut should be resurrected and broadened to capture the dynamics of the new post-Thatcher local government system.

In Britain a 'new community-regime', distinguished from American regimes by (a) the institutional context (such as the direct controlling role of central government in certain activities), (b) the traditional limited entrepreneurial role of business and (c) the weakened role of local authorities, has its genesis in the changes of the last decade (on the USA see Stone, 1989, Logan and Molotch, 1987; Logan and Swanstrom, 1990). Agencies such as UDCs and TECs administering large government grants can be as significant for a local community as the local council. In Britain it is probable that in public–private partnerships and centrally controlled agencies the private component will be more significant than the public for two reasons. First, the government has ensured that private sector representatives dominate the boards of agencies such as UDCs and TECs in the ILG sector. And, second, for urban development private funding will be much more important proportionally than public contributions.

### *The Constitutional Status of Local Government*

The alacrity with which local government has been stripped of many of its traditional functions and the indifference with which these changes have been received by voters – with the exception of the poll tax's direct fiscal impact – suggests a political culture uninterested in maintaining or strengthening local government (Bogdanor, 1992). The local elections (outside London) on 7 May 1992 gave the Conservatives their best results since 1977, despite the erosion of local government powers, and Labour its worst results since 1982, with even less support than in the general election of 9 April.

Politically and financially power in the British polity resides at the centre and not outside Whitehall. The British tradition of local government is a long one but its political resonance is not powerful. The distinguished scholarship about normative theories of local government (Hill, 1974; Magnusson, 1986) needs to be revived to address recent reforms. There is a crisis about the normative status of local government and to date how this crisis might be resolved has received paltry consideration (Jones and Stewart, 1985; King, 1989).

Local government in Britain lacks constitutional status; it is subject to *ultra vires*, empowered to undertake those functions only deliberately granted it by Parliament. In most European states local governments are granted powers of general competence or specified autonomy within which they conduct policy. There are of course limitations upon the powers of local government in these countries but such restrictions operate within a constitutional guarantee of general competence. In Britain the Constitution provides no support for local government, a position formalised by the Widdicombe Report: 'local government has no independent right to exist. Its continued existence is based on the contribution it can make to good government. It needs to be able to demonstrate that it is a more effective means of government than local administration' (*Report of the Committee of Inquiry into the Conduct of Local Authority Business*, 1986, p.55).

This constitutional vulnerability poses a key question: as an institution should local government be subject to substantial restructuring by the national government or should its status be distinct and guaranteed as such in constitutional law? This question is peculiarly pertinent in Britain where the power of the national government to restructure local government is absolute. There are two arguments for a statement guaranteeing the status of local government.

First, local governments are manifestations in part of local communities. There is a geographical and communal basis to the division of institutional power across local territories resting in tradition and historic ties. The fact that citizens form loyalties to local government institutions because these are considered to represent their community provides a rationale for ensuring that such affiliations are not ruptured arbitrarily by national whim and directive. Such feelings will be enhanced if there is a return to the old county boundaries.

Second, guaranteeing local government institutions constitutionally increases their autonomy and especially their autonomy in dealing with the national government. It is a necessary dimension of a mature polity that local government enjoys sufficient independence to structure its relations with the national government. Such constitutional guarantees would facilitate a reasoned and judicious reform of local government which combined financial, functional and structural arrangements. The last twenty-year cycle of piecemeal reforms in all three aspects has contributed to the decline of local government in the British polity.

# PART TWO
# Public Policy

# 10

# Economic Policy

**STEPHEN WILKS**

Success in managing the economy has come to be regarded as the key to electoral success, and economic policy is conventionally given pre-eminence in analyses of contemporary politics. It is curious therefore that the Conservatives should have won their election victory in April 1992 in the face of the most serious recession since the 1930s; and that British membership of the European Monetary System (EMS), while it lasted, prompted speculation about 'the end of macro-economic policy' (Britton, 1992, p.138). The link between individual prosperity and political popularity has not been broken but economists are now far less certain about the merits of competing theories; the main political parties are closer together in their views of economic policy than they have been for twenty-five years; and analysts are floundering around trying to find new interpretations of the British economic predicament and its implications for policy.

Uncertainty over the economic policy of the 1992 Major government was intensified by Black Wednesday. The events of 16 September 1992 constitute the most dramatic and momentous turning point in macro-economic policy since Thatcher's election in 1979. Membership of the European Exchange Rate Mechanism (ERM) at a parity of DM 2.95 had been the central tenet of Conservative policy, affirmed in the boldest and most uncompromising terms by the Chancellor and Prime Minister in speech after speech. Yet during that Wednesday the inner Cabinet and the European financial community watched in mesmerised fascination as tidal waves of selling took the pound to its ERM floor. As the markets closed Britain 'suspended' its ERM membership and allowed the pound to float. By the end of the month it had fallen by 27 pfennigs from its ERM floor to DM 2.50.

Withdrawal from the ERM was a stunning blow to the credibility of Major and Lamont. It re-opened the dispute about Europe and the Maastricht Treaty within the Conservative Party, and within the Labour Party as Bryan Gould resigned from the Shadow Cabinet. But in destroying the central target of economic policy – the defeat of inflation through defence of the parity – ERM withdrawal opened up a new set of options and a need to redefine a basis for macro-economic policy. Monetary policy was relaxed, interest rates were cut and it seemed that a greater priority might be given to the promotion of industrial growth.

This chapter briefly reviews the nature of macro- and micro-economic policy and the institutions which administer it. This leads into an examination of the recent record of macro-economic policy and British experience since joining the ERM on 8 October 1990. The argument that macro-economic policy is increasingly channelled by European constraints takes us into an analysis of micro-economic (supply-side) policy and a discussion of deregulation, social market policies and prospects for an industrial policy.

## Macro- and Micro-economic Policy: the Great Divide

Macro-economic policy is concerned with the overall level of economic activity and addresses policy targets such as inflation, unemployment, growth and the balance of payments. It operates through monetary and fiscal policy. In contrast micro-economic policy is directed at the detailed workings of industry, either at individual industrial sectors such as steel or brewing, or at specific activities associated with industrial productivity such as research, training or export promotion. Clearly the two levels interact. Interest rates affect investment, government spending has a differential impact on industries such as defence or construction, and exchange rate policy affects exports. But one of the prime failures of post-war British economic policy has been the inability to make constructive

links between these levels. In practice macro- and micro-policy
have been conducted in isolation from one another, with
priority being given to macro-economic policy and, since
1979, overwhelming attention given to the defeat of inflation
at the expense of all other priorities.

This division of economic policy is reflected in institutional
divisions within central government and is expressed in
fundamental conflicts over the conduct of policy. Macro-
economic policy is conducted by the Treasury working closely
with the Bank of England (and nowadays constrained by the
Bundesbank). Traditionally considerable attention was paid to
City opinion, and international financial markets must be
constantly catered to. Policy is conducted with an eye to
market reaction and is concerned to create credibility and
manipulate expectations. Micro-economic policy, on the other
hand, is the province of the Department of Trade and Industry
(DTI) in conjunction with other departments like Employment, the Scottish Office and science staff in the Cabinet
Office. It is concerned with far longer-term issues ranging from
energy planning to the tax position of small business. Its
primary constituency is the Confederation of British Industry
(CBI) and especially the range of organisations representing
manufacturing industry.

If anything the centrality and power of the Treasury
increased during the 1980s. It was entrusted with the government's central economic goal and was bolstered by theories of
monetarism, balanced budgets and neoclassical economics
which emphasised anti-inflationary policies (Allsopp *et al.*,
1991, p.71). These prescriptions reinforced the independence
of the Treasury and required that it be supported in cutting
spending and speaking with credibility over monetary policy.
Even more so than in previous regimes the relationship
between the Chancellor and the Prime Minister became the
dominant Cabinet alliance. When the alliance collapsed, most
dramatically with the resignation of Nigel Lawson in October
1989 after disputes with Margaret Thatcher and her personal
economic adviser, Sir Alan Walters, the government as well as
the Prime Minister began to totter (for cameos on these events
see Ranelagh, 1992, Chapter 13). At the other end of the see-
saw the DTI shrank in importance and prestige as government

steadily wound down micro-economic policy measures in favour of market solutions. At the beginning of the 1990s, however, all the signs were of a revival of micro-economic policy and a reappraisal of the theoretical base and the importance of macro-economic policy. This reversal revolves around British integration into the administrative and economic system of the EC, and is worth spelling out in a little more detail as the main theme of this chapter.

In effect the UK signalled its willingness to surrender macro-economic sovereignty in October 1990 when it joined the ERM. It made that surrender a reality in agreeing the bulk of the programme of Economic and Monetary Union (EMU) at the Maastricht Summit in December 1991. That surrender was born of a growing disillusion with British policy which had generated an over-valued pound in the early 1980s, had produced a sharp reminder that this was not permanent when sterling fell to $1.03 in 1985, and was clearly unable to control inflation in the 'Lawson boom' of 1987–88. During 1990 inflation rates were exploding towards 10 per cent, thereby undermining many of the hard-won gains of the early 1980s and revealing Thatcher's claims of an economic miracle to be delusory. Her refusal to align policy with European practice played a large part in her downfall. She had to be 'bounced' into membership of the ERM by her Chancellor, John Major, and her Foreign Secretary, Sir Geoffrey Howe, at the Rome European Council in October 1990.

Membership of the ERM tied British exchange rates into a 'wide band' of 6 per cent around the European average. The EMU programme (see Table 10.3, p.230) envisages a progression from this 'semi-fixed' status to complete monetary union by 1 January 1999, at which point eligible countries would abandon their national currencies in favour of the European Currency Unit (ECU). With fixed exchange rates, and interest rates used solely to defend the currency, monetary policy would no longer be made in London but in Germany by the Bundesbank. There would be a significant stabilising role for fiscal policy, but even here budget deficits and borrowing would be limited by rules of fiscal convergence. The implications of this loss of control were evident during 1992 when ERM membership meant that the UK was locked into a high exchange rate, high interest rate posture despite a steadily deepening recession. In aligning itself with Bundesbank monetary policy Britain found itself gratuitously paying a price for the high German interest rates occasioned by the cost of German reunification.

In these circumstances prolonged high inflation or a rise in unit costs creates a lack of industrial competitiveness, balance of payments crises, even higher interest rates to defend the currency parity and a penalty in the form of lowered economic activity and higher unemployment. The way out of this vicious circle is to increase industrial efficiency through micro-economic policies. Suddenly the supply-side issues of invest-ment, innovation, training and sectoral planning take on a new importance. As long as European monetary cooperation remains a goal of government we can expect a shift in the bias of economic policy-making during the 1990s away from the Treasury and towards the DTI.

## Macro-economic Policy: the Record

The Conservatives under Thatcher had the ambitious aim to turn the tide of economic history and reverse Britain's relative economic decline. For a short euphoric period in 1987–89 when productivity rates began to exceed those across Europe it seemed that they had succeeded (Hannah, 1989, pp.40, 48). That illusion was shattered during 1990–91 as the old problems reasserted themselves and rising inflation, deteriorat-ing balance of payments and falling industrial production led Britain into deep and prolonged recession.

Over the longer term a sober review of growth rates indicates an improved British performance relative to Europe during the 1980s but not the qualitative improvement for which the Conservatives had aimed. Table 10.1 updates the statistics from a classic study of Britain's relative decline (Caves and Krause, 1980, p.18). It dramatically highlights the failure to perpetuate the growth improvement of the mid-1980s. Along with the USA Britain entered the recession earlier, and was hit harder, than its main competitors. The negative GDP growth from 1988–92 was particularly disappointing.

TABLE 10.1   Average annual percentage growth rates of OECD countries, 1957–92

| Country | 1957–67 | 1967–78 | 1980–88 | 1988–92 |
|---|---|---|---|---|
| Japan | 10.4 | 7.2 | 3.4 | 2.9 |
| USA | 4.1 | 3.0 | 1.9 | 0.2 |
| Germany | 5.5 | 3.8 | 1.7 | 2.3 |
| France | 5.6 | 4.4 | 1.4 | 1.4 |
| Britain | 3.1 | 2.3 | 1.7 | −0.6 |
| **All OECD** | **4.8** | **3.8** | **2.0** | **1.0** |

*Sources*: Whiteley (1990, p.193); OECD Main Economic Indicators.

John Major's talk of a country 'at ease with itself' belied any revivalist pretensions. His emphasis was on low inflation rather than high growth. While attempting to fight off devaluation during September 1992, Major told his CBI audience that 'we must bite the anti-inflation bullet or accept that we will be forever second-rate in Europe' (*Financial Times*, 11 September 1992). However, although the rate rapidly fell from the peaks of 1990 to reach historically low levels in 1992, rates were still lower elsewhere in Europe, as is shown in Table 10.2.

TABLE 10.2   OECD inflation and unemployment rates, June 1992

|  | Inflation (%) | Unemployment (%) |
|---|---|---|
| Japan | 2.3 | 2.1 |
| USA | 3.1 | 7.4 |
| France | 3.0 | 10.3 |
| Germany | 4.3 | 4.5 |
| Italy | 5.4 | 9.9[1] |
| Spain | 6.2 | 16.9[2] |
| UK | 3.9 | 10.5 |
| **OECD Europe** | **6.8** | **9.2** |

*Source*: OECD Main Economic Indicators; inflation (May); unemployment (June) (1 = Jan, 2 = Feb), OECD standardised rates.

In evaluating the impact upon competitiveness, relative inflation trends are key. Major recognised this when in July 1992 he reiterated the old goal of Thatcher and Lawson of 'zero' inflation and talked of sterling replacing the mark as the strongest currency in the EMS. His pretensions were regarded by industry as dangerous and by financial analysts as ludicrous; a *Financial Times* columnist described him as a King Lear who has 'made himself look silly' (Anthony Harris, *Financial Times*, 3 August 1992). Nonetheless Major was underlining the continuing main goal of macro-economic policy, the defeat of inflation. Britain is said to be 'inflation prone', to have an 'inflationary mentality': the self-defined goal of the 1992 Major government was finally to eliminate this syndrome even at the cost of massive rises in unemployment.

In many respects, the goal of zero inflation was in fact the most important of Thatcher's legacies to Major. It was, moreover, one which she had consciously engineered. In conceding ERM membership to Major (as Chancellor) and Hurd in October 1990, Thatcher nevertheless insisted on the crucial condition that sterling enter the ERM at a rate of DM 2.95. This was a penal rate which, if adhered to, would at least have the clear Thatcherite merit of squeezing inflation out of the British economy. As it turned out, DM 2.95 became unsustainable, and the alternative Thatcherite goal of British withdrawal from the ERM was enacted.

The policy of sacrificing all goals on the altar of zero inflation was thus shattered by Black Wednesday. Suddenly the criteria by which policy was to be judged became the subject of widespread debate. A return to monetary targets, a consideration of asset values and government borrowing were all touted by the Chancellor as indicators in addition to the exchange rate. As uncertainty dragged on the damage to John Major's leadership steadily mounted. Criticism from within the Conservative Party became overt and the split over whether the Maastricht Treaty should be ratified widened. A *Sunday Times* leader (27 September 1992) could declare that 'the British government is damaged goods and John Major needs to undertake a radical rethink of strategy and policy if he is to restore its fortunes, and his own . . . the whole edifice of official policy has crumbled into a shambles'. This was a remarkable reversal for a government which had won an historic victory only six months earlier. It was not all bad news. Those who wanted to give a higher priority to growth and employment saw a sudden opening up of opportunities, a positive outcome especially since the portents for unemployment seemed so gloomy.

From its trough early in 1990 unemployment rose remorselessly by over half a million to overtake the European average during 1991. The ability of the Conservatives to win an election in the face of such high unemployment, and of forecasts of 3 million unemployed in 1993, reinforced the message of 1983: that unemployment no longer loses elections. The debate over unemployment therefore stresses long-term unemployment, the growing phenomenon of 'non-employment' (people expecting never to work), and of course the social despair, deprivation and disruption implied by a large and marginalised body of the unemployed.

As recession obstinately continued during 1992 and the economy, in the Bank of England's vivid phrase, continued to 'bump along the bottom', so the resumption of growth appeared to be constrained by several exceptional factors. One of the most worrying was the balance of payments deficit. The UK was continuing to run a substantial trade deficit even at the trough of the recession when in theory demand conditions should have been generating a surplus. Since 1983 this had included a deficit on manufactured goods and with the gradual decline in North Sea oil production there was by 1991 also a small deficit on fuels trade. This constraint opened up the classic British predicament of increased growth sucking in imports, creating a currency crisis and requiring a further bout of deflation: the classic 'Stop–Go' syndrome. The answer to this problem again lay on the supply-side with an urgent need to expand the manufacturing base which had been so decimated in the recession of the early 1980s.

A more unusual problem lay in the debt legacy of the Lawson boom and the 'Yuppie-years'. An increase in liquidations and in personal bankruptcy was dramatised by the despair of formerly secure and prosperous Lloyd's 'names' brought down by three years of record insurance losses. Meanwhile the decline of the housing market brought a new topic into economic discussion, the question of declining wealth, debt overhang and consumer caution. Net housing wealth fell by an extraordinary 24 per cent between the third quarter of 1989 and the first quarter of 1992. As estimates put the proportion of people with 'negative equity' in their houses (mortgages higher than valuation) above 1 million, and as repossessions escalated, so people became far less willing to spend. The same problem was evident elsewhere in the world economy and especially in the crashes of the Japanese property and stock markets. With all the traditional major 'engines of growth' in Japan, Germany and the USA facing problems, commentators talked of recession giving way to depression and to 'the greatest world economic crisis since the Thirties. It is now wholly out of the Government's control' (William Rees-Mogg, The *Independent*, 7 September 1992).

## Economic Policy and Europe

Although there remains considerable uncertainty about the prospects for full Economic and Monetary Union by 1999, it is indisputable that European institutions and policies will provide the context which will increasingly dominate British economic policy. Accordingly it is productive to study the specifics of the Maastricht programme in order to appreciate the direction and the emphases which will be embodied in moves to European economic union during the 1990s.

The December 1991 Intergovernmental Conference at Maastricht drew up a Treaty, signed in February 1992, which embodies extensive revision of the 1957 Rome Treaty to provide for 'European Union', institutional reform and a series of new EC 'competences' such as culture, health and foreign policy (see Chapter 3). The Treaty is therefore far wider than the economic proposals but it is these that have attracted most controversy, giving rise to a protocol which allows Denmark and the UK to remain outside the final stage of EMU. The proposals for monetary union embody the timetable set out in Table 10.3.

The institutional provisions are especially important. As the programme progresses into Stage II macro-economic policy

TABLE 10.3   The Maastricht Treaty programme for economic and monetary union (agreed December 1991)

---

*Stage I*
1 July 1990

- Currency linkage through EMS
- Abolition of all controls over capital movements
- Initiate convergence process towards four criteria
    - Inflation within 1.5% of three lowest
    - Interest rates within 2% of three lowest
    - Budget deficit not excessive
    - No downward devaluation over past two years
- Process monitored by Council of Ministers, Economic and Finance Ministers (ECOFIN)
- Completion of Single European Market (SEM)

*Stage II*
1 January 1994

- Creation of European Monetary Institute (EMI) to replace Committee of Central Bank Governors and to implement EMU
- Convergence monitored with greater vigour
- Report on progress by ECOFIN on 31 December 1996 detailing EMU membership and timetable

*Stage III*
1 January 1999 (unless otherwise specified)

- Creation of European System of Central Banks (ESCB) comprising the European Central Bank (ECB) and the national Central Banks
- ECB and national banks to become fully independent
- ESCB objective is 'price stability'
- ECU becomes common currency in substitution for national currencies
- Procedures for controlling budget deficits strengthened
- Official foreign exchange reserves to be managed by ECB

---

*Source*: Maastricht Treaty; see extracts in Gros and Thygesen (1992, pp.427–59).

will be increasingly supervised and influenced by a European body in the shape of ECOFIN and its proposed new economic and financial committee. The Treaty is clear that this body will 'formulate a draft for the broad guidelines of the economic policies of the Member States and of the Community, and shall report its findings to the European Council' (Article 103, para.

2). By 1999, the European Central Bank (ECB) would be a major arbiter of British economic policy and prosperity. We have already received a taste of this as British commentators have begun to analyse the activities of the Bundesbank on which the ECB is modelled. Statements from the Bundesbank are now subject to detailed dissection, its slablike Frankfurt headquarters appear on news bulletins, and its President has become an influence over domestic policy. It was Bundesbank views on the desirability of currency realignment, expressed in an indiscreet interview with *Handelsblatt* by its President, Dr Helmut Schlesinger, that provoked the decisive selling surge on Black Wednesday and the decided cooling in Anglo–German relations including unprecedented public recriminations between Schlesinger and Lamont. It was not hard to see why Euro-sceptics in both major parties had strong reservations about Stage III of EMU and about transferring economic sovereignty to such an independent body.

In the short period since Britain entered the EMS we have therefore experienced a transformation in macro-economic policy. Old certainties have evaporated as policy instruments have changed, the theoretical debate has shifted, radical new institutional structures are being constructed and it has become impossible to study British policy in isolation from the wider European picture. If Britain went so far as to join EMU she would become simply a region in a wider economic area. The economic implications of this are far from clear. Prognoses range from low inflation and a competitive revival to regional stagnation and mass unemployment. What is certain is that policy-making has changed with bewildering rapidity, the momentum of European integration has become so considerable that even those nominally in control appear almost the victims of events. The French referendum of 20 September 1992 on Maastricht, with a narrow 51 per cent endorsement, offered some clarity. It allowed European leaders to reaffirm support for the Treaty on the basis of a Franco-German axis which left Britain increasingly isolated in its reluctance to ratify the Treaty. Major faced an almost impossible balancing act in fulfilling the leadership responsibilities of the Presidency of the European Council whilst placating the Euro-sceptics within his own Party.

In this atmosphere of a more hesitant but still determined move towards European economic union Britain's policy choices revolved around three options:

(1)  To remain outside the ERM and curb inflation through a 'traditional' mix of monetary, fiscal and floating exchange rate policy. Although widely regarded as impractical this appeared to be the preference of Norman Lamont who talked (in Parliament on 24 September 1992) of policy 'tailored to the needs of the British economy'.
(2)  To pursue ERM entry as a medium-term goal up to two years away and 'when conditions are right' and to relax policy in the meantime to limit the worst damage from the recession.
(3)  To make a firm commitment to rejoin the ERM as soon as possible at a more realistic parity but with policy attuned to German monetary policy in order to stabilise the currency.

None of these options could be evaluated in purely economic terms, they also involved fundamental foreign policy choices. For the pro-Europeans options (1) and (2) reawakened the nightmare of the late 1980s of a 'two-tier' Europe. A 'franco-mark' zone which embraced the Benelux countries, Austria and Switzerland opened up the prospect of a narrower monetary union which would dominate British economic policy – as the USA dominates Canada – but which would be immune from British influence.

Hence options for macro-economic policy had become entangled with much wider and even emotional issues of policy towards Europe as a whole. But none of this could hide the fact that Britain's weakness within the ERM, its lack of credibility in the financial markets, and its powerless bargaining position with EC finance ministers all derived from the long-standing deterioration in the 'real' economy. It is to these supply-side considerations that we now turn.

## 'Supply-side' Policy in Context

Relative economic decline has provided a sombre backdrop to economic policy-making for the past thirty years (Gamble,

1990). In 1962 British GDP per capita was the fifth highest in the world: in 1992 with a per capita GDP of $16 600 the British economy had grown, individuals were wealthier, but Britain as a nation was now sixteenth in the world league table as the poorest of the 'G7' group of advanced industrial nations. Economic trends of such persistence are clearly very deep-seated and explanations for decline accept a long-term British problem of low productivity obstinately entrenched in the supply-side of the economy.

In their responses to decline governments have seized upon a variety of explanations and policies. In 1979 Thatcher's winning election manifesto declared that 'Our country's relative decline is not inevitable. We in the Conservative party think we can reverse it'. This was a bold claim but the reversal of decline lay at the heart of the Thatcherite 'mission'. The process of making Britain great again involved economic success as well as an assertive foreign policy. In 1987–88 when Nigel Lawson was riding the crest of the economic boom serious observers were suggesting that a century of relative decline had been stemmed. The recession of 1990-92 quickly pricked this bubble of euphoria but if the battle for growth was still being waged the battle for ideological victory had surely been won. The terms of the debate over economic policy had shifted decisively from the left–right confrontation of the 1960s and 1970s towards a new common ground defined by the right and by the market.

Despite the popular attention which it receives, macro-economic policy, with its dramas of interest rate changes and budget strategies, is at best only half the story of economic policy. Fiscal and monetary policy are vitally important with a greater potential for harm than for good but the real, long-term and decisive determinants of economic health lie on the so-called 'supply-side' of the economy. In its common-sense usage the term 'supply-side' refers simply to the supply of goods and services: the type, quantity, quality and price at which they are produced and the responsiveness of production to changes in economic conditions. The focus here is on two simple words: 'international competitiveness'. This ubiquitous phrase encap-sulates one of the most complex, widely analysed yet imper-fectly understood aspects of economic policy (Porter, 1990).

Competitiveness of goods is affected by design, availability, reliability of supply, novelty, status, marketing, financing and a myriad other factors in addition to simple price. Getting this mix of factors right is extraordinarily difficult and is a task in which government can perform only a peripheral role. In the contemporary capitalist world it is companies rather than nations or governments which compete. No other area of policy is more important for government, yet in no other area is it so powerless. Governments can facilitate, cajole, exhort, even subsidise but it is the 'private sector' that competes.

The question of how to achieve international competitiveness is in many countries a question of technical discussion and pragmatic policy choice. In the UK it has provided the central ideological confrontation between Labour and the Conservatives. Labour has historically favoured planning, intervention and public ownership, which is still enshrined in the famous 'Clause IV' of the Party's constitution. In complete contrast, and consistent with their representation of capital rather than labour, the Conservatives have favoured the free market, minimal intervention and limited regulation. The story of the 1980s has been the complete and unambiguous victory of the Conservative prescription as the vision has been converted into reality and a 'new right' exhortation to free market forces has been enshrined in policy initiatives stretching well beyond competitive industry to education and the health service. Thatcherism was about many things, and about style as well as substance, but a good part of the substance of Thatcherism was the implementation of market-based policies within the industrial economy (there is a huge literature on Thatcherite economic policy but see especially Gamble, 1988; Michie, 1992).

Thatcherism transformed the parameters of industrial policy debate. No serious observer could have predicted such profound change not only in policies but also in norms and expectations. The extent of transition can be illustrated by four areas across which a substantial element of cross-party consensus existed prior to 1979. Each of these areas can be summed up in slogans, emotive phrases which were touch-stones of political faith for thirty years. First is the idea of the 'mixed economy', the notion that a benign mix of public and private industries was normal. Privatisation has wholly transformed the picture. With plans to privatise British Rail, British Coal and the Post Office after the 1992 election there is almost literally nothing left to sell. Secondly the idea of 'strategic industries' has similarly been undercut to a substantial extent. Part of the reason for the mixed economy was nationalisation of industries considered vital for the long-term health of the nation: industries such as coal and steel, motor vehicles, computing and aerospace. Not only have many of these industries been privatised, but Conservative governments in the 1980s declared that they were willing to accept the outcome of international market forces which could dictate their shrinkage or collapse. Britain would then simply import rather than produce. In 1985 Nigel Lawson even went so far as to argue that he could tolerate the decline of the entire manufacturing sector if market signals indicated that Britain's future lay with service industries (Wilks, 1987). The practical effect of this stance was to reduce and eliminate the sometimes huge subsidies that went almost as a matter of course to such industries. Thus the budget of the DTI has been reduced to under £1 billion – virtually invisible – and European comparisons in Table 10.4 now show that Britain has one of the lowest levels of industrial subsidy in the EC. The pit closure fiasco at the end of 1992 served to modify, if not wholly transform, the Major government's stance in this regard. It is clear from the energy review that not all industries will now be left to the free play of market forces.

Thirdly, and in a similar vein, Conservative policy has abandoned big prestige projects in research and development. Thus 'scientific leadership' in areas like aerospace (Concorde), atomic research (nuclear reactors), air defence science (missiles) and data processing (computers and chips) is no longer held out as a goal. Instead the emphasis has moved to the encouragement of innovation and information flows, to the commercialisation of science and the incorporation of research into competitive products.

Running through these three areas is a subordination of political to market choice. As we saw above, the Conservative

TABLE 10.4    Annual average state aid to manufacturing:
European comparisons, 1986–88

|  | Million ECU | As per cent of GDP | ECU per person employed [a] |
|---|---|---|---|
| UK | 3 570 | 0.6 | 670 |
| France | 5 664 | 0.7 | 1 250 |
| Germany (West) | 7 639 | 0.8 | 960 |
| Ireland | 408 | 1.6 | 1 950 |
| Italy | 9 563 | 1.5 | 1 900 |
| Spain | 2 930 | 1.2 | 1 210 |
| **Twelve EC countries** | **33 714** | **0.9** | **1 150** |

*Source*: *European Economy* (1991, p.34).

[a] Figures rounded to nearest ten.

interpretation of how the economy works conveyed the
message that government could do little about unemployment. The fourth abandoned totem is therefore 'full employment', although in fairness this was abandoned in practice if
not in name by the Labour Government in 1975. But in
abandoning full employment the Conservatives also pursued
an alternative goal of a free labour market which required
acute limitation of union power and the rejection of the
concept of 'tripartism'. This move away from tripartism
reveals the essence of the new Conservative approach to
economic management and distinguishes the British model
clearly from the practices typical of France, Italy and
especially Germany. Tripartism involved consultation, discussion and compromise between government and the 'two sides'
of industry: capital and labour, the CBI and the TUC. It was a
variant of neocorporatism in that business and union organisation were taken to represent the interests of their members and
were incorporated into governmental decision-making. This
was done quite formally. Agencies such as the Manpower
Services Commission (MSC) – now abolished – were managed
by Boards drawn from unions and business as well as
government. The arrangement met its apogee in the National
Economic Development Council (NEDC) which was created

by the Conservatives in 1962 as a forum for industrial diplomacy. The NEDC included the leaders of business and the unions and seemed to lead a charmed life, continuing to meet throughout the 1980s until its abolition was announced by Norman Lamont in June 1992 (see Chapter 14).

Radical change in the 1980s constituted a move away from traditional certainties but also put in place an alternative set of concepts and slogans chief of which was the idea of the 'enterprise economy'. Much has been written about whether the stress during the Thatcher years on incentives, individualism, materialism and the celebration of 'wealth creation' either provoked or reflected a genuine shift in political culture (Crewe, 1988). The virtues of free competitive markets however had become the orthodoxy. Government policy has become dominated by neoclassical market principles and by the more dynamic market analysis associated with Hayek and Schumpeter. The former dictates that markets and competition should be introduced into hitherto protected areas like financial services, health care, prisons and even the civil service. The latter recognises that entrepreneurs deserve rewards, that monopoly is sometimes proof of success and that regulation must operate sympathetically (see Gamble, 1988; Hahn, 1988; Helm *et al.*, 1991).

In some respects Major distanced himself from Thatcherism, and is regarded as a 'social-market conservative' more at home with the idea of social responsibility and motivated more by instinct than by ideology. But on supply-side policy Major's instincts were wholly to endorse the Thatcherite principles of free choice and market economics, and to adhere to what he called the central economic 'truths' of the 1980s. Thus in the quintessentially Thatcherite forum of the fifteenth anniversary dinner of the Adam Smith Institute, Major told his audience that:

> we have privatised State-owned industries. We have cut taxes. We have liberated businessmen [*sic*] and investors. We have deregulated and opened markets. We have spread wealth and we have spread ownership. We have seen a phenomenal growth in personal pensions and savings.
> There is no going back on this (Major, 1992).

**From 'Pure-market' to 'Social-market'?**

Until the 1992 election, pre-existing policies on privatisation, training, science, small business and so on were simply perpetuated by the Major government and, symbolically, the Thatcherite Peter Lilley was retained at the head of the demoralised DTI. Lilley presided over a Department which had become essentially regulatory, advisory and reactive under a series of ideologically right-wing ministers. Business groups such as the CBI, and business leaders, regularly complained that they could find no sympathetic ear in government and that Lilley was unimpressive, showing no talent or even interest in communicating with industry. Similarly Major was preoccupied with Europe, the poll tax, the health service and the impending election. He gave every indication of being content with the minimalist, hands-off relationship with industry and the 'pure-market' approach.

This groundswell of industrial discontent is illustrative of one of the curiosities of Conservatism which became particularly marked under Thatcherism. Although widely perceived as the 'party of capital' Conservatives have an uneasy relationship with big manufacturing companies, marked by suspicion and mutual incomprehension. The Conservative Party is much more at ease with the City and Thatcherism was orientated towards small business and the individual entrepreneur. Partly as a result 'big business' in Britain is politically weak (Leys, 1985) and the CBI projects a hesitant voice which is often ignored by Conservative ministers (Grant, 1993). Nonetheless business, in Belloc's lines, which Macmillan liked to quote, 'always keeps a hold of nurse, for fear of finding something worse'. A pre-election survey of 235 Board-level executives from Britain's top 500 companies found that 80 per cent thought Labour policies would harm their companies (*Financial Times*, 16 March 1992). Business criticism of the government was muted for fear of giving Labour electoral ammunition, and for the first time in an election campaign the CBI abandoned its political neutrality to endorse the Conservative Party.

One important area of concern which became open criticism after the Conservatives had safely won the April 1992 election concerned competition policy and regulation. The processes of liberalisation and privatisation had produced an unprecedented level of freedom and exposure to market forces but also allowed companies to take perhaps too much advantage of legislative relaxation. Massive financial frauds by the BCCI managers and by Robert Maxwell; operation of restrictive practices by brewers and motor retailers; and exploitation of monopoly power by privatised utilities such as BT and the electricity generators: all these caused concern. The inevitable response was an increase in regulation.

Regulation involves the development of consistent rules either through legislation or agreement (self-regulation) which establishes clear parameters within which free competitive activity can take place. From an economic point of view regulation involves counteracting market failures, especially monopoly and restrictive practices. From a legal perspective it ensures honest and ethical behaviour. From a new right 'public-choice' perspective, however, it implies a lobbying process whereby companies secure advantageous restrictions which help them avoid competition. The neoliberal wing of the Conservative party has always been most suspicious of any extension of regulatory activity (Veljanovski, 1990). Of course regulation is a complex and subtle process which is used to secure a whole range of goals from environmental protection to equal rights. What most concerned business in the post-privatisation world of private monopolies was the abuse of monopoly power.

The established agencies of competition policy and monopoly control are the OFT (Office of Fair Trading) and the MMC (Monopolies and Mergers Commission). They became more prominent and active during the 1980s as did the EC agency Directorate-General IV (DG IV) which, under Commissioner Sir Leon Brittan, became active in controlling restrictive practices, state aids and the largest mergers. To these have been added a new tier of special-purpose competition agencies which combine administrative and quasi-judicial functions. The most significant are OFTEL (1984), OFGAS (1986), OFWAT (1989) and OFFER (1990) (see Chapter 9). These agencies monitor and regulate price, profit, consumer satisfaction, quality of service, limits on competition and so on.

Every move and statement of their Director-Generals, such as Professor Stephen Littlechild of OFFER, is scrutinised and analysed with as much care as if they were ministers. Share prices move and corporate strategies are amended in response to their opinions. Professor Littlechild is lobbied intensively by industrial users to reduce bulk energy tariffs, by Age Concern to protect pensioners in the winter and by PowerGen to recognise the high costs of generating electricity from British coal. This is a new breed of 'industrial statesmen' whose regulative powers also provide latent powers to pursue an industrial policy. Whether such a policy will materialise lies in the hands of the Secretary of State.

## Prospects for an Industrial Policy

The appointment of Michael Heseltine as Secretary of State for Trade and Industry in April 1992 marked a significant change in industrial policy. For most of his predecessors since Sir Keith Joseph in 1979 the very words 'industrial policy', and certainly 'industrial strategy', were an irrelevance and a delusion. The task of government was to create and sustain a free competitive market – nationally, internationally and within every specialised area of the economy. The behaviour of individuals and companies within those markets, and the outcomes in terms of profits, market share and growth were no concern of government. Any attempt to 'intervene', to be selective or to 'pick winners' was by definition counter-productive. The logical extension of this argument was that the DTI itself was redundant. Indeed, Sir Keith and several of his successors actually advocated its abolition. It became a Cinderella Department with decimated budgets, minimal prestige, demoralised staff and a series of disastrous ministerial appointments which included eleven Secretaries of State over 13 years and such ideologues as Sir Keith Joseph, Cecil Parkinson, Norman Tebbit, David Young and Nicholas Ridley. This extreme application of neoliberal doctrine was widely regarded as destructive, and was certainly at odds with the traditions and practices of Britain's major foreign competitors (see Marquand, 1988). In a modern industrialised economy in which government affects competitive performance in a myriad ways on a daily basis, civil servants struggled to be helpful and positive in the face of ministerial scepticism.

Heseltine took little trouble to hide his impatience with the doctrinal intransigence of the libertarian wing of the Conservative Party. In 1986, after his dramatic Westland resignation, he wrote a thoughtful and well-received book which outlined a manifesto for an active industrial policy. He declared that 'the prime immediate need is for the Conservatives to formulate a national strategy for industry' and included ideas which were anathema to the Thatcherites. Government, he said, 'cannot pretend that it is not involved in decisions about the future of key "platforms" of industry . . . There are industries, such as the steel industry, the car industry and the airframe industry which cannot be allowed to fail if Britain is to remain an advanced economy' (Heseltine, 1987, pp.5, 111). His views were wholly compatible with the 'social market' approach of pragmatic policy typical of Germany. Heseltine's views were carefully thought through and deeply held. It was clear that having been denied the prize of the party leadership, the Industry portfolio was the best consolation prize.

No minister holding such views would have been appointed to the DTI under Thatcher. Heseltine's appointment therefore created expectations that he would refashion government relations with industry and mobilise government to enhance industrial competitiveness in a systematic fashion. The appointment was seen as a personal boost for the DTI and he received a warm welcome at No. 123 Victoria Street. In an act typical of his taste for theatre he resurrected the traditional title of President of the Board of Trade which allowed his officials to refer to him as 'the President'. Certainly President Heseltine was relatively unfettered by manifesto commitments. The Conservative election manifesto had promised little change with more deregulation and modest changes to encourage training and research. The most tangible items were commitments to privatise coal and rail and to make some minor reorganisation in government.

Heseltine therefore took over a DTI significantly strengthened by the abolition of the Department of Energy and the shifting of its responsibilities to the DTI; by the acquisition of responsibility for small firms from the Department of Employment and also a more formalised responsibility to liaise with TECs over training. In compensation the DTI lost responsibility for investment regulation including the SIB (Securities and Investment Board) and regulation of investment management, brokers, unit trusts and the bulk of City activities. Partly to conform to European practices, and partly in recognition of DTI shortcomings in respect of scandals such as Barlow Clowes, BCCI and Maxwell, these powers were transferred to the Treasury even though reservations about split responsibilities were expressed by several City bodies. Elsewhere in Whitehall a very significant development lay in the naming of William Waldegrave, the Chancellor of the Duchy of Lancaster, as Minister for Science, the first time since 1964 that this had been a formal Cabinet portfolio. This promised a greater salience for the promotion of innovation and R&D in conjunction with the DTI.

The early days of the new government saw two important organisational changes in respect of industrial policy. In June 1992 the Chancellor, Norman Lamont, announced the abolition of the NEDC and its associated secretariat. Although there was much surprise at this move which John Smith described as an act of 'industrial vandalism', the NEDC had become totally marginalised and its formal abolition was of largely symbolic significance (for a history see Middlemas, 1988). The NEDC represented the last vestige of indicative planning, interventionism and tripartism; its abolition could be seen as clearing the way for a more activist and interventionist role by the DTI itself to which several NEDO staff, including the Director-General, transferred. In July Heseltine announced a fundamental reorganisation of the DTI which consigned to the garbage can the candyfloss organisation and title of Lord Young's 'Department of Enterprise' and instead returned to traditional principles of industrial sponsorship and sectoral organisation. DTI officials are once again being required to open 'an informed dialogue and a constructive partnership' with industry and to 'relate more closely to individual sectors of industry'. All the signs are that Heseltine is anxious to give substance to his newly enunciated goal to 'help British companies to win' (Heseltine, 1992), a goal that won immediate support from Howard Davies, the new Director-General of the CBI. However, critics wondered whether he had the resources, political support and administrative capability to make that goal attainable.

As the debate over supply-side policies develops over the mid-1990s three areas of conflict will be decisive. The first is the classic battleground of British economic policy between the Treasury and the DTI. As the powerhouse of British administration with responsibility for macro-economic policy and public spending the Treasury has consistently over-ruled and out-manoeuvred the Industry Department. It dislikes the possible spending implications of industrial support, whether they be for vocational training or research costs written-off against corporation tax. Equally it has consistently resisted adjusting macro-economic policy instruments, especially interest rates and exchange rates, to cater to the needs of manufacturing.

The second battleground is the minefield of interdepartmental coordination embodied in the Cabinet committee system. An industrial policy demands cooperation from a range of other ministries such as Employment, Defence, the Foreign Office and the regional (Scottish, Welsh and Northern Ireland) Offices. Above all it needs the personal support of the Prime Minister. It is significant that Heseltine does not chair any of the key Cabinet committees announced under the 'open government' initiative (see Chapter 8).

The third battleground is relations with the European Commission. Whole swathes of domestic policy are now dominated or influenced by European policies and directives. This is especially marked in the field of industrial policy where European programmes on regional policy, science and technology, competition and merger policy, state aids, public purchasing, workers' rights, indirect taxation and the whole 'social charter' provide strict limits on room for manoeuvre. European priorities will not necessarily conflict with domestic preferences and the 1992 programme of completion of the Single Market is strongly supported by the government. Nonetheless a complex, subtle and often acrimonious process of consultation and compromise with the Commission will mark any attempt to develop a more active industrial policy.

## Supply-side Policy from the Bottom of the Cliff

Many of the supply-side policies pursued during the 1980s may well have been overdue and have prepared British industry for a more successful and competitive future. This could particularly be said of the reform of industrial relations, the restoration of incentives, the privatisation of commercial industries and the elimination of industrial subsidies. There remains much to be done. Policy on R&D is a mess and British research spending actually declined during the 1980s. Similarly there is a very long way to go on training and the TECs are stumbling from crisis to crisis. In other areas like environmental protection and sympathetic regulation the government's stance is inadequate. The timebomb for the 1990s, however, is the contraction in British manufacturing and the trade deficit in manufactured goods.

British industry has suffered a remorseless relative decline over the post-war period with a steady loss in share of exports and an increase in imports (for an excellent polemic see Pollard, 1984). The apotheosis of this problem came in 1983 when, for the first time since the industrial revolution, British trade in manufactured products went into deficit. At the time this caused considerable excitement and agonising but the financial implications were hidden by windfall gains made from North Sea oil. Britain has been extraordinarily fortunate in having this external constraint alleviated by oil exports and it is doubtful whether the benefits have been used wisely. In any event, as North Sea output begins a slow decline the debate on manufacturing trade gains a new urgency.

## Conclusion

The 1992 Conservative manifesto (p.9) argued that 'a vigorous manufacturing sector is essential to a healthy British economy'. By 1992 manufacturing employment had shrunk by a third since 1979 to 21 per cent of the workforce and the UK was running a huge visible trade deficit even in the depths of recession (when it might be expected to move into surplus). It was feared that any resumption of growth would suck in imports, generate a currency crisis, necessitate domestic deflation and choke off growth. This is exactly the policy problem that had dogged British governments since 1945 and it is these brutal realities of the 'economic fundamentals' that lay behind the debate over the over-valuation of the pound within the ERM and the events of Black Wednesday. These spectacular currency crises are epiphenomena, important in their own right but not nearly as important as the essential facts of industrial performance and institutional weakness which underlie them.

# 11

# Social Policy

**CHRIS PIERSON**

With the return of a Conservative government at the 1992 general election, it has been suggested that real change in British politics came from within the Conservative Party, with the replacement of Margaret Thatcher by John Major in the autumn of 1990. It has also been argued that, after the turmoil of the Thatcher years, there is now a 'new consensus' emerging amongst the major parties about the future conduct of social policy and about the broad parameters of the welfare state. In fact, social policy in the 1990s is a strange amalgam of both continuity and change, with elements of a 'new consensus' set beside unresolved disputes and long-standing problems.

## The 1990s: 'A New Era for Social Policy'?

Formally, at least, there is a marked continuity between present Conservative social policy and that of the last Thatcher government. Glennerster *et al.* (1991, p.389), write of the period between 1988 and 1990 under Thatcher seeing 'the most decisive break in British social policy since the period between 1944 and 1948', the years in which the modern British welfare state was created. As well as implementation of the government's Social Security Act 1986, these years witnessed the passage of the Education Reform Act 1988, the Housing Act 1988, the National Health Service and Community Care Act 1990 and the implementation of wholesale reform of the NHS following the publication of the White Paper *Working for Patients* in January 1989 (Department of Health, 1989a). The

246

current policy climate is set by the contested process of putting these reforms into practice. It will be some time (probably several years) before we can come to a measured judgement of their consequences. Attention here is focused upon the intended nature of the changes, the rationale that underlies them and an interim assessment of their likely consequences for British social policy.

## Education

The Education Reform Act 1988 has been described as 'the most important and far-reaching piece of educational law-making for England and Wales since the Education Act of 1944' (Maclure, 1989, p.v). It provided for the following changes:

(1) Inauguration of a *national curriculum* for all maintained schools.
(2) A policy of *open enrolment* under which parents are free to choose schools for their children.
(3) Under the *local management of schools*, responsibility for the running of schools is transferred from Local Education Authorities to schools' own governing bodies.
(4) All secondary schools and larger primary schools may seek to *opt-out* of local authority control and become grant-maintained schools, directly funded by central government.
(5) New funding and planning arrangements are established for both universities and polytechnics.
(6) Provision is made for the establishment of *City Technology Colleges*.
(7) The Inner London Education Authority (ILEA) is abolished.

This process of reform was further developed in the government's 1992 White Paper *Choice and Diversity* which, as well as changing aspects of the national curriculum and encouraging 'specialisation' within particular schools, sought to hasten the move towards a system of 'decentralised' grant-maintained schools, by simplifying the process of opting-out and transferring further powers from local authorities to a new regional Funding Agency for Schools (Department for Education, 1992).

*Education Reformed*

The government's educational reforms were greeted by both its admirers and its critics as a radical innovation. The government insisted that educational standards could be raised by increasing parental *choice* and encouraging inter-school *competition*, while at the same time centralising control of the school *curriculum*. Its intention was to marginalise the influence of local government (which had previously taken much of the responsibility for running the education system through local education authorities) and the power of teachers, their unions and the 'educational establishment', which the government held to be largely responsible for a long-term decline in educational standards. The ambition is to establish a system of opted-out, self-managed schools, directly funded by government, operating their own selection criteria and competing with other schools for student numbers. The best (and most popular) schools will be able to expand, while competition will encourage the less successful schools to improve their performance and make themselves more attractive to parents. Increased competition is also to be the watchword of reform in higher education, with funding reflecting the capacity of institutions to attract students and their ability to provide courses at lowest cost.

Critics of the government's reform have very serious reservations about its outcomes. Many fear the centralisation of power represented by the Secretary of State's control over the national curriculum. Others condemn the loss of democratic control and the capacity for effective localised planning which the marginalisation of local authorities entails. A number of commentators insist that the nation's educational 'under-performance' (if it really exists) is not attributable to poor teaching methods or poor management systems, but much more directly to inadequate resources. They fear that the mechanisms of competition and selection will further concentrate cultural and financial resources in the hands of middle-class parents and their children and will precipitate a (still) less equitable and egalitarian educational system. Any lingering sense of public education as part of a shared citizenship will be lost in the process.

It is still very early to judge the outcome of the government's reforms. Yet the introduction of local management has already had a substantial impact upon the ways in which schools are run, as has the implementation of the national curriculum following closely upon the latest phase of reorganisation of the examination system. In the short term, there is evidence of the sort of unanticipated and perverse outcomes which attend most policy innovations. Difficulties in establishing the content of the national curriculum and the disputes that have arisen in several schools between headteachers and newly-empowered governors (most notoriously in the borough of Stratford in east London), suggest that the government's aspiration for educational 'decentralisation' may well be frustrated by the repeated need for ministerial intervention. A 1992 OECD Report which found that in the late 1980s Britain was spending less on education than almost any other developed country suggests that there may be some merit in the suggestion that Britain's educational problems are a result of under-funding (OECD, 1992). In the longer term and more generally, given that too great an emphasis upon equality was seen as one of the weaknesses of the old system, it is not perhaps unreasonable to suppose that the reforms are likely to widen the inequality of educational outcomes. Here as elsewhere in the reform process, it may be that more efficiency will mean less equity.

*Health*

In the late 1980s, the government embarked upon a still more controversial and high-risk strategy of reform in public health care. The National Health Service (NHS) had been at the heart of the welfare consensus before 1979 and even after 1983 Conservative ministers were anxious to stress that the NHS was 'safe in their hands'. However, while the *principle* of public health care free at the point of use and funded from general taxation remained very popular, by 1987 there was evidence of growing dissatisfaction with the general *performance* of the NHS

(Bosanquet, 1988). In a context in which the government had increased funding for the NHS in real terms by nearly 30 per cent between 1979 and 1987, it found itself criticised for persistently under-funding public health care. The government determined that a better use of the very substantial resources devoted to health care (estimated at £25.7 billion for 1990–91) could be secured by a wholesale reorganisation of the internal workings of the NHS. After a rather faltering review process, the government's reform proposals emerged in the White Paper *Working for Patients* in 1989. It stipulated the following changes:

(1) *Delegation of decision-making* to district, hospital or individual GP level.
(2) Hospitals and other units may seek to opt-out of local health authority control and acquire *self-governing trust status*. Trusts have the freedom to sell their services to other health authorities, to budget-holding GPs and to the private sector. They may establish their own management structures and determine their own terms and conditions of employment.
(3) *Health authorities are free to buy services* from within their own area, from other health authority areas, from opted-out hospitals and from the private sector.
(4) *GP fundholding*: larger general practices will have their own budgets.
(5) *GPs contracts are redrafted* to give greater financial incentives, to stipulate certain statutory requirements and to limit the prescription of certain drugs.
(6) *Reform of the NHS along more business/managerial lines.*
(7) *Greater auditing* of quality and value for money.
(8) Encouragement of *greater cooperation with the private sector.*

As with education, so in the health service, the government's reforms concentrate upon dividing the *purchasers* of health services from the *providers* of those services. While retaining a commitment that 'NHS services are available to all, paid for mainly out of general taxation; and mostly free at the point of use', the government look to the introduction of competition and choice to deliver more effective care without a major increase in the level of resources devoted to health care. The remit is to make the health service more responsive to the consumer (the patient or, more normally, the patient's surrogate, i.e., the GP or the health authority as purchaser). As with opting-out under the education reforms, the government has encouraged the expansion of trust status and argued that 'in time, Trust status will become the natural organisational model for units providing patient care' (NHS Management Executive, 1990, p.3).

## Health Reformed

Since their inception, the government's health reforms have come under sustained attack. Labour's contention that the Conservatives intended to 'privatise' the health service was bitterly contested throughout the period preceding the 1992 general election and health policy provoked some of the bitterest exchanges of the election campaign itself. The government also faced opposition from the main health service unions and professional associations, including a high-profile campaign by the doctors' organisation, the British Medical Association (BMA). It was argued that the government's reforms would eliminate effective national and local planning and accountability, replacing this with a surfeit of over-mighty managers. It was insisted that the reforms drew attention away from the *real* problem which beset the NHS, which was not its maladministration, but its persistent under-funding. Some argued that the new contractual arrangements would set up perverse incentive structures, encouraging GPs to avoid taking onto their lists the most costly (and medically needy) patients, or denying patients in some areas ready access to certain forms of NHS treatment (for example, dental services). From the BMA came the objection that under the new arrangements commercial criteria might interfere with doctors' clinical judgement, while the Labour Party made much of the emergence of a 'two-tier' health service and of the possibility that eventually the government might break up the NHS. All of these claims were fiercely resisted by the government.

As with the education reforms, there was some hesitation in responding to the government's initiative before the general election, but the Conservatives' electoral victory should mean that by the middle of 1993 two-thirds of NHS hospital and community units will be organised as trusts (*Scotsman*, October 1992). Under these circumstances, it is too soon to make any reasoned judgement about the overall outcome of the government's reforms. Such piecemeal evidence as has become available is highly selective and politically contentious. For example, government figures released shortly *before* the election showed a very substantial fall in the number of those waiting more than a year for an operation, whilst statistics published *after* the election showed that those waiting up to a year for an operation (who made up some 90 per cent of the waiting population) had increased by 7 per cent (*Guardian*, May 1992). There is evidence that some of the earliest and most prestigious hospital trusts (including Guy's Hospital in London), soon found themselves facing acute financial difficulties. In some areas, it appeared that the patients of budget-holding GPs were receiving preferential access to hospital treatment and the buying and selling of services across health authority boundaries has had some perverse outcomes in terms of meeting the clinical needs of patients. In the wealthier parts of the south of England, substantial numbers of dentists under the new contract 'opted out' of the provision of NHS treatment and in the summer of 1992 members of the British Dental Association (BDA), in dispute with the government over payments, balloted against the registration of new NHS patients. By contrast, the government's own first review of the NHS reforms suggested that more patients were being treated, waiting lists were falling and that patients endorsed the new trust organisation of hospitals (NHS Management Executive, 1991).

At this early stage in the working through of the reform process, three comments seem in order. First, in comparison with other developed states, Britain devotes a low proportion of its GDP to health care and at an unusually low administrative cost. In 1985, Britain devoted 6.1 per cent of GDP to health, compared with 10.7 per cent in the USA and an OECD average of 7.3 per cent. Of this expenditure, as little as 3 per cent was officially attributed to administrative costs in the pre-reform NHS (Le Grand *et al.*, 1990, p.99). However much efficiency the government's reforms may inject into the system, it is difficult to see that they can redress problems that arise from wholesale under-spending on health care. Secondly, it has long been recognised that ill health has a social class and regional component (with higher rates of mortality and morbidity amongst manual workers and their families and in the less prosperous regions of the country), and that middle-class patients have often been better able to gain access to the resources that the health service provides (Goodin and Le Grand, 1987). There has apparently been some success in addressing this inequality over the past twenty years through the national redistribution of health service spending (Le Grand *et al.*, 1990). Given the devolution of decision-making and the government's over-riding concern with efficiency in the reform process, it is not clear that the trend towards greater equity in health care can be sustained. Thirdly, it is notoriously difficult to measure health outcomes (though some advances in this area have been made by health economists over the past decade). The government's reforms and particularly its measures for medical audit are meant to get past the barrier of simply measuring *inputs* (how much money is spent on health care) and to look at *outcomes* (how many patients are treated for what conditions and at what cost). Yet such data is still a surrogate for what we really want to measure, which is any improvement in the nation's health and well-being. There is still a suspicion that the NHS is primarily a national *medical* service rather than an integrated service for the promotion and maintenance of good health. Given that so much of the improvement in the nation's health over the last century has been gained through the improved diet, better housing and improved working conditions atten-dant upon economic growth, it may be that the most important contribution that the government could make to improving the nation's health is to address the problems of poverty and mass unemployment. Whilst the government's 1992 White Paper *The Health of the Nation* recognised the importance of preventative measures and the impact of 'lifestyle' upon peoples' well-being, there was little real attempt to address these aspects of the social aetiology of public health (Department of Health, 1992).

*Housing*

Housing is a particularly instructive area of government social policy, since the break with the prevailing order dates not from the late 1980s but from the earliest days of the first Thatcher government. We may thus consider the consequences of policy change over a much longer period. Housing is also exceptional in that it is the one area of social expenditure where the government has achieved a real cut over the past decade. In real terms, the government's housing budget is now less than one half of what it was in 1979 (HM Treasury, 1991). As we shall see, this does not, however, necessarily reflect a net saving of housing costs to the public exchequer.

Since 1979, Conservative housing policy has pursued the complementary ambitions of promoting owner-occupation as the preferred form of tenure and minimising the role of local authorities in the provision of housing. In line with this policy, the Housing Act 1980 gave local authority tenants the 'Right to Buy' their properties at substantial discounts and during the 1980s almost 1.5 million local authority and new towns, properties were sold to their occupiers. The 1980 Act also changed the mechanism under which central government provides funds for local authority housing, effectively obliging councils to raise the general level of their rents. As general subsidies to local government fell and rents increased, the main burden of subsidising housing costs has fallen upon the means-tested Housing Benefit (which rose to £5.3 billion by 1990–91). The government also sought to revive the privately-rented sector which, while accounting for some 90 per cent of all households in 1900, had subsequently fallen to little more than 10 per cent (CSO, 1991; HM Treasury, 1991.)

These policy intentions were reinforced under the government's 1988 Housing Act. This had four main elements:

(1) A further attempt was made to *encourage the private rented sector*, with rent deregulation and tax concessions.
(2) Local authority tenants were encouraged to exercise a '*tenant's choice*' to enable them to transfer the ownership and management of their estates to a private landlord or housing association.

(3) The government was given powers to create *Housing Action Trusts* (HATs) which would take over and manage on behalf of central government (particularly difficult) local authority estates.

(4) The act legislated further central government control over local authority housing and identified *Housing Associations* as the preferred form of 'social' housing (see Glennerster *et al.*, 1991, pp.398–403).

The outcome of this latest range of reforms is as yet unclear. Given the current regime for owner-occupiers and the further fall in the privately-rented sector to about 7 per cent of households by 1990, it is to be doubted whether the government can induce a major expansion of the private-rental sector. Despite voting arrangements which are heavily weighted in favour of a change of status, tenants have shown remarkably little interest in a transfer away from local authority control or in favour of HATs. By 1990, housing associations accounted for about 3 per cent of all households, and the government hopes to see an expansion of about 40 000 homes per annum in this sector from 1992–93. However, the new financial regime is likely to see a steep rise in housing association rents, perhaps reaching twice the level of local council rents and it is not clear that housing associations will be able fully to meet the remit for social housing that the government has in mind (Duke of Edinburgh, 1991).

Certainly, the government's principal aspiration to expand owner-occupation has largely been realised in the course of the 1980s. Owner-occupation, which accounted for 55.3 per cent of households in 1979, had risen to 67.6 per cent in 1990 (Council of Mortgage Lenders, 1991). Owner-occupation is seemingly in tune with the Conservative themes of self-reliance and independence from the state in the welfare area and certainly it receives very little in the way of direct subsidies from government. But owners do benefit from a very favourable tax regime. Mortgage holders enjoy income tax relief on mortgages up to £30 000, a net cost to the public exchequer of £7.8 billion in 1990–91. Owner-occupiers pay no tax on 'the imputed rent' of their home (the value of living in their own house), nor do they pay tax on capital gains in the value of their property. At the same time, there is evidence that as the public sector has shrunk (and the most desirable public properties have been sold off under the 'Right to Buy' legislation), so it has come to constitute a residual housing sector confined to those who are unable to take advantage of the inducements offered to take up owner-occupation (Hills and Mullings, 1990).

In the early 1980s, this was, at least electorally, an extremely successful policy. It is suggested that many of the skilled manual workers whose shift to the Conservatives had helped them to win the election of 1979 were the principal beneficiaries of discounted council house sales and that this helped to cement their support for the Conservative party. In the housing boom of the late 1980s, especially in the Tory heartlands of the south of England, owners made huge capital gains as house prices raced ahead of general inflation. At the same time, the 1980s saw an unparalleled rise in homelessness, with the figure doubling in England between 1978 and 1986. Given the decline in the public sector housing stock, there was a still steeper rise in the numbers of households in temporary accommodation, often in extremely unsatisfactory bed and breakfast establishments.

In the early 1990s, the position for owner-occupiers looked much less rosy. In a context of rising unemployment and consistently high real interest rates, many mortgage holders faced increasing difficulties in servicing their debt. Repossessions of houses by building societies and banks rose from an annual figure of 3 480 in 1980 to 36 607 in the first half of 1991 alone. At the same time, real house prices, which had already fallen substantially from their highest point in 1988, fell by a further 6 per cent in the year to May 1992. Both of these processes were most pronounced in the Conservatives' electoral heartland of the south of England, where the fall in the year prior to the General Election was widely in excess of 8 per cent (Halifax Building Society, 1992). Any initial recovery in the housing market may be stalled by the very large overhang of properties – said to be worth some £8 billion – which the building societies have not yet repossessed because of dire market conditions.

The experience of Conservative housing policy is peculiarly instructive. First, it is clear that the Conservatives have had considerable success in curtailing the role of local authorities and in shifting the balance between owner-occupation and the public-rented sector. One consequence was the increasing residualisation of public sector housing, which increasingly became a second-choice form of tenure for those who could not afford the preferred form of owner-occupation. However, this is not the whole story and the housing experience illustrates a number of more general points about social policy and its political consequences. First, it is extremely difficult to reduce the social expenditure budget. The housing budget is the one area in which the government has made real cuts in the 1980s. Yet, the withdrawal of funds to local authority housing has probably been matched by the increasing costs of Housing Benefit (an element of the Social Security Budget) and by tax expenditures on income tax relief on mortgages. What is involved is a *redistribution* of costs and benefits rather than a large net saving of public funds. Secondly, the housing experience gives evidence of the *inter-connectedness* of social policy with other areas of government activity. Britain has an unusually high level of home-ownership and an unusual amount of the nation's (and most individuals') wealth is tied up in the housing stock. The housing market thus has an unusually powerful effect upon the general well-being of the national economy. The depression of the housing market in the early 1990s posed acute economic and political difficulties for the government. Its desire to expand the economy in the run-up to the 1992 election was constrained, not only by the new discipline of the ERM, but also by the depressed state of the housing market and consumer spending. The perverse consequence of the increased concentration upon home-ownership and the boom of the late 1980s was to make it extremely difficult to revive the economy in the early 1990s. That the Conservatives, under the weight of all these disadvantages, were still able to secure a fourth consecutive electoral victory tells us something remarkable about the nature of the British electorate. It also points us towards an important and more general conclusion about the nature of the welfare state. While popular sentiment may still see the welfare state as an expression of society's benevolent attitude to the less privileged, this is a quite inadequate account of its (near-universal) emergence in market-based societies. The welfare state exists in part to provide those public goods which markets cannot deliver or where market provision will have perverse outcomes. A more balanced tenure structure (similar to that of many of our European neighbours) may actually deliver *efficiency* gains in terms of overall economic performance.

## Continuity and Change in British Social Policy: the 1990s

We are now in a better position to make an overall evaluation of the recent past and the immediate future of British social policy. First, given the radical intentions of the Conservatives after 1979 and the burst of legislative activity in the late 1980s, it is as well to stress the elements of long-term *continuity* in welfare policy. While the growth of spending has indeed been restrained throughout the 1980s (a process which had already begun under the 1974–79 Labour government), social spending has proven to be remarkably resilient. In real terms it has risen by more than 20 per cent since 1979. Much of this increase has been required simply to meet the costs of rising and permanent mass unemployment and it certainly does not mean that there has been a matching improvement in the living conditions of those who are primarily dependent upon the state for an income. Nonetheless, wholesale cuts in social expenditure have been avoided. Secondly, despite the government's enthusiasm for 'targeting' benefits, the state continues to be a provider of health, education and retirement pensions to a mass public. Undoubtedly there has been some residualisation of public provision over the past decade, but this has been concentrated upon those who were already worst off, for example, those on state income support and in public sector housing. This pattern of resources rather more generously directed towards the 'mass' welfare state, with retrenchment concentrated in the 'minority' or stigmatised areas (such as unemployment benefit and one-parent benefit) is not especially new.

There have however been significant changes, above all in the pattern of service delivery. The unifying themes of the reforms initiated in the late 1980s were the government's determination to divide welfare purchasers from welfare providers, the encouragement of private provision, the wish to relocate welfare 'within the community' and (wherever possible) the marginalisation of local government. This has led both to a *devolution* of day-to-day authority into the hands of local managers and a *concentration* of formal powers in the hands of central government (as, for example, in the provisions of the Education Reform Act and in the centralisation of financial control over public sector housing). At the same time, there has been an expansion of 'private' (though often publicly-subsidised) welfare for those who can afford it. There has thus been an enhancement of personal pension rights and private health care for those in secure and well-paid full-time employment.

For some commentators, these changes presage a wholesale dismemberment of the welfare state in the 1990s. They anticipate a process of residualisation throughout the welfare state as those who can afford private provision opt-out of state-provided services and consequently become more reluctant to pay the taxes to support them. This is reflected in the view that we are becoming a 'Two-Thirds, One-Third' society, in which that third of the population excluded from the welfare-generating world of full-time permanent work and dependent upon state support (particularly women, ethnic minorities and one-parent families) fall ever further behind the standards of living enjoyed by 'mainstream' society.

Certainly, there is the possibility of reaching a watershed of 'mainstream' defection from public welfare which might move Britain towards an 'Americanised' residual welfare state. But there are some countervailing pressures. First, the expansion of private welfare is easily over-stated. The rapid growth in private health insurance (often as an occupational benefit funded by employers) has slowed and the private insurers face actuarial difficulties in extending their cover into a wider population which is both more prone to illness and less able to meet the rising costs of insurance. Again, while the numbers in private education have risen, this represents a long-term post-war trend and the overall numbers are still low. The character of public health care and education may be changed by the government's recent reforms, but the great majority of the population (some 90 per cent) still rely upon the public health and education services. Secondly, members of the middle class, who might be thought the most likely to defect from public services, actually do rather well out of the welfare state. Spending on higher education, for example, tends to redistribute wealth *upwards* since the student population is disproportionately middle class. Similarly, the extension of owner-occupation continues a long-term post-war trend and if we define the welfare state broadly enough to include fiscal policy, we see that owner-occupation is subject to a very substantial public subsidy (of about £8 billion in 1990–91). Fourthly, opinion polls indicate a high, indeed a rising level of support for the welfare state across all social classes. In the 1990 British Social Attitudes survey, 56 per cent of voters favoured the option of increasing taxes to spend more on health, education and social benefits (compared with a figure of 32 per cent in 1983). The survey revealed a long-standing preference for increased spending on the mass-consumed (and most expensive) services (health, education and pensions), and a lower level of support for social security benefits, which were seen to be directed towards a 'less deserving' minority (Taylor-Gooby, 1990). Whilst some doubt has been cast upon the salience of these figures, there is little evidence of a wholesale shift in public opinion away from state-funded welfare services. Finally, if the government were to succeed in delivering a more cost-effective, consumer-responsive (though less equitable and less egalitarian) service, we might expect not so much a wholesale residualisation of public welfare as a further bifurcation of the welfare state, in which the mass services enjoyed whatever improvements in funding were available, while the position of those poorest and most dependent upon the state declined further.

## The Continuing Failures of British Social Policy

This brings us to the continuing *failures* of the British welfare system. Since 1979, Conservative social policy has been predicated upon reversing the failures it associated with the previous period of broadly social democratic government. Yet, after more than a decade of Conservative government, it is not clear that their social policy objectives have been any more effectively secured. The replacement of the 'nanny state' with the 'enterprise state' was supposed to unleash entrepreneurial skills, to galvanise investment and to transform the supply-side of the British economy. Yet, despite the undoubted economic and labour market changes of the 1980s, in the early 1990s many of the problems of the British economy look singularly untransformed. But perhaps the most culpable failure of British social policy is its inability to address the problem of poverty. This seems even more blameworthy under a regime which abandons the universal or 'citizenship' model of the welfare state in favour of 'targeting' help where it is most needed. Given the limited aspirations of a residual social policy, it should at least not worsen the position of the poor. Defining and measuring poverty is inherently controversial. Nonetheless, it seems clear that the position of the poor in Britain has indeed worsened over the past ten years. Barr and Coulter, in an extremely careful and measured analysis of the 1980s, insist that 'whatever the poverty line used, the number of poor individuals and families rose substantially . . . the number of individuals in poor households rose from 5.1 million [1979] . . . to 9.4 million in 1985' (Barr and Coulter, 1990, p.333). Poverty was especially concentrated amongst single pensioners and single parents, groups which are disproportionately female. In this most basic area of income maintenance, the welfare state has probably failed women more comprehensively than any other group.

## Policy Challenges in the 1990s

We may expect the development of social policy in the early 1990s to be shaped by the working through of the government's major public service reforms in circumstances of continuing financial stringency. But the context will also be set by a range of new or continuing long-term developments which are likely to place a substantial strain upon the social policy apparatus, especially upon the welfare state budget.

(1) *The Europeanisation of social policy*: If Britain is to become more closely integrated within the legal and economic ambit of European institutions (as still seems likely though not certain), European law on social policy and European Court rulings on British government practice are likely to have an increasing effect upon policy outcomes. Throughout the 1980s and into the 1990s, the British government has sought to avoid the enactment of European-wide reform of welfare policy and the labour market (the Social Charter, the Social Action Programme, the 'social chapter' of the Maastricht agreement). This will become increasingly difficult if integration progresses through the 1990s. Since European social policy is generally more comprehensive and more generous than UK provisions and, in particular, since it gives much more extensive rights to workers, it will represent a very real challenge for any government that seeks to continue the policies of the Thatcher and Major administrations.

(2) *An ageing population*: Britain, in common with other advanced industrial states, is an ageing society. Some have argued that the welfare state, which is substantially a system of support for the elderly, will break down in the twenty-first century as the rising costs of supporting a growing elderly population fall upon a diminishing proportion of wage-earners. It is likely that this 'problem' has been over-stated. Nonetheless, an ageing population (particularly the growing proportion of the 'very elderly' amongst the aged), will place increasing pressure upon the State's resources. Concern about the escalating costs of providing through the social security budget for the residential care of the elderly was a major impetus to the government's community care legislation of 1990, which sought to relocate the responsibility for such provision with local authorities and 'the community'. Financial pressure will probably require further policy changes in the future (including a likely change to the retirement age).

(3) *Changing family structure*: Pressure on the welfare budget is likely to be further increased by continuing changes in patterns of family structure. It is a part of the government's ambitions for 'care in the community' to return welfare responsibility from the state to the family. In fact, such a policy aspiration is rather misleading, since the greater part of welfare provision

has always been provided informally within the family, and disproportionately by women. Yet there are social trends which make it likely that growing numbers will be unable to rely upon these traditional family structures for welfare support. Marital breakdown is a major cause of welfare dependency, particularly for lone mothers, and Britain has the second highest divorce rate in the EC. By 1989, one-quarter of all households in Britain were one-person households, double the number in 1961. By 1987, 14 per cent of all families with dependent children in the UK were headed by a lone parent, again nearly twice the proportion in 1971. It is likely that the growth of households will run ahead of the general growth in the population, and that a disproportionate number of these new households will be headed by a single person. While we may be uncertain about the precise consequences of these changes, it is likely that they will increase the need for the state (or at least state funding) to replace or augment the family (CSO, 1991).

(4) *Increasing childcare*: Female labour force participation has increased throughout the industrialised world over the past twenty years. This trend looks set to continue. Under these circumstances, and given that traditional division of labour in which care for children has been disproportionately the responsibility of women, the state will come under increasing pressure to improve the provision of childcare facilities for the under-5s (which is already very limited in Britain compared with many of her European neighbours) So far the government has instituted some very minor tax changes to encourage workplace nurseries. Pressure to extend this provision is certain to increase.

(5) *Community care*: Government policy, particularly that embodied in the NHS and Community Care Act 1990, has been increasingly directed towards shifting care out of institutions and into 'the community'. As a result, individual carers and community agencies, such as Community Health Councils (CHCs), are now becoming the focus of care policy which previously would have been managed through psychiatric hospitals and other long-stay institutions. The challenge this generates for individual carers, for GPs and for local authority social services departments is substantial, and may become

excessive. Although some of the savings made from closing down long-stay institutions are being transferred to care in the community, it is not clear that these will prove sufficient to meet the needs which are now developing.

(6) *New health challenges*: The government is also likely to face a number of new health challenges as the structure of the population and patterns of social behaviour change. AIDS, for example, already represents a significant and rising cost to the health budget and there is at least a possibility that its may come to constitute a very substantial welfare cost. At present, the health and social costs of AIDS and AIDS-related conditions are extremely difficult to estimate, because projections of the likely spread of the disease are so variable. But it has already upset the actuarial calculations of private insurers (and triggered a number of problems of civil rights and confidentiality), and it is also likely to have a long-term impact upon the costs and delivery of public health care.

## Conclusion: Towards a New Welfare Consensus?

After the ideological excitement of the Thatcher years and the sharply leftward turn of the Labour party in the early 1980s, it has been suggested that the early 1990s are witnessing a return to 'consensus politics', though a consensus shaped by the rightward move of the 1980s and the perilous location of the British economy in a European and world order over which we have precious little control. How far does this idea extend to the welfare field?

In some senses, the idea of a 'new' consensus is rather misleading. In the face of the rhetoric of both government and opposition, the Conservative record on social policy over the last decade is marked quite as much by continuity (especially with the record of the Labour government after 1976), as by radical change. There has been no wholesale transfer of welfare services into the private sector. There has been a slowing of growth of social expenditure, but not the sort of reversal which was recommended at the turn of the 1980s. The failure to address the problem of poverty and the redistribution of resources upwards are (unhappily) long-standing features of the British welfare state.

However, there have been some real changes which are even now becoming institutionally and socially entrenched. It is hard to imagine that these would or indeed could be reversed simply by a change of government. While Labour is committed to remedy what it sees as the more coercive and residualising changes introduced by the Conservatives, it does seem that the government's commitment to divide welfare purchasers and providers is here to stay. On the other hand, the Conservatives have moved back towards the 'mainstream', with their manifesto commitment to sustain the value of Child Benefit and their greater emphasis upon securing value and efficiency within the public services, rather than their wholesale replacement with a private sector alternative. At the same time, all the major parties share at least a rhetorical commitment to put power into the hands of the welfare consumer or citizen and to give the individual contractual rights of redress against public authorities. Thus, Major has made much of the improvements in the performance and accountability of the public services which are supposed to follow from the inauguration of his much-vaunted 'Citizen's Charter'. There is also widespread support for the de-institutionalisation and debureaucratisation of welfare care and for the State to offer support to community-based welfare services rather than seeking to replace them with statutory interventions. (Consensus here is tempered however by a suspicion amongst the government's opponents that their enthusiasm for community care is finance-led.) There may also be a general recognition (rather infrequently articulated) that the 'social engineering' ambitions of both left and right have failed and consequently some downplaying of social policy as an agent of social reform. There is perhaps also a keener understanding, certainly compared with the consensus before 1979, that social policy and economic policy are intimately connected. The view that social policy has been a constraint upon successful economic policy is, following the evidence of the 1980s, less boldly and less frequently advanced. More often do we find the (rather bleak) recognition that only a more successful economic policy (or still more simply, a more successful economy) holds out the prospect of any substantial improvements in public welfare provision.

This sets British social policy in its proper and broader context. For all the rhetoric of choice and citizenship, the single most important political consideration surrounding the welfare state over the last twenty years has been its cost. The major reforms of the late 1980s sought efficiency gains, so as to extract a greater welfare output from a welfare input which could not rise in line with either social expectations or demographically-driven need. The recent past and the foreseeable future of British social policy is thus dominated by the constraint of cost in a context of comparative economic decline. Whatever government holds power in the 1990s, the pressures for an improvement of public welfare services are likely to remain, and whilst there may be a new impetus for policy reform and innovation from beyond these islands, the main barrier to reform will remain the sluggish condition of the British economy.

# 12

# Environmental Politics

## JOHN McCORMICK

In terms of its place on the British political agenda, the environment has recently been riding a rollercoaster. Until 1988, it was given relatively little attention. The major political parties lacked coherent or comprehensive environmental policies, and while public attention continued to focus on areas of traditionally greater prominence, such as foreign and economic policy, the environment remained little understood and barely regarded by central or local government.

In 1989, it seemed that this was all about to change. Green consumerism achieved a new prominence, the Green Party won 15 per cent of the vote in the 1989 European elections, opinion polls regularly placed the environment among the three most important public concerns, there was wide-ranging public debate about approaches to environmental protection, and even Margaret Thatcher (who had once described the environment as a 'humdrum' issue) acknowledged that protecting the balance of nature was one of the 'great challenges of the late 20th Century' (McCormick, 1991). It seemed that the environment had finally entered the public policy mainstream.

By the early 1990s, however, the environment had once again become an issue of secondary importance. In part this was due to a shift of political attention back to foreign policy issues (notably the Gulf War, changes in eastern Europe, and the Maastricht debate), but in large part it was due to economic recession. Despite opinion polls indicating that environmental protection continued to have wide public support, the environment is ultimately a 'quality of life' issue, meaning that public and political interest in the environment is often determined by economic factors. Generally speaking, when the economy is strong, and inflation and unemployment low, people feel they can afford to attend to issues such as the state of the environment; when the economy is troubled, people attend to more immediate bread-and-butter issues such as jobs and the cost of living.

The prominent role played by John Major at the June 1992 Earth Summit in Rio de Janeiro gave a brief fillip to political interest in the environment. However, continuing recession – coupled with upheavals in European currency markets in autumn 1992 – ensured that interest had subsided once again by the start of 1993. The environment will doubtless continue to peak and trough in the public and political consciousness – as do all issues (Hogwood, 1992) – but at least it is now a permanent part of the policy agenda. Thanks to a combination of compelling scientific evidence, public opinion, the growing power of the environmental lobby, the consequences of privatisation, and the demands of EC law, the Major administration has found itself obliged to develop more coherent policies and to reorganise the machinery of environmental policy-making. Previous British governments may have found few votes in the environment, and thus largely ignored the issue, but no British government will ever again be able to afford to ignore the environmental dimension of economic development.

## The Policy Debate

Environmental policy concerns itself with the relationship between people and their natural environment. Ideally, the goal of environmental policy should be to ensure that economic and social development is productive and profitable, but also sustainable (i.e., that human demands of natural resources do not exceed – or interfere with – supply).

Britain has traditionally had a curious approach to environmental management. On the one hand, the British people value their countryside and wildlife, and Britain has had an impressive record in recognising and responding to environmental degradation (including passing the world's first comprehensive air pollution control Act in 1956, and creating the world's first Cabinet-level environment department in 1970). On the other hand, central government has proved slow to recognise and understand the environment as a distinct policy area. There are several possible explanations for this contradictory record.

Firstly, there are substantial disagreements on the best approach to environmental management. Given continuing scientific uncertainty about cause and effect (particularly with regard to bigger issues, such as global warming), governments are loath to make broad policy commitments, and instead dabble in the kind of ad hoc responses described by Lindblom as 'disjointed incrementalism'. Instead of approaching problems methodically or through a comprehensive reform programme, policy-makers often make small or incremental changes to existing policies (Braybrooke and Lindblom, 1963).

The problem has been compounded in recent years by a debate over whether to take a regulatory approach to the environment, or to leave environmental protection to the free market. Much of this debate was triggered by the 1989 Pearce report, which argued in favour of changes in the way economic progress is pursued, and of integration of environmental concerns into economic policy (Pearce *et al.*, 1989).

Secondly, because many policy-makers think of themselves as custodians of the public interest, and feel that they understand the best interests of the public with minimal reference to the public itself, environmental policy in Britain continues to be made in closed policy communities. Throughout the 1980s, one of the strongest such communities was that consisting of farmers, represented mainly by the National Farmers' Union (NFU), and the Ministry of Agriculture, Fisheries and Food (MAFF). So close was the relationship between the two that their representatives had almost daily meetings to consult and discuss policy. However, partly due to the success of attempts by environmental interest groups to draw attention to threats posed by modern farming to the countryside (Shoard, 1980, 1987), the NFU–MAFF relationship has weakened in recent years.

Thirdly, local government has traditionally been responsible for much environmental regulation, but given that relatively few voters have much interest in local politics, local authorities are held less accountable (Vogel, 1986). Consistent local government policies are also compromised by the often different priorities of different local authorities. In the Midlands, South Wales and Scotland, for example, local economic priorities have led to a prevailing unwillingness by local authorities to meet the additional expenses of controlling pollution. Meanwhile, areas downwind or downstream of the sources of pollution argue in favour of action.

Finally, because the environment has for so long been such a minor issue on the British policy agenda, relatively little time or thought has been expended on designing an effective and rational institutional and legislative structure. The result is that it is difficult to say exactly who is responsible for making and implementing environmental policy in Britain.

The Department of the Environment (DoE) would seem to be most obviously responsible, but its name does not reflect its true interests. The very title Department of the 'Environment' is misleading, because environmental policy is a small (and not very important) part of the DoE's overall responsibilities. Only 10 per cent of the staff of the department actually deal with environmental issues, and the department routinely gives most of its attention to its responsibilities in local government and housing. In 1989–91, for example, most of its attention was focused on implementation of the poll tax. The role of the DoE is further weakened by the fact that few Environment Secretaries have shown any particular interest in the environment, and by the way that other government departments have responsibilities that impact the environment, but are subject to only marginal DoE control (e.g., transport, energy supply, housing, and trade).

Although at first glance it may not appear to be an environmental agency, MAFF arguably plays a more central role in British environmental policy (certainly countryside policy) than does the DoE. MAFF has traditionally focused on encouraging food production, and has been the subject of repeated criticism by environmental groups for pursuing policies aimed at improving the efficiency and productivity of agriculture at the cost of Britain's natural heritage, notably woodlands and hedgerows. In recent years, MAFF has come to see itself increasingly as a ministry for the countryside, and has been active in assessing countryside issues, notably through its study on Alternative Land Uses and the Rural Economy (ALURE).

## Policy Developments

Current government policy on the environment is based on a combination of regulation and economic measures (in the form of tax incentives, grants and loans). Specific responses to shortfalls in environmental policy have been encapsulated in three main initiatives: the 1990 White Paper on the environment, the 1990 Environmental Protection Act, and changes in policy-making institutions.

The White Paper, published in September 1990 under the title *This Common Inheritance*, listed more than 350 measures already being taken by the government on the environment, along with proposals for new legislation or new activities. Among the few initiatives were: creation of a ministerial energy efficiency committee aimed at countering global warming, new proposals to protect the countryside (including more protection for hedgerows), changes in institutional arrangements for environmental policy-making (including the naming of ministers with environmental responsibilities in each government department) and a programme to combat noise nuisance.

Among media, opposition parties and environmental groups, the White Paper was almost universally condemned as disappointing, tentative, and a missed opportunity. For many critics, it confirmed that the British government still had a limited and unimaginative definition of environmental policy. *The Times* (26 September 1990) noted that, although some of the brightest minds in the DoE had been brought to bear on the White Paper, the principal civil servants involved 'had an intimate knowledge of housing and local government policy but, at the beginning of the exercise, much less knowledge or experience of environmental questions'. Their involvement illustrated 'the lowly status long accorded the issue of environmental protection in the government department normally entrusted with its care'. The White Paper also seemed to prove once again that economic interest groups still had considerable influence within Whitehall. Notable among these were the transport, oil and gas, and business lobbies. Despite its growing public support, the environmental lobby still had not been able to convert public sympathy into substantial political influence.

Also in 1990, the Environmental Protection Act was passed, covering a broader range of issues than had been addressed by any previous environmental legislation. One of the major innovations of the Act was the principle of integrated pollution control (IPC). IPC is based on the argument that government should take a precautionary approach to pollution control, preventing pollution at source, recognising the integrated nature of the environment, and encouraging polluters to pay; pollution should be controlled using the 'best practicable environmental option' (BPEO).

For the opposition parties and other critics of government environmental policy, the White Paper and the Environmental Protection Act 1990 were both fundamentally undermined by institutional confusion. As well as the DoE and MAFF, environmental policy is influenced by a pot-pourri of additional agencies. Among these are various state conservation agencies, Her Majesty's Inspectorate of Pollution (HMIP), the Royal Commission on Environmental Pollution (RCEP), the National Rivers Authority (NRA), and the Office of Electricity Regulation (OFFER) and its water industry equivalent, OFWAT. HMIP was itself only created in 1987 through an amalgamation of the inspectorates of industrial air pollution, radiochemicals, and hazardous wastes, while the NRA was created in 1989 in response to EC requirements for the existence of an independent water pollution control authority.

Particular concern was expressed by environmental pressure groups about the government's decision to increase institutional confusion – and, it was alleged, diminish environmental safeguards – by breaking the nation-wide Nature Conservancy Council (NCC) into three separate agencies covering England, Scotland and Wales. Despite a storm of protest, this change was legislated by the 1990 Act, and came into force on 1 April 1991. The three new bodies are English Nature, the Nature Conservancy Council for Scotland, and the Countryside Council for Wales. A Joint Nature Conservation Committee has been created to coordinate UK-wide initiatives, but it is doubtful whether it can maintain the level of expertise and impact that was generated by the NCC.

Against this background, the third focus of recent government policy has been further institutional reform. Demands for the creation of a more unified and centralised body akin to the US Environmental Protection Agency were finally met in 1992, when the government announced plans to create a new watchdog, the Environment Agency, which would combine the duties of HMIP, the NRA, and local government waste-regulation departments. Fragmentation of the NCC remains a matter of regret to environmentalists.

## Britain and the EC

Against a background of variable government interest in environmental regulation, the role and influence of the EC in environmental policy-making has grown. The environment received no mention in the Treaty of Rome, but since 1972 the EC has become increasingly active in setting environmental standards (Haigh, 1987). This has happened most notably since passage of the 1987 Single European Act (SEA); part of the process of harmonisation needed to create the single market necessitated setting common environmental standards across the Community.

The EC is now arguably the single most important and effective influence on British environmental policy and politics. Milton argues, for example, that 'the most striking feature of the government's policy on pollution is the extent to which it is dictated by EC directives' (Milton, 1991). Among the air pollution standards that have been set by EC law rather than British law are those on smoke, sulphur dioxide, nitrogen oxides, lead, and motor vehicle emissions. EC law has had particularly notable effects on British policy on water quality and acid pollution.

Britons have long prided themselves on the quality of their drinking water, assuming that it was as good as – if not better – than standards elsewhere in Europe. However, once EC standards were compared with those in Britain, it immediately became obvious that Britain fell short. The EC has now passed more than 25 directives dealing with drinking water, bathing water, and surface water, all of which have led to improvements in the quality of British water. EC law has also led to institutional changes in Britain. When the Thatcher government first mooted the idea of privatising the water supply industry in 1986, it proposed passing on pollution control responsibilities to the new private water companies. This was however found to be illegal under EC law, compelling the Thatcher government to create the NRA, an independent watchdog with increased powers over pollution control.

Similarly, after many years of intransigence and opposition to action, the British government was finally obliged to take action on acid pollution by the 1987 EC directive on large combustion plants. This obliges Britain and its EC partners to make substantial reductions in emissions of sulphur dioxide and nitrogen oxides, the basic constituents of acid pollution. The change of policy was notable partly for the fact that it came after many years of pressure on Britain from the Scandinavian countries that received much of Britain's acid pollution, and partly for the fact that it obliged the Thatcher administration – long ardently opposed to acid pollution regulation – to make a notable policy U-turn (McCormick, 1989). In short, EC law was able to achieve what many years of domestic and foreign pressure on the British government had failed to achieve. This created an interesting irony; while the water industry was privatised (and thus freed of direct government control), it was also made subject to considerably stronger environmental regulation.

In other policy areas, the European Commission has proved itself to be an important actor. Particularly controversial in Britain was the October 1991 decision of EC environment commissioner Carlo Ripa di Meana to call a halt to seven British construction projects on the grounds that they had failed to comply with the EC's 1985 Environmental Assessment Directive. This requires environmental impact assessments to be submitted before any major project can proceed. The seven projects were the M3 extension at Twyford Down, the Channel Tunnel rail link (including the King's Cross terminal in central

London), the M11 link road in Hackney, east London, an incinerator at South Warwick Hospital, a soft-drinks plant and can-making factory at Brackmills, Northampton, the East London River Crossing through Oxleas Wood, and the extension of a British Petroleum refinery in Falkirk. At the end of July 1992, the EC dropped legal action against the first five of these seven projects, but continued to pursue the final two. Ultimately, it could take Britain to the European Court of Justice.

Other bodies are also able to make use of EC machinery in holding the British government to account on environmental matters. A particular source of contention has been the issue of water and beach standards, following the EC's 1975 Bathing Water Directive. Persistent unwillingness on the part of the government to enforce this directive provoked Lancashire County Council to attempt to persuade the Commission to prosecute the British government over the issue of sewage on Blackpool beach (Young, 1993).

However, it may be that EC competence in these matters will be scaled down during the course of the 1990s. One of the issues caught up in the subsidiarity debate which swept the Community in 1992 was environmental regulation. At the Edinburgh Summit of December 1992, the decision was taken to return some policy-making competence to national governments. This may reduce the ability of the EC to enforce environmental standards throughout the Community. Needless to say, it would not only be the British government which would breathe a sigh of relief were this to happen. Indeed, the southern European states have far worse records than does Britain in complying with EC environmental directives.

**The International Dimension**

British policy has also been determined increasingly by broader international pressures. Unlike most other policy issues, environmental problems cannot always be addressed solely at the national level. The international dimension of environmental policy has become increasingly prominent, beginning with the debate during the 1980s over acid rain, progressing through concerns over global warming and threats to the ozone layer, and leading in 1992 to the debates generated by the UN Conference on the Environment and Development (the Earth Summit), held in Rio de Janeiro in June 1992.

Considerable controversy surrounded Britain's performance prior to the conference. A consortium of more than 100 interest groups declared that Britain, the USA, and Saudi Arabia had the worst records in the preparations for the conference. Their criticism was based partly on Britain's initial delay in signing the biodiversity treaty on the protection of global wildlife and plant species, and partly on British reluctance to promote a strong new UN body to follow-up on the agreements reached at the summit.

In the event, despite concerns among British ministers that signing the biodiversity treaty would incur considerable expenses for the wealthier industrialised countries, John Major signed both the biodiversity treaty and the global warming treaty. In his speech to the Earth Summit, he went on to promise £100 million of new aid to help address global environmental problems, a 'Darwin initiative' that would place the expertise of British research centres at the disposal of the world's scientific community, and a 'global technology initiative' to promote the transfer of clean technologies to poorer countries. There were also indications that the environment secretary, Michael Howard, had played an important role in securing changes in the global warming convention signed at the summit, thereby encouraging an initially reluctant USA to attend the conference. George Bush became the only Western leader not to sign the biodiversity treaty, despite attempts by John Major to persuade him otherwise.

Global warming has posed an entirely new set of challenges to policy-makers in Britain, as elsewhere. Britain argues that the control of global warming is a communal obligation in which every country should play a part, and that government should create the framework within which individuals can make the decisions needed to phase out greenhouse gases (Milton, 1991). Current British policy is to phase out chlorofluorocarbons (CFCs) by the end of the century, and to stabilise carbon dioxide emissions at 1990 levels by the year

2005. In part this will be achieved by greater efficiency in electricity production. For the time being, government policy is to encourage renewable energy and energy conservation, while promoting a growing place for nuclear energy. Although electricity privatisation publicly revealed for the first time that nuclear power generation was uneconomical, the coal pit closures announced in October 1992 were at one with projections that nuclear power and gas would provide an increased share of Britain's electricity generation capacity.

Whether or not the Rio summit ultimately proves successful, it confirmed once again the international dimension of many environmental problems, and the extent to which policy in Britain will continue to be influenced by debates over shared problems and shared resources.

## The Changing Environmental Lobby

Private environmental groups, traditionally the source of the greatest domestic pressure on the British government to amend its policies, have seen their support and their influence continue to grow since 1989. Although large and well-supported at the beginning of the 1980s, the environmental lobby had less political influence than its numbers suggested (Lowe and Goyder, 1983). However, by 1990, the membership of the lobby had doubled (from about 2.5–3 million members to about 5 million members), its income had more than tripled to nearly £200 million, and all the larger groups had seen substantial increases in staff numbers. Most of the growth has been concentrated in the last five years, and the groups with the fastest growth have been those that are either more activist (such as Greenpeace and Friends of the Earth (FoE)) or which have international interests (such as the World Wide Fund for Nature (WWF)). The lobby is also making ever more effective use of the media to promote public debate on environmental issues, and – through parliamentary committees and the EC – has had access to substantial new channels for political influence.

The growth in support for environmental groups may be part of an undercurrent of radicalisation occurring in the environmental movement. Certainly, more groups have become more overtly politically active, largely in response to frustration with the apparent unwillingness of government to respond to what are seen as increasingly critical issues. Radicalisation helps explain why there is more overlap between the membership of the Green Party and that of Greenpeace and FoE than there is between the Green Party and more traditional environmental groups.

As they have grown, environmental groups have also changed their tactics. Concerns about their charitable status made many reluctant to become overtly politically active a decade ago. Today, the more traditional groups are more politically influential, while (ironically) the more activist groups of the early 1980s (such as Greenpeace) have become more conservative, and more centrally a part of the 'establishment' environmental lobby. There has been a tendency for groups to move away from complaint and criticism, and towards both research-based appeals to policy-makers, industry and the public, and the provision of services and solutions.

Traditionally activist groups like Friends of the Earth are now finding themselves under challenge from even more radical groups which feel that FoE and Greenpeace are becoming too respectable. When the government announced plans to extend the M3 across Twyford Down, thereby threatening two Sites of Special Scientific Interest (SSSIs), two Scheduled Ancient Monuments and one Area of Outstanding Natural Beauty, among the (intentionally) highly visible groups which amassed to object was the British arm of the American group, Earth First!, which has some 1 000 UK supporters. This group adopts aggressive tactics in its defence of the environment, including inflicting damage on machinery. It has been joined on the radical fringe of British environmentalism by an Earth Liberation Front.

The more traditional interest groups have also placed a new emphasis on the role of the individual in the creation of environmental problems, and on proposing solutions to problems, rather than simply warning of their consequences. In addition, groups have built on their traditional ad hoc coordination and cooperation, and have issued more joint statements on government policy, such as those on water and electricity privatisation. Groups are increasingly working towards more or less pre-agreed sets of goals, and complementing each other. For example, FoE, in working with other groups on changes to the water privatisation bill, was often cast as the confrontational group. By taking on this role, it attracted enough of the ire of ministers to allow other groups to portray themselves as less confrontational, and to succeed in having some of their proposals accepted.

There have also been many changes relating to the access of environmental groups to the policy-making process. In the area of countryside conservation, the reduced power of the NFU has combined with growing criticism of MAFF to reduce the influence of the agricultural lobby, while allowing environmental groups more influence. The British government still lacks a countryside policy, and many of the changes in the countryside against which groups campaigned so actively in the early 1980s continue unabated. Nevertheless, there has been a discernible shift in public opinion and sympathy away from the agricultural lobby and towards the conservation lobby.

The work of parliamentary committees has also led to an increase in opportunities afforded to groups to influence parliament and political parties, with several groups for the first time appointing parliamentary liaison officers. With the realisation that an increasing amount of British environmental policy and law is now influenced by or decided in Brussels, there has also been a tendency for groups either to increase their direct representation at the Community level, or to pay more attention to EC legislation and its implications for Britain. FoE, Greenpeace and WWF have all appointed Brussels lobbyists for the first time.

Another clear change in tactics has involved environmental groups paying more attention to public attitudes and behaviour. The growth of the green consumer movement since 1989 (see below) was at least in part an outcome of the public awareness activities of the environmental lobby during the 1980s. As green consumerism grew, groups found a new and potentially fruitful means of influencing public policy through encouraging changes in consumer demands. Not only were groups now exerting pressure on the British government through the EC, but – by building an environmentally educated consumer population – they could exert further pressure for policy change.

## Green Consumerism and Green Politics

Perhaps the most significant development of the last few years has been the emergence of green consumerism in Britain. Consumer preferences have in turn had an impact both on the attention given by government to the environment, and on the policies pursued by government.

Although consumers were becoming more concerned about their health, diet and fitness a decade or more ago, the most recent wave can be dated specifically from the September 1988 publication of *The Green Consumer Guide* (Elkington and Hailes, 1988). A practical guide for consumers, it became an immediate bestseller, and spawned Green Consumer Weeks, Green Shopping Days, many other similar guides, and a new interest in environmentally-conscious consumerism.

The consequence of this was to bring about substantial changes in the practices of business and industry, and to make government more aware of the demand for stronger environmental legislation. It became common for companies to boast their green credentials, and to use the environment as a positive selling point. In some cases, entirely new businesses (such as The Body Shop) have been created around green consumer principles, while the demand for green technologies has spawned a new business sector. While it is still too early to be sure about the origins of green consumerism, it is arguable (ironically) that it was both a consequence of and a reaction to the Thatcherite enterprise culture, with its emphasis on consumption, competition, and greater responsiveness to the needs of customers. Green consumerism might be interpreted as a reaction to the values of 'low-conscience' free enterprise.

Coincident with the growth of green consumerism, the Green Party attracted new and growing support after 1988. Having never won more than 1.5 per cent of the vote at general elections, or 5.9 per cent of the vote at local elections, it surprised almost everyone (including itself) by winning 15 per cent of the vote at the June 1989 European Parliament elections. This was more than twice the combined share of the Liberal Democrats and Social Democrats.

While this did not result in British Greens winning any seats in Strasbourg, it nevertheless prompted much discussion about green ideology, and a response from other parties, which had until then given relatively little attention to the need for well-considered environmental policies. The creation of Tory Green Initiative in 1988 was accompanied by the reconstitution of the Liberal Ecology Group as the Green Democrats. For its part, Labour decided to build a network of sympathisers inside environmental groups to advise the party on how to build its green credentials.

Support for the Greens quickly fell to 7–8 per cent in opinion polls following the European elections, and by the time of the 1992 general election was down to less than 2 per cent; in the 1992 local government elections in England, the Greens won just 1.5 per cent of the vote. Given the closeness of the 1992 general election, and the depth of the recession, the major parties focused their campaigns on more traditional issues, the environment was given little attention, and those who had voted Green as a protest in 1989 switched back to the main parties. For the foreseeable future, it seems more likely that the major parties will adopt elements of the Green platform than that the Greens themselves will experience a resurgence.

## The Changing Place of Environmental Policy

A decade ago, neither the government nor the opposition parties took the environment seriously, and none had a comprehensive environmental policy, nor a coherent set of positions on particular issues. Environmental law was patchy, and the methods used to protect and manage the environment were largely held hostage to the wishes of vested economic interests, particularly the business, transport and agricultural lobbies. The network of government environmental agencies was incoherent, confused, and largely ineffective. The environmental lobby was big and active, but it was politically marginalised. For many people, 'the environment' meant simply protection of the countryside. Among political scientists, almost no attention was paid to the environment as a political or policy issue.

By 1992, the position had changed considerably. The support given to the Greens in 1989, the emergence of green consumerism, and the continued growth in support for environmental interest groups had all clearly emphasised the depth of public support for sound environmental policies. The response of both the government and the opposition was hesitant and conditional, and the much-heralded 1990 White Paper proved hugely disappointing to the environmental lobby. While there is little immediate sign that the Conservative government is doing much to push Britain into the first rank of environmental achievers, alongside Germany, the Netherlands, and the Scandinavians, it can no longer afford to ignore growing public demands for improved environmental protection.

The most substantial changes since 1989 have come in the growth of green consumerism, and in the size, influence and tactics of the environmental lobby. Membership and income grew dramatically, and the lobby continued to build on its functions as the only real force for improved environmental management in Britain. Its access to government has improved, and while this may not yet always have resulted in direct changes in policy, the lobby has backed up its appeals to government with enormously successful appeals to public opinion.

Despite changes in public will, political will remains confused. Few in government would now disagree that the problems of the environment must be addressed, but there is no consensus on how best to promote sustainable development. Institutional structures remain confused and legal arrangements patchy. In the short term, it seems likely that the greatest pressure for change will continue to come from the environmental lobby and the EC. In the absence of government leadership, the combination of growing public demands for change (promoted – and, in some cases, effected – by interest groups) and the legal obligations imposed by Brussels are ultimately compelling the government to follow, and to take action where otherwise they might have delayed.

**Future Challenges**

Future problems in the environmental sphere will continue to be substantial. From the dangers of nuclear power to the continuing population explosion, from resource depletion to the many problems generated by biotechnology, and from worsening problems of energy supply to mounting problems relating to poverty, it is clear that politicians in Britain (and throughout the world) are being faced by escalating global difficulties which demand far more imaginative solutions than those so far proposed. More to the point, those solutions urgently need to be applied.

However, there is no consensus concerning the way in which environmental problems should be addressed. Indeed, three distinct sets of responses have emerged.

(1) Contemporary elite orthodoxy tends to hold that environmental problems are manageable provided that certain limits are respected. There are, it is argued, trade-offs to be made in all spheres of politics: the environment must take its place alongside the demands of economic growth and other human wants. Thus, while limits will be placed on carbon dioxide emissions and the use of CFCs, for example, supporters of this view argue that we should avoid giving the environment too much political prominence.

(2) Dating back to the 'Prophets of Doom' debate in the 1960s, there is the view that environmental problems have been under-stated, and that dire environmental consequences will follow if action is not taken immediately to save the planet. According to this conception, the very survival of the earth hangs perilously in the balance. The entire basis of our economic, social and political arrangements must be altered forthwith if the planet is to be saved. The environment must be placed at the very top of the policy agenda if we are to survive as a species.

(3) Contrasting with the pessimism of the Prophets of Doom, there are those who argue that the problems of the environment have been over-stated by the environmental movement. This view holds that the earth is a cornucopia, that all human needs can be met in perpetuity by a global system which is self-adjusting, and which is highly unlikely to

be fatally damaged by the kinds of human activities which have been undertaken for centuries without leading to ecological disaster. This view holds that no drastic revision of our current socio-economic policies is necessary.

Given these very different sets of views, agreeing and implementing environmental policy continues to be an enormously complex proposition. Politics, by its very nature, is all about compromise. However, the kinds of compromises we must make in order to design effective environmental policies remain unclear. Reaching those compromises is handicapped by the lack of scientific certainty over the causes and effects of environmental problems. In short, the environment poses challenges to policy-makers unlike those posed by any other area of policy.

# 13

# Foreign and Defence Policy

**DAVID SANDERS**

The international situation that confronts nation-states changes constantly. New international organisations develop, others atrophy and decay. Trade patterns vary as new markets and sources of supply are found and old ones lost. Friendships and antagonisms rise and fall as domestic political conditions in different states change. There are occasions, however, when the character of the international system changes so rapidly and fundamentally that major policy adjustments are required on the part of all international actors. The revolutionary changes in the Soviet Union and eastern Europe that began in the mid-1980s and culminated, in December 1991, in the dissolution of the USSR itself constituted precisely such a transformation of the international system. With the disappearance of the old certainties, and risks, of the Cold War, British foreign policy-makers have sought to identify the dangers, challenges, and opportunities of the new situation. As will be seen, however, in order to accomplish this task, they have been inclined to use old conceptual models that may not be entirely appropriate to the changed conditions in which they are being employed.

## The End of the Cold War

The 'bipolar' conditions of the Cold War informed Britain's foreign policy strategy for most of the post-war era. For forty years, Britain sought to protect its own security through the

North Atlantic Treaty Organisation (NATO), a defensive alliance between north America and western Europe that was intended to deter further Soviet expansion in Europe. London encouraged the development of the European Economic Community (EEC), which it subsequently joined in 1973, in part as an economic bulwark against the communist threat. And it pursued policies towards the Third World – even when it was obliged to relinquish the Empire in the 1950s and 1960s – that were designed to insulate indigenous regimes from the appeals and subterfuges of communism. Although it was widely recognised that the notion of a simple bipolar capitalist/communist divide required qualification, the sense that Britain's interests were coterminous with those of the capitalist West in general, and that western interests were collectively threatened by the expansionism and aggression of Soviet communism, dominated the thinking of the British foreign policy elite. In its view, the industrialised world was partitioned into two hostile camps which not only confronted one another in the European theatre but also competed for spheres of influence in the 'Third World', where the 'loss' of a state from one side's sphere was typically regarded as a 'gain' for the other.

In the mid-1980s, however, things began to change. The liberalisation of Soviet communism initiated by Gorbachev after 1985 set in train a series of events that, by 1990, had seen non-communist governments take power throughout eastern Europe and a considerable softening of all aspects of Soviet foreign policy. Indeed, in July 1990, the NATO powers issued the 'London Declaration' which stated unequivocally that the countries of the now-defunct Warsaw Pact were no longer regarded as enemies: that the Cold War was effectively over. Notwithstanding this marked change in the West's public stance, however, lingering doubts remained that conservative forces in the Soviet Union might still try to reverse the Gorbachev reform process and seek to reintroduce the sort of hard-line regime that had provoked the West into its confrontational Cold War posture in the first place. These doubts were themselves entirely dispelled by the extraordinary developments that followed the abortive putsch against

Gorbachev which took place in August 1991. Although Gorbachev was briefly restored to power, the Soviet people's response to the coup presented Boris Yeltsin, the non-communist president of the Russian Republic (which, at that stage, was still part of the Union of Soviet Socialist Republics), with an opportunity to wrest political and economic power from both Gorbachev and the Union. In the months following the coup, Yeltsin's government gradually extended its constitutional powers whilst simultaneously curtailing those of the centre. Indeed, by December 1991, Gorbachev had resigned and the Union had been terminated; fifteen new sovereign, non-communist states had declared independence and been duly recognised by the West; and a loose 'Commonwealth of Independent States' (CIS) had been instituted, consisting of only eight of the original fifteen Soviet republics.

The implications of the changes were evident to everyone. The dangerous enemy, which had been suspected of either direct or indirect involvement in almost every challenge to western interests that had been mounted during the previous four decades, had simply ceased to exist. The ubiquitous and malign Soviet threat that the NATO alliance had been expressly created to deter had disappeared. The bipolar partitioning of the global system into mutually hostile communist and capitalist camps, each headed by a superpower armed to the teeth with strategic nuclear weapons, had ended. A whole new set of possibilities for international cooperation opened up. The UN Security Council, for so long paralysed by the threat of the Soviet veto, could once again contemplate taking decisive action to counter aggressive challenges to the existing international order – as it did against Iraq in the spring of 1991. With only one superpower now remaining, there was even talk – originating in Washington – of a New World Order in which respect for sovereignty, democracy and human rights (at least as defined on Capitol Hill) would flourish. There was also a huge potential for a 'peace dividend'. The demise of the Soviet threat meant, in principle, that the massive arsenals of the West could be substantially reduced and the resources thus released diverted to more socially productive uses.

In addition to the ending of the Cold War, there were two other major international developments in the late 1980s and early 1990s to which Britain's foreign policy-makers were also obliged to respond. One was the dramatic revival of Islamic consciousness throughout the Middle East and parts of Asia and Africa, which had occurred in the aftermath of the Islamic revolution in Iran in 1979. The collapse of the Soviet Union offered fertile ground for Islamic fundamentalists to extend their religious and political influence. Several of the newly-independent republics had sizeable Muslim populations whose religious aspirations had previously been heavily curtailed, if not actively suppressed: the abandonment of state-sponsored Marxism produced an ideological vacuum that Islamic proselytisers were only too willing to fill. A second development, much closer to home, was the consolidation and revitalisation of the EC integration process that arose out of the signing of the Single European Act (SEA) in 1986. This measure not only provided for the completion of the free internal EC market by 1992, but also extended the powers of the European Parliament and the opportunities for the Council of Ministers to take (qualified) majority decisions, thereby overriding the express objections of individual member states in certain specified policy areas.

Taken together, these three sets of changes – the end of the Cold War, the resurgence of Islam and the renewed supranational momentum of the EC – posed a serious strategic problem for Britain's foreign policy elite. Should Britain soldier on more or less as before, seeking to maximise British interests by adjusting its policies incrementally as circumstances dictated? Or should it recognise that major changes to the international order in turn required major adjustments in policy – that Britain's international role and responsibilities required fundamental review? In the wake of the Conservatives' re-election in April 1992, there was little obvious sign that any such review was indeed taking place. There had certainly been a Defence Review published in 1990, but this assessment of military needs and priorities necessarily paid scant attention to wider questions of economic, political and security strategy.

## UK Defence and Foreign Policy Strategy in the 1990s: the Strategic Options

During the Thatcher period, the role that Britain pursued in international affairs was broadly in line with that adopted by successive governments since 1945. London was content to play a support role behind Washington, assisting the latter's efforts to keep the world safe for capitalism and democracy. To facilitate the performance of this support role, Britain sought to maintain the trappings of world power status which were embodied in its permanent seat on the United Nations Security Council and its possession of an 'independent' nuclear deterrent. The Atlantic connection, moreover, continued to be the focus of Britain's defence policy: as far as London was concerned, an American military presence in Europe remained an essential prerequisite of geostrategic stability. Thatcher's instinctive Atlanticism in the political and security spheres, however, did not blind her to the fact that Britain relied on other EC countries for over 50 per cent of its export markets. (In 1950, UK exports to what were to become the twelve EC countries as a percentage of total UK exports stood at 11.2 per cent. By 1960, the equivalent figure had risen to 15.4 per cent; by 1970 to 29.2 per cent; by 1980 to 43.4 per cent; and by 1988 to 50.2 per cent. At the start of 1993 a figure of 57 per cent had been reached.) The Atlanticism that characterised much of Britain's foreign policy during the 1980s was accordingly tempered in economic matters by the Prime Minister's vision of a European Community (of nation-states rather than of individuals) committed to the free movement of capital, goods, labour and services across national frontiers.

Thatcher's removal, of course, together with the changes in the international system described above, produced a situation in the early 1990s that could have resulted in a decisive shift in Britain's international role. Britain's responsibilities, after all, had been dramatically reduced. The empire was long gone. Hong Kong, though still under British control until 1997, had effectively been negotiated away in 1984. The Falkland Islands were still a problem, but the relatively small garrison stationed there was probably enough to deter any Argentine ambitions for the foreseeable future. Australia had taken over Britain's former defence obligations in south east Asia. And, most important of all, the disappearance of the Soviet threat meant that British assistance was no longer required either to defend western Europe against a Warsaw Pact blitzkrieg or to assist American efforts to resist Soviet expansionism in the Third World. In these circumstances, John Major's government was faced with a fairly clear strategic choice. On the one hand, Britain could continue in the Thatcherite vein, pursuing broadly Atlanticist policies, aspiring to maintain the symbols of its world role, and ensuring that a distinctive British voice was still heard in the international corridors of power. On the other hand, it could recognise the facts of Britain's long-term economic decline; accept that London's position within the revitalised Security Council resulted from the geostrategic conditions of 1945 rather than from the political realities of the 1990s; and adopt an international role commensurate with Britain's status as a middle-income, middle-sized European power whose best interests probably lay in coordinating its economic and security policies with those of its European neighbours.

In the event, the Major government opted for incremental adjustments to the status quo rather than radical revision. Major's foreign policy strategy, like that of his predecessor, was founded on three simple precepts: the importance of maintaining the Anglo–American connection or, failing that, the Euro–American connection; the need to sustain Britain's role and status as a major world power; and the desirability of maximising economic, political and military cooperation among independent, sovereign states. The operation of these principles can be variously observed in four different policy contexts: in Britain's behaviour during the Kuwait crisis of 1990–91; in the emphasis that it accords to different international organisations; in the priorities that were announced in the 1990 Defence Review; and in Britain's stance on the question of a common EC foreign policy.

*The Kuwait crisis (August 1990 – April 1991)*

Saddam Hussein's invasion of Kuwait was widely regarded as the 'first test' of the post-Cold War era. Gorbachev made it clear from the outset that the Soviet Union would not oppose western efforts to remove Iraqi forces from Kuwait. Accordingly, the USA, Britain and France used their Security Council positions to ensure that sanctions were imposed against Iraq and that, when these failed to achieve their desired effect, the necessary force was deployed in order to liberate Kuwait. Throughout the crisis Britain showed very little interest in the various (unsuccessful) EC efforts to develop a common Community policy towards Iraq. On the contrary, Britain's behaviour was consistently Atlanticist. At the diplomatic level, London's activities were concentrated on supporting American efforts to ensure that the formal resolutions to exert maximum pressure on Iraq were passed in the Security Council. In military terms, although Britain's contribution to the multinational force was unavoidably modest, the fact that British forces were committed early and placed under American strategic command constituted an important symbolic legitimation of American policy that helped to build the necessary momentum for assembling a genuinely multinational force that could be used against Iraq. Moreover, once Iraqi forces had been duly expelled from Kuwait, in April 1991, London also backed Washington's decision not to pursue Saddam to Baghdad and subsequently joined with the Americans in establishing 'safe havens' for the Kurdish minority in northern Iraq.

Two main points need to be made about Britain's behaviour in the Kuwait affair. First, under both Thatcher and Major, Britain's view was that, regardless of the particular international institution that was used as the legitimising cloak for military action (and the UN was employed in this instance simply because it promised to yield the widest array of participants in the multinational force), effective action could only be taken by a group of determined and like-minded states acting in concert: it was inconceivable that a supranational decision-making body (such as the EC Commission) could summon the necessary will or resources to take the sort of unpalatable decisions that were clearly required. Second, it would be wrong to infer from the subordinate role played by Britain in support of US diplomacy and military operations that Britain was simply 'protecting its interests by identifying them with those of the United States'. Rather, London was following the course of action that its policy makers believed was appropriate to the exigencies of the situation. Crucially, policy makers in London and Washington strongly concurred both on the nature of the problems that Saddam's behaviour had created and on what needed to be done to remedy them: Iraq's actions against a weak and defenceless neighbour constituted an unacceptable infringement of the principle of respect for the territorial integrity of other sovereign nations; it was a violation of international norms that had to be resisted, if necessary by force, in order deter further violations either by Iraq itself or by states equally delinquent in their objectives. Britain's Atlanticist stance in the Kuwait crisis, in short, was not a reflection of John Major blindly following George Bush's lead. It resulted, rather, from the similarity of analysis favoured by key decision makers in the White House and Downing Street. As far as the British government was concerned, Saddam's aggression required a resolute response; and it was Washington and the UN, most certainly not Brussels, that offered the best prospect of achieving one.

*Priorities Towards Different International Organisations (1990–92)*

The continued Atlanticism of Britain's external policy was also evident in the priorities that the Major government accorded to different international organisations. In the economic sphere, Britain's intimate connections with the EC were, of course, of paramount importance. In the context of the stalled Uruguay Round of GATT negotiations, however, Britain generally pedalled a softer line towards Washington than its EC partners on the main issue that divided the USA and Europe – the question of subsidies to the aviation industry and to agriculture. The British government was also very alert to what it regarded as the potential dangers of the establishment of a North American Free Trade Area (covering Canada, the US and Mexico) which it feared might prejudice British exporters' access to North American markets.

This sympathy for the Atlantic connection was even more apparent in Britain's stance on defence and security matters. Essentially, the Major government's position was to resist any institutional developments that might weaken Washington's attachment to Europe and to welcome any that might strengthen it. Thus, London insisted that NATO remain the cornerstone of western Europe's defence. It opposed diluting the organisation by extending its membership to include former adversaries in eastern Europe, though it enthusiastically accepted the creation of the North Atlantic Cooperation Council, in November 1991, as a forum in which the former NATO and Warsaw Pact opponents could discuss matters of mutual concern. It also welcomed Dutch proposals, endorsed by NATO Secretary-General Manfred Worner in May 1992, that NATO should be prepared, in principle, to participate in peacekeeping activities throughout the European theatre – a considerable departure from NATO's original core function of collective defence. The British government also made clear its preparedness to see NATO forces used as a means of enforcing the recommendations of the Conference on Security and Cooperation in Europe (CSCE), provided that it was understood that CSCE would possess no powers of instruction in this context.

Britain also sought to ensure that the Western European Union (WEU, created under the terms of the 1948 Brussels Pact, but effectively relaunched with the admission of West Germany in 1955) should develop in ways that were compatible with NATO's continued primacy in European defence. France and Germany endeavoured to present the WEU as the focus for an EC defence policy, the core of which would be a Franco–German 'rapid reaction force' of about 35 000 troops. London, however, insisted that WEU should never be more than a supplement to NATO: it might be allowed to assist in the development of a 'European security identity', but only within the context of a defensive alliance which maintained a strong American presence.

London's antipathy towards an enhanced defence role for WEU was mirrored in its insistence that the EC itself should not be permitted to develop such a role. Britain consistently argued for a clear separation between security policy and defence policy. Security policy was taken to cover arms reduction talks, non-proliferation negotiations, confidence-building measures and the creation of formal and informal mechanisms for peaceful conflict resolution; defence policy to connote questions of military hardware, manpower provision and contingency and strategic planning. In the British view, it was entirely appropriate to seek to develop security policies at EC level, provided that they were arrived at through procedures which allowed for the exercise of the national veto. However, since Community-level defence policies would imply a diminution of NATO's role, these matters should remain outside the EC's purview: for London, keeping the Americans committed to Europe's defence remained far more important than efforts to strengthen the Community's internal coherence through the development of a common defence policy.

### 'Options for Change' and Britain's Defence Priorities

The 'Options for Change' Defence Review, published in July 1990, was the British government's first (and, so far, only) formal attempt to adjust its defence policy in response to the ending of the Cold War. The broad policy outlines of the Review were simple. Now that it was no longer necessary to deploy large numbers of troops in Germany in order to deter a surprise land-based attack from the east, army manpower could be cut by approximately 40 000 to 116 000. Not surprisingly, right-wing Conservative MPs strenuously resisted the plans for troop reductions. Their case was considerably strengthened by the upsurge in inter-communal violence in the former Yugoslav states of Bosnia and Croatia during 1991–92. This was precisely the sort of conflict that was likely to recur throughout eastern Europe – and elsewhere – in the future. Yet the international community, whether it was under the auspices of the UN or the EC (or both, as in the case of the London agreement on the Balkans in August 1992), could only hope to undertake successful peacekeeping operations if adequate infantry resources were available. If Britain retained any aspirations to an international peacekeeping role (which, as a permanent member of the UN Security Council, it did), it would be obliged to maintain a sizeable infantry force and to reverse its planned manpower cuts.

Given the reduced air and sea threat to Britain itself that had been engendered by the collapse of Soviet power, 'Options for

Change' also proposed small reductions in the number of RAF squadrons and in the size of the surface fleet. (The number of RAF squadrons was to be reduced from 24 to 18; the number of Royal Navy frigates and destroyers to be reduced from 48 to 40.) However, the four-boat Trident submarine programme, with its 512 independently-targeted nuclear warheads, would proceed as planned – on the grounds that such a force already contributed the minimum credible deterrent available.

This protection of the 'independent deterrent' in the face of cuts to conventional forces spoke eloquently of the government's conception of Britain's future international role. The independent deterrent had originally been acquired in the 1950s, partly as an 'insurance policy' against any future American withdrawal from NATO, and partly as a 'second decision centre' whose reaction the Soviets would be obliged to consider if they were contemplating either a nuclear or a conventional assault on NATO territory. Yet, even with the collapse of the Soviet threat, Britain determined to retain its independent deterrent. The government's express explanation for this decision was that there was no telling who might get hold of the nuclear weapons dispersed around the former Soviet Union; or who might autonomously develop a nuclear capability in the future. Although at least one academic expert (Wallace, 1992a) dismissed the implied fears of an 'Islamic bomb' as 'risible', the government's response was simple: the continued British possession of nuclear weapons provided a security guarantee for the British people of an order that could not otherwise be sustained in what was still a dangerous and uncertain world. In response to suggestions that a specifically British and independent deterrent would not be required if Britain were simply to rely on the Americans or join with other EC countries to develop a European deterrent, the government's supporters argued that the nature of international politics was such that complete reliance could never be placed on the good behaviour of other international actors, no matter how close relations might appear at any given time.

The express motivation underpinning the retention of the British deterrent, then, was centred on the government's continuing conception of Britain as an independent, sovereign nation which ultimately had to rely on its own efforts in order to protect itself. Yet there were two other sets of considerations, relating to the symbolism of the deterrent, that were also important. First, the fact that Trident was an American-built missile system which Washington sold exclusively to London was one of the few remaining, visible expressions of the 'special' Anglo–American relationship: only the British were trusted sufficiently to merit being supplied with such devastating American military technology. Second, maintaining the deterrent symbolised Britain's continuing Great Power status. There was precious little objective reason in the 1990s why Britain (or, for that matter, France) should remain one of the five permanent members of the UN Security Council. In terms of economic strength and conventional military capabilities, Britain had long since been very much in the second division. Its diplomatic experience certainly counted for something, but that could never compensate for Britain's simple lack of economic and military muscle. In these circumstances, being a major nuclear power was the one public justification that Britain could provide for maintaining its privileged diplomatic position within the UN. And, of course, it was through the UN – and through London's connections with Washington – that Britain could continue to aspire to perform its world role. In essence, the question of the independent deterrent was the point at which the two major elements of the British government's post-Cold War role conception converged: its Atlanticism and its desire to continue to play a world role. Small wonder that the government should have been so insistent on retaining it.

## The Question of a Common EC Foreign Policy

Throughout the 1970s and 1980s, there were various efforts, first through the Davignon procedure and later through European Political Cooperation, to coordinate the foreign policies of EC member-states. One of the hopes at Maastricht in December 1992, particularly among the French and German delegations, had been that the Community might introduce a system of qualified majority voting (which weights votes according to national population size) in the Council of Ministers on certain foreign policy matters. These efforts were strongly resisted by John Major's negotiating team, which succeeded in retaining the ministerial veto in the foreign policy, security and defence spheres – thereby effectively scuppering the prospect of a common foreign policy that would be binding on all member-states.

There were two main arguments in favour of a move towards a commonly-determined EC foreign policy. First, a single loud voice stating a single position would carry more weight in international negotiations than several smaller voices – even if they were expressing more or less the same sentiment. Second, and perhaps more cynically as far as the British and French were concerned, a common EC foreign policy would be one way of exercising influence over a newly-united Germany set on using its economic pre-eminence in Europe to extend both its involvement in eastern Europe and its activities on the world stage. For Major's government, however, neither of these arguments was compelling. For one thing, a meaningful single voice would be very difficult, if not impossible, to achieve. For another, the notion that a democratic Germany either could or should be moderated in its foreign policy strategy by virtue of its EC membership was both unrealistic and offensive. Moreover, a common EC foreign policy based on majority voting – qualified or otherwise – was simply an unacceptable constraint on Britain's freedom to determine how it should respond to external challenges and opportunities: a constraint that was especially unacceptable in view of Britain's continuing Atlanticist and world role aspirations.

It was also thought to be highly unlikely that, in any crisis short of common external attack, a group of nation-states with diverse interests would be able to agree on a concerted and decisive course of action. Indeed, for London, the EC's impotence during the Kuwait crisis was a clear demonstration of this precise problem. It was a problem, moreover, that was compounded by the abysmal failure of EC diplomacy during the Yugoslavian crisis of 1991–92. Right from the outset, the Community could not agree on either the procedures for, or the likely consequences of, formally recognising the seceding republics of Croatia, Slovenia, Bosnia–Herzegovina and Macedonia. The Germans argued that early recognition would oblige Serbia to withdraw the federal army (which it controlled) from Croatia and Bosnia because the Serbs would not want to risk EC disapproval by engaging in aggression against what would then be independent sovereign states. The British, in contrast, favoured delay on the grounds that recognition would leave the Serbs with no other option but to escalate the violence in order to secure their *de facto* hold on Serbian enclaves in the two other republics. In the event, the German position prevailed but the British analysis proved correct. Recognition was granted to Croatia in January 1992 and to Bosnia in February. The subsequent efforts of the EC's peace mission, however, proved totally ineffectual in securing even a lasting cease-fire, let alone any kind of diplomatic settlement between the warring republics. For the British, the message of these failures was clear: the concept of a common EC foreign policy that involved anything more than the voluntary coordination of nationally-determined positions was a nonsense. Foreign policy, for the foreseeable future, was something better left to the nation-state – or at least to the Security Council of the UN, where powerful and autonomous nation-states could act in concert, if they so chose, in order to modify the behaviour of recalcitrant pariah states.

## The Foreign Policy-making Process

Any discussion of the British desire to maintain national decision-making autonomy, of course, immediately begs the question as to who it is that actually makes British foreign policy. As in the domestic sphere, the process is a complex one involving pressures from, and consultation with, a wide range of bureaucratic and political elites. The main institutional actors inside Whitehall and Westminster are described schematically in Figure 13.1. It should be emphasised, however, that it is Cabinet that remains the key decision-making centre in matters of policy strategy, with a pivotal role being played by its Defence and Overseas Policy Committee (DOPC). Traditionally, DOPC's main source of policy-relevant information was the Foreign and Commonwealth Office (FCO), though during the Thatcher years – partly as a result of the

299

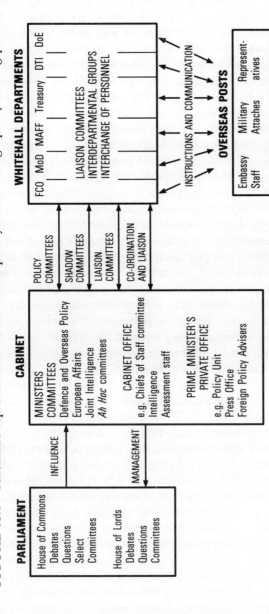

FIGURE 13.1  Schematic representation of the contemporary British foreign policy-making process

KEY
FCO   Foreign and Commonwealth Office          DTI   Department of Trade and Industry
MoD   Ministry of Defence                      DoE   Department of the Environment
MAFF  Ministry of Agriculture, Fisheries and Food

*Source*: Michael Clarke, 'The Policy-Making Process' in Smith *et al.* (1988) p. 86 (Figure 4.1).

close relationship between the Prime Minister and her foreign policy adviser, Charles Powell – the FCO's advice tended to be downgraded in favour of that supplied by Downing Street's own Policy Unit. (Indeed, a favourite joke of the Thatcherites was that the main function of the Foreign Office was to look after the interests of foreigners.) Under John Major, given both the lack of a Powell-like figure at No. 10 and the closeness of the relationship between the new PM and Douglas Hurd, FCO advice has counted for rather more than it did before November 1990. Major has nonetheless continued his predecessor's predilection for close involvement in all major foreign policy matters – as he demonstrated in his handling both of the Kuwait crisis of 1991 and of the Balkan crisis of 1991–92.

But if the DOPC has continued to reign supreme in matters of security and 'high' diplomacy, the same cannot be said of economic affairs. It has often been suggested that, since 1945, the game of international politics has become less about the control of territory and populations and more about attracting foreign investment and promoting overseas trade. For a medium-sized power like Britain, the ironic feature of this sort of change has been that just as economics has become more important, the internationalisation of markets and of production has simultaneously robbed the nation-state of its ability independently to pursue foreign economic policies aimed at maximising the interests of its people. Britain's accession to the EC in 1973 in part reflected a recognition of this reduction in national autonomy. Indeed, London's foreign economic policies since 1973 have increasingly been formulated in collaboration with Britain's European partners. During Britain's membership of the ERM (October 1990 – September 1992), Britain's currency and interest rate policies were even more tightly constrained than ever before. This lead, in turn, to an enhanced policy-making role for ad hoc meetings of EC Finance Ministers (such as the one held at Bath in September 1992) and to a diminution of the influence of the Treasury. In the short term, the suspension of Britain's ERM membership may engender a partial restoration of Treasury influence. However, any future 'deepening' of the EC will further inhibit the capacity of Whitehall (and perhaps even Downing Street) to influence British foreign economic policy –

that is, if there is a specifically 'British foreign economic policy' to be influenced at all.

## Explaining Britain's Foreign Policy Strategy

In spite of these economic developments, Britain's foreign and defence policies in the early 1990s, in all other important respects, remained staunchly Atlanticist. The government remained committed to the preservation of Britain's 'world role' (such as it was); and London continued to resist the efforts of other EC countries to build a common foreign policy that might in any sense reduce British decision-making autonomy in the political or security spheres. The intriguing question, of course, was why, in the post-Cold War era, this approach should have been so insistently pursued. The answer – and it has already been hinted at – lay in the way in which members of the British foreign policy elite continued to think about international politics. Britain's foreign policy-makers during the Cold War era were understandably committed to a state-centric, 'Realist' conception of the international system. In simple terms, Realism asserts that, in the absence of a single 'world government', the nation-state can never be sure that it is safe from external attack. Every state permanently risks being confronted by at least one potential aggressor which, if it is given the opportunity to do so, will seek to dominate and exploit any other state weaker than itself. Under such conditions, argues the Realist, the overriding objective of a nation-state's foreign policy must be the maintenance of its security (Sanders, 1990).

Viewed through the lens of Realism, it is easy to see why, for Britain's policy-makers, the end of the Cold War made very little difference to their conception of Britain's international role. One arch-enemy – the Soviet Union – had disappeared, but another – a militant Islamic alliance, perhaps – might conjure itself at any moment. In these circumstances, it was better to keep faith with an old and trusted ally – the USA – and to cling to any resources – the independent deterrent and the permanent Security Council seat – that might conceivably be of use in any joint action taken with the USA in times of crisis. It was also better to participate in an EC whose rules did not restrict the British government's freedom to follow its own judgement in the intricate and constantly changing world of international politics.

The crucial question for the future, of course, is whether this sort of Realist thinking is any longer appropriate to the actual international situation that Britain now confronts. Critics of the government's current foreign policy strategy pursue two main sets of ideas. One strand of thinking (Burton *et al.*, 1984) challenges the entire notion of Realism. Its proponents argue that in an age of interdependence – of economic interpenetration and mutual vulnerability to ecological and nuclear disasters – conceptual models that emphasise cross-national and trans-national cooperation are far more appropriate than the conflictual, state-centric world-view of the Realist. The main implication of this critique is clear: if the assumptions underlying Britain's foreign policy strategy are themselves incorrect, then the strategy is unlikely to achieve its desired objective of maximising the interests of the British people.

A second line of criticism suggests that, even if the Realist frame of reference is accepted, Britain's overall strategy is still inappropriate, and for at least two reasons. First, the implicit assumption of the Thatcher/Major approach – that there is a clear bifurcation between economic and security interests – cannot be sustained indefinitely. During the 1970s and 1980s, Britain was able to participate fully in the economic activities of the EC but at the same time remain broadly aloof from the Community in matters of foreign and defence policy, concentrating instead on NATO and its connection with the USA. The apparent readiness of other EC members – crystallised at Maastricht – to extend Community activities into the security and defence fields, however, suggests that in future Britain may find it more difficult to retain the economic benefits of EC participation whilst simultaneously focusing its defence and security policies in the Atlantic sphere.

The second objection to Britain's current foreign policy strategy from within the Realist perspective is that Britain does not possess the resources necessary to support it (Sanders, 1990). Playing the role of America's 'universal and indispensable number two' is expensive. The commitment to an out-of-area capability and an independent nuclear deterrent are luxuries that a nation with an historically low growth rate simply cannot afford to sustain indefinitely. On this account, Britain's policy-makers would do best to recognise that Britain is a middle-ranking European power whose main interests, in both the economic and defence spheres, lie in close cooperation with other middle-ranking European powers; that London should stop being in thrall to Washington and cease to pose, ineffectually, on the world stage; that Britain should embrace the EC rather than resist it; that the British, having moved towards Europe for the last thirty years, should finally become 'good Europeans'.

## Problems for the Mid-1990s

Whatever conceptual models the British elite eventually adopts in its efforts to determine Britain's foreign policy strategy for the 1990s, there are several key problems that will have to be confronted. The most pressing will almost certainly be the economic and political crisis in eastern Europe and the former Soviet Union. The nationalist and ethnic tensions released by the collapse of communism, compounded by the accumulated effects of years of economic failure, constitute an explosive cocktail that will need to be handled with considerable finesse, as well as compassion. The development of militant Islam, especially when it is combined with the likelihood of nuclear proliferation, will similarly require close monitoring and sensitive diplomacy. As far as the present British government is concerned, these are problems for the industrialised world as a whole, not just for Europe. This is why it insists on the need for Europe to maintain its strong Atlantic connections. It is why it resists any developments within the EC that might strengthen the ever-present isolationist tendencies in American foreign policy. For the Major government, global problems require global, not just European, solutions. In its view, American disengagement from the affairs of Europe would be disastrous because it would not only risk damaging Euro–American trade but also substantially reduce the opportunities for successful Euro–American collaboration in global crisis-management in the future. It is therefore very keen to support the Clinton Administration's commitment to resolving problems in Eastern Europe and the former Soviet Union, and to warn against the negative consequences of any protectionist moves in America.

There is, however, a further dimension to Britain's concern to maintain the Atlantic connection. The emergence of Germany as the pivotal European power presents Britain with a major problem within the EC, for British policy has for many years has been predicated on the need to prevent the continent from being dominated by a single power. The fact that Germany is already beginning to take a more aggressive diplomatic stance, as was seen in its pre-emptive recognition of Croatia and Bosnia at the start of 1992, only serves to make this problem more pressing. Indeed, the clear danger is that the EC could become little more than a German zone. In these circumstances, maintaining the Atlantic connection gives Britain the option of releasing itself from a European arena in which power imbalances have become substantial.

It is for these reasons that London clings both to the 'special relationship' and to its 'world role' even though the Soviet threat which nurtured them both has now disappeared and Britain has, for a very long time indeed, lacked the relative economic strength to sustain either of them. In spite of the end of the Cold War, Britain's foreign policy-makers still seem to be committed to Realist modes of thinking. As a result, the UK looks set to carry on 'muddling through' in its foreign and defence policies throughout the 1990s.

# PART THREE
## Current Issues

# 14

# Organised Interests After Thatcher

**IAN HOLLIDAY**

On the whole, organised interests did not fare well under Thatcher. At the level of political doctrine, they found their role in the policy process – which had developed throughout the post-war period – dismissed as illegitimate. At the level of political practice, they accordingly found themselves excluded from many key points in the process of policy-making and implementation. In short, organised interests were subjected to a series of shocks in the Thatcher years. At the end of those years, many of them had substantially diminished power and influence.

Yet no sooner was Thatcher gone than organised interests began to be courted by politicians in ways which were entirely familiar pre-Thatcher, but which had been scorned by ministers throughout the 1980s. Indeed, one of the first acts of Michael Heseltine on his return to government as Environment Secretary in November 1990 was to invite consultation with the local government associations on the form of local taxation which should replace the calamitous poll tax. Similarly, on subsequently establishing a Local Government Commission with a much broader remit, Heseltine indicated that its mode of inquiry would be consultative. At the Treasury, the pressure of policy failure also gradually persuaded Norman Lamont that discussion of British economic policy with organised interests might be advisable. In each case, such an approach would have been unthinkable in the Thatcher years.

By the end of 1992, even trade unions – widely held to be the greatest casualties of Thatcherism – appeared to be experiencing something of a renaissance, being at the forefront of public outcry over the pit closure programme proposed by Heseltine in his new incarnation as Trade and Industry Secretary. The irony that Arthur Scargill should lead the campaign against pit closures – and that he should receive in many respects a sympathetic press, when Thatcher herself had long since departed No. 10, and was moreover no longer lauded by the media – was not lost on commentators. Indeed, the symbolism of Scargill outlasting Thatcher suggested that the trade unions had perhaps not been 'defeated' by Thatcherism after all.

The role of organised interests after Thatcher is therefore a less straight-forward matter than might have seemed likely – certainly to Thatcher herself – when conviction politics held sway in Downing Street and the self-proclaimed mission of politicians was to deny 'sectional interests' a role in policy-making. Indeed, even under Thatcher things never worked out as well in practice as was required by the prevailing doctrine of the time. Yet there is no doubt that liberal corporatism no longer functioned with Thatcher in power.

## The Strange Death of Liberal Corporatism

Liberal corporatism was (intended to be) an arrangement whereby government and a series of peak organisations came together to plan the British economy. Established in stages after the Second World War, it most publicly comprised a tripartite arrangement involving government, trade unions represented by the TUC, and business represented by the CBI. Each had equal representation on the National Economic Development Council (NEDC), the chief institutional embodiment of British liberal corporatism through which economic planning was conducted from the early 1960s onwards. Subsidiary institutions were developed at various sectoral levels. Through the developed procedures of liberal corporatism, policy-makers checked policy with key interest groups, who often possessed important powers of veto.

At the end of the 1970s, the liberal corporatist regime collapsed. Like liberal England 60 years earlier (Dangerfield, 1966), it died of a combination of internal and external causes.

Internally, it was always characterised by contradictions, for it never succeeded in developing mechanisms whereby its constituent elements could deliver on agreements made. On the one hand government consistently adopted a 'hands-off' approach to economic intervention. On the other its two partners frequently demonstrated that they could not in any case ensure that the interests which they represented would abide by any agreement struck at national level. Most notorious in this regard were the trade unions, which seemed to be beset by indiscipline in the late 1960s and 1970s (Dorfman, 1983). Business was, however, equally prone to problems created by a lack of national control (Grant, 1993). In truth, organised interests in Britain were not sufficiently organised to ensure that liberal corporatism worked.

The system was, then, somewhat unstable in years before 1979. On more than one occasion incomes policies, which were central to its operations, fell apart. Importantly, the fourth stage of the Callaghan government's incomes policy disintegrated in the winter of 1978–79, as both trade unions and business sought to circumvent its 5 per cent limit on pay increases. The ensuing Winter of Discontent was one major factor in the Conservatives' May 1979 election victory.

At this point, the chief external factor in the demise of liberal corporatism came into play. The Thatcher governments were determined that such arrangements would cease, and although the NEDC was not abolished by Thatcher, its importance was substantially downgraded. More generally, the whole ethos of government changed, from policy-making by consensus to a more centralised mode. This is not to say that consultation with organised interests simply ceased in 1979. Indeed, in many policy areas it continued much as before, at least for several years (Jordan and Richardson, 1987). At the public level of government consultation with trade unions and business, May 1979 did, however, represent a watershed.

## Thatcherism's Critique of Liberal Corporatism

Thatcherism had a number of objections to the way in which Britain was run prior to 1979. High on its list of criticisms was the damaging place in the policy process occupied by organised interests. In part this critique reflected party political calculation. As the sorry experience of the Heath government had demonstrated, the Conservatives simply found it very difficult to govern a country in which the trade union movement played a key role in policy-making (Bulpitt, 1986). In part it reflected traditional liberal commitments to a market economy. An important wing of the Conservative Party, associated with Enoch Powell in the 1960s, and with Thatcher and her mentor, Sir Keith Joseph, in the 1970s, had always maintained a principled opposition to government intervention in the market order, and found itself able to influence government policy in the 1980s. In part it reflected – in a largely instinctual fashion – an explanation of British decline which was only fully developed in the 1980s.

This explanation of a century of relative economic decline places most weight on 'institutional sclerosis' (Olson, 1982) which, it is argued, increasingly characterised the British political order in the post-war years. It is by no means incompatible with others. It can, for example, be partnered with cultural explanations (Wiener, 1981) and with critiques of the political and administrative elite which led Britain out of the Second World War and into what it hoped would be the New Jerusalem (Barnett, 1986). It is, however, distinctive.

Its key argument is that a mature political society with a long history of peaceful, incremental change will gradually become infested, and eventually overrun, by distributional coalitions which pursue not the general good, but merely their own sectional interests. Japan and West Germany experienced economic miracles in the post-war period because the totalitarian regimes which took them to war succeeded in ridding them of a large number of interest groups. Defeat accounted for many more. In effect, these two countries entered the post-war period without the encumbrances with which the British state had to deal, and were consequently able to adapt to the challenges of the post-war order and to achieve strong growth. Britain, by contrast, entered the post-war period with a system of interest group representation which was painstakingly restored by the Attlee government to its pre-war condition (Hennessy, 1992). This system reduced its capacity to adapt to change, and restricted its growth rate accordingly.

It was just this sort of interpretation of British decline that Thatcherism developed. For party political and principled reasons, the British state needed to be freed from the constraints of interest group pressure. Moreover, if Britain was to join the likes of Japan and Germany on high growth paths, institutional sclerosis had to be overcome. Notice was served that organised interests would find life very different under Thatcher government.

## Organised Interests Under Thatcher

Organised interests – or pressure groups – divide into a number of categories. Jordan and Richardson (1987) note that they can differ both in terms of the goals they pursue (which can be either sectional or promotional) and in terms of the strategy they adopt in order to attain that goal (which involves taking insider or outsider status). The examples they give of sectional interests with insider status and therefore privileged access to government are the British Medical Association (BMA) and the National Farmers' Union (NFU). Promotional groups held by them to have insider status are the Howard League for Penal Reform and the RSPCA. Among those groups identified as being outside the normal channels of the policy process are the National Union of Ratepayers' Association (sectional) and CND and the Animal Liberation Front (promotional). Building on this four-fold categorisation, it might be noted that sectional groups may be further divided into professional groups (such as the BMA), and those with a more commercial interest (such as a vast range of business organisations).

In the Thatcher years, even interests which had hitherto enjoyed insider status were often forced by government refusal to negotiate and bargain to adopt the tactics of outsiders. The BMA, a classic insider throughout the post-war period, was obliged by Kenneth Clarke's intransigence over a new contract for GPs to take its campaign to the British people. A controversial and very high profile poster campaign put the question, 'What do you call a man who ignores medical advice?', and answered it, 'Mr Clarke'. Despite this, the contract was imposed on GPs in 1990. As it happens, most GPs have done very well out of it (Holliday, 1992b). Other venerable professional groups, such as the Bar Council and the Law Society, as well as more mundane groupings of university lecturers, teachers, and the like, were also forced into a confrontational stance by the Thatcher administration. In many sectors of industry, old collaborative relations were similarly transformed. All sectoral associations now find themselves more pressurised by government, and are consequently a great deal more publicity-conscious than was previously the case. The brewing industry, for example, certainly did not expect to be opposed by government, but when challenged on monopolistic practices was forced into the political arena.

However, not all organised interests fared badly under Thatcher. A fair few – such as the Institute of Directors (IoD), a series of interest groups in the financial sector, interests representing big energy producers, the British Roads Federation (BRF), and so on – even had a rather good 1980s. Yet this was not because the Thatcher administration maintained consultative contacts with privileged interest groups, for government–interest group consultation was reduced (though not abolished) across the board in the 1980s. Thatcher had very little respect for representative status, and consulted (if at all) on a much more ad hoc basis than had any of her immediate predecessors. Rather, it was because the broad trend of government policy happened to favour some interest groups above others. Thus, interest groups in the financial services sector fared well in the 1980s, less as a result of direct lobbying than as a consequence of the overall temper of government policy. Similarly, the BRF prospered in the 1980s – as it had also done in many previous decades – largely because of Thatcher's antipathy towards rail transport. New policy space was therefore created in the 1980s, and generated opportunities for a range of interest groups. This, however, was more the consequence of new biases created in the system by Thatcherite doctrine, than of a direct process of lobbying.

The world of organised interests was therefore transformed by a decade of Thatcherism. The central theme of the decade was increased uncertainty, as a number of interest groups found places in the policy process which they had come to take for granted abruptly challenged. Local government associations, the education profession, even doctors and a range of business interests found themselves in a more tenuous – or even calamitous – position than had hitherto been the case. Oddly, one classic outsider campaign, organised by poll tax demonstrators (heirs to Jordan and Richardson's National Union of Ratepayers' Association), became a success story of the late Thatcher years, contributing in fact to her downfall.

## Trade Unions After Thatcher

Many organised interests were affected by the demise of liberal corporatism. Its chief casualties were, however, the trade unions. Not only were they denied their former role in policy-making, they also found themselves confronted by a government which sought to undermine the very foundations on which they had developed in previous years. Henceforth, trade unions were to be denied legitimacy and, through this denial, strength (Holmes, 1985).

There is no doubt that both these objectives had been substantially accomplished by the time Thatcher left office. Trade union membership was down from 12 million in 1979 to 8 million in 1991. Trade union militancy was also down, with strike levels in the late 1980s and early 1990s at their lowest for half a century. Trade union access to government and to policy-makers more generally had been substantially reduced (Marsh, 1992).

Yet no single factor accounts for this change. Certainly government action was important. On the one hand the Thatcher administration did indeed act to undermine trade union legitimacy, cutting contact to a bare minimum, and creating a climate in which unionism was seen to be counter-productive. On the other hand it also mounted a direct, if graduated, attack on unionism, both through legislation and through a long series of public sector strikes, most of which the government was seen to win. Most important in this regard was the year-long miners' strike of 1984–85 (Adeney and

Lloyd, 1986). But these were not the only reasons for the retreat of trade unionism in the 1980s.

Also significant were factors partly or wholly outside the control of government. The massive rise in unemployment at the start of the 1980s – for which, admittedly, Thatcherism must take a good deal of responsibility – was of the first importance in undermining trade union power because it created a large reserve army of labour. Similarly, the changing nature of British industry in the 1980s, prompted in part by the big shake-out at the start of the decade, had an adverse effect on unionism because it involved a general shift from large-scale manufacturing to small-scale manufacturing and service industries, which are less heavily unionised. Linked changes in the world economy only served to reinforce this process (Bassett, 1987).

Trade union power may well therefore have declined in the 1980s under any government. The Thatcher governments simply ensured that the decline was substantial, and that it was fully reflected in legislation. The importance of these two exercises should not be under-estimated. By the end of the third Conservative term, legislation enacted in stages since 1979 had (1) removed all legal immunities from the closed shop, (2) outlawed all secondary action, (3) established a requirement that trade unions hold pre-strike ballots, (4) forced some internal democratisation on unions, and (5) made a number of other minor changes to industrial relations law.

In the long run-up to the 1992 general election it was nevertheless possible to envisage an important role for trade unions in British politics in the 1990s. To begin with, though they had certainly been battered during the 1980s, they had not been totally undermined. In particular, their workplace strength had remained remarkably intact, as is shown by UK wage rates which grew at or above inflation throughout the 1980s (Longstreth, 1988). Beyond this there was the possibility that a Labour government, though pledged to reverse only a few of the Conservatives' reforms, would enact a number of beneficial measures.

Pivotal Labour commitments in 1992 included a national minimum wage, an extension of rights to part-time workers, a new trade union recognition law, and the various elements included in the EC's Social Chapter (such as legislation on working time, and mandatory works councils for larger companies), which a Labour government was pledged to sign. Whilst Labour's central intention was to extend rights to all workers, rather than simply to trade unionists, there is little doubt that trade unions would have benefited both from these specific measures, and from the increased status which they would have enjoyed under a Labour government. Indeed, there was even a chance that a neocorporatist arrangement would emerge, with the two sides of industry coming together with government to discuss Labour's proposed National Economic Assessment.

The return of the Conservatives for a fourth term signalled that formal re-incorporation of the trade union movement into the policy-making process would not take place, and that the trend of the 1980s towards deregulation of the labour market and encouragement of individualism at work would continue. Indeed, Norman Lamont's announcement in June 1992 that NEDC – the central institution of British liberal corporatism – was to be abolished at the start of 1993 was a symbolic reaffirmation of key Thatcherite tenets. The 1990s can be expected to witness increases in individual employer–employee contracts in the private sector, in performance-related pay in the public sector, and in flexibility all round. Furthermore, the Conservatives intend to extend their legislative programme by enacting such measures as (1) new rules governing automatic 'check-off' of trade union dues, (2) 7-day notice of strikes, (3) postal as opposed to workplace ballots on strike action, and (4) removal of TUC regulation of the trade union movement.

Yet it is not clear that trade unions can be written out of the policy process as easily as either Thatcher or her successors would like. At sub-national levels of the policy process it is, for example, evident that the decision almost entirely to exclude trade unionists from participation in Training and Enterprise Councils (TECs) was a mistake, and that they will need to be brought back into British training policy-making if that policy is to work. A more dramatic mistake – both legally and politically – was Heseltine's failure to consult mining unions over the pit closure programme announced in November 1992. Furthermore, by this date even Treasury ministers were starting to revive contacts with trade unionists. Indications that some form of neo-corporatism might be reconstituted were therefore evident as Major's second term proceeded.

This is not, however, to argue that trade unions are actually likely to regain the prominent place in the policy process that was accorded to them in the years leading up to 1979. Then, they were even made formally responsible for the level of income tax which resulted from the Healey budget of 1976 (Healey, 1989). Today, such overt dealing with peak organisations is no part of the Chancellor's strategy. A gradual reconstitution of neocorporatist arrangements nevertheless remains a clear possibility.

Trade unions have themselves sought to change both their role in British politics and their structures as a means of meeting the new challenges of the 1990s. Immediately after Labour's defeat in the 1992 general election both the Labour Party and a number of trade unions recognised that ties between the two wings of the labour movement would have to be reduced and perhaps severed altogether if the party was to have a chance of winning a future general election. On the part of Labour, strategists sought to release the party from trade union influence in policy-making. On the part of the unions, it was recognised that money might more profitably be spent not on financing the Labour Party (more than 50 per cent of running costs up to 1992) and its election campaigns (90 per cent of costs in 1992), but on European lobbying, industrial campaigns, and local government. New agendas that unions plan to pursue in the 1990s include training and control of pension funds.

The structure of the trade union movement is also changing, not because Labour lost in 1992, but because the fall in union membership during the 1980s – 1 million members in the TGWU alone – put pressure on their finances and forced them to seek mergers. In May 1992 the AEU engineers and EETPU electricians merged to create a new union with 0.9 million members. There is a good chance that the MSF will also soon join to boost membership to 1.6 million. On the day before the 1992 general election three large public sector unions, NALGO, NUPE and COHSE, announced that in July 1993 they would together form Unison, with a total of 1.4 million members, making this the biggest public sector union in Britain. Finally, there is even the possibility that the two largest general unions, the TGWU (1.2 million members) and the GMB (0.9 million), will soon merge, restoring the TGWU to the position it has held for 60 years as Britain's largest union. There is every chance that by the end of the decade five or six dominant super-unions will have been created. In these circumstances, the TUC itself may collapse, as super-unions seek to direct their own campaigns.

The development of super-unions is in many ways odd. The trend in the economy as a whole is towards fragmentation, and company bargaining. In these circumstances it is in some senses unclear what additional assistance super-unions will be able to offer individual trade unionists at the company level. The most likely development is that they will compete to offer the best fringe benefits – such as pension and other financial packages – to their members. In an increasingly deregulated labour market, trade unions will continue to shift from political to financial activities. Moreover, like many other organisations, they will be forced to lobby more often in Europe, both alone and in collaboration with other European unions, through EuroTUC. The importance of the European arena has already been recognised by unions such as the GMB, which opened a Brussels office in January 1992. Yet the ability of the trade union movement to revive neocorporatist arrangements in the domestic sphere can only be enhanced by the move towards super-unionism.

The gradual revival of British trade unionism is, however, no more than one example of change in the role of organised interests since Thatcher. Government–interest group relations which had been carefully nurtured in the years leading up to 1979 were certainly treated with a great deal less respect in subsequent years. Since 1990, however, a reverse movement has started to take place.

## Organised Interests in the 1990s

Policy style undoubtedly changed with the replacement of Thatcher by Major, and in many areas – notably the conduct of Cabinet government – commentators point to the reappearance of a more consensual style of policy-making. In the world of organised interests there is clearly no possibility of a simple return to the situation which existed before 1979. Yet under pressure of policy failure, even a post-Thatcher Conservative administration has been forced to revive a number of contacts with organised interests. In part, this reflects a rather less dogmatic approach to policy-making. In addition, it is evidence of a realisation that Thatcherite modes of operation were not always ideal.

Indeed, removal of organised interests from the policy process in the Thatcher years often tended to generate the sort of policy mess which led policy-makers to question whether it actually makes sense to act unilaterally within the policy process. In some fields, it would actually have been very difficult to make the sorts of changes which Thatcherism sought by consultative means. Some aspects of trade union reform are good examples. In others, however, Thatcherism's own ends would have been advanced by a more inclusive and corporatist style. Here, numerous examples may be cited. Reform of local government finance is a classic case. By the time policy-makers came to develop the poll tax, their contacts with local government had diminished almost to zero. The consequences were predictably catastrophic. Other examples – in education, health and a series of additional spheres – may readily be cited (Marsh and Rhodes, 1992). In these circumstances, the very possibility of running a state on Thatcherite lines must be called into question.

It is, however, important to be clear about the precise terms of the question that is being asked of Thatcherite strategy. Much of the Thatcherite case against the British policy style was premised on the contention that the British policy process in the years up to 1979 was programmed to produce certain outcomes by the very nature of its policy-making arrangements. What Thatcherism understood very clearly – and objected to very strongly – was the fact that the British policy style had a procedural bias towards consensus politics. If the post-war consensus was to be undermined, the British policy process had to be fundamentally reconstructed. Thatcherite policy could not simply be fed through existing mechanisms.

Thus it would be wrong to argue that Thatcherism should at all times have respected policy-making modes which had been established during the post-war period. To have done this would have placed substantial constraints on Thatcherite radicalism. It can, nevertheless, be maintained that in cutting (on some occasions all) contacts with organised interests, Thatcherism almost wilfully created policy mess.

It is not entirely clear how the process of rebuilding government–interest group relations will develop. When many – though by no means all – structures have been destroyed, a straightforward return to the status quo ante is impossible. Furthermore, it has already been argued that liberal corporatism British-style never did work as intended, and could not be expected to do so now. A simple return to its modes of operation is therefore neither feasible nor desirable. In these circumstances it is likely that the uncertainty which characterised the 1980s will be extended into the 1990s. Contacts will be resumed, but in an ad hoc manner. Piecemeal reincorporation of organised interests is the most likely development.

## Conclusion

Organised interests after Thatcher operate in an environment which is changing in three main ways. To begin with, the individualistic drive which Thatcher did as much as anyone else to champion in the 1980s could develop yet further in the 1990s, requiring interest groups to develop accordingly. Here, the biggest challenge faces trade unions, which are built on a collectivistic ethos. If they are to play an important part in British politics in the 1990s, they may have to develop a more individualistic orientation, setting themselves up perhaps as defenders of individual rights at work.

Other organised interests may not face this difficulty, but they will be equally affected by the other two main changes to the British policy environment. The first is the changing nature of the policy process and, indeed, of the British State itself. As the old monolithic State structure is increasingly fragmented and politicised, so the uncertainty facing organised interests mounts and their tactics and resources have to be diversified. The second is the developing European dimension. Already many policy areas and processes have been Europeanised, and already British interests have started to respond by joining European associations. Beyond this, many organised interests, and notably a number of businesses, have begun to recognise that if they are to play a full part in the new Europe which is forming, they may need new types of representation. The result is that even if, as seems likely, many European ideals suffer setbacks over the years to come, the Europeanisation of much policy will in all probability continue apace.

Increased pluralism in a reshaped and extended policy domain is therefore the chief challenge to face all organised interests after Thatcher. Even interests which were long privileged by the British State – indeed, in the case of the trade unions, especially those interests – are being forced to adapt to a more uncertain policy-making environment. Their tactics and resources are altering to take account of the increased insecurity which they face. Yet there are signs as the Major government lurches from one crisis to another that a piecemeal revival of quasi-corporatist arrangements will be the theme of the 1990s.

# 15

# Migration and the Politics of Race*

## JOHN SOLOMOS and LES BACK

Migration and racism are not new issues in Britain. For many
years they have been politically salient. However, during the
late 1980s and early 1990s they have started to feature in
political debates in new ways. Issues surrounding the Rushdie
affair, the role of religious differences, immigration from Hong
Kong, and refugee and asylum policy have highlighted the
changing dynamics of the politics of race and ethnicity (which
may revolve around religious, language, and national identities, as much as around race). Moreover, there have been
persistent concerns that tension in many inner city areas
between the police and young blacks may lead to further
urban unrest such as that which occurred in 1981 and 1985.
Above all, it has become abundantly clear in all liberal
democracies that political conflicts about race and ethnicity
are not just the residual hangovers from pre-modern societies
which liberals and Marxists used to believe.

### Recent Trends in Europe

Across much of western Europe migration and the politics of
race have become major aspects of political mobilisation, and

* Parts of this chapter draw on a research project on the politics of race and
social change which has been supported by the Economic and Social
Research Council (award number R 000 23 1545). We are grateful to the
ESRC for its support.

321

some countries have experienced a sharp growth in racism and hostility to migrants. Neofascist and right-wing political parties everywhere are using migration as a means of attracting support, and making electoral headway in a previously unprecedented fashion (Husbands, 1991; Balibar, 1991). In France, the Front National under Jean-Marie Le Pen has polled up to 14 per cent of the nation-wide vote, and won seats widely in regional and European elections. In Germany support for the right-wing Republikaner Party has also surged in regional elections. In Belgium the far right Vlaams Blok taps Flemish nationalism, and in Italy the neofascist MSI party has revived its appeal, particularly in the south.

Additionally, there is increasing evidence of the involvement of right-wing movements in the growth of violence aimed at migrants and refugees. Serious outbreaks of radical right violence in Germany during 1991 and 1992 aimed at persecuting migrants have in some cases been apparently tolerated or approved by substantial sections of the population, especially in the former East Germany. Outside the EC, conflict in the former Yugoslav territories has descended into all-out civil war marked by horrific 'ethnic cleansing', and politics in other parts of the former Soviet empire has taken on a strong racialist dimension. These human disasters are forcible reminders of the seriousness of unconstrained ethnic politics, and of how little 'modernity' alone can do to constrain the spiral of racist and ethnic conflicts once it has been inaugurated.

Two immediate factors are often singled out as helping to shape recent developments. First, it is argued that developments in eastern Europe and the former Soviet Union have helped to create 'fears' about the likelihood of mass migration from the former Communist states to countries as diverse as Germany, Italy and Austria. This issue has indeed been widely debated in the period since 1989, though it is not easy to draw any clear conclusions about future patterns of migration or to predict the nature of political responses that are likely to arise (Cohen, 1991). Second, it is argued that the question of migration from North Africa has become a key political issue in France and other societies. Here, the contention is that political instability and demographic change could generate pressures to migrate across the North African region as a whole, and that this could have a major impact on Mediterranean countries such as France, Spain and Italy.

Although there are still strong national political differences, the past decade has nonetheless witnessed a number of Europe-wide trends. First, new patterns of migration and settlement have had an impact on Europe as well as other parts of the world, and have led to the arrival of new groups of migrants from a range of social and economic backgrounds. Second, a growing number of refugees and asylum-seekers have been displaced by a combination of political instability, economic and natural disasters and the threat of genocide. The extent of such displacement has helped to put the question of refugees and asylum-seekers high on the political agenda of many countries in Europe and elsewhere.

Third, these transformations have taken place at a time of uncertainty and confusion over the economic and political orientation of the 'New Europe'. Questions are being asked about what is meant by talk of constructing a new 'European identity', and the interplay with established national and ethnic boundaries. It is perhaps not surprising, therefore, that in this environment the position of ethnic and racial minorities who are already in Europe is intimately tied to the over-arching issue of the politics of migration.

Fourth, the rapid transformation experienced by a number of societies over the past two decades, particularly in terms of growing levels of unemployment and the persistence of large-scale joblessness, has provided fertile ground for extreme right-wing parties and movements to target ethnic and racial minorities as 'enemies within' who are ultimately 'outsiders'. At a simplistic level calls for the expulsion of 'foreigners' can command substantial electoral support, while even violence against particularly stigmatised groups (such as gypsies in many European societies) may be passively tolerated by large numbers of people.

In the broader European context the key issue in recent debates about migrant workers is the complex question of 'citizenship rights' and how these should be reconceptualised in the context of the 'New Europe'. Some important elements of this debate are discussions about: (1) the political rights of minorities, including the issue of representation in both local and national politics; (2) minority religious and cultural rights, and their role in the context of a society which is becoming more diverse; (3) the role of legislative interventions to protect the rights of minorities and develop extensive notions of citizenship and democracy in the 'New Europe'. At the broadest level these developments raise urgent questions. Are we seeing the emergence of a new racism? Does it take similar forms in all European countries? What can best be done to develop policies to tackle the root causes of racism in contemporary Europe?

## Is Britain the Exception?

Britain has not witnessed a rapid growth of extreme right-wing political parties, despite the fact that immigration and race remain heavily politicised issues. In the 1987 general election the two major British fascist parties – the British Movement (now the British National Party: BNP) and the National Front (NF) – did not contest any seats. In 1992, however, the two parties put up 27 candidates (the NF 14 and BNP 13) and polled 12 000 votes (*Runnymede Trust Bulletin*, May 1992). However, all of these candidates lost their deposits of £500 and only two candidates polled much more than 1 per cent of the vote. Compared with the success of fascist parties in continental Europe the electoral showing of the NF and the BNP was insignificant.

The conventional wisdom of Labour and Conservative politicians has attributed this lack of extreme right-wing success to the fact that Britain has operated 'twin-track' policies of strictly controlling immigration (using laws which critics argue themselves embody racial discrimination), but also enforcing anti-discrimination laws internally. On this account British voters have not supported extremists because they are confident that the existing social balance will not be radically changed, while British domestic law and institutions have substantially improved the climate of race relations and racial equality domestically.

Some observers argue that racist and far-right parties have also failed to grow because since 1979 the Conservative Party has successfully presented itself as able to control immigration, and has been able to maintain the support of voters who might otherwise be attracted to the extreme right (Husbands, 1992). During the 1992 general election some Tory politicians made a clear attempt to present a firm position on the question of immigration control. Sir Nicholas Fairbairn, warned a few days prior to the election that a Labour government would mean a major influx of primary immigration, whereby Britain would be 'swamped by immigrants of every colour and race and on any excuse of asylum or bogus marriage, or just plain deception' (*Runnymede Trust Bulletin*, May 1992). This resulted in a series of tabloid headlines warning about 'human tides' of migrants (*Sun*, 4 April 1992). The Conservative leadership was quick to distance itself from any suggestion that immigration control was connected to race; however John Major did state that he was in favour of immigration control that was 'firm and fair'.

The Conservatives' ability to avoid any rivals on their right is partly the consequence of Britain's plurality rule electoral system, which does not allow small political parties to flourish. During the general election leading Conservative politicians used the emergence of far-right political groupings as both an argument for strong immigration control and against proportional representation. In the aftermath of Fairbairn's intervention Kenneth Baker, then Home Secretary, connected the emergence of the far right in Germany to these issues:

In the state of Baden Wurtemburg, the fascist Republikaner Party received 11 per cent of the vote [in regional elections]. Previously it had received 1 per cent. This dramatic growth in support for the fascists was due to one issue. That issue was the flood of migrants and would-be asylum seekers whose continuing numbers have aroused public concern about this rising tide . . . If proportional representation turned out to have the same results in Britain, it would be a pact with the devil. Mr Kinnock and Mr Ashdown are preparing for Britain a deadly political cocktail (*Conservative Party News*, 6 April 1992).

The significance of this intervention is that the blame for fascism is not ascribed to the political cultures of Europe but to the presence of migrants who 'trigger' these responses. Equally, the choice of metaphors which refer to 'rising tides of migrants' connects very closely with previous notions of Britain being 'swamped by other cultures'. The end result is that the Conservatives cater to the anti-immigration lobby and exploit the politics of race and contemporary racism without invoking racism in a direct way. The responsibility for any future 'deadly political cocktail' is instead placed squarely with the opposition parties. On 7 April 1992, just two days before the General Election, the *Daily Express* ran the headline 'BAKER'S MIGRANT FLOOD WARNING – LABOUR SET TO OPEN DOORS'.

Broader explanations of the absence of a significant racist right in Britain also point to its limited appeal outside of a few specific localities like East London (Husbands, 1992). It is not possible to draw a direct comparison, for example, between the situation in France and Britain. The discussion in Britain about race and race relations in not to be found in other European societies (Bovenkerk *et al.*, 1990; Lloyd, 1991).

These differences are important but Britain continues to suffer from serious problems of racism. Recent years have seen a significant growth in racial attacks and in many parts of the country violence has taken place. It is currently estimated that 70 000 racist incidents are occurring each year (Campaign Against Racism and Fascism, 1992). Perhaps one of the most alarming patterns which is emerging is that this violence seems to be occurring most frequently in suburban areas. In July 1992, Ruhullah Aramesh was brutally beaten by a gang of white male youths in the South London suburb of Thornton Heath, Croydon. Aramesh, a refugee from Afghanistan, intervened when four white youths started harassing his female relatives. The youths left initially only to return with reinforcements. Aramesh was surrounded by a crowd of young men shouting racist taunts and armed with metal bars and baseball bats; two days later he was dead. Other examples of this kind of violence include the stabbing of Roland Adams on the Thamesmead Council Estate, Woolwich, South East London in 1991, and the attack on Sultana Ahmed from behind by two white youths, who set her sari on fire with lighter fuel in Ilford, Essex.

Critics also argue that to focus only on very overt racism, such as these horrific incidents, may give a misleading picture. Robert Miles has recently argued that perhaps what is novel about contemporary forms of racism is not the proliferation of racist social movements but an intensification of ideological and political struggle around the expression of a racism that often claims not to be racist – as in Baker's warning about migrants noted above (Miles, 1989). Racism should be seen not as a monolithic set of ideas but as an ideology that takes particular forms within given social and political relations. In Britain, for example, issues such as employment, housing, education, and law and order have been racialised (Solomos, 1993).

## Political Mobilisation by Ethnic Minorities

Members of minority races and ethnic groups are not passive observers or victims of racism in British society. They are increasingly shaping their own and the country's political futures. Evidence of increased minority representation in political institutions began to emerge in the 1980s, but it was only during the early 1990s that the full impact of this process was witnessed. The past decade has seen the election of a sizeable number of black and ethnic minority local councillors in London, Birmingham, Bradford, Leicester and other localities (Back and Solomos, 1992a). At the same time there has been more limited evidence of change at the level of national party politics with the election of five black Labour Members of Parliament and one black Conservative.

During the general election all the political parties claimed that race was no longer an issue in British political life. All of the black Labour MPs elected in 1987 were returned to Parliament, many of them with significantly increased majorities. Keith Vaz in Leicester East won a 10 per cent swing to Labour. Equally, Bernie Grant in the north London constituency of Tottenham managed the second largest swing to Labour of 9 per cent. Despite the defeat of Ashok Kumar, who was elected as Labour MP for Langbaurgh in a 1991 by-election, two new black MPs were also elected to Westminster. Piara Khabra held the Labour seat of Ealing Southall and Nirj Deva became the first black Conservative MP in Brentford and Isleworth.

In all, more than twenty black candidates stood: ten for the Labour Party, eight for the Conservatives and four for the Liberal Democrats. The success of black candidates in the election was offered as evidence that Britain was becoming a multiracial democracy, by contrast with the European trends reviewed above. Yet during the election campaign it was also clear that despite the conspicuous participation of black people in the political process, the claim that race was no longer an important feature of the electoral process was premature in its optimism. In the Tory-held constituency of Cheltenham John Taylor, the Conservative candidate and black barrister, failed to be elected despite endorsement by John Major. Taylor's selection and campaign took place amid accusations of racism from the Liberal Democratic opposition and within Cheltenham's Conservative Association.

These are not the only signs that the issue of political representation has become a key question. During the past few years there has been evidence in a number of local contexts that the question of minority access to political influence is an issue that has had a major impact on the Labour Party, and to a lesser extent the Conservative Party. Recent controversies in Small Heath in Birmingham about the selection of the Labour candidate for the 1992 general election highlighted the contested nature of power and influence in many inner city constituencies (Back and Solomos, 1992b). At the same time, controversy over Taylor's selection in Cheltenham showed that the Conservative Party is by no means immune from such conflicts.

Britain's ethnic minorities are questioning whether they are fully included in and represented through political institutions. It is not surprising, therefore, that an important concern in recent years has been the issue of citizenship and minority rights in British society. There is a growing awareness of the gap between formal citizenship and *de facto* restriction of the economic and social rights of minorities as a result of discrimination, economic restructuring and the decline of the welfare state. It is also the result of increasing influence by minority political activists in particular localities, who have attempted to use political participation as a route to political office.

A number of cases have recently highlighted the increased prominence of religious and cultural issues in current ethnic politics. The chief example is the Rushdie affair when the Ayatollah Khomeini issued a *fatwa* against the author Salman Rushdie for an allegedly anti-Islamic book, the novel *The Satanic Verses*. Essentially this edict was a religious pardon for any devout Muslim who should kill Rushdie, prompting the author to retreat into a secret life under continuous police protection, and generating a storm of protest concerning the balance between free speech and respect for different religions. In Britain the Rushdie affair polarised British Muslims, since it seemed to put religious duty against respect for the law, and it provided a potent pretext for racist feelings to find expression. Growing public interest in the role of fundamentalism among sections of Muslim communities in various countries has given a new life to debates about the issue of cultural differences and processes of integration.

## Conclusion: the Future for Multiculturalism

The key question raised by these trends concerns prospects for the development of multiculturalism in the present political environment. Hostile media coverage of the Rushdie affair strongly reinforced the view that minorities which do not share the dominant political values of British society pose a threat to social stability and cohesion. Some commentators have used these events to criticise 'multiculturalism' and 'anti-racism', and assert the need for 'melting-pot' policies which are aimed at the full integration of ethnic minorities rather than respect for their separate cultural identities.

There are clearly at this stage quite divergent perspectives about how best to deal with all of these concerns. There is a wealth of discussion about what kind of measures are necessary to tackle the inequalities and exclusions which confront minority groups. At the same time there is clear evidence that existing initiatives are severely limited in their impact. A number of commentators have pointed to the limitations of legislative and public policy interventions in bringing about a major improvement in the socio–political position of minorities (Hammar, 1985; Layton-Henry, 1990). The very plurality of categories used in current debates seems to indicate that the objectives pursued are by no means clear and are in fact essentially contested notions. In particular, researchers and practitioners do not concur on what they mean by terms such as 'equality of opportunity' and 'anti-discrimination', or what they consider to be evidence of a move towards the stated goals of policies.

Some observers argue that the development of equal opportunity policies is the outcome of a process of political negotiation, pressure group politics and bureaucratic policy-making. However, others emphasise the need to look beyond stated objectives and public political negotiations and explore ways in which deeply-entrenched processes of discrimination may be resistant to legal and political interventions while inegalitarian social relations structure society as a whole. If existing strategies are indeed failing, then what policies could tackle discrimination more effectively? What links could be made between policies on immigration and policies on social and economic issues? What kind of positive social policy agenda can be developed to deal with the position of both established communities and new migrants in the 1990s and beyond?

There are no easy answers to these questions and the experience of the past two decades indicates that any set of policies will by no means achieve unanimous support in society as a whole. But perhaps a starting point for future policy agendas is the recognition that there is a need for a coordinated public policy to deal with various social, political and cultural aspects of the position of ethnic minorities. In the past British policy initiatives have been at best ad hoc and piecemeal. Although public policy has been committed for some time to the pursuit of equal opportunity and multi-culturalism, there is no clear political and social consensus in society about what these goals mean, either ideologically or practically. For example, there is little agreement about what public policies need to be developed to deal with discrimination in such areas as education, social policy and employment. Opponents of new initiatives in effect deny that racism is endemic in British society.

The policy areas where most clarification of objectives is needed include: (1) links between anti-discrimination legislation and its role is creating greater opportunities and providing remedies for ethnic minorities and new migrants; (2) connections between multicultural and anti-racist initiatives which address the situation in areas such as employment, education, social services and housing; (3) inter-relationships between national UK policies and initiatives developed by the EC and other transnational institutions and bodies in response to specific issues.

What we are witnessing in the current period is the development of new forms of racism, and to some extent the resurgence of older forms in some national contexts. Extreme right-wing political movements have mobilised to oppose these new patterns of immigration. At the same time, ethnic minorities are better mobilised than in the past to defend their interests. For both reasons there is an increasing awareness that the question of the social and political rights of established minorities is likely to prove one of the most difficult social issues to handle in the near future. The next decade is likely to see renewed debate about the socio–political rights of both ethnic and other minority communities. Such debates are likely to increase in intensity in the future.

# 16

# The Media and Politics

**DAVID MARSH**

Much has been written on the role of the media in British politics. However, most existing studies concentrate on assessing the influence of television and the press on voting. For the most part, they fail to address broader questions concerning the role the media plays in relation to democracy. This chapter aims to address this deficiency. Initially, I identify three conflicting views in the literature of the proper role and status of the media in democratic society before establishing how these are related to broader normative views of the form British democracy should take. Subsequently, I aim to assess which view of the media most accurately describes British practice through a brief analysis of three areas which have attracted a great deal of attention: media bias; media influence on voting; and government manipulation of information.

## The Role of the Media

The role which the media does, and should, play in relation to democracy is contested. Miller (1991) identifies three contrasting views of the proper role and status of the media which have been held in Britain and elsewhere: mobilising; libertarian; and public service. In the mobilising view, the media should be subordinate to the State; the government is the guardian of the national interest and the media should promote that national interest as 'defined by the State/government. In the libertarian view, the media should have the freedom to publish/broadcast and the public should have the freedom to read/view, subject to very limited constraints imposed by the State/government to protect national security and, possibly, public morality. In the public service view, the media has a right, indeed for some a duty, to scrutinise government, holding it accountable for its actions and being responsive to the public.

## Views of Democracy and Views of the Media

Of course these views on the appropriate role of the media are invariably related to broader views about the proper relationship between governors and the governed; that is on the type of democratic government Britain should have. The conservative view of democracy, which of course is not inevitably and certainly not exclusively associated with the Conservative Party, places the emphasis upon leadership; upon strong, centralised efficient government, rather than responsive government (Marsh and Tant, 1989; Tant, 1993). The argument here is that a more open participatory form of government would mean inefficient government as politicians and civil servants would be forever looking over their shoulders, thus avoiding taking actions which are necessary, if unpopular. This is a top-down, leadership, view of democracy, which would advocate: a simple plurality electoral system, strong party discipline and executive dominance of the legislature, because these would produce a decisive majority and hence strong government; limited access to information about government, because access to information reduces efficiency; low levels of participation, because participation leads to excessive demands, conflict and hence inefficiency; and a unitary political system, to ensure centralised, consistent government. It would also imply a mobilising view of the media; the government knows best what is in the national interest and the media should forward that interest.

In contrast, a participatory view of democracy emphasises the need for government to reflect the attitudes and preferences of the population; to be responsive to the electorate. Here, more openness and responsiveness mean fairer, more democratic government. This view would advocate: proportional representation (PR), because it ensures that the legislature more accurately reflects the political views of the electorate; increased power for the legislature in relation to the executive, in order to hold the executive more accountable between elections; freedom of information, so that the executive can be held accountable; greater participation, because participation increases the representativeness and the responsiveness of government; and devolution of power to sub-national government, to ensure participation and responsiveness. It would also imply a public service view of the media, with the media acting as a crucial check on government power.

Historically, these are the two views of democracy which have informed the British political tradition although as I, and others, have argued it is the conservative view which is dominant and has underpinned the institutions and processes of British government (Tant, 1993). However, in the more recent period an alternative view of democracy has gained ground in Britain, as elsewhere; a view which closely identifies democracy and the market. Following Hayek, it is suggested that governments, both politicians and bureaucrats, seek to reshape the social world by State economic management and the redistribution of resources. This is oppressive because it attempts to regulate the lives and activities of individuals. In this view democracy is not an end but a means, 'a doctrine about the manner of determining what will be law' (Hayek, 1960, p.103); the end is to ensure continued and expanded individual freedom. A democratic system should be designed to underpin, and reflect, a free-market society and a 'minimal state'. This is not the place to discuss this view but it enshrines a clear tension; it is difficult to see how the mechanisms of the democratic system can ensure its policy outputs reduce State intervention and bolster individual freedom. Thatcherism resolved this tension by stressing the need for a strong State to ensure a free economy (Gamble, 1988).

To Thatcherites the argument was that Britain had suffered from 'over-government'. Successive governments had intervened more in the economy responding to pressure from powerful interests. This led to the reduction of individual freedom and the imposition of constraints on the operation of the market. As such, the British variant on this position tended to be associated with the conservative view of how political institutions should be structured. The rhetoric of Thatcherism emphasised the need for strong decisive government in order to promote individual freedom and the operation of the market. This rhetoric also implied a libertarian view of the media; the media should not be an agent of the State, still less should its purpose be to hold government to account, all that was necessary was the establishment of the conditions within which a free market could flourish. As we shall see, the practice of the Thatcher governments was rather different from the rhetoric. In effect, the Thatcher governments were informed by a conservative, rather than a 'new right', view of democracy and, as such, operated with a mobilising view of the proper role of the media in a democracy.

## Examining the Media's Role

It is impossible in this brief chapter to deal with all aspects of the question I wish to pose in this section: which view of the media most accurately describes British practice? Here, I concentrate exclusively on three areas: media bias, particularly in the context of elections; media influence on voting patterns; and government manipulation of information.

### Media Bias

No reader of the British tabloid press can be in any doubt that media bias exists in this sphere. The *Sun*'s election day issue in April 1992 represents only the most obvious example of this bias. As far as the press is concerned there are three related problems. First, ownership of the press is highly concentrated. Second, the press overwhelmingly supports the Conservative Party. Third, this support becomes increasingly overt during an election campaign.

Table 16.1 indicates the extent of concentration; 57 per cent of daily sales and 66 per cent of Sunday sales were by newspapers owned by two companies, News International and Mirror Group Newspapers. Of course, this situation may change, depending on the fate of the Mirror Group. Why do certain individuals want to own newspapers? Simon Jenkins

TABLE 16.1    Readership shares of newspaper owners, May 1992

| By owner | Per cent of Daily readership | Per cent of Sunday readership |
|---|---|---|
| News International (*Sun, Today, Times, News of the World, Sunday Times*) | 31 | 36 |
| Mirror Group Newspapers (*Mirror, Record, Sunday Mirror, People*) | 26 | 30 |
| United Newspapers (*Express, Star, Sunday Express*) | 16 | 10 |
| Associated Newspapers (*Mail, Mail on Sunday*) | 12 | 12 |
| Daily Telegraph (*Telegraph, Sunday Telegraph*) | 7 | 3 |
| Guardian/Manchester Evening News (*Guardian*) | 3 | – |
| Newspaper Publishing (*Independent, Independent on Sunday*) | 3 | 2 |
| Pearson (*Financial Times*) | 2 | – |
| Lonrho (*Observer*) | – | 3 |
| Apollo (*Sunday Sport*) | – | 2 |
| Total | 100 | 100 |

examines this question and comes to a clear conclusion. There is precious little profit involved; only the *Sun* makes much money. Rather, the press barons are in newspapers for power, influence and easy access to the establishment and glory (Jenkins, 1986).

Anyone who wants more detailed documentation of the bias of the press need turn no further than the work of Mark Hollingsworth (1986). He presents enormous detail of press distortion of coverage of individuals, like Benn or Livingstone, or issues, like the miners' strike or the nuclear power issue. If only a fraction of his evidence is accurate, and it is documented at great length, then the tabloid press is a major constraint on the operation of democracy rather than a key means of keeping governments responsive.

Only one daily newspaper, the *Mirror*, is committed to the Labour Party. In fact, 70 per cent of daily readers and 62 per cent of Sunday readers were urged to vote Conservative in 1992 by their newspapers. What is most noticeable, and perhaps more noticeable in the 1992 election campaign than previously, is the extent to which newspapers are willing to serve, rather than merely support, the Conservative Party. Research carried out for the *Guardian* by the Communications Research Centre (CRC) at Loughborough University showed that the daily tabloids – with the exception of the *Daily Mirror* – surpassed their previous reputation for Tory bias (see also Billig *et al.*, 1992). In particular, in the first three weeks of the campaign the CRC found that the tabloids always portrayed the Conservatives as presenting their policies or attacking Labour policies, never as defending their own policies. In contrast, the Labour Party was portrayed as defending its policies rather than attacking Conservative ones. The clear aim was to present a negative image of the Labour Party. This intention was graphically illustrated on the morning after the polls reported a startling 7 per cent lead for Labour (1 April). *Today*, the *Sun*, the *Daily Star* and the *Daily Mail* all failed to make the Labour surge the lead story; indeed the *Sun* relegated the story to a couple of inches on page 4. The exception was the *Daily Express* which put the story on the front page but carried a leader entitled 'Time to Trumpet Tory Triumphs' which concluded: 'The change of tune must begin today' (see also Harrop and Scammell, 1992.)

It would be misguided however to see most tabloid newspapers as simply the creature of the Conservative Party. While, as Jenkins claims, most proprietors are not in business simply to make profits, they must beware of falling too far out of step with their readers. Two recent developments illustrate this point. The *Sun* has had great difficulty challenging the *Daily Record*, the sister paper of the *Mirror*, in Scotland. For this reason, the Scottish *Sun* began to campaign for independence with an editorial on 23 January 1992 which proclaimed: 'Rise now and be a Nation again'. Its support for the SNP was not unequivocal, in particular it opposed the party's socialist policies, but there is little doubt that this conversion represented one element in a strategy designed to reposition the *Sun* in the Scottish newspaper market. In the English context, the tabloids' attitude to the Conservative government's management of the economy from mid-1992 provides similar evidence that newspapers must be aware of their readerships' interests. Here, growing unemployment and its particular effect on those sections of the population which buy tabloid newspapers must have played a significant role in prompting this shift in the tone and target of the editorials of the *Sun* and other tabloids.

Overall, the last Royal Commission on the press in 1977 was guilty of under-statement when it claimed:

> Over most of this century, the Labour movement has had less newspaper support than its right wing opponents and . . . its beliefs and activities have been unfavourably reported by the majority of the press (HMSO, 1977).

The question of bias in the electronic media is much more problematic. For example, there is a lively debate about the treatment of trade unions. The Glasgow Media Group (1976, 1980) argued that supposedly neutral television news broadcasts often present trade unions, strikes and radicals in very unfavourable ways. The Group's first, and probably best, book *Bad News* examined all television reports of a month-long strike at British Leyland's Cowley plant. The dominant theme of the news was that strikes, rather than, for example, poor management or inadequate investment, were the cause of Leyland's problem. The Group's work has been subject to strong methodological criticisms (Harrison, 1985). However, other work does support its conclusion. Although Jones' (1986) study of the miners' strike concludes that bias was limited, this conclusion sits unhappily with some of his evidence which indicates the consistent emphasis of television news on picket-line violence.

As far as television is concerned, the bias seems to come more from the nature of the medium than from any conscious decisions on the part of producers or editors. As the Royal

Commission on Broadcasting argued: 'the broadcasters were not guilty of deliberate and calculated bias. But that coverage of industrial affairs is in some respect inadequate and unsatisfactory is not in doubt'. Television presents brief, visual images:

They too-often forget that to represent the management at their desks, apparently the calm and collected representatives of order, and to represent shop stewards and picket lines stopping production, apparently the agents of disruption, gives a false picture of what strikes are about. The broadcasters have fallen into the professional error of putting compelling camera work before news (HMSO, 1977).

There is no doubt that coverage of election campaigns on TV and radio is more balanced than that in the press, particularly the tabloid press. Indeed, Miller's (1991) detailed study of media coverage of the 1987 election campaign indicates that TV news was pervasive, undifferentiated and relatively unbiased. Nevertheless, Miller does highlight three ways in which TV news coverage was biased, and two of these strongly favoured the Conservatives. First, news references to the main parties and their leaders were invariably positive; this obviously contrasted noticeably with press coverage. Second, in effect the Conservatives received twice as much coverage as other parties, because they had two bites at the cherry: they received coverage as the government and as one of the competing parties. Third, TV news had its own agenda which did not reflect public interest, at least as measured by opinion polls. In the later stage of the campaign, TV news paid a great deal of attention to defence which was a Conservative issue; that is, an issue which heavily favoured the Conservative Party (Miller, 1991, p.77).

As yet, we have no detailed academic study of the 1992 campaign. However, the CRC study referred to previously closely monitored TV coverage in the four weeks of the campaign (see also Harrison, 1992, Gavin, 1992). It does not report on coverage of the government as distinct from the Conservative Party but it does highlight three sources of pro-Conservative bias. First, the Conservatives received a greater share of news coverage during the election campaign. The actual figures were: 35.3 per cent to the Conservatives and 30.6 per cent to Labour on BBC 1; 38.1 per cent: 30.7 per cent on ITV; 40.0 per cent: 30.7 per cent on Channel 4; and 35.7 per cent: 31.4 per cent on Radio 4. The Conservatives were also twice as likely to get first 'sound bite' on the news as the Labour Party. Second, and perhaps more significantly, there was a clear tendency as the campaign progressed for commentators from the City to be used as independent experts on the parties' economic policies, despite the fact that these commentators were likely to support the Conservative Party (*Guardian*, 6 April 1992; this view is also supported by Gavin, 1992, p.610).

Two key points emerge from the discussion in this section. First, there is a marked concentration of ownership and control in the media. As far as newspapers are concerned, there is little doubt that proprietors own newspapers not for profit but for status and influence. Second, there is no doubt that there is a pro-Conservative bias in the media. In particular, the tabloid press, especially in an election campaign, appears the servant, rather than just the supporter, of the Conservative Party. Of course, this might not be regarded as important if the media had no influence upon voting; but as we shall see that is not the case.

*The Media and Voting Behaviour*

The role of the media in relation to voting behaviour has been a contentious area but in the more recent period a clear pattern seems to be emerging from most studies. Dunleavy and Husbands argue that newspapers exerted a very clear effect on voting patterns during the 1983 general election:

> the Conservative vote is some 30 percentage points lower amongst people primarily exposed to non-Tory messages than it is amongst readers of the Tory press, a high level of association that has few parallels amongst either social background or issue influences (Dunleavy and Husbands, 1985, p.115).

Harrop in contrast, takes a more circumspect view. He criticises Dunleavy and Husbands for their methodology and argues that although papers can influence the party preference of those readers who have none, the main effect of the press is limited to reinforcement of existing voting intentions (Harrop, 1987).

Harrop's conclusion alludes to a major analytic problem: whether there is any way of definitively establishing how far newspapers influence their readerships and/or how far readers buy newspapers which reflect their political view. Newton argues that, while there is an interdependence between the press and its readers, politics plays little part in that reciprocity, particularly for the tabloids (Newton, 1992) This conclusion is supported by Kellner and Worcester's (1982) study which showed that during the 1979 election campaign, 9 per cent of the *Sun*'s readers thought it supported no party, 33 per cent thought it supported Labour and 25 per cent did not know which party it supported. In fact, 68 per cent (8.6 million) of *Sun* readers did not know its party political position. While the *Sun* was the extreme case, the equivalent figures for other papers were: *Daily Mail* 20 per cent; *Daily Express* 19 per cent; *Daily Mirror* 27 per cent; *Daily Telegraph* 8 per cent. Overall, 37 per cent of the readers of these five papers (13.9 million people) failed to identify their paper's party politics.

Newton has employed a novel methodology which goes some way to overcoming the problems of causation. He attempts to establish a newspaper effect by considering only 'cross' readers, those whose newspaper reading does not 'match' their voting intention, whilst controlling for those readers' political views. He concludes:

> the newspaper effect is statistically and substantively significant. Moreover, its impact seems to vary from one election to another according to political circumstances, and to be greatest when the election result is closest. (Newton, 1992, p.68)

Miller's (1991) analysis overcame the problem of cause and effect by examining the extent to which the voting intentions of readers of a given newspaper changed over the campaign. His figures are startling and tend to confirm Dunleavy and Husband's conclusion. He found:

(a) The right-wing papers improved their readers' image of Kinnock and the Labour Party (p.197).
(b) The press had a particularly strong influence on the attitudes of Labour identifiers, especially towards the end of the campaigning (p.198).
(c) In his panel of voters the Conservatives' lead over Labour increased by 34 per cent among *Sun/Star* readers but by a mere 2 per cent amongst *Mirror* readers, which suggests the tabloids were able to influence their readers (p.198).
(d) The Conservatives' lead increased by 50 per cent amongst political uncommitted *Sun/Star* readers but not at all amongst uncommitted *Mirror* readers (pp.198–9).

Such evidence certainly makes Neil Kinnock's claims that the Tory tabloids won the 1992 election for the Conservatives sound less like sour grapes. According to a Mori Poll, based on a large sample of 22 700 voters, there was a 4 per cent swing to the Tories among *Sun* readers in the last week, 9 per cent among *Daily Express* readers and 2 per cent for the *Daily Mail*. This would mean that up to half a million readers of these papers swung to the Conservatives in the last week, enough to turn a potential Labour victory into defeat in a large number of target seats. As one example, in Basildon, where 50 per cent of the electorate read the *Sun*, the Conservatives retained a very vulnerable seat when there was only a 1.26 per cent swing to Labour. However, there was also a significant swing among *Mirror* readers which suggests that the late swing cannot be explained mainly, if at all, in terms of a newspaper effect. Certainly, the Miller study suggests that the tabloids' influence was exercised over an extended period rather than in a few brief days.

Although all the evidence suggests that electors regard television and radio as less biased and a more trustworthy source of information, there is no evidence that the electronic media has much influence on voting behaviour. The reason, of course, is clear; television's coverage is relatively undifferentiated and impartial, it does not set out to convert voters. Certainly, Miller's study confirms this view. He emphasises:

Political attitudes were very largely determined by partisanship but not completely. Even with stringent controls for partisanship and ideology, multiple regression analyses show that the press, but not television, had a significant influence on voter preferences (Miller, 1991, p.198).

## Government Manipulation of Information

The essential backdrop to the role of the media as a check upon executive power in Britain is the secrecy of British government. Two points are particularly important. First, the British system of government is one of the most secretive among liberal democracies (Tant, 1993). Second, it remains that way because it suits the executive, which does not wish to introduce a more open system. So, for example, in many ways the Conservative government intensified official secrecy in the 1989 Official Secrets Act. This obsession with secrecy makes it difficult for the media to hold government accountable, even should it wish to do so.

The position of the media is also constrained by the 'D notice' system which is administered by the Defence, Press and Broadcasting Committee composed of press and government nominees, chaired by a senior civil servant, with an 'independent' secretary chosen by the Committee. The Committee was established in 1906 as an alternative to formal press censorship. It 'advises' newspapers not to publish supposedly sensitive material and its decisions are underpinned by an informal system of letters, phone calls and chats with editors and political journalists. There is little doubt that such a system also prevents material which would be damaging to government, as distinct from State, interests being published.

The Thatcher governments were particularly concerned to control information. They took an especially dim view of investigative journalism, at least when it investigated, or had an effect upon, government. A brief example will illustrate the point. On 19 January 1987, with an election in the offing, it was reported that a film in the BBC documentary series *The Secret Society* had been withdrawn by the BBC because it might threaten national security. The film revealed that the Ministry of Defence (MoD) had secretly launched a £500 million electronic surveillance project without informing Parliament, although it had previously agreed that any defence projects costing more than £250 million would be disclosed to the House of Commons PAC. The thrust of the programme was thus about parliamentary accountability rather than national security. The BBC denied that it had been subject to government pressure. However, subsequently the government successfully sought an injunction to prevent Duncan Campbell, the maker of the programme, from talking or writing about the contents of the documentary. The injunction was not served before an article by Campbell appeared in the *New Statesman* reporting the accusations against the MoD; as a consequence, the government gained injunctions for a police search of Campbell's house and the *New Statesman*'s offices. A great deal of material was taken away and a few days later the police obtained a warrant to search the BBC Scotland Offices and removed documents and 200 containers of film and slides. All these warrants were obtained under the Official Secrets Act but no prosecution of Campbell was initiated. Indeed, as Ewing and Geery (1990, p.151) argue, the Act had 'served its purpose of intimidation'.

All British governments have aimed to control information, and one of the chief means used has been the lobby system. The system was created in 1884 and permitted certain accredited journalists privileged access to Westminister and to MPs and ministers, on the condition that they did not directly attribute what they were told. Bernard Ingham was appointed Press Secretary to Margaret Thatcher in September 1979 and proceeded over the next eleven years to dominate the lobby. If only a fraction of Robert Harris' (1990) book *Good and Faithful Servant* is true, and it appears well researched and documented, then it offers a depressing picture of the manipulation of information. Indeed, Sir Frank Cooper, commenting upon his experience as Permanent Secretary in the MoD during the Falklands War, attacked Ingham's role in very specific terms:

the aim now is the management of the media with a very much higher degree of central control from Number 10

Downing Street and with the connivance of a part of the media. There is now public relations – which I would define as biased information. I suggest that the post of Chief Information Officer at Number 10 Downing Street is in fact a political job in a party sense and not a job which it is proper for a civil servant to fill unless he or she resigns from the Civil Service on appointment (cited in Harris, 1990, p.99).

The Westland affair presents another example of media manipulation. The core of the affair concerned the leaking by the DTI of a letter from the Solicitor General, Sir Patrick Mayhew, criticising the Secretary of State for Defence, Michael Heseltine, for 'material inaccuracies' in a letter he had written to the European consortium he supported in the battle for Westland, a helicopter company. The letter was leaked by Colette Bowe, Chief Information Officer at the DTI. She claimed that she had been ordered to do so by Ingham. Ingham denies this charge (Ingham, 1991, pp.335–7), although Harris (1990, p.132) argues that 'circumstantial' evidence clearly substantiates Bowe's account. We shall never know the truth, but what is clear is that someone in the Government Information Service leaked information in order to undermine a Cabinet minister and present Thatcher's position in the best possible light. Indeed, it is difficult not to agree with Harris' conclusion:

> The media had to be briefed in order to cause the maximum amount of public damage to Heseltine's credibility. Indeed, it is a misnomer to speak of a 'leaked letter'. It was not a letter but two words ('material inaccuracies'), taken out of context, which were leaked. It was a smear (Harris, 1990, p.133).

It is also worth noting that when the House of Commons Select Committee on Defence subsequently investigated the Westland affair, its enquiries were effectively undermined by the government's refusal to permit any of the civil servants involved to testify. The accountability of the executive to Parliament took a distant second place to the need to protect the government from serious political embarrassment.

It is also important to deal briefly with the changes which have occurred since the election of John Major. Bernard Ingham was immediately replaced by Gus O'Donnell who had been Major's media adviser in the Treasury. It is too early to pass judgement on the new era for the lobby, but it is significant that the *Guardian* which, together with the *Independent* and the *Scotsman*, had left the lobby in 1986 because of the nature of Ingham's briefings, rejoined in 1991 claiming that the 'atmosphere was less polluted'. Even so, it must be emphasised that the lobby system has always existed so that the government can manipulate the use of information; in essence what are involved are 'authorised' and 'doctored' leaks.

There have also been some small moves toward greater openness since the 1992 general election. John Major authorised: release of information about the number and membership of Cabinet committees; naming of the Head of the Security Services; and publication of the secret ministerial rule-book, *Questions of Procedure for Ministers*. However, these are very limited concessions. There is no intention to introduce a Freedom of Information Act and without it scrutiny of the executive by the media, or indeed anyone else, is greatly hampered; which is why, of course, the government has no intention of introducing a Freedom of Information Act.

## The Media and Democracy – Revisited

The institutions and practices of the media in relation to government are underpinned by elements of each of the three views of the proper role and status of the media; mobilising, libertarian and public service. However, there is no doubt that it is the mobilising view which has dominated the attitudes and actions of British governments towards the media, particularly since 1979.

The libertarian model has some validity. There are few legal limitations on individuals' freedom to publish, or their freedom to read or view what they wish. However here, as elsewhere, there is nothing about freedom which can guarantee full expression of divergent opinions or provide a check upon any government misuse of power. In fact, the pattern of concentration and bias within the media, particularly the press, is such that a few people control the 'free market in ideas'; yet such a free market is the core of the libertarian view. The Thatcher governments took steps to introduce a greater emphasis upon market forces into the media but they had little interest in ensuring greater diversity of opinions.

The public service model operates to an extent as far as broadcasting is concerned. However, the BBC, which is the bastion of public service broadcasting, has come under severe pressure in recent years. The Conservative government criticised the BBC over its coverage of the Falklands, the American air strike against Libya and, more frequently, Northern Ireland (Walters, 1989). In addition, there were claims that Thatcher interfered in the appointment of BBC Governors. In fact, Alistair Milne, dismissed by the Governors as Director General in January 1987, claims in his autobiography that the BBC senior management:

> shared a growing concern about the politicisation of the Board. Time and time again the BBC put forward what seemed to us perfectly proper names for consideration by the Government – and time and again such names were rejected, usually, we were told, by No 10, and people of obvious political complexion appointed (Milne, 1988, p.82).

Of course, this may be sour grapes. Walters presents a very balanced analysis of relations between the Conservative government and the BBC. He argues:

> the Thatcher government cannot be regarded as having disturbed a stable and harmonious relationship between the BBC and government. It is arguable that the politics of broadcasting in the eighties would have been fraught whoever was in power. A lack of consensus in defining 'responsible' broadcasting and a general unease at the professional broadcasters' presumption in claiming the right to define it for themselves posed unresolved problems and carried over from the seventies (Walters, 1989, p.391).

As Walters argues, in its early years the BBC was very cautious in its coverage of politics. However, this tradition changed as the world and technology changed; by the 1960s 'broadcasters . . . saw their role as providing a critique, not simply an exposition, of the political world' (Walters, 1989, p.389). The key point is that in the 1970s and 1980s governments had a very different conceptualisation from the BBC on the 'responsibilities' of the media. Thatcher merely developed, she did not initiate, this government view of responsibility; the media's responsibility at times of conflict, indeed whenever the 'national interest' was concerned, was to support the government view, seen as synonymous with the national interest. Walters highlights the broader problem:

> The viability of a politically independent but publicly funded broadcasting institution presupposes a willingness on the part of government to tolerate a pluralistic structure of power in society. It must be willing to respect the right of such an institution to use its power in accordance with its own definition of the public interest. The government must accept the legitimacy of definitions of the public interest other than its own; it must in other words, tolerate a plurality of values. However, Mrs Thatcher's is a self-proclaimed 'conviction' government – and it is supremely confident of its convictions. Furthermore, it legitimises its right to impose those convictions by invoking its electoral accountability: only government which is accountable to the people through Parliament can lay down an authoritative definition of the public interest. The BBC is vulnerable to the monopolistic value system of such a government (Walters, 1989, pp.347–98).

In essence, the Thatcher governments were operating with a mobilising view of the proper role of the media. This is very evident throughout Bernard Ingham's memoirs. He argues consistently that the media was irresponsible, anxious to undermine government authority:

> Current affairs television in Britain is in a most unhealthy State. But so is that similar and inter-active clique in newspaper journalism. Never look for merit in British media awards: only look for the official backside-booting which the

nominees have indulged in. There is only one qualification for a media award these days: the undermining of elected authority (Ingham, 1991, p.356).

Ingham conflates two things which are seen as synonymous by advocates of leadership democracy and a mobilising role for the media. They must be separated. In his view, questioning the actions and motives of government, particularly a conviction government like Thatcher's, is equivalent to undermining the national interest because government knows best. However, in the public service view a key role of the media is to question elected authority. Obviously, such questioning, and even undermining, of elected authority, stands or falls on the quality of the investigative journalism involved and the veracity of the story. One would have more sympathy with Ingham's defence if he accepted that the exposure of government failings was a legitimate task for the press. He frequently mentions Watergate, but only to castigate British current affairs television by characterising it as constantly in search of such headlining-grabbing stories. Yet the Watergate investigation led to the exposure of illegal activities and a massive cover-up in American government and to the downfall of a President. It is also revealing that the British tabloid press, which is the real villain of this piece, receives no criticism. It is difficult not to believe that this is because, with the exception of the *Mirror*, the tabloids were as loyal to Margaret Thatcher as was Bernard Ingham.

# PART FOUR
# Theorising British Politics

# 17

# Political Theory and British Politics

**DAVID BEETHAM**

In this chapter I propose to examine a number of theoretical ideas and debates about constitutional issues – about the nature of sovereignty, the meaning of democracy, the character of political representation – which emerged in British politics during the 1980s, and which will be of increasing salience as the 1990s progress.

With some oversimplification, we could say that the dominant agenda of normative political theory in the 1980s was provided by the new right, and focused almost exclusively on the question of how much the State should do, how far it should intervene in economy and society, for what ends and by what means. The central new right idea of freeing the market from a multiplicity of historically accumulated constraints was justified equally on the grounds of individual freedom (through the extension of consumer choice), of economic growth (through the releasing of individual initiative), of distributive justice (through the entitlements derived from a 'fair exchange') and of social welfare (through the 'trickle-down' effect of incentives for the able and wealthy to make money) (see King, 1987, Chapters 3–5). These different components of new right thought were connected by the common organising idea of the free market – an idea that has historically proved enormously effective in Britain in incorporating the chief virtues of the liberal tradition, and in enabling individual self-interest to be pursued with an easy conscience.

Although each of the component elements of new right thinking mentioned above has been subjected to sustained criticism from the Left, the latter has been unable to develop an equally cogent organising principle to give the different aspects of its critique sufficient popular resonance in an age when the ideas of socialism and collectivism have become discredited. In particular, theorists from the left have proved unable to offer a sufficiently compelling account of a positive role for the state in the productive economy, of how to link redistributive justice with economic growth, or of how to render growth compatible with environmental concerns. It should be said that this is no easy task, and it may well be that there is no single organising idea or principle that can encompass it.

However, the construction of a new intellectual synthesis as a counterweight to the totalising logic of the free market is one of the necessary tasks of political opposition in the 1990s, if the stranglehold of the Conservatives over British public life is ever to be broken. What that stranglehold demonstrates is that a party with a secure following among two-fifths of the electorate can govern indefinitely in the UK, if the opposition to it is intellectually and organisationally divided. And it can do so in a manner that denies most alternative ideas or political forces any effective public role, given the concentration of power in the hands of the central executive which the political system allows.

## Sources of a Different Agenda

The experience of political exclusion in a state dominated by one party is only one of the factors that has brought a different, constitutional agenda to the forefront of debate, and called into question many of our most fundamental political ideas. The traditional British conception of sovereignty as a monopoly of legislative authority over a given territory, located in a single set of institutions, has been under challenge from a number of different directions: from the surrender of legislative powers to the EC; from the continuing crisis of political authority in Northern Ireland; from the pressure for devolution or outright independence in Scotland; from the debate on the role of local government and its place in a Europe of the regions. Moreover, the monopolistic conception of sovereignty has seemed particularly inadequate when conjoined with the idea of democracy as majority rule, since the latter can readily be used to justify the curtailment of dialogue, the subordination of minorities, or the erosion of civil rights. And the idea of majority rule itself is rendered acutely problematic by a system of representation that gives two-fifths of the electorate a 'majority' voice, and skews the Parliamentary composition of the ruling party so heavily towards the South of England. What can 'representative government' mean when parliament is, in these and other ways (such as its social composition) so unrepresentative?

These issues – of sovereignty, democracy, representation – comprise a quite different agenda from the market-oriented debates which preoccupied political theorists in the 1980s. They concern not what the State should do, but how it should be institutionally and spatially organised to do it; not how little or much the State should involve itself in society, but how it can be rightfully authorised by society, and in what manner should be accountable to it.

Constitutional questions of this sort are often held to be a narrow concern of the so-called 'chattering classes', in comparison with the bread-and-butter issues of economic organisation and social distribution. At the end of the day, however, no issue is more basic than the legitimacy of a society's political arrangements, and no political question more fateful than whether the State can rightfully require obedience from its subjects. It is because the legitimacy of the UK's system of government is now becoming more contested, on the mainland as well as in Northern Ireland, that a reconsideration of what we understand by the concepts of sovereignty, democracy and representation, and of the disputes about them, is such an important theoretical task.

## Sovereignty: Monopolistic or Multiple?

The idea of sovereignty as exclusive jurisdiction over a given territory, embodying a monopoly of law-making, adjudicating and enforcing power, was evolved by political thinkers at the time of the emergence of the European state system in the sixteenth and seventeenth centuries, and has since become an integral component of our thinking about the modern state. From the outset the idea had both an external and an internal point of reference (Beitz, 1991, pp.236–44). *Externally*, it was used to resist the claims of powers outside the territory to jurisdiction over it, or over aspects of its affairs as, for instance, the Catholic Church had historically done. Here sovereignty meant independence, or self-determination: the right to legislate without interference from outside, or 'limitation by any external source of law.

Of course, sovereign states could enter into alliances and incur treaty obligations that limited their actions in various ways, in return for enhanced effectiveness internationally. But in so far as such relationships were entered into voluntarily, and could always in principle be dissolved, they did not constitute an infringement of sovereignty, any more than entering into personal relationships or commitments by an individual could be said to infringe his or her autonomy. States today, like individuals, may have widely differing powers or capacities. Yet they are all equally acknowledged to have the right to legislative self-determination, or sovereignty; and nothing is more strongly resisted by a State than any attempt from outside to infringe this right, through interference in its domestic affairs.

At the *internal* level, on the other hand, the idea of sovereignty was developed to resolve competing claims to jurisdiction from inside the territory, whether they came from different regional centres, from competing dynastic families or from different bodies within the State itself. Here sovereignty meant the existence of an institution, or set of institutions, which was acknowledged as the ultimate source of law-making and adjudication by everyone within the territory, and which had the capacity to enforce its writ across the land. The idea was associated historically with a process of internal unification or pacification, and with the clarification of the relationship between the different institutions and levels of government within a given territory. In the case of the UK the ultimate source of legislative authority came to be defined as residing in Parliament, or the Crown in Parliament to be precise: a conception which we know today as the principle of parliamentary sovereignty.

It is worth emphasising at this point that sovereignty, in its internal aspect, is not necessarily the same as unlimited power, or a centralised uniformity of government. There is certainly a tradition of English theorising, from the political theorist Thomas Hobbes through legal theorists such as Blackstone and Dicey, which can be interpreted in this manner (Hobbes, 1960, Chapter 18; Blackstone, 1765, Chapter 2; Dicey, 1886, Chapter 1). In practice, however, the ultimate legislative authority of the Westminster Parliament has in the past proved compatible with a substantial devolution of power, whether to local authorities throughout the UK, or to a separate Parliament as in Northern Ireland; it has also been superimposed on top of a quite separate legal, educational and religious system, as in Scotland. Indeed, the tolerance of such diversity, or dispersal of power, has been argued to be a necessary condition for holding the UK together at all (Crick, 1991, pp.102–4).

The meaning of parliamentary sovereignty here has been that such dispersal has been legally validated by Parliament, which has always retained the ultimate right to vary or override it if sufficiently compelling circumstances demanded. The principle of parliamentary sovereignty has therefore excluded any constitutionally guaranteed position for subordinate levels of government independently of Parliament, such as exists in a federal system, where the powers of different tiers of government are guaranteed and adjudicated by an independent constitutional court. In sum, parliamentary sovereignty has included diversity and pluralism, but excluded any independent constitutional guarantee for it.

We need to be clear, then, what the concept of 'sovereignty' has meant, in both its external and internal aspects, if we are to understand why it has now become such a problematic and contested idea in the UK. Among the different factors that have contributed to this situation we should distinguish once again between the external and internal dimensions. At the external level, most obvious is the development of the EC into a fully fledged law-making body, whose legislation takes precedence over that of the UK Parliament. Whatever benefits the UK gains from membership, subordination to such a body is not only a substantial diminution of parliamentary sovereignty; it also undermines a central claim historically implicit in the idea of sovereignty – that the independent State constitutes the most effective political institution for protecting and promoting the interests of its citizens. It may be that the claim was always a dubious one; but the development of the EC makes clear that, in an increasingly interdependent world, the idea of sovereignty as independence is becoming anachronistic (see Held (ed.), 1991, pp.212–22).

A second area where the idea of sovereignty in its external aspect has been eroded has been in relation to Northern Ireland, through the Anglo–Irish Agreement. The acknowledgement that another State has a legitimate interest, and a significant role to play, in UK internal affairs is unique. Although less far reaching in its implications for sovereignty than the EC, this development nevertheless embodies a similar recognition that the traditional conception of sovereignty is inadequate to cope with the complexity of the contemporary world, in this case with the aspirations of minority ethnic, cultural or national groupings, especially where their allegiances cross existing State boundaries. Indeed, the situation in Northern Ireland is only one example of a problem which the break-up of the USSR and Yugoslavia has demonstrated as chronic, and whose solution lies more in internationally guaranteed rights for minorities than in a monopolistically defined and defended State sovereignty. At this point the supranational framework provided by the EC may actually help resolve such conflicts within its member-states, by lessening the significance of existing national boundaries, and developing an EC-wide conception of citizenship that is common to all (Boyle, 1991, pp.75–8).

If in its external aspect, then, the idea of parliamentary sovereignty is being substantially eroded, in its internal aspect it has become much more sharply accentuated, as the doctrine of Parliament as the supreme legislative authority has been used by successive governments to enhance the power of the central State at the expense of all other levels of government, and indeed all other established bases of diversity within the public sphere. The more that has been surrendered externally, the more the internal paramountcy of Westminster has been asserted, to the point where the idea of sovereignty as the

ultimate legislative authority has come to mean unlimited
jurisdiction and unrestricted power. This process can be seen in
the imposition and maintenance of direct rule in Northern
Ireland; in the erosion of the separate Scottish legal and
educational systems; and in the successive emasculations of
local government, to the point where it has become simply an
administrative arm of Whitehall. The doctrine of parliamentary sovereignty, in short, has both allowed, and served to
justify, a progressive centralisation of decision-making and an
increasing uniformity of public life throughout the UK.

Not surprisingly, this process has provoked resistance, and in
the name of the very same principle of self-determination that
is central to sovereignty itself. The resistance has been most
pronounced where the assertion of Westminster supremacy has
infringed a deep-rooted sense of collective identity, as in
Scotland, and in different manner in Wales and Northern
Ireland. Appeal to the principle of self-determination is less
effective in defence of local government, since any sense of local
political identity has been substantially eroded over time, as
boundaries and names have chopped and changed in the
interest of administrative tidiness. In Scotland, in contrast, the
principle of Westminster sovereignty has come to be resented
as an assertion of English hegemony over Scotland, and of
Conservative hegemony over an electorate that is predominantly anti-Conservative, and whose political culture is
markedly antipathetic to a purely free-market philosophy.
Here the principle of the self-determination of peoples has been
most consistently invoked to sustain the claims for a Scottish
assembly (Edwards, 1989, pp.13–53). Although the situation
in Northern Ireland is much more complex, in view of the
division between its communities, it seems unlikely that the
claims for self-determination in either country can be satisfied
in the long term without a separate Parliament, whose
constitutional position is protected against future dissolution
by Westminster; and any such provision would have predictable consequences for the status of Wales as well.

Where, then, do these developments leave the idea of State
sovereignty in general, and the doctrine of parliamentary
sovereignty in particular? Long term trends point to an
inexorable shift away from the monopolistic sovereignty of

the nation-state towards a world of multiple jurisdictions and differentiated or partial sovereignties. This is required by the increasing interdependence and international scale of political decision-making, on the one hand, and in order to satisfy the pluralism of national, ethnic and regional identities, on the other. Societies with federal systems of government are already familiar with such a conception of sovereignty, and with the multiple political allegiances that it entails. In the UK, however, we can expect to see a determined resistance to such a process on behalf of a traditional conception of sovereignty, and on the part of its dominant nationality, the English, who have never had to worry whether they were more English than British because the two have been effectively synonymous. So a conflict between these competing conceptions of sovereignty, the monopolistic and the multiple, in both their external and internal aspects, is likely to be one of the key issues of the 1990s, and to continue to cause division within the parties as well as between them.

## Democracy: Majority Rule, Pluralism or Citizens' Rights?

The increasing centralisation and uniformity of government in the UK has called into question not only the concept of sovereignty, but also the meaning of democracy itself. Just as centralisers have been able to trade on an ambiguity in the meaning of sovereignty – between ultimate legislative authority and unlimited power – so they have also appealed to a particular conception of democracy as majority rule. According to this conception, majorities must by definition be more representative of the people as a whole than minorities; and, therefore, whichever party wins a parliamentary majority is entitled to execute its programme without qualification, because it represents the 'popular will'. Any restraint on that authority, whether by opposition parties, organised groups or powerful institutions, would be a frustration of the popular will, and hence undemocratic.

Historically, the 'majority rule' conception of democracy has been more associated with the left than the right of the political spectrum, since it can be used to empower a deprived majority against a privileged minority. It can be seen in the Jacobin tendency of the French revolution, and in the Marxian concept of 'proletarian dictatorship': the determined use of majority power to expropriate the minority class of privileged property owners (Draper, 1986, Chapter 11). In diluted form it has also found its place in the British Labour Party. What was novel about Thatcher's administrations was that the idea was successfully appropriated by the Right, and employed to denounce and disempower a quite novel set of supposedly self-serving minorities acting to frustrate the 'popular will': trade union leaders, public service professionals, Whitehall mandarins, even elected Town Hall politicians. In the name of democracy many intermediate sources of power between the central state and the citizen, capable of resisting government policy, were demobilised.

This determined exercise of democracy as majority rule has provoked objection in the name of two different conceptions of democracy, which are usually associated with the liberal tradition, and with the liberal components in the portman-teau concept of 'liberal democracy'. The first of these is the idea of tenderness to minorities: majority rule should be tempered by a readiness to listen to and accommodate minority interests and viewpoints, if it is to be government by consent rather than by imposition (see Mill, 1991, pp.292–301). Denounced as a wishy-washy 'consensus', this view appeals to the key liberal idea of pluralism – of independent groups, ideas and interests within civil society – and to the sceptical liberal intuition that what is good for society can only be discovered in the free interplay between differing view-points, and cannot be known with certainty as a final truth.

This 'minority-sensitive' conception of democracy can also be justified on grounds of democratic, as well as liberal, principle. Thus it can be argued that democracy means, literally, rule by the people, and this signifies the people as a whole, not the rule of one part of it, however large, over another. Such a conception requires procedures of debate which ensure that all significant points of view are heard, and decisional procedures, such as those of amendment, which allow an initial majority position to be modified to take account of other viewpoints. If at the end of the day decisions have to be taken by majority vote, this can be nothing more than a procedural device for dealing with irreconcilable disagreement, not the acme of democratic perfection. So while democratic institutions may require a majoritarian voting procedure to ensure that decisions cannot be determined or blocked by a minority, democratic principle requires that such a procedure should always be used as a last, and not a first, resort.

A 'minority-sensitive' conception of democracy, then, is one alternative to the idea of majority rule that can be derived from the liberal political tradition, and hence from the tradition of British politics itself. Another, overlapping, conception is the idea of democracy as a set of guaranteed citizens' rights, to be protected if need be against the majority: in the first instance the key political and civil rights such as the right to vote, to associate with others, to free expression and movement, to information about government, to a fair trial by one's peers, and so on. What distinguishes these as *democratic* rights is that they are necessary if the people are to influence and control the process of public decision-making, and those who take such decisions, on an ongoing basis. A democracy, on this view, is a society where such rights are guaranteed to individuals if necessary against majority rule, when the majority might find it desirable to infringe or revoke them (Dworkin, 1977, Chapter 7; IPPR, 1991, Introduction).

Again, such a conception has a historical place in the British tradition of politics. Yet the claim that individual civil rights are sufficiently protected by the courts and the common law, or else by Parliament, looks very threadbare in the light of the succession of recent examples of their infringement, and in a context where the common law can be so readily over-ridden by parliamentary statute, and Parliament itself has become so much the creature of the executive (Index on Censorship, 1988; Thornton, 1989). The issue for debate here is less whether individual liberties need more effective protection, than how it should best be done: whether through reform of the second chamber, and the power of a joint parliamentary committee to obstruct legislation that might infringe recognised civil liberties; or through incorporation of the European convention of civil and political rights into domestic law, and an associated reform of the judiciary (Ewing and Gearty, 1990, Chapter 8).

Whatever the precise mechanism that is advocated, the underlying idea is one of democracy as a set of institutionally guaranteed rights, which require protection against a conception of democracy as majority rule, such as has held sway under recent Conservative administrations. What we have experienced since 1979, so it is argued, has been the introduction of liberal economics by means of an illiberal conception of politics; the development of an economically limited State through the exercise of politically unlimited power. And although, now that the Thatcher 'revolution' has reached the stage of consolidation, we may see a return to a more consensual and open form of government under Major, the argument of the constitutional reformers is that this is more a matter of style than substance; and that in any case the protection of individual rights, or the powers of local government, or the influence allowed to Scottish public opinion, should not be dependent upon the grace and favour of the executive, but should be institutionally secured in a reformed (and written) constitution.

Conservatives will claim that their exercise of majority rule has not been oppressive, as constitutional reformers imply, because its aim has been to free individuals from the power of the state, and to expand the powers of the citizen. However, we should note, finally, two very different conceptions of citizenship at work here, which go to the heart of the current debate about democracy. On the one side the citizen is defined primarily as a consumer, and civil society primarily as a market place. On this view, the extension of citizenship is to be found in the expansion of consumer powers in the market; and the important rights to guarantee, as in the Citizens' Charter, are the rights of consumer choice and consumer redress in respect of those services that remain in the public sector (Seldon, 1990, Chapter 5). On the other side civil society is seen more as a forum, or place of collective discussion and organisation, and the important rights to guarantee are those which enable citizens to exercise some *collective* influence and control over the circumstances of their shared life, in its different aspects and at its various levels (see Elster, 1986). It is only through the exercise of these rights, it can be argued, and through the control over collective decisions that they allow, however imperfectly, that people have historically been able to offset the economic inequities caused by the market, to limit its damaging consequences, and to prevent its intrusion into every sphere of social life. Where the balance should be struck between these two competing accounts of citizenship will be one of the recurring issues of the 1990s.

## Representation: Proportional or Disproportional?

The most obvious objection to a majority rule conception of democracy as applied to the UK is that no parliamentary majority since 1945 has enjoyed the support of a majority of the electorate; and that since 1970 no governing party has secured even 45 per cent of the popular vote. What we have experienced is minoritarian government operating according to a starkly majoritarian conception of democracy; and it is this combination that has most directly put the issue of constitutional reform, and especially reform of the electoral system, onto the political agenda. Whenever two parties have monopolised the electoral contest in the UK, the plurality or 'first-past-the-post' system has produced results that are broadly proportional to the popular vote. But whenever a substantial third force has emerged with popular support, as in the period from 1900 to the 1930s, and again since 1970, there has developed a considerable and arbitrary disproportion between the vote for the parties nationally, and the party composition in the House of Commons. In such periods the demand for electoral reform has gathered momentum (Bogdanor, 1981, pp.119–74).

Why does proportionality matter? Is it the only consideration relevant to choosing between different electoral systems? We talk about our kind of political system as one of 'representative government', and these two terms help define the two main tasks of an electoral system: to produce an elected assembly that is representative of the people, and a government that is effective and accountable to them. In a parliamentary system elections have to accomplish both tasks simultaneously; and it is the possible conflict between the two tasks – of representation and government formation respectively – that is the main source of disagreement about our electoral system. In what follows, these two different aspects will be considered in turn.

The concept of political representation is highly complex. Here I shall concentrate on only one sense in which an elected assembly can be said to represent the electorate: that it is representative of them, as a smaller body can be said to be representative of a larger one (the so-called 'microcosmic' conception of representation) (Birch, 1972, pp.15–21). Now it can readily be shown that all liberal democracies, in one way or another, strive to ensure that their elected assemblies are representative of their electorates in this sense. They do so because of a very basic principle of democracy, that of political equality: every elector should count for one, and none for more than one. It follows that, if this principle is applied systematically, then the resulting composition of Parliament will be representative of the whole electorate in a microcosmic sense. The crucial question, however, is *how* the principle of political equality should be applied, and *in what respect* representativeness should be sought (Beetham, 1992).

There are broadly three different interpretations of representativeness currently in contention. These are that the House of Commons should be representative of the electorate according to its geographical distribution; according to the distribution of its votes between the parties; or according to its social characteristics. We could no doubt try to achieve all three together; but the chief dispute is about which should be paramount. Supporters of what is called 'proportional representation' (PR) put the main weight on the second feature, but all three embody their own ideas about proportionality. The question is: which is the most appropriate conception of proportionality or representativeness?

The existing electoral system is based upon a geographical concept of representativeness, and a correspondingly spatial definition of political equality. Its conception is that Parliament should be representative of the geographical distribution of the population; and that all votes should count for the same, regardless of where people happen to live. This principle is evident in the work of the Boundary Commission, whose task is to equalise the size of constituencies, so that all parts of the country get equal representation according to their population, and all votes carry equal weight as between each constituency. Here political equality is being interpreted in primarily spatial terms. The result is a House of Commons that is highly proportionate geographically, and one that mirrors the distribution of the electorate across the country (give or take some moderation of the principle in favour of Wales, Scotland and Northern Ireland).

Supporters of so-called 'proportional representation' argue for a different conception of proportionality, and a different account of political equality: Parliament should mirror the distribution of the national or regional vote between the parties; and the vote of each elector should count for the same, regardless of which party he or she happens to vote for. Advocates of this conception of proportionality do not necessarily discount geographical considerations, but they argue that they should not be made exclusive. In their view, the problem with the plurality system is that it is based upon a conception of representation relevant to a society that has long since disappeared, when constituencies embodied natural communities, and elections were a matter of choosing who would best represent the interests of the locality in Parliament. Nowadays, however, when elections are primarily a choice between national party programmes, and when constituencies are largely artificial slices of the electorate, the relevant respect in which Parliament should be proportionate, and political equality should be secured, is in respect of how people vote. After all, why should strenuous efforts be made to ensure that the worth of a vote is the same in Winchester as in Liverpool, and not also to ensure that the vote of a Liberal Democrat voter is the same as that of a Conservative or Labour one? If the purpose of the Boundary Commission is to ensure that each person's choice carries equal weight, then the effect of the plurality system is to ensure that Conservative votes in the South of England count for far more than Conservative votes in Scotland, and both for far more than Liberal Democrat voters in most parts of the country.

A third conception of proportionality argues that Parliament should be representative of the electorate in respect of its social characteristics; and that each elector should have an equal chance of being represented by someone with their own characteristics, who therefore shares some of their key experiences. The chief characteristics currently urged are those of race and gender, on the grounds that the House of Commons is almost exclusively white and also disproportionately male. There is no disputing that it is grossly unrepresentative in both these respects. Indeed, effective equality of opportunity to stand as a representative is as important a democratic principle as the equal value of votes between citizens.

However, there are two objections typically advanced against incorporating such considerations into the formal requirements of an electoral system. One is that there are many other characteristics that might be considered relevant – age and class, for example, since the House of Commons also largely comprises middle-aged professionals – and that deciding which to include in a formal specification of electoral candidacy is arbitrary. A second objection is that a person's sex, race or whatever, tells us little about the policies they are likely to support, even on issues affecting women or racial minorities respectively; so such candidates cannot be taken to be representative of the relevant electorate in any unproblematic way (see Phillips, 1991, pp.73–8).

The choice of which of these three conceptions of representativeness or proportionality should be given priority comes down to the question of what elections are mainly about. Are they about selecting the best person to serve local interests, about choosing between national party programmes, or about identifying the candidate who will most closely reflect one's own social characteristics? Since most people would say that the second feature is the most important, and certainly behave as if it were, it follows that securing the proportionality of Parliament according to the distribution of the party vote, and ensuring equality between citizens regardless of which party they vote for, should take priority over other considerations; though this would not rule out giving considerations of locality or social composition a secondary place in an electoral system, if we so chose.

It is significant that opponents of 'proportional representation' are rarely able to find fault with it on grounds of the representative aspect of elections, but only for its consequences for government formation. Here the issue revolves almost entirely around our attitude to coalition government. From a democratic point of view, two objections are usually advanced to a system that requires coalition government as the norm. One is that it removes the process of government formation from the direct control of the electorate, and puts it in the hands of party managers meeting in 'smoke-filled rooms'. The second is that it can give a small 'hinge' party such as the Liberal Democrats a weight in government out of all proportion to its degree of electoral support. Attitudes towards electoral reform are almost entirely a question of whether we take these objections seriously; and, if so, whether we judge them of sufficient importance to outweigh the manifest inequality of the plurality system (Plant, 1991, pp.33–5).

Supporters of 'proportional representation' argue that both objections are over-stated. The first overlooks the fact that existing parties are themselves coalitions, over whose composition and balance the electorate has little control; that any party taking part in coalition discussions is publicly accountable to its voters for its actions; and that if, in such negotiations, manifesto commitments which do not have the support of a majority of the electorate have to be abandoned, there can be nothing undemocratic about that. Voters for a coalition partner would presumably rather have some influence over government than none at all, as in a loser-gets-nothing system.

But would that influence be excessive? It would only be undemocratic if it could be shown that a party representing a minority of the population consistently enjoyed an influence over the whole range of government policy, and a share of ministerial posts, that was quite out of proportion to its degree of electoral support. Whether such a defect is inherent and unavoidable in a system of PR remains a key question for debate. However, any deficiency in this regard can be expected to appear progressively less significant, as the UK's one-party State further extends its life under the existing electoral arrangements.

## Conclusion: Legitimacy Deficit or Legitimation Crisis?

The concept of 'legitimacy' was brought into some disrepute in the 1970s when political theorists spoke too glibly about a 'legitimation crisis' in the advanced capitalist societies (e.g., Habermas, 1976). What we can more correctly speak about in this particular advanced capitalist country is a significant legitimacy gap or deficit, which derives from the fact that traditional justifications for the constitutional arrangements now lack credibility, whether at the level of sovereignty, democracy or representation. In the first case this is because of the combined erosion of sovereignty externally and opposition to its reinterpretation as unlimited power internally; in the second case, because a liberal conception of democracy has proved to be impotent against the determined assertion of majority rule; in the third, because that assertion is made, not on behalf of a majority, but by a highly unrepresentative Parliament. The legitimacy of a government is not only a question of whether it achieves and exercises power according to established rules; but of whether the rules are themselves justifiable according to principles widely accepted within the society (Beetham, 1991, Chapter 1). It is that which is now in doubt.

Not surprisingly, the legitimacy deficit is recognised more clearly by non-Conservatives than by Conservatives, and is experienced more sharply the further one moves away from the South of England. However, we should distinguish between the recognition of a legitimacy deficit, and the active delegitimation of government through the public withdrawal of consent, which is necessary to produce an actual crisis of political authority, or legitimation crisis. Such a public withdrawal of consent has occurred repeatedly in Northern Ireland, on the part of different groups of actors: by civil rights marchers against the Stormont system in 1968; by striking Protestants against the power-sharing executive in 1974; by IRA violence against Westminster rule continuously since the 1970s. It began to take place in Scotland with organised civil disobedience against the poll tax during the last years of Thatcher, and may take other forms over the coming period.

At the same time, the delegitimation of government through the collective withdrawal of consent is not the only possible outcome of a legitimacy deficit. There are also the less dramatic forms of disaffection, whereby only the most grudging cooperation is accorded government policies by those whose support is needed, when they not merely disagree with them, but refuse to acknowledge the government's moral authority to impose them. Governments may survive such minimalism indefinitely; whether they can secure the degree of cooperation needed to overcome complex societal problems is more open to doubt.

What prospect is there, finally, of closing the legitimacy gap? In principle there are three different ways of doing so. The first is to invent new justifications, or refurbish old ones, for the rules of the political game that have become discredited. This is unlikely to be effective, since it is how the rules are experienced in practice, not the manner of their intellectual justification, that lies at the heart of the problem. A second solution is for the government to modify its own behaviour, since it is the manner in which it has interpreted the rules that has contributed to bringing them into discredit. However, the problems are only partly of the government's making; and, in any case, a change of policy, for example to allow alternative political forces some publicly effective role, may only serve to underline that they are there on the government's sufferance, not as a matter of constitutional right. The third route is through changing the rules themselves, whether by piecemeal or wide-ranging constitutional reform. For the reasons given in this chapter, pressure for such reform can be expected to continue throughout the 1990s, though it may only be through the election of a non-Conservative government that any changes will actually come to be made.

# Guide to Further Reading

### Chapter 2  The Constitution

A critical approach to Britain's existing constitutional arrangements can be found in Harden and Lewis (1988). Two works which give particular attention to the relationship between Conservative government and constitutional practice are Ewing and Gearty (1990) and Graham and Prosser (1988). A more recent edited collection is Lewis, Graham and Beyleveld (1990). Brazier (1991) offers a more bipartisan approach.

Views from the right of the political spectrum include Vibert (1991) and Mount (1992). Hailsham (1992) is also of interest given its author's earlier contribution to constitutional debate.

### Chapter 3  The European Dimension

The literature on the EC, and on Britain and the EC, has expanded and improved considerably in recent years. For an account of the history of the EC see Urwin (1991). Nugent (1992), Laffan (1992), Archer and Butler (1992), and Nicoll and Salmon (1990) provide general texts on the government, the politics, and the policies of the EC. A 'hands-on' feel of the EC can be obtained by consulting the Treaties, which are published in several forms, and the bi-monthly *Bulletin of the European Communities*, which gives a detailed summary of all significant EC activities and developments. George has written two histories of Britain's relations with the EC: one brief (1991) and one substantial (1990). He has also edited a book which analyses the impact of EC membership on the British political system (1992). An overall assessment of the costs and benefits of EC membership for Britain is found in Bulmer *et al.* (1992).

### Chapter 4  Territorial Politics

Good general surveys of different aspects of territorial politics are Madgwick and Rose (1982), Bulpitt (1983), and Crick (1991b). Kearney (1989) provides 'a four nations' history of the British Isles. The territorial dimension of Scottish politics and public policy is expertly analysed in Midwinter *et al.* (1991), while Marr (1992) has written a very accessible history of the struggle for constitutional reform in Scotland. The political economy of UK regions is explored in Martin (1989). Northern Ireland is best approached through Whyte (1991) and McGarry and O'Leary (1990) and (1993).

## Chapter 5   Voting and the Electorate

The best introduction is Harrop and Miller (1987); its international focus is a plus. On Britain, Denver (1989) is succinct and sensible and Denver and Hands (1992a) is a valuable package of articles on recent issues and controversies, although stronger on long-term than short-term influences.

Butler and Stokes (1974) is the first and classic national survey study of British voters; some conclusions are dated – it stops in 1970 – but the analytic framework is not. Subsequent survey studies include: Sarlvik and Crewe (1983) on the 1970s (issue-voting); Heath *et al.* (1985) and Dunleavy and Husbands (1985) (the 'radical model') on the 1983 election and Miller *et al.* (1990) on 1987, which examines campaign effects. Analysing the full 1964–87 set of British Election Studies, Heath *et al.* debunk fashionable ideas about recent electoral change.

Two studies of class and party, broadly corroborating class dealignment, are Franklin (1985) and Rose and McAllister (1986); geographical polarisation is documented and partly explained in Johnson *et al.* (1988).

On the 1992 election, King (1992) and the October 1992 issue of *Parliamentary Affairs* are useful collections of articles, covering more than voting.

Reference works worth consulting are Craig (1989) for election statistics in historical perspective and Crewe *et al.* (1991) for survey trends since 1963. The periodicals most likely to publish recent research are the *British Journal of Political Science*, *Electoral Studies*, *Parliamentary Affairs* and the *British Parties and Elections Yearbook*.

## Chapter 6   The Political Parties

General descriptions of British parties (like this chapter itself) are hampered by the difficulty that no single author can be equally knowledgeable about all of them. Conservative and Labour traditions are both complex and require careful 'reading' to appreciate them, while the Liberal Democrats (and their predecessors) have elusive ideas and are in any case chronically under-studied.

On the Conservative party, see Gamble (1988, especially Chapter 6 on ideology), and Norton (1992). A number of books have been published by prominent Conservatives, each of them appearing to express the broad philosophy but in fact expounding rather sectarian versions of their faith. The traditional far right view is set out by Scruton (1980), while the classic Tory paternalist case is well stated by Gilmour (1977). The technocratic moderniser view is captured in Heseltine (1987) and the market liberal view is best set out in pure form by Lawson (1981). A book by a former market liberal turned Major loyalist is Willetts (1992).

On the Labour party the existing literature is highly outdated, preoccupied with a historic agenda dominated by old Fabianist ideas and almost ignoring the key debates now wracking the party, such as electoral reform, how to diminish union influence, the moderniser versus traditionalist disputes, and how Labour can broaden its electoral appeal. The Fabian legacy is restated in traditionalist guise by Hattersley (1987) while the 1980s' preoccupations of the Labour left are covered in Seyd (1987). A long, well-informed but highly partisan defense of the trade union-dominated operations of the Labour machine is given by Minkin (1991).

On the Liberal Democrats there is little written of any substance. The former Liberal party's internal politics are covered by the essays in Bogdanor (1983).

The process of party competition in the UK is not often analysed in the analytic way that would be normal in US political science. Some useful summary material is contained in McLean (1987) and (1982, Chapters 1–4), Dunleavy and Husbands (1985, Chapters 2–4) and Dunleavy (1991, Chapters 4 and 5).

## Chapter 7   Parliament

The most substantial general work on Parliament published in recent years is Griffith and Ryle (1989), which is particularly strong on the procedures of the two Houses, and contains a wealth of useful statistics about, for instance, legislative proceedings and parliamentary questions. Adonis (1990) also provides an excellent general overview, illustrated with many charts, diagrams and tables. Drewry (1989) examines the work of select committees, particularly in the period 1979–87. Shell (1992) is the standard work on the House of Lords. Garrett (1992) has written a provocative 'insider's' account of the limitations of Parliament in the 1990s. On the more specialised aspects of parliamentary scrutiny, mention should be made of Rush (1990), who tackles the subject of Parliament and pressure politics, and Carstairs and Ware (1991), who examine Parliament's role in foreign affairs. Both these works contain interesting case studies.

## Chapter 8   Government at the Centre

It is too soon for anything other than speculative accounts of the effect of Major on the central State to have appeared. The best place to start on the core executive is the special edition of *Public Administration* (Spring 1990), though most introductory textbooks say something and most say the same. Hennessy (1986) and his update (1991) are still the most detailed accounts of the work of cabinet committees. Rose (1987) has not been bettered as a general account of departments, containing data which whilst several years old still reflect useful departmental comparisons. The Crossman (1976) and Castle (1980, 1984) diaries are still worth reading for insider accounts of the functioning of cabinets. Ranelagh (1992) is an account of many of the personalities of the Thatcher years, and provides a counterpoint to organisational and structural accounts. Greenaway, Smith and Street (1992) is an excellent book of case studies on central government decision-making which should be read by all students of British government.

On the civil service, Hennessy (1990) is long and anecdotal providing good background reading, Drewry and Butcher (1991) a useful and simple introduction. Dowding (1993) attempts a more theoretical treatment, explaining why the civil service is changing and what the likely results will be.

Little has been written on the effects of the EC on the central executive as virtually all of the expanding literature is policy-oriented. Bendor (1991) gives an insider's account of the work of the European Secretariat, whilst Mazey and Richardson (1993) is a collection of articles on the effects of the EC on lobbying and policy networks. Dowding (1993) considers the effects upon British administration of the increasing competence of the EC.

## Chapter 9   Government Beyond Whitehall

For competent introductions to British local government see Byrne (1988), Gyford (1984), Hampton (1991) or Rhodes (1988). Useful reviews of the most recent changes can be found in Butcher *et al.* (1990), Cochrane (1991), Goldsmith (1992), Stewart and Stoker

(1989) and Stoker (1991). Local political activity is thoroughly reviewed in the Widdicombe Report (Report, 1986) and the accompanying research volumes. Discussions of theories of local government and urban politics are covered effectively in Dunleavy (1980), Gurr and King (1987), Jacobs (1992), Jones and Stewart (1985) Keating (1991), King and Pierre (1990) and Wolman and Goldsmith (1992). For discussion of normative questions about local government see King (1989), Magnusson (1986), Gyford (1991) and Hill (1974). On local government finance see Travers (1986).

## Chapter 10   Economic Policy

The *Financial Times* is essential for current developments. On Britain's relative decline the best brief study is Pollard (1984). For the political and institutional context see Gamble (1988, 1990) and Marquand (1988). On recent economic policy the *National Institute Economic Review* (quarterly) provides first-class technical analysis, Allsopp *et al.* (1991) give a thorough grounding. Michie (1992) looks at most aspects of policy from a critical perspective while Keating *et al.* (1992) are more forward looking.

   Material on the 'supply-side' and industrial policy is patchy. Work by Grant (e.g., 1993) is most useful. It is often best to turn to journals such as *Government and Opposition* (political science interpretation), *Political Quarterly* (description and political comment), *Public Money and Management* (detailed dissection of policy). Also valuable are the badly under-used reports from House of Commons Select Committees, especially the Treasury and Civil Service Committee and the Trade and Industry Committee. The literature on the European dimension has grown rapidly and is often of poor quality, but see Swann (1992).

   For the more theoretically ambitious the economic theories are nicely reviewed in Mair and Miller (1991) while the politics of the industrial economy are well treated by Middlemas (e.g., 1991). The changing role of the Treasury is dealt with in Thain and Wright (1993).

## Chapter 11   Social Policy

For a general treatment of British social policy in its theoretical, historical and international context, the most comprehensive and up-to-date source is Pierson (1991). Some interesting questions about the nature of social policy are raised by Glennerster in Bulmer, Lewis and Piachaud (1989). For detailed empirical material on the period 1974–89 in the UK, see the several contributions in the excellent Hills (1990). A less statistical review of the major policy areas is available in McCarthy (1989). A useful survey of the reform process between 1988 and 90 is offered by Glennerster, Power and Travers (1991). The Welfare State Programme (at the Suntory–Toyota International Centre for Economics and Related Disciplines at the London School of Economics) has published a succession of valuable and well-informed discussion papers on the social policy reform process in the UK. On the government's education reforms see Maclure (1989) and David in Hills (1990). On health reform, see Department of Health (1989a), Grand, Winter and Woolley in Hills (1990) and Allsop in McCarthy (1989). For a brief and critical review of the government's housing policy, see Duke of Edinburgh (1991). Popular attitudes to the welfare state are reviewed in Bosanquet (1988) and Taylor-Gooby (1990). On Europe and the Social Charter, see Rhodes (1991), on the consequences of an ageing population, see Pierson (1991), and on changing household composition and its policy consequences, see Millar (1989) and CSO (1991).

## Chapter 12  Environmental Politics

Key full-length studies of current British environmental policy and politics include McCormick (1991) and Robinson (1992). Shorter studies of recent policy can be found in Blowers (1987) and Lowe and Flynn (1989). A useful comparison of policies in Britain and the USA is offered by Vogel (1986). Discussion of the influence of the EC on British policy is covered by Haigh (1987). Green politics are covered by Porritt (1984), Porritt and Winner (1988), and Dobson (1990).

## Chapter 13  Foreign and Defence Policy

The best sources for recent developments in British foreign policy are two journals published by the Royal Institute of International Affairs: *International Affairs* and *The World Today* (see, for example, Wallace, 1992b). On policy during the post-war period in general, see Sanders (1990). For a good review of the Thatcher years see Byrd (1988). For a more theoretical approach, see Smith *et al.*, (1988). For an excellent review of the Anglo–American 'special relationship', see Louis and Bull (1986). On the imperial origins of Britain's current 'world role' aspirations, see Porter (1984). On defence policy, the best exposition remains Baylis (1984).

**Chapter 14    Organised Interests After Thatcher**

A classic, though also long and quite demanding, analysis of the
operations of British liberal corporatism is Middlemas (1991). A
more accessible account can be found in Kavanagh (1990). The
comprehensive source on British trade unionism before, during and
after the Thatcher years is Marsh (1992). The best guide to the
changing role of business in British politics and policy-making is
Grant (1993). On the role of organised interests in the policy process,
Jordan and Richardson (1987) is a good, if slightly dated, introduction, whilst Mazey and Richardson (1993) adds useful material on
the emergent European dimension.

**Chapter 15    Migration and the Politics of Race**

For an overview of the history and politics of race in British society,
see Solomos (1993). For a broader theoretical survey of ideas about
race and racism, see Miles (1989). Attempts to analyse broader
trends in Europe as a whole can be found in Hammar (1985),
Bovenkerk *et al.* (1990) and Layton-Henry (1990). Recent political
trends in Europe are looked at in Balibar (1991), Husbands (1991)
and Lloyd (1991). The changing forms of minority political
participation in Britain are looked at in Back and Solomos (1992a,
1992b). An exploratory account of the differences between Britain
and other European societies can be found in Husbands (1992).

**Chapter 16    The Media and Politics**

For an overview of different models of democracy, see Held (1987).
On the nature of democracy in Britain and the British political
tradition, the established texts are Birch (1979) and Beer (1982). A
more recent critical work which develops the argument advanced in
this chapter is Tant (1993).

   On the role of the media in relation to democracy see Keane
(1991). The best extant work on the media and voting is Miller
(1991). However, this deals with the 1987 general election. On the
1992 election see the chapters by Harrison and Harrop and
Scammell in Butler and Kavanagh (1992). The biography of
Bernard Ingham by Harris (1990) should be required reading for
anyone interested in the operation of British democracy. However,
for balance it should be read in conjuction with Ingham (1991).

**Chapter 17   Political Theory and British Politics**

An excellent account of new right ideas in the context of British politics is King (1987). Different perspectives on the market economy are to be found in Gray (1992) and Plant (1984). A left agenda for the 1990s is set out in Blackstone *et al.* (1992). Recent discussions about the concept of sovereignty in relation to the UK are to be found in Crick (1991a), and in relation to Europe and the international order in Beitz (1991) and Held (ed.) (1991). Different perspectives on democracy and constitutional reform are offered by Ewing and Gearty (1990), Graham and Prosser (1988), Holme and Elliott (1988), Marquand (1988), Norton (1982) and Oliver (1991). The implications of concepts of representation for electoral systems are considered by McLean (1991), Plant (1991), Reeve and Ware (1992) and Rose (1983). Arguments for PR are to be found in Lakeman (1982) and against in Hain (1986); and are considered more dispassionately in Bogdanor (1984). Finally, the concept of legitimacy and its significance for contemporary British politics are discussed in Barker (1990) and Beetham (1991).

# Bibliography

Adeney, M. and Lloyd, J. (1986) *Loss Without Limit: The Miners' Strike of 1984–5*, London, Routledge and Kegan Paul.

Adonis, A. (1990) *Parliament Today*, Manchester, Manchester University Press.

Allsopp, C. *et al.* (1991) 'The Assessment: Macroeconomic Policy', *Oxford Review of Economic Policy*, special issue on 'Economic Policy in the 1980s', vol. 7 no. 3 (Autumn).

Archer, C. and Butler, F. (1992) *The European Community: Structure and Process*, London, Pinter.

Back, L. and Solomos, J. (1992a) 'Black Politics and Social Change in Birmingham: An Analysis of Recent Trends', *Ethnic and Racial Studies*, vol. 15, pp.327–51.

Back, L. and Solomos, J. (1992b) 'Who Represents Us? Racialised Politics and Candidate Selection', *Research Papers, no. 2*, Department of Politics and Sociology, Birkbeck College.

Baker, D., Gamble, A. and Ludlam, S. (1992) 'More "Classless" and Less "Thatcherite"? Conservative Ministers and New Conservative MPs after the General Election', *Parliamentary Affairs*, vol. 45, pp.656–68.

Baker, D., Gamble, A. and Ludlam, S. (1993) 'Whips or Scorpions? The Maastricht Vote and the Conservative Party', *Parliamentary Affairs*, vol. 46, pp.151–66.

Balibar, E. (1991) 'Es Gibt Keinen Staat in Europa: Racism and Politics in Europe Today', *New Left Review*, vol. 186, pp.5–19.

Barker, R. (1990) *Political Legitimacy and the State*, Oxford, Clarendon Press.

Barnett, C. (1986) *The Audit of War: The Illusion and Reality of Britain as a Great Nation*, London, Macmillan.

Barr, N. and Coulter, F. (1990) 'Social Security: Solution or Problem?', in Hills (1990).

Bassett, P. (1987) *Strike Free: New Industrial Relation in Britain*, London, Macmillan.

Bates, T.St J.N. (1991) 'European Community Legislation Before the House of Commons', *Statute Law Review*, vol. 12, pp.109–34.

Baylis, J. (1984) *Anglo–American Defence Relations, 1939–1984*, 2nd edn, London, Macmillan.

Beer, S.H. (1982) *Modern British Politics: A Study of Parties and Pressure Groups*, 3rd edn, London, Faber.

Beetham, D. (1991) *The Legitimation of Power*, London, Macmillan.

379

Beetham, D. (1992) 'The Plant Report and the Theory of Political Representation', *Political Quarterly*, vol. 63, pp.460–7.

Beitz, C.R. (1991) 'Sovereignty and Morality in International Affairs', in Held (ed.) (1991), pp.236–54.

Bendor, B.G. (1991) 'Governmental Processes: Whitehall, Central Government and 1992', *Public Policy and Administration*, vol. 6.

Billig, M. *et al.* (1992) 'In The Hands of the Spin-Doctors: Television, Politics and the 1992 General Election', in Miller, N. (ed.), *Current Debates in Broadcasting*, Manchester, Manchester University.

Birch, A.H. (1972) *Representation*, London, Macmillan Press.

Birch, A.H. (1990) *The British System of Government*, 8th edn, London, Unwin Hyman.

Blackstone, T. *et al.* (eds) (1992) *Next Left*, London, Institute for Public Policy Research.

Blackstone, W. (1765) *Commentaries on the Laws of England*, vol. 1, Oxford, Clarendon Press.

Blondel, J. (1963) *Voters, Parties, Leaders*, Harmondsworth, Penguin.

Blondel, J. *et al.* (1970) 'Legislative Behaviour: Some Steps Towards a Cross-National Measurement', *Government and Opposition*, vol. 5, pp.67–85.

Blowers, A. (1987) 'Transition or Transformation? Environmental policy under Thatcher', *Public Administration*, vol. 65, pp.277–94.

Bogdanor, V. (1981) *The People and the Party System*, Cambridge, Cambridge University Press.

Bogdanor, V. (1983) *Liberal Party Politics*, Oxford, Clarendon Press.

Bogdanor, V. (1984) *What is Proportional Representation?*, Oxford, Martin Robertson.

Bogdanor, V. (ed.) (1987) *The Blackwell Encyclopaedia of Political Institutions*, Oxford, Blackwell.

Bogdanor, V. (1992) 'Neighourhood Watchdog for Whitehall', *The Guardian* (27 July).

Bosanquet, N. (1988) 'An Ailing State of National Health', in Jowell, R., Witherspoon, S. and Brook, L. (eds.), *British Social Attitudes: the 5th Report*, Aldershot, Gower.

Bovenkerk, F., Miles, R. and Verbunt, G. (1990) 'Racism, Migration and the State in Western Europe: A Case for Comparative Analysis', *International Sociology*, vol. 5, pp.475–90.

Boyle, K. (1991) 'Northern Ireland: Allegiances and Identities', in Crick (ed.), (1991) pp.68–78.

Braybrooke, D. and Lindblom, C.E. (1963) *A Strategy of Decision*, New York, Free Press.

Brazier, R. (1991) *Constitutional Reform*, Oxford, Clarendon Press.

Britton, A. (1992) 'From EMS to EMU', in Keating *et al.* (1992).

Browne-Wilkinson, Lord (1992) 'The Infiltration of a Bill of Rights', *Public Law*, pp.397–410.

Budge, I. and Farlie, D. (1983) *Explaining and Predicting Elections*, London, George Allen & Unwin.

Bulmer, M., Lewis, J. and Piachaud, D. (1989) *The Goals of Social Policy*, London, Unwin Hyman.

Bulmer, S., George, S. and Scott, A. (1992) *United Kingdom and EC Membership Evaluated*, London, Pinter.

Bulpitt, J. (1982) 'Conservatism, Unionism, and the Problem of Territorial Management', in Madgwick P. and Rose R. (1982).

Bulpitt, J. (1983) *Territory and Power in the United Kingdom*, Manchester, Manchester University Press.

Bulpitt, J. (1986) 'The Discipline of the New Democracy: Mrs Thatcher's Domestic Statecraft', *Political Studies*, vol. 34, pp.19–39.

Burton, J. *et al.* (1984) *Britain Between East and West: A Concerned Independence*, Aldershot, Gower.

Butcher, H., Law I., Leach, R. and Mullard, M. (1990) *Local Government and Thatcherism*, London, Routledge.

Butler, D. (1953) *The Electoral System in Britain 1918–1951*, Oxford, Clarendon Press.

Butler, D. and Kavanagh, D. (1992) *The British General Election of 1992*, London, Macmillan.

Butler, D. and Stokes, D. (1974) *Political Change in Britain*, 2nd edn, London, Macmillan.

Butt Philip, A. (1985) 'Pressure Groups in the European Community', University Association of Contemporary European Studies, *Working Paper*, No. 2.

Butt Philip, A. (1992) 'British Pressure Groups and the European Community', in George (1992).

Byrd, P. (ed.) (1988) *British Foreign Policy Under Thatcher*, London, Philip Allan.

Byrne, T. (1988) *Local Government in Britain*, Harmondsworth, Penguin.

Campaign Against Racism and Fascism (1992) *Racist Murders*, (leaflet).

Carstairs, C. and Ware, R. (eds) (1991) *Parliament and International Relations*, Milton Keynes, Open University Press.

Castle, B. (1980) *The Castle Diaries 1974–76*, London, Weidenfeld & Nicolson.

Castle, B. (1984) *The Castle Diaries 1964–70*, London, Weidenfeld & Nicolson.

Caves, R. and Krause, L. (1980) *Britain's Economic Performance*, Washington, The Brookings Institution.

Central Statistical Office (1991) *Social Trends, 21*, London, HMSO.

Chapman, R.A. (1988) 'The Next Steps: A Review', *Public Policy and Administration*, vol. 3, pp.3–10.

Chartered Institute of Public Finance and Accountancy (1992) *The Competitive Edge: Early Trends in Compulsory Competitive Tendering*, London, CIPFA.

*Citizen's Charter* (1991) Cm 1599, London, HMSO.

Clutterbuck, R. (1981) *The Media and Political Violence*, London, Macmillan.

Cochrane, A. (1991) 'The Changing State of· Local Government: Restructuring for the 1990s', *Public Administration*, vol. 69, pp.281–302.

Cohen, R. (1991) 'East–West and European migration in a global context', *New Community*, vol. 18, no. 1, pp.9–26.

Council of Mortgage Lenders (1991) *Housing Finance*, no. 12.

Craig, F. (1989) *British Electoral Facts 1832–1987*, Aldershot, Parliamentary Research Services.

Crewe, I. (1987) 'Why Mrs Thatcher Was Returned with a Landslide', *Social Studies Review*, vol. 3, no. 1, pp.2–9.

Crewe, I. (1988) 'Has the Electorate become Thatcherite?', in Skidelsky (1988).

Crewe, I. (1991) 'Labour Force Changes, Working Class Decline, and the Labour Vote: Social and Electoral Trends in Postwar Britain', in Piven, F. F. (ed.), *Labor Parties in Postindustrial Societies*, Oxford, Polity Press.

Crewe, I. (1992) 'Why did Labour Lose (Yet Again)?', *Politics Review*, vol. 2, no. 1, pp.2–11.

Crewe, I. and King, A. (1993) 'Are British Elections Becoming More "Presidential"', in Mann, T. and Jenings, M. Kent (eds) [forthcoming title].

Crewe, I., Day, N. and Fox, A. (1991) *The British Electorate 1963–1987*, Cambridge, Cambridge University Press.

Crick, B. (1991) 'The English and the British', in Crick (ed.) (1991), pp.90–104.

Crick, B. (ed.) (1991) *National Identities*, Oxford, Blackwell.

Crosland, A. (1956) *The Future of Socialism*, London, Cape.

Crossman, R.H.S. (1964) 'Prime Ministerial Government', reprinted in King (1985).

Crossman, R.H.S. (1976) *The Diaries of a Cabinet Minister*, London, Hamish Hamilton.

Crozier, M. (1970) *La société bloquée*, Paris, Seuil.

Cunningham, M. (1992) 'British Policy in Northern Ireland', *Politics Review*, vol. 2, no. 1 (September) pp.30–3.

Curtice, J. (1988) 'One Nation?', in Jowell, R., Witherpoon, S. and Brook, L. (eds), *British Social Attiudes: the 5th Report*, Aldershot, Gower.

Curtice, J. (1992) 'The North–South Divide', in Jowell, R., Brook, L., Prior, G. and Taylor, B. (eds), *British Social Attitudes: the 9th Report*, Aldershot, Gower.

Curtice, J. and Steed, M. (1982) 'Electoral Choice and the Production of Government: The Changing Operation of the UK Electoral System since 1955', *British Journal of Political Science*, vol. 12, pp.249–98.

Curtice, J. and Steed, M. (1992) 'The Results Analysed', in Butler, D. and Kavanagh, D. (1992).

Dahl, R. (1961) *Who Governs?*, New Haven CT, Yale University Press.

Dangerfield, G. (1966) *The Strange Death of Liberal England*, London, MacGibbon & Kee.

Denver, D. (1989) *Elections and Voting Behaviour in Britain*, London, Philip Allan.

Denver, D. and Hands, G. (1992b) *Issues and Controversies in British Voting Behaviour*, London, Harvester Wheatheaf.

Denver, D. and Hands, G. (1992b) 'Constituency Campaignng', *Parliamentary Affairs*, vol. 45, pp.528–44.

Department for Education (1992) *Choice and Diversity: A New Framework for Schools*, London, HMSO.

Department of Health (1989a) *Working for Patients*, London, HMSO.

Department of Health (1989b) *The Health of the Nation*, London, HMSO.

Department of Health (1992) *The Health of the Nation: A Strategy for Health in England*, Cm 1986, London, HMSO.

Department of Health and Social Security (1985) *The Reform of Social Security*, Cmnd 9517, London, HMSO.

Department of the Environment (1986) *Paying for Local Government*, Cmnd 9714, London, HMSO.

Department of Trade and Industry (1992) Press Release on Reorganisation, 3 July.

Dicey, A.V. (1886) *The Law of the Constitution*, 2nd edn, London, Macmillan.

Dobson, A. (1990) *Green Political Thought*, London, Unwin Hyman.

Dorfman, G. (1983) *British Trade Unionism against the Trades Union Congress*, London, Macmillan.

Dowding, K.M. (1991) *Rational Choice and Political Power*, Aldershot, Edward Elgar.

Dowding, K.M. (1993) *The Civil Service*, London, Routledge.

Draper, H. (1986) *Karl Marx's Theory of Revolution, vol.3: The Dictatorship of the Proletariat*, New York, Monthly Review Press.

Drewry, G. (1988) 'Legislation', in Ryle M. and Richards, P.G. (eds), *The Commons Under Scrutiny*, London, Fontana, pp.120–40.

Drewry, G. (ed.) (1989) *The New Select Committees*, 2nd edn, Oxford, Clarendon Press.

Drewry, G. and Butcher, T. (1991) *The Civil Service Today*, 2nd edn, Oxford, Basil Blackwell.

Drucker, H. (1978) *Doctrine and Ethos in the Labour Party*, London, Allen & Unwin.

Duke of Edinburgh (1991) *Inquiry into British Housing: Second Report*, Joseph Rowntree Foundation.

Dunleavy, P. (1980) *Urban Political Analysis*, London, Macmillan.

Dunleavy, P. (1989) 'The United Kingdom: Paradoxes of an Ungrounded Statism', in Castles, F. (ed.), *The Comparative History of Public Policy*, Cambridge, Polity Press.

Dunleavy, P. (1991) *Democracy, Bureaucracy and Public Choice*, Hemel Hempstead, Harvester Wheatsheaf.

Dunleavy, P. (1992) 'Democracy in Britain: A Health Check for the 1990s', in Crewe, I. *et al.* (eds), *British Elections, Parties and Public Opinion Yearbook, 1991*, Hemel Hempstead, Harvester Wheatsheaf.

Dunleavy, P. and O'Leary, B. (1987) *Theories of the State: The Politics of Liberal Democracy*, London, Macmillan.

Dunleavy, P. and Husbands, C. (1985) *British Democracy at the Crossroads: Voting and Party Competition in the 1980s*, London, Allen & Unwin.

Dunleavy, P. and King, D.S. (1990) 'Middle-Level Elites and Control of Urban Policy-Making', paper to the PSA Urban Politics Group (June).

Dunleavy, P. and Rhodes, R.A W. (1990) 'Core Executive Studies in Britain', *Public Administration*, vol. 68, pp.3–28.

Dunleavy, P. and Weir, S. (1991) 'The Making of a Euro-Brit', *Guardian*.

Dunleavy, P., Jones, G.W. and O'Leary, B. (1990) 'Prime Ministers in the House of Commons 1868–1988', *Public Administration*, vol. 68, pp.123–41.

Dunleavy, P., Margetts, H. and Weir, S. (1992) *Replaying the 1992 General Election: How Britain Would Have Voted Under Alternative Electoral Systems*, London, Joseph Rowntree Reform Trust and LSE Public Policy Group.

Dworkin, R. (1977) *Taking Rights Seriously*, London, Duckworth.

Edwards, O.D. (ed.) (1989) *A Claim of Right for Scotland*, Edinburgh, Polygon.

Efficiency Unit (1988) *Improving Management in Government: The Next Steps* (The Ibbs Report), London, HMSO.

Elkington, J. and Hailes, J. (1988) *The Green Consumer Guide*, London, Gollancz.

Elster, J. (1986) 'The Market and the Forum', in Elster, J. and Hylland, A. (eds), *The Foundations of Social Choice Theory*, Cambridge, Cambridge University Press, pp.103–32.

European Communities (1992) *Treaty on European Union*, Luxembourg, Office for Official Publications of the European Communities.

*European Economy* (1991) 'Fair Competition in the Internal Market: Community State Aid Policy', Commission of the EC no. 48, (September).

Ewing, K.D. and Gearty, C.A. (1990) *Freedom under Thatcher: Civil Liberties in Modern Britain*, Oxford, Clarendon Press.

Finer, S.E. (ed.) (1975) *Adversary Politics and Electoral Reform*, London, Anthony Wigram.

Franklin, M. (1985) *The Decline of Class Voting in Britain*, Oxford, Clarendon Press.

Franklin, M., Mackie, T., Valen, H. *et al.* (1992) *Electoral Change: Responses to Evolving Social and Attitudinal Structures in Western Countries*, Cambridge, Cambridge University Press.

Fry, G.K., Flynn, A., Gray, A., Jenkins, W. and Rutherford, B. (1988) 'Symposium on Improving Management in Government', *Public Administration*, vol. 66, pp.429–45.

Fulton Committee (1968) *The Civil Service*, Cmnd 3638, London, HMSO.

Galbraith, J.K. (1992) *The Culture of Contentment*, London, Sinclair-Stevenson.

Gamble, A. (1988) *The Free Economy and the Strong State: The Politics of Thatcherism*, London, Macmillan.

Gamble, A. (1990) *Britain in Decline*, 3rd edn, London, Macmillan.

Garrett, J. (1992) *Westminster: Does Parliament Work?*, London, Gollancz.

Gavin, N. (1992) 'Television News and the Economy: The Pre-Election Coverage', *Parliamentary Affairs*, vol. 45 pp.596–611.

Gellner, E. (1983) *Nations and Nationalism*, Oxford, Oxford University Press.

George, S. (1990) *An Awkward Partner: Britain in the European Community*, Oxford, Oxford University Press.

George, S. (1991) *Britain and European Integration Since 1945*, Oxford, Blackwell.

George, S. (ed.) (1992) *Britain and the European Community: The Politics of Semi-Detachment*, Oxford, Clarendon Press.

Gilmour, I. (1977) *Inside Right*, London, Quartet.

Glasgow University Media Group (1976) *Bad News*, London, Routledge.

Glasgow University Media Group (1980) *More Bad News*, London, Routledge.

Glennerster, H., Power, A. and Travers, T. (1991) 'A New Era for Social Policy: A New Enlightenment or a New Leviathan?', *Journal of Social Policy*, vol. 20, pp.389–414.

Goldsmith, M. (1992) 'Local Government', *Urban Studies*, vol. 29, pp.393–410.

Goodin, R.E. and Le Grand, J. (1987) *Not Only the Poor: The Middle Classes and the Welfare State*, London, Allen & Unwin.

Graham, C. and Prosser, T. (eds) (1988) *Waiving the Rules*, Milton Keynes, Open University Press.

Grant, W. (1989) *Pressure Groups, Politics and Democracy in Britain*, Philip Allan, Chapter 5, 'Pressure Groups and the European Community', pp.90–112.

Grant, W. (1993) *Business and Politics in Britain*, 2nd edn, London, Macmillan.

Grantham, C.M. (1989) 'Parliament and Political Consultants', *Parliamentary Affairs*, vol. 42, pp.503–18.

Gray, J. (1992) *The Moral Foundations of Market Institutions*, London, Institute of Economic Affairs.

Greenaway, J., Smith, S. and Street, J. (1992) *Deciding Factors in British Politics: A Case Studies Approach*, London, Routledge.

Grief, N. (1991) 'The Domestic Impact of the European Convention on Human Rights as Mediated through Community Law', *Public Law*, pp.555–67.

Griffith, J.A.G. (1991) *The Politics of the Judiciary*, 4th edn, Oxford, Clarendon Press.

Griffith, J.A.G. and Ryle, M. (1989) *Parliament: Functions, Practice and Procedure*, London, Sweet & Maxwell.

Gros, D. and Thygesen, N. (1992) *European Monetary Integration*, London, Longman.

Gyford, J. (1984) *Local Politics in Britain*, 2nd edn, London, Croom Helm.

Gyford, J. (1991) *Consumers, Citizens and Local Politics*, London, Macmillan.

Gurr, T. R. and King, D.S. (1987) *The State and the City*, Chicago, University of Chicago Press and London, Macmillan.

Habermas, J. (1976) *Legitimation Crisis*, London, Heinemann.

Hahn, F. (1988) 'On Market Economics' in Skidelsky (1988).

Haigh, N. (1987) *EEC Environmental Policy and Britain*, London, Longman.

Hailsham, Lord (1992) *On the Constitution*, London, HarperCollins.

Hain, P. (1986) *Proportional Misrepresentation*, Aldershot, Wildwood House.

Halifax Building Society (1992) *House Price Index, 48*, Halifax Building Society.

Hammar, T. (ed.) (1985) *European Immigration Policy: A Comparative Study*, Cambridge, Cambridge University Press.

Hampton, W. (1991) *Local Government and Urban Politics*, 2nd edn, London, Longman.

Hannah, L. (1989) 'Mrs Thatcher, Capital Basher?', in Kavanagh, D. and Seldon, A. (eds), *The Thatcher Effect*, Oxford, Clarendon Press.

Harden, I. and Lewis, N. (1988) *The Noble Lie: The British Constitution and the Rule of Law*, London, Hutchinson.

Harris, R. (1990) *Good and Faithful Servant*, London, Faber.

Harrison, M. (1985) *TV News: Whose Bias?*, Hermitage, Berks, Policy Journals.

Harrison, M. (1992) 'Politics on the Air', in Butler, D. and Kavanagh, D. (1992).

Harrop, M. (1987) 'Voters', in Seaton, J. and Pimlott, B. (eds), *The Media in British Politics*, Aldershot, Avebury.

Harrop, M. (1990) 'Political Marketing', *Parliamentary Affairs*, vol. 43, pp.277–91.

Harrop, M. and Miller, W. (1987) *Elections and Voters: A Comparative Introduction*, London, Macmillan.

Harrop, M. and Scammell, M. (1992) 'A Tabloid War', in Butler, D. and Kavanagh, D. (1992) pp.180–210.

Hart, J. (1992) *Proportional Representation: Critics of the British Electoral System 1820–1945*, Oxford, Oxford University Press.

Hattersley, R. (1987) *Choose Freedom: the Future for Democratic Socialism*, London, Penguin.

Hayek, F.A. (1960) *The Constitution of Liberty*, London, Routledge and Kegan Paul.

Held, D. (1987) *Models of Democracy*, Cambridge. Polity Press.

Healey, D. (1989) *The Time of My Life*, London, Michael Joseph.

Healey, N.M. (ed.) (1993) *Britain's Economic Miracle: Myth or Reality?*, London, Routledge.

Heath, A. and Paulson, B. (1992) 'Issues and the Economy', *Political Quarterly*, vol. 63, no. 4, pp.432–47.

Heath, A., Jowell, R. and Curtice, J. (1985) *How Britain Votes*, Oxford, Pergamon Press.

Heath, A. *et al.* (1991) *Understanding Political Change: The British Voter 1945–1987*, Oxford, Pergamon Press.

Held, D. (1991) 'Democracy, the Nation-State and the Global System', in Held (1991), pp.197–235.

Held, D. (ed.) (1991b) *Political Theory Today*, Cambridge, Polity Press.

Helm, D. *et al.* (1991) 'The Assessment: Microeconomic Policy in the 1980s', *Oxford Review of Economic Policy*, vol. 7 no. 3 (Autumn).

Hennessy, P. (1986) *Cabinet*, Oxford, Basil Blackwell.

Hennessy, P. (1990) *Whitehall*, revised edn, London, Fontana.

Hennessy, P. (1991) 'How Much Room at the Top? Margaret Thatcher, the Cabinet and Power Sharing', in Norton (ed.) (1991).

Hennessy, P. (1992) *Never Again: Britain 1945–51*, London, Cape.

Heseltine, M. (1987) *Where There's a Will*, London, Hutchinson.

Heseltine, M. (1992) 'Setting the Agenda', speech to *Sunday Times* Conference (1 June).

Hill, D. (1974) *Democratic Theory and Local Government*, London, Allen & Unwin.

Hills J. (ed.) (1990) *The State of Welfare: The Welfare State in Britain Since 1974*, Oxford, Clarendon Press.

Hills, J. and Mullings, B. (1990) 'Housing: A Decent Home for All at a Price within their Means?' in Hills (1990).

HMSO (1977) *Royal Commission on the Press 1974–77*, Cmnd 6810, London, HMSO.

HMSO (1991) *A Rough Guide to Europe: Local Authorities and the EC*, London, HMSO.

HM Treasury (1991) *Public Expenditure Analyses to 1993–4*, Cm 1520, London, HMSO.

Hobbes, T. (1960) *Leviathan*, Oxford, Basil Blackwell.

Hogwood, B.W. (1992) 'Ups and Downs: Is There an Issue–Attention Cycle in Britain?', *Strathclyde Papers on Government and Politics*, no. 89.

Holliday, I. (1992a) 'Scottish Limits to Thatcherism', *Political Quarterly*, vol. 63, pp.448–59.

Holliday, I. (1992b) *The NHS Transformed: A Guide to the Health Reforms*, Manchester, Baseline Book Company.

Hollingsworth, M. (1986) *The Press and Political Dissent*, London, Pluto Press.

Holme, R. and Elliott, M. (eds) (1988) *1688–1988: Time for a New Constitution*, London, Macmillan.

Holmes, M. (1985) *The First Thatcher Government, 1979–83*, Brighton, Wheatsheaf.

Houlder, V. (1992) 'Glimmer of Northern Light on Tyne', *The Financial Times* (3 July).

Husbands, C. (1991) 'The Mainstream Right and the Politics of Immigration in France: Major Developments in the 1980s', *Ethnic and Racial Studies*, vol. 14, pp.170–98.

Husbands, C. (1992) 'Why has there been No Extreme Right in Great Britain?', *LSE Magazine* (Spring) pp.4–8.

Index on Censorship (1988) 'Britain', *Index on Censorship*, 17.1.

Ingham, B. (1991) *Kill the Messenger*, London, Fontana.

Institute for Public Policy Research (IPPR) (1991) *The Constitution of the United Kingdom*, London, IPPR.

Jackson, P.M. (1992) 'Economic Policy', in Marsh, D. and Rhodes, R.A.W. 1992, pp.11–31.

Jacobs, B.D. (1990) 'Business Leadership in Urban Regeneration: Towards a Shared Vision?', in King and Pierre (1990).

Jacobs, B.D. (1992) *Fractured Cities*, London, Routledge.

Jenkins, S. (1986) *The Market for Glory*, London, Faber.

Johnson, N. (1980) *In Search of the Constitution: Reflections on State and Society in Britain*, London, Methuen.

Johnston, R.J. and Pattie, C.J. (1992) 'Unemployment, the Poll Tax and the British General Election of 1992', *Environment and Planning C: Government and Policy*, vol. 10, pp.467–83.

Johnston, R.J., Pattie, C.J. and Allsopp, J.G. (1988) *A Nation Dividing?*, London, Longman.

Jones, B.D. (1990) 'An Uneasy Certitude in Urban Political Economy', *Urban Affairs Quarterly*, vol. 25, pp.524–31.

Jones, G. and Stewart J. (1985) *The Case for Local Government*, 2nd edn, London, Allen & Unwin.

Jones, N. (1986) *Strikes and the Media: Communication and Conflict*, Oxford, Basil Blackwell.

Jordan, A.G. and Richardson, J.J. (1987) *British Politics and the Policy Process: An Arena Approach*, London, Unwin Hyman.

Judge, D. (1992) 'The "Effectiveness" of the Post-1979 Select Committee System: the Verdict of the 1990 Procedure Committee', *Political Quarterly*, vol. 63, pp.91–100.

Kavanagh, D. (1990) *Thatcherism and British Politics: The End of Consensus?*, 2nd edn, Oxford, Oxford University Press.

Keane, J. (1991) *The Media and Democracy*, Cambridge, Methuen.

Kearney, H. (1989) *The British Isles: A History of Four Nations*, Cambridge, Cambridge University Press.

Keating, G. *et al.* (1992) *The State of the Economy 1992*, London, Institute of Economic Affairs.

Keating, M. (1991) *Comparative Urban Politics*, Aldershot, Edward Elgar.

Kellas, J. (1989) *The Scottish Political System*, 4th edn, Cambridge, Cambridge University Press.

Kellner, P. and Crowther-Hunt, Lord (1980) *The Civil Servants: An Inquiry into Britain's Ruling Class*, London, MacDonald, Futura Publishers.

Kellner, P. and Worcester, R. (1982) 'Electoral Perceptions of Media Stance', in Crewe, I. and Harrop, M. (eds), *Political Communications: The General Election Campaign of 1977*, London, Allen & Unwin.

King, A. (ed.) (1985) *The British Prime Minister*, 2nd edn, London, Macmillan.

King, A. (ed.) (1992) *Britain at the Polls 1992*, Chatham, N.J., Chatham House.

King, A. (1992) 'Over-the-Shoulder Politics', in King, A. (ed.) *Britain at the Polls 1992*, Chatham, N.J., Chatham House.

King, D.S. (1987) *The New Right*, London, Macmillan.

King, D.S. (1989) 'The New Right, the New Left and Local Government' in Stewart and Stoker (1989).

King, D.S. (1993) 'The Conservatives and Training Policy 1979–92: From a Tripartite to a Neoliberal Regime', *Political Studies*, vol. 41, pp.214–35.

King, D.S. and Pierre, J. (eds) (1990) *Challenges to Local Government*, London, Sage.

Laffan, B. (1992) *Integration and Co-operation in Europe*, London, Routledge.

Lakeman, E. (1982) *Power to Elect: The Case for Proportional Representation*, London, Heinemann.

Lawson, N. (1981) *The New Conservatism*, London, Conservative Political Centre.

Layton-Henry, Z. (ed.) (1990) *The Political Rights of Migrant Workers in Western Europe*, London, Sage.

Le Grand, J. (1990) 'The State of Welfare', in Hills (1990).

Le Grand, J., Winter, D. and Woolley, F. (1990) 'The National Health Service: Safe in Whose Hands?' in Hills (1990).

Lewis, N., Graham, C. and Beyleveld, D. (eds) (1990) *Happy and Glorious: The Constitution in Transition*, Milton Keynes, Open University Press.

Lewis-Beck, M. (1988) *Economics and Elections*, Ann Arbor, University of Michigan Press.

Leys, C. (1985) 'Thatcherism and British Manufacturing: A Question of Hegemony', *New Left Review*, vol. 151.

Lloyd, C. (1991) 'Concepts, Models and Anti-Racist Strategies in Britain and France', *New Community*, vol. 18, pp.63–73.

Logan, J.R. and Molotch, H.L. (1987) *Urban Fortunes: The Political Economy of Place*, Berkeley and London, University of California Press.

Logan, J.R. and Swanstrom T. (eds) (1990) *Beyond the City Limits*, Philadelphia, Temple University Press.

London Docklands Development Corporation (LDDC) (1988) *Reports and Accounts 1987–88*, London, LDDC.

Longstreth, F.H. (1988) 'From Corporatism to Dualism?: Thatcherism and the Climacteric of British Trade Unions in the 1980s', *Political Studies*, vol. 36, pp.413–32.

Louis, W.R. and Bull, H. (eds) (1986) *The Special Relationship: Anglo–American Relations Since 1945*, Oxford, Clarendon Press.

Lowe, P. and Flynn A. (1989) 'Environmental Politics and Policy in the 1980s', in Mohan, J. (ed.), *The Political Geography of Contemporary Britain*, London, Macmillan.

Lowe, P. and Goyder, J. (1983) *Environmental Groups in Politics*, London, Allen & Unwin.

McCarthy, M. (ed.) (1989) *The New Politics of Welfare: An Agenda for the 1990s?*, London, Macmillan.

McCormick, J. (1989) *Acid Earth: The Global Threat of Acid Pollution*, London, Earthscan.

McCormick, J. (1991) *British Politics and the Environment*, London, Earthscan.

McGarry, J. and O'Leary, B. (1993) *The Politics of Antagonism: Understanding Northern Ireland*, London, Athlone Press.

McGarry, J. and O'Leary, B. (eds) (1990) *The Future of Northern Ireland* Oxford, Oxford University Press.

McKenzie, R.T. (1965) *British Political Parties: The Distribution of Power Within the Conservative and Labour Parties*, London, Heinemann.

McLean, I. (1982) *Dealing in Votes: Interactions between Politicians and Voters in Britain and the USA*, Oxford, Martin Robertson.

McLean, I. (1987) *Public Choice: An Introduction*, Oxford, Basil Blackwell.

McLean, I. (1991) 'Forms of Representation and Systems of Voting', in Held (ed.) (1991), pp.172–96.

Maclure, S. (1989) *Education Re-formed: A Guide to the Education Reform Act*, London, Hodder & Stoughton.

Madgwick, P. and Rose, R. (eds) (1982) *The Territorial Dimension in United Kingdom Politics*, London, Macmillan.

Magnusson, W. (1986) 'Bourgeois Theories of Local Government', *Political Studies*, vol. 34, pp.1–18.

Mair, D. and Miller, A. (1991) *A Modern Guide to Economic Thought*, Aldershot, Edward Elgar.

Mair, P. (1992) 'The Question of Electoral Reform', *New Left Review*, no. 194, pp.75–96.

Major, J. (1992) 'The Next Phase of Conservatism: The Privatisation of Choice', speech to the Adam Smith Institute (June).

Marquand, D. (1988) *The Unprincipled Society*, London, Fontana.

Marr, A. (1992) *The Battle for Scotland*, Harmondsworth, Penguin.

Marsh, D. (1992) *The New Politics of British Trade Unionism: Union Power and the Thatcher Legacy*, London, Macmillan.

Marsh, D. and Read, M. (1988) *Private Members' Bills*, Cambridge, Cambridge University Press.

Marsh, D. and Rhodes, R.A.W. (eds) (1992) *Implementing Thatcherite Policies: Audit of an Era*, Milton Keynes, Open University Press.

Marsh, D. and Tant, A. (1989) 'There is No Alternative: Mrs Thatcher and the British Political Tradition', *Essex Papers in Politics and Government*, No. 69.

Marsh, I. (1986) *Policy Making in a Three Party System*, London, Methuen.

Marshall, G., Newby, H., Rose, D. and Vogler, C. (1988) *Social Class in Modern Britain*, London, Hutchinon.

Martin, R. (1989) 'Regional Imbalance as Consequence and Constraint in National Economic Renewal', in F. Green (ed.), *The Restructuring of the UK Economy*, Brighton, Harvester Wheatsheaf, pp.80–97.

Martin, R. (1992) 'The Economy' in Cloke, P. (ed.), *Policy and Change in Thatcher's Britain*, Oxford, Pergamon.

Mason, D. (1985) *Revising the Rating System*, London, Adam Smith Institute.

Mather, G. (1988) 'Government by Contract', paper given to the RIPA conference, Kent (September).

Mazey, S.P. and Richardson J.J. (1992) 'British Pressure Groups: the Challenge of Brussels', *Parliamentary Affairs*, vol. 45, pp.92–107.

Mazey, S. and Richardson, J.J. (eds) (1993) *Lobbying in the European Community*, Oxford, Oxford University Press.

Michie, J. (ed.) (1992) *The Economic Legacy 1979–1992*, London, Academic Press.

Middlemas, K. (1979) *Politics in Industrial Society: The Experience of the British System since 1911*, London, André Deutsch.

Middlemas, K. (1988) *Industry, Unions and Government: 21 Years of NEDC*, London, Macmillan.

Middlemas, K. (1991) *Power, Competition and the State: Vol. 3: The End of the Post-War Era*, London, Macmillan.

Midwinter, A., Keating, M. and Mitchell, J. (1991) *Politics and Public Policy in Scotland*, London, Macmillan.

Miles, R. (1989) *Racism*, London, Routledge.

Mill, J.S. (1991) *On Liberty and Other Essays* (ed. J. Gray), Oxford, Oxford University Press.

Millar, J. (1989) *Poverty and the Lone Parent: the Challenge to Social Policy*, Aldershot, Avebury.

Miller, W. (1991) *Media and Voters*, Oxford, Claredon.

Miller, W. *et al.* (1990) *How Voters Change*, Oxford, Clarenon Press.

Milne, A. (1988) *DG: Memoirs of a Broadcaster*, London, Hutchinson.

Milton, K. (1991) 'Interpreting Environmental Policy: A Social Scientific Approach', *Journal of Law and Society*, vol. 18, pp.4–17.

Minkin, L. (1991) *The Contentious Alliance: Trade Unions and the Labour Party*, Edinburgh, Edinburgh University Press.

Moore, C. (1990) 'Displacement, Partnership and Privatization: Local Government and Urban Economic Regeneration in the 1980s' in King and Pierre (1990).

Morison, H. (1987) *The Regeneration of Local Economies*, Oxford, Clarendon Press.

Mount, F. (1992) *The British Constitution Now: Recovery or Decline?*, London, Heinemann.

Nairn, T. (1981) *The Break-Up of Britain*, new edn, London, NLB/ Verso.

National Audit Office (1988) Report by the Comptroller and Auditor General, *Department of Environment: Urban Development Corporations*, London, HMSO (May).

Newton, K. (1992) 'Do People Read Everything They Believe in the Newspapers? Newspapers and Voters in the 1983 and 1987 Elections', in Crewe, I. and Norris, P. (eds), *British Parties and Election Yearbook*, London, Simon & Schuster, pp.51–74.

NHS Management Executive (1990) *Working for Patients NHS Trust: A Working Guide*, London, HMSO.

NHS Management Executive (1991) *NHS Reforms – The First Six Months*, London, HMSO.

Nicoll, W. and Salmon, T.C. (1990) *Understanding the European Communities*, London, Philip Allan.

Norton, P. (1982) *The Constitution in Flux*, Oxford, Martin Robertson.

Norton, P. (1984) 'Parliament and Policy in Britain: Parliament as a Policy Influencer', *Teaching Politics*, vol. 13, pp.198–221.

Norton, P. (1985) 'Introduction: Parliament in Perspective', in Norton, P. (ed.), *Parliament in the 1980s*, Oxford, Basil Blackwell.

Norton, P. (1990) ' "The Lady's Not for Turning", But What About the Rest?', *Parliamentary Affairs*, vol. 43.

Norton, P. (1991) 'Parliament Since 1945: A More Open Institution?', *Contemporary Record*, vol. 5, pp.217–34.

Norton, P. (1992) 'The Conservative Party', in King, A. (1992).

Norton, P. (ed.) (1991) *New Directions in British Politics?*, Aldershot, Edward Elgar.

Nugent, N. (1992) *The Government and Politics of the European Community*, London, Macmillan.

Oakeshott, M. (1962) *Rationalism in Politics*, London, Methuen.

Official Journal of the European Communities (1992) *C168* (4 July).

O'Leary, B. (1985) 'Explaining Northern Ireland: A Brief Study Guide', *Politics*, vol. 5, no. 1, pp.35–41.

O'Leary, B. (1990) 'Northern Ireland and the Anglo–Irish Agreement', in Dunleavy, P. *et al.* (eds), *Developments in British Politics 3*, London, Macmillan.

Oliver, D. (1991) *Government in the United Kingdom*, Milton Keynes, Open University Press.

Olson, M. (1982) *The Rise and Fall of Nations*, New Haven, CT., Yale University Press.

Organization for Economic Co-Operation and Development (OECD) (1992) *Education at a Glance: OECD Indicators*, Paris, OECD.

Pearce, D., Markandya A. and Barbier E. (1989) *Blueprint for a Green Economy*, London, Earthscan.

Phillips, A. (1991) *Engendering Democracy*, Cambridge, Polity Press.

Pierson, C. (1991) *Beyond the Welfare State? The New Political Economy of Welfare*, Cambridge, Polity.

Plant, R. (1984) *Equality, Markets and the State*, Fabian Tract, 494, London, Fabian Society.

Plant, R. (ed.) (1991) *Interim Report of the Working Party on Electoral Reform*, London, Labour Party.

Policy Studies Institute (1992) *Urban Trends 1*, London, Policy Studies Institute.

Polsby, N.W. (1975) 'Legislatures', in F.I. Greenstein and N.W. Polsby (eds), *Handbook of Political Science*, vol. V, Reading, Mass., pp.257–319.

Porritt, J. (1984) *Seeing Green*, Oxford, Basil Blackwell.

Porritt, J. and Winner, D. (1988) *The Coming of the Greens*, London, Fontana.

Porter, B. (1984) *The Lion's Share: A Short History of British Imperialism*, London, Longman.

Porter, M. (1990) *The Competitive Advantage of Nations*, London, Macmillan.

Pollard, S. (1984) *The Wasting of the British Economy*, 2nd edn, London.

Rabinowitz, G. and Macdonald, S.E. (1989) 'A Directional Theory of Issue Voting', *American Political Science Review*, vol. 83, pp.93–121.

Ranelagh, J. (1992) *Thatcher's People*, London, Fontana.

Reeve, A. and Ware, A. (1992) *Electoral Systems*, London, Routledge.

*Report of the Committee of Inquiry into the Conduct of Local Authority Business* (1986) *The Conduct of Local Authority Business* (chairman Mr David Widdicombe QC), Cmnd 9798, London, HMSO, and *Research Volumes I–IV*.

Rhodes, M. (1991) 'The Social Dimension of the Single European Market: National versus Transnational Regulation', *European Journal of Political Research*, vol. 20, 1991.

Rhodes, R.A.W. (1988) *Beyond Westminister and Whitehall*, London, Unwin Hyman.

Richardson, J.J. and Jordan, A.G. (1979) *Governing Under Pressure: The Policy Process in a Post-Parliamentary Democracy*, Oxford, Martin Robertson.

Ridley, F.F. (1991) 'Using Power to Keep Power: The Need for Constitutional Checks', *Parliamentary Affairs*, vol. 44, pp.442–52.

Robinson, M. (1992) *The Greening of British Party Politics*, Manchester, Manchester University Press.

Rose, R. (1983) 'Elections and Electoral Systems', in Bogdanor, V. and Butler, D. (eds), *Democracy and Elections*, Cambridge, Cambridge University Press, pp.20–45.

Rose, R. (1987) *Ministers and Ministries: A Functional Analysis*, Oxford, Clarendon Press.

Rose, R. and McAllister, I. (1986) *Voters Begin To Choose: From Closed Class to Open Elections in Britain*, London, Sage.

Rush, M. (ed.) (1990) *Parliament and Pressure Politics*, Oxford, Clarendon Press.

Sanders, D. (1990) *Losing an Empire, Finding a Role: British Foreign Policy Since 1945*, London, Macmillan.

Sanders, D. (1991) 'Government Popularity and the Next Election', *Political Quarterly*, vol. 62, pp.235–61.

Sanders, D. (1992) 'Why the Conservative Party Won – Again', in King, A. (1992), pp.171–222.

Sanders, D., Marsh, D. and Ward, H. (1993) 'The Electoral Impact of Newspaper Coverage of the UK Economy, 1979–87', *British Journal of Political Science*, vol. 23, no. 2, pp.xxx–xxx.

Sarlvik, B. and Crewe, I. (1983) *Decade of Dealignment*, Cambridge, Cambridge University Press.

Scruton, R. (1980) *The Meaning of Conservatism*, Harmondsworth, Penguin.

Seldon, Anthony (1990) 'The Cabinet Office and Coordination 1979–87', *Public Administration*, vol. 68, pp.103–21.

Seldon, Arthur (1990) *Capitalism*, Oxford, Basil Blackwell.

Seyd, P. (1987) *The Rise and Fall of the Labour Left*, London, Macmillan.

Shell, D. (1992) *The House of Lords*, 2nd edn, Hemel Hempstead, Harvester Wheatsheaf.

Shoard, M. (1980) *The Theft of the Countryside*, London, Maurice Temple Smith.

Shoard, M. (1987) *This Land is Our Land*, London, Paladin.

Skidelsky, R. (ed.) (1988) *Thatcherism*, London, Chatto & Windus.

Smith, J. and McLean, I. (1992) 'The UK Poll Tax and the Declining Electoral Roll: Unintended Consequences?', *Warwick*

*Economic Research Papers*, no. 398, Department of Economics, University of Warwick.

Smith, M. (1991) 'From Policy Community to Issue Network: Salmonella in Eggs and the New Politics of Food', *Public Administration*, vol. 69, pp.235–55.

Smith M., Smith, S. and White, B. (eds) (1988) *British Foreign Policy: Tradition, Change and Transformation*, London, Unwin Hyman.

Solomos, J. (1993) *Race and Racism in Britain*, 2nd edn, London, Macmillan.

Steiner, J. and Dorff, R.H. (1980) 'Decision by Interpretation: A New Concept for an Often Overlooked Decision Mode', *British Journal of Political Science*, vol. 10, pp.1–13.

Stewart, J. and Stoker, G. (eds) (1989) *The Future of Local Government*, London, Macmillan.

Stoker, G. (1991) *The Politics of Local Government*, 2nd edn, London, Macmillan.

Stone, C.N. (1989) *Regime Politics: Governing Atlanta 1946–1988*, Lawrence, University Press of Kansas.

Stone, C.N. and Sanders, H.T. (eds) (1987) *The Politics of Urban Development*, Lawrence, University Press of Kansas.

Studlar, D. and McAllister, I. (1992) 'A Changing Politial Agenda? The Structure of Political Attitudes in Britain, 1974–87', *International Journal of Public Opinion Research*, vol. 4, pp.148–76.

Swann, D. (ed.) (1992) *The Single European Market and Beyond*, London, Routledge.

Tant, T. (1993) *British Government: the Triumph of Elitism*, Aldershot, Dartmouth.

Taylor-Gooby, P. (1990) 'Social Welfare: The Unkindest Cuts', in Jowell, R. Witherspoon, S. and Brook, L. (eds), *British Social Attitudes: the 7th Report*, Aldershot, Gower.

Thain, C. and Wright, M. (1993) *The Treasury and Whitehall*, Oxford, Oxford University Press.

*The Times* (1992) *The Times Guide to the House of Commons April 1992*, London, Times Books.

Thornton, P. (1989) *Decade of Decline: Civil Liberties in the Thatcher Years*, London, NCCL.

Travers, T. (1986) *The Politics of Local Government Finance*, London, Allen & Unwin.

Urwin, D.W. (1991) *The Community of Europe: A History of European Integration Since 1945*, London, Longman.

Veljanovski, C. (1990) 'The Political Economy of Regulation', in Dunleavy, P. *et al.* (eds), *Developments in British Politics 3*, London, Macmillan.

Vibert, F. (1990) *Constitutional Reform in the United Kingdom: An Incremental Agenda*, London, IEA.

Vibert, F. (1991) (ed.) *Britain's Constitutional Future*, London, IEA.

Vogel, D. (1986) *National Styles of Regulation*, Ithaca, Cornell University Press.

Wade, H.W.R. (1991) 'What Has Happened to the Sovereignty of Parliament?', *Law Quarterly Review*, vol. 107, pp.1–4.

Walker, J. (1983) 'The Origins and Maintenance of Interest Groups in America', *American Political Science Review*, vol. 77, pp.390–406.

Walkland, S.A. (1976) 'The Politics of Parliamentary Reform', *Parliamentary Affairs*, vol. 29, pp.190–200.

Walkland, S.A. (1977) 'Whither the Commons?', in Walkland, S.A. and Ryle, M. (eds), *The Commons in the 70s*, London, Fontana, pp.238–56.

Wallace, W. (1992a) 'But What Are We Deterring?', *Guardian* (30 January).

Wallace, W. (1992b) 'British Foreign Policy After the Cold War', *International Affairs*, vol. 68, pp.423–42.

Walters, P. (1989) 'The Crisis of "Responsible" Broadcasting', *Parliamentary Affairs*, vol. 42, pp.380–98.

Weber, M. (1978) 'Parliament and Government in a Reconstructed Germany', Appendix II, *Economy and Society*, vol. 2 (eds G. Roth and C. Wittich), Berkeley, University of California Press.

Weir, S. (1992) 'Waiting for Change: Public Opinion and Electoral Reform', *Political Quarterly*, vol. 63, pp.197–221.

Whiteley, P. (1990) 'Economic Policy', in Dunleavy, P. *et al.* (eds), *Developments in British Politics 3*, London, Macmillan.

Whiteley, P. and Seyd, P. (1992) 'Labour's Vote and Local Activism: The Impact of Local Constituency Campaigns', *Parliamentary Affairs*, vol. 45, pp.582–95.

Whyte, J. (1990) *Interpreting Northern Ireland*, Oxford, Oxford University Press.

Wiener, M.J. (1981) *English Culture and the Decline of the Industrial Spirit 1850–1980*, Cambridge, Cambridge University Press.

Wilks, S. (1987) 'From Industrial Policy to Enterprise Policy in Britain', *Journal of General Management*, 13 (Summer).

Willetts, D. (1987) 'The Role of the Prime Minister's Policy Unit', *Public Administration*, vol. 65, pp.443–54.

Willetts, D. (1992) *Modern Conservatism*, Harmondsworth, Penguin.

Wolman, H. and Goldsmith, M. (1992) *Urban Politics in Britain and the United States*, Oxford and New York, Blackwell.

Wood, L. (1992) 'Tecs Pressure Shephard on Training Policy', *Financial Times* (27 April).

Wright, A. (1987) *Northern Ireland: A Comparative Analysis*, Dublin, Gill and London, Macmillan.

Wynn Davies, P. (1992) 'Development Losses of £67m a "Scandal"', *The Independent* (13 July).

Young, H. (1989) *One of Us: A Biography of Margaret Thatcher*, London, Macmillan.

Young, S. (1993) 'Environmental Politics and the EC', *Politics Review*, vol. 2, no. 3, pp.6–8.

# Index